ADVANCE PRAISE FOR THE BOOK

'In this pathbreaking and deeply researched book, Dhirendra K. Jha builds a compelling portrait of M. S. Golwalkar, the RSS's early and most influential supremo and sarsanghachalak. In Jha's able hands we see the evolution of a figure that is hugely ambitious, resentful, anxious and insular as he faces a new India based on secular and democratic principles. Jha shows convincingly that the proliferation of RSS organizations in many domains in Indian society, presenting themselves as cultural, non-political and patriotic outfits, was a direct response to how the RSS's political ambitions were thwarted after Partition and the murder of Gandhi. Drawing on a wealth of original sources, Jha has given us a book that anyone interested in understanding modern India must read—now and in the decades to come.'—**Thomas Blom Hansen, author, *The Saffron Wave: Democracy and Hindu Nationalism in Modern India***

'Based on first-hand material, this erudite book reveals important biographical information about one of the most secretive public figures of post-independence India. But it is more than a biography. Writing on Golwalkar, Dhirendra K. Jha explains how the RSS became a mass organization influencing not only politics, but also society in a decisive way.'—**Christophe Jaffrelot, author, *The Hindu Nationalist Movement and Indian Politics, 1925 to 1990s***

'A striking feature of the contemporary scene in India is the emergence of the RSS, purportedly a cultural organization, as a major *political* player. M. S. Golwalkar, the subject of this study, succeeded the founder Dr. Hedgewar as the head of the RSS in 1940 and remained at the helm till his death in 1972, steering the organization through the crucial pre- and post-independence years. Dhirendra K. Jha has rendered an invaluable service by giving us the first exhaustive and objective study of Golwalkar's life and work, based on original primary sources, including interviews and archival material, including police records consulted for the first time. It is also a disturbing book, because its revelations on the inner working of the organization, based on hierarchy, doublespeak, secrecy, and divisive and sectarian anti-minority ideological worldview, do little to inspire confidence in its professed nationalist and democratic credentials.'—**Mridula Mukherjee, Professor (retd.), Modern Indian History, Jawaharlal Nehru University**

PRAISE FOR *GANDHI'S ASSASSIN*

'A frightening dive into the violent subculture of the RSS.'—**Jacobin**

'A credible account of Gandhi's assassination and how it was linked to Hindu far-right groups such as RSS, Hindu Mahasabha, and their leaders including Vinayak Damodar Savarkar.'—**Al Jazeera**

'Dhirendra K. Jha's meticulously researched book leaves no stone unturned in its earnest endeavour to decipher the pernicious ideological roots and simultaneously map the bigoted individual thought processes that eventually culminated in the brutal assassination of Mahatma Gandhi.'—**The Telegraph**

'[This] biography of a potently totemic figure for Hindutva busts several long-standing myths.'—**Business Standard**

'Deeply researched and lucidly written, *Gandhi's Assassin* does a good job in its portraiture of Nathuram Godse and in reporting details of the plot to kill MK Gandhi.'—**Hindustan Times**

'[A] page-turner, *Gandhi's Assassin*... shows that the myth about the killer of the Mahatma was a lie the RSS manufactured to conceal its bloody vision.'—**Ajaz Ashraf, Mid-Day**

'In *Gandhi's Assassin*, Dhirendra K. Jha has anatomized, with calm resourcefulness, the politics and psychology of a fanatic. He has also written a secret and sinister history of modern India—the one we need to understand our ruinous present.'—**Pankaj Mishra**

'This book goes beyond the plot that resulted in Mahatma Gandhi's assassination. It is indeed highly revealing of the omnipresence of the RSS on the Indian political scene in the 1940s. If the organization did not fight British colonialism and did not contest elections, it was intimately related to Savarkar's Hindu Mahasabha, the first Hindutva party, and, more importantly, organically linked to the Hindu Rashtra Dal, a militant body co-founded by Nathuram Godse—a man who, as Dhirendra K. Jha shows, never left the RSS.'—**Christophe Jaffrelot**

'Dhirendra Jha's book is not just a very readable and credible account of the plot and the people behind Gandhi's murder, including a psychological analysis of his assassin, but a comprehensive study of the wider politics of the Hindu Mahasabha, the RSS and their leaders, including Savarkar, which makes it a must-read and highly relevant in today's context.'—**Mridula Mukherjee**

GOLWALKAR

GOLWALKAR

THE MYTH BEHIND THE MAN, THE MAN BEHIND THE MACHINE

Dhirendra K. Jha

SIMON &
SCHUSTER

London · New York · Sydney · Toronto · New Delhi

First published in India by Simon & Schuster India 2024

1 3 5 7 9 10 8 6 4 2

Simon & Schuster India
818, Indraprakash Building,
21, Barakhamba Road,
New Delhi 110001.

www.simonandschuster.co.in

Simon & Schuster: Celebrating 100 Years of Publishing in 2024

Hardback ISBN: 978-81-979492-3-4
eBook ISBN: 978-81-979492-4-1

Typeset in India by SÜRYA, New Delhi
Printed and bound in India by Replika Press Pvt. Ltd.

CONTENTS

Preface

In 1939, months before Hitler forced the world into a catastrophic global war, a book that proposed a Hindu nationalist approach to India's minority communities, especially Muslims, along the lines of the Nazi treatment of Jews in Germany, was published quietly in India.[1] The book's author, Madhav Sadashiv Golwalkar, was thirty-three years old. He was slim and spirited and smoked cigarettes continually. His dark eyes were bright and communicative, and his long black hair merged with the overgrown bushy beard that gathered below his chin, elongating his thin face. He had grown up in mofussil towns of central India and studied Zoology at Banaras Hindu University in the quintessential holy city of Varanasi on the Ganga. At the time, Golwalkar was yet to be thoroughly assimilated into the Rashtriya Swayamsevak Sangh, a Hindu militia set up in 1925, although he had been hovering around its leader, Dr. K. B. Hedgewar, for more than a year. The publication of the book, *We or Our Nationhood Defined,* may have been a subdued affair, but it served Golwalkar well. His status grew rapidly, and a little over a year later, upon the death of Hedgewar in 1940, he shot to the top of the RSS, becoming its second leader.

1. See for detail M. S. Golwalkar, *We or Our Nationhood Defined*, Bharat Publications, Nagpur, 1939.

In short order, even as everyone's attention was on the Second World War, Golwalkar set out to take full control of the RSS. With his book as the guiding force, he restructured the RSS to an unprecedented degree and packed it with highly passionate Hindu radicals given to strict subordination, discipline and devotion. These ceaselessly active individuals lent the RSS an intimidating tone and turned it into a powerful political instrument that was to work in mission mode to satisfy his craving for power and authority. In his effort to be everything at once, he became its chief architect, its principal organizer, the author of its ideology, its supreme teacher, its master tactician and its demagogic leader.

From its start, the RSS was ideologically rooted in *Hindutva: Who is a Hindu?*, the 1923 text by Hindu supremacist ideologue Vinayak Damodar Savarkar that claimed the whole of (pre-Independence) India for Hindus by virtue of the fact that they alone, and not Muslims or Christians, considered its territory sacred. But it was through Golwalkar's prescriptions in *We or Our Nationhood Defined* that the RSS obtained Nazi anti-Semitism as a model for dealing with India's minorities. Golwalkar's political clarity, which now became central to the ideological training of the RSS men, brought to the militia a sense of confidence it had never experienced before. It ensured that the credo of Indian Muslims as a 'foreign race' wielded the most lasting ideological influence upon members of the RSS.

Golwalkar found himself imperiled only once, when a member of his organization, Nathuram Vinayak Godse, assassinated Mahatma Gandhi on 30 January 1948. The sense of loss from Gandhi's death was so colossal that it numbed the newly independent nation of India and gave way to a violent public fury and a massive government crackdown against the RSS and its leaders. Golwalkar was put behind bars, and the RSS was banned. But a little over a year later, in July 1949, he made his way out of jail, and got the ban on the RSS revoked, by accepting all conditions of the government and promising complete loyalty to India's secular, democratic Constitution.

Golwalkar now stopped talking about *We or Our Nationhood Defined*. But the book's thesis continued to remain at the core of the RSS ideology, a fact that was noted by J. A. Curran Jr., an American researcher who produced the first well-investigated book on the RSS two years after the ban was revoked. Following his extensive interactions with Golwalkar and a large number of RSS leaders and cadres,[2] Curran concluded in his 1951 book that despite the ban and massive public outrage against the RSS in the wake of Mahatma Gandhi's assassination, the organization's real ideology continued to be based on *We or Our Nationhood Defined*. '*We* can be described as the R.S.S. "Bible",' Curran wrote. 'It is the basic primer in the indoctrination of the Sangh volunteers. Although this book was written twelve years ago, in a national context different from the contemporary one, the principles contained in it are still considered entirely applicable by the Sangh membership.'[3]

Golwalkar led the RSS for more than three decades—from 1940 until his death in 1973—extending the organization across the entire country, infusing its ranks with his political vision and exercising the most significant influence on generations of Hindu supremacist leaders, including Narendra Modi, the prime minister whose reign since 2014 has witnessed massive efforts to steer the national discourse to treat Muslims as the 'other'. Hate speeches, overt Islamophobia, lynchings of Muslims and the anti-intellectual environment in which dissent, even disagreement, often gets portrayed as 'anti-national' have become frequent in recent times. These, as well as the Modi government's attempts to push forward

2. J. A. Curran, Jr., *Militant Hinduism in Indian Politics: A Study of the R.S.S.*, Institute of Pacific Relations, New York, 1951, p. 3.

3. Ibid., p. 28.

its Hindu majoritarian agenda, including a citizenship law seen to directly discriminate against Muslims, mark the triumph of an ideological project set forth by Golwalkar in *We or Our Nationhood Defined*. And yet, Golwalkar's life history has continued to remain virtually an uncharted territory. All existing biographies are the works of Golwalkar loyalists who had reasons to glorify him. Instead of basing their arguments on facts, these biographers preferred to write allegorically, as if dealing not with a human being but an object of worship, a demi-god. On inspection, the efforts at concealment and the glorification of his personality did not begin after his death; they started under the supervision of Golwalkar himself.

When I set out to explore Golwalkar's life, I wondered how much he resembled Hitler and how much the demi-god of the Hindu Right; I wondered how his pervasive self-awareness of being an orthodox Brahmin placed him in total harmony with these two images; and I wondered how it was that some Indians considered him one of the biggest communal instigators, bent on destroying India's plural ethos and secularism, and yet others, regarding him as an ascetic figure and a messiah, could weep in their homes and in the streets on his death. I wondered, too, how Golwalkar influenced the historical processes of the age and how he himself got influenced by them.

It was with these questions in mind that I began to read archival records and books about Golwalkar, to talk to people who knew him and to discover as much as I could about his life. Sense also had to be made of the interconnections between him and his times across the long span of his active presence in the politics of the Hindu Right. In itself, Golwalkar's personality was oddly pallid and expressionless; it acquired tension and fascination and became compelling only in the context of the politics of the Hindu Right and the RSS. Consequently, the story of Golwalkar's life is an essential element of the Right in India. In the book, the background of his life history plays up more prominently than is customary in conventional biographies; Golwalkar is shown against his own—and the Hindu Right's—nostalgias, anxieties and resentments as well as events in the wider world that conditioned, promoted and drove him, and sometimes panicked him.

Madhu the *Ekpathi*

When, in 1939, Madhav Sadashiv Golwalkar published his maiden book, he quietly morphed from a former lab demonstrator in the Zoology department of Banaras Hindu University into an ex-professor. In the opening pages of *We or Our Nationhood Defined*, the author introduces himself as 'M.S. Golwalkar, M.Sc., L.L.B. (Sometime Professor, Benares Hindu University)'.[1] Eight years earlier, upon taking up the job, he had written to a friend in a letter dated 2 September 1931: 'I am working as a demonstrator in the Department of Zoology here [BHU]. This is a temporary post caused by a leave vacancy.'[2] The job lasted seventeen months, and its completion in the beginning of 1933 marked the end of Golwalkar's stint with the BHU.

Yet, at the time of the book's publication, none of his acquaintances questioned his assumption of a fake identity. In fact, they never did. They rather deluged everyone with extravagant claims on his behalf. His efforts at pretension seemed to pique no one's curiosity.

1. M. S. Golwalkar, *We or Our Nationhood Defined*, Bharat Publications, Nagpur, 1939, title page.

2. M. S. Golwalkar to Vamanrao Deshpande, *Shri Guruji Samagra*, Vol. 6, Suruchi Prakashan, New Delhi, 2014, p. 243.

It is uncertain why he resorted to this falsehood. But it was not a mistake. Even biographical accounts on him written subsequently under his own supervision repeated the lie and affirmed without exception that he had indeed been a professor—and not a lab assistant—at the BHU. His acquaintances and followers, who called him Guruji or the Teacher, simply believed it. In effect, he successfully communicated how he would like to be seen and what he would like known about him.

Apparently, Golwalkar had a sense of himself as an intellectual since his early days, and this might have led him to harbour an ambition to become a professor one day—a position that commanded respectability in society, especially among middle and lower middle classes. Though his ambition remained unfulfilled, by telling the world that he had once been a 'professor', he seemingly hoped to enhance popular admiration for himself as a learned person.

His efforts to conceal his past occupation while still on the cusp of becoming the chief of the Rashtriya Swayamsevak Sangh (RSS) also revealed how conscious he had become of his calling early on. In the years ahead, it would assume a pattern and shape his style of leadership.

RSS leaders of Golwalkar's vintage hardly ever encouraged accounts that dwelt on personal aspects of their past lives. For them, their organization and its militant ideology mattered above all else. But Golwalkar had a penchant for the glorification of his personality. This particular preference seemed stamped upon almost every text written about him—by his own guiding will—down to the last days of his life. One of the fallouts of Golwalkar's obsession with his persona was that these accounts, which introduced a note of allure into his portrait, read his childhood strictly through the prism of the adult Golwalkar's political career and ideology. They portrayed him as a born leader and a child prodigy who had distinguished himself from other boys of his age group and had had a mind of his own from a very early age.

As leaders from obscure backgrounds become famous, it is conventional for legends to be built about them, and often claims are made that some of their past accomplishments were much more profound than they seemed. In Golwalkar's case, the word was that his intellectual prowess was beyond any contestation. To his acquaintances and followers, who looked at him with definite awe, it might only have appeared normal for an intellectual of Golwalkar's calibre to have served, even if for a brief while, in the capacity of a professor. At the time of the publication of his book in 1939, his intelligence and diligence had been recognized in the RSS. His essential qualities, too, were noted by his acquaintances: he was thoughtful, intuitive and quick-witted, and was superbly multilingual with a good command over English, Sanskrit, Hindi and Bengali, apart from Marathi, his mother tongue.

However, nobody felt that his obsession of stylizing his persona existed in him to an abnormal degree.

II

Golwalkar was thirty-three when *We or Our Nationhood Defined* was published. A decade later, in 1949, appeared his first official biography, written by a close aide, Gangadhar Indurkar.[3] It presented Golwalkar's birth as if it were one of someone entrusted with a destiny higher and more exalted than that of ordinary people.

---

3. Gangadhar Indurkar, a Maharashtrian Brahmin, was born in 1918 and grew up in Allahabad in modern-day Uttar Pradesh. He started his journalistic career as a local reporter for a Varanasi-based Hindi newspaper in 1940 and soon joined *Kesari*, the Pune-based Marathi newspaper started by Congress conservative Bal Gangadhar Tilak in the late nineteenth century. *Kesari* now acted as the mouthpiece of the Hindu Mahasabha and the RSS. Indurkar joined the RSS sometime in the early 1940s. In 1949, the year he published the biography *Guruji: Rashtriya Swayamsevak Sangh ke Sarsanghchalak Shri Madhav Sadashiv Golwalkar ka Jeevan Charitra*, he was already recognized as one of the staunchest Golwalkar loyalists outside Maharashtra.

'Guruji was born at four-thirty in the morning of 19 February 1906 at Nagpur, the capital of Central Provinces,' writes Indurkar.

> Incidentally, when he was born the air was filled with the sound of morning drum-beats emanating from the palace of Nagpur's Bhonsale royal family. Who can say that drum-beats did not foretell Guruji's illustrious future? [...] In those days the family lived in deep poverty. But after his birth, there was no scarcity of any kind in the family.[4]

This description of his birth was repeated in biographies written subsequently by other aides during his lifetime. Narayan Hari Palkar,[5] whose biography, *Shri Ma Sa Golwalkar,* appeared in 1956, sought to wrap his master's birth in a similar aura. 'The rooster crowed announcing it to be the auspicious day of February 19, 1906,' Palkar writes.

> As the first rays of the sun heralded the arrival of dawn, in the house of Mr. Balkrishnapant Raikar, a son was born to Laxmibai. The very first sounds that fell on the ears of this babe must have been of the "choughada" from the imperial palace of Nagpur's Bhonsale. It was as if the call of the clarion at dawn was reminding him of the grandeur of the times gone by.
>
> Although this boy was given the name "Madhav", everyone

4. Shri Gangadhar Indurkar, *Guruji: Rashtriya Swayamsevak Sangh ke Sarsanghchalak Shri Madhav Sadashiv Golwalkar ka Jeevan Charitra*, Sangh Vastu Bhandar, Delhi, 1949, pp. 1-2.

5. N. H. Palkar was a Maharashtrian Brahmin who was born in 1918 and grew up in Pune. He joined the RSS in 1933 while still in school. He completed matriculation in 1936 but could not continue his college education, apparently due to health-related problems. After dropping out of college, he actively worked for the RSS in Thane and Pune districts and was among the first to become a Pracharak in 1942. When the RSS was banned in the aftermath of the assassination of Mahatma Gandhi and differing voices started emanating from within the outfit, Palkar stood firmly with Golwalkar. Once the ban on the RSS was lifted, he set out to write a comprehensive biography of the RSS chief. The book was published to mark Golwalkar's fiftieth birthday.

> took to calling him "Madhu". After the child's birth the family's fortunes took a turn for the better. Madhav's young [maternal] aunt took the birth of her nephew to be the cause of this shift and announced his arrival to be akin to the coming of "Sawai Madhavrao" to the household.[6]

Such hyperbolic descriptions of his birth became a part of the sentimental embroidery and melodramatic touches that embellished the Golwalkar personality cult in later years. Yet, the fable cloaking Golwalkar's birth could not hide the obvious signs of the condition into which he was born—the dominant feature of the picture being the nervous instability of a family looking for signs of security and respectable solidity.

Golwalkar, like Indurkar and Palkar, belonged to the Brahmin caste, an elite social group that is held by legend to have emerged from the brain of Lord Brahma, the mythical creator of the universe. Brahmins see themselves as upholders of Hinduism, a religious system defined by its characteristic stress on birth-based hierarchical arrangement of endogamous social groups—castes. Theologically, Brahmins occupy the apex of Hinduism's social pyramid, enjoying a bewilderingly complex set of privileges and observing a baffling combination of restraints. Originally, they were, as per Hindu mythology, mendicants and philosophers living apart from the material world and its temptations, but through centuries they transformed into a priestly class.

For a time, centuries ago, Golwalkar's ancestors lived in considerable affluence at Golwali, a village in the hills of the Western Ghats in Ratnagiri district of modern-day Maharashtra. The village's oral history holds that in those days, they went by the surname 'Padhye'. The village is part of the Konkan region, the land that, as per a local legend, Lord Parashurama had reclaimed

6. N. H. Palkar, *Shri Ma Sa Golwalkar*, published by N. H. Palkar, Mumbai, 1956, pp. 5-6.

by shooting an arrow into the Arabian Sea. The oral history, however, traces the origin of the village to the time when most of western India was under the rule of the Chalukya dynasty.

'The village came into existence in the seventh century when Chalukya king Pulkesin II donated revenue-free land to our ancestors in this area along with exclusive rights of *pourohitya* [priestly rights] in 72 neighbouring villages in the doab region of Garh and Saptalingi rivers,' said Anant Purushottam Padhye, a resident of Golwali and a distant relative of M. S. Golwalkar. 'Our ancestors were deeply religious and totally given to study of Vedas and other Hindu scriptures. They performed priestly duties in the donated villages and ran a Gurukul [Sanskrit-medium school] that attracted students from far and wide.'[7]

For almost a millennium, Golwali's affairs were relatively quiet. The village lived in near total isolation, its residents managing the Gurukul and performing priestly duties in the 72 donated villages. Golwali's oral history holds that the arrangement survived even after Maratha Chhatrapati Shivaji set up his kingdom in the region in the seventeenth century. But the quietude of the village abruptly ended under the Peshwas, the Brahmin rulers of the Maratha empire, about a year before they fought the Third Battle of Panipat in 1761. Earlier, the Peshwas had served as subordinates to the Chhatrapati. But by now the prime ministership had become hereditary and the Peshwas the de-facto rulers, relegating the Chhatrapati to the position of a mere figurehead.

Golwali's oral history contains at least two versions of what happened to them in the watershed year that preceded the Third Battle of Panipat. In one, the reigning Peshwa, Balaji Baji Rao, who was also known as Nanasaheb, deceived the Padhyes of Golwali by transferring their priestly rights over the 72 villages

7. Based on an interview with Anant Purushottam Padhye at Golwali village in Maharashtra's Ratnagiri district on 26 October 2021.

in Garh-Saptalingi doab to his own relatives. As expected, the Padhyes flew into uncontrollable rage. They cursed the Peshwas, packed their belongings, put Golwali on fire and set out across the Maratha kingdom.[8]

'Nothing survived that fire in Golwali except the stone foundation of the Gurukul, which is the sole remnant of the rage triggered by Peshwa Nanasaheb's deceit,' said Anant Padhye.[9] He and many other residents of Golwali still believe that the curse did not go in vain. The very next year, in 1761, the Peshwas were routed in the Third Battle of Panipat, fought far away north of Delhi, in which the Maratha side was arrayed against the Durranis, the Rohillas and the Awadhis. Balaji Baji Rao lost his son, Vishwas Rao, in the battle and died from the shock a few months thereafter.

A second version, which is supported by an account written by Royal Asiatic Society's Bombay president, John Wilson, and published in 1877, holds that what happened in Golwali was a reflection of Balaji Baji Rao's extremely inimical attitude towards Karhade Brahmins after he came to know that the latter had been secretly practising human sacrifice as part of their ritual. Karhades are one of the three traditionally endogamous subgroups of Maharashtrian Brahmins, the other two being Chitpawans and Deshasthas. The Padhyes of Golwali belonged to the Karhade subgroup, while the Peshwas were Chitpawan Brahmins.

In *Indian Caste*, John Wilson gives an account of the so-called Karhade practice of human sacrifice and claims that Balaji Baji Rao was so appalled on getting to know about one such ritual killing in Poona (or Pune) that he branded all Brahmins of this subgroup as dangerous criminals and ordered their general persecution. Writes Wilson:

---

8. Ibid.

9. Ibid.

> The tribe of Brahmans called Karhadi had formerly a horrid custom of annually sacrificing to their deities (Shaktis) a young Brahman. The Shakti is supposed to delight in human blood, and is represented with three fiery eyes, and covered with red flowers. [...] The prayers of her votaries are directed to her during the first nine days of the Dasara feast; and in the evening of the tenth day a grand repast is prepared, to which the whole family is invited. An intoxicating drug is contrived to be mixed with the food of the intended victim, who is often a stranger whom the master of the house has for several months, perhaps years, treated with the greatest kindness and attention; and sometime to lull suspicion, given him his daughter in marriage. As soon as the poisonous and intoxicating drug operates, the master of the house, unattended, takes the devoted person into the temple, leads him three times round the idol; and on his prostrating himself before it takes this opportunity of cutting his throat. He collects with the greatest care the blood in a small bowl; which he first applies to the lips of this ferocious goddess, and then sprinkles it over her body; and a hole having been dug at the feet of the idol for the corpse, he deposits it with great care to prevent discovery. After perpetration of this horrid act, the Karhadi Brahman returns to his family, and spends the night in mirth and revelry, convinced that by this praiseworthy act he has propitiated the favour of his blood-thirsty deity for twelve years.[10]

By Wilson's account, the practice discontinued when a young Brahmin, who had escaped the fate despite being nurtured for such a sacrifice by a 'cruel Brahman' of the subcaste and who had been privy to the ritual killing of another youth in his own place, came scampering to Balaji Baji Rao and recounted the whole sordid story of the gruesome murder.

---

10. John Wilson, *Indian Caste*, Vol. II, Times of India Office, Bombay, 1877, p. 22.

> Orders were instantly given to seize every Karhadi Brahman in the city of Puna, and particularly the infamous perpetrator of the horrible deed. He was, with a number of others similarly convicted, put to death; and all the sect were expelled [from] the city, and strict injunctions laid on the inhabitants to have in future as little connection with them as possible.[11]

As per the second version, it was this general persecution of Karhades that resulted in the forfeiture of the Golwali Padhyes' *pourohitya* rights over 72 neighbouring villages. Infuriated by this unexpected attack on their traditional rights and devastated by the sudden loss of the major source of their livelihood, the Padhyes of Golwali decided to emigrate. In any event, the disaster that fell on the Padhyes during the reign of Balaji Baji Rao changed the course of their history. Little is recalled about the intervening generations except that some of their descendants returned to Golwali after the decline of the Maratha empire and that one section of emigrants, in loving memory of the village they had to abandon, later changed their surname from 'Padhye' to 'Golwalkar'.

III

The only qualification Golwali's emigrants possessed was their ability to perform priestly acts and teach Sanskrit scriptures. The biggest branch of these emigrants, therefore, aimed for a place where they could survive on what they knew best. They went eastward and, crossing the Western Ghats and travelling about 300 km, chose the famous pilgrimage town of Pandharpur as their new abode.[12] The town, frequently visited by a sizeable community of Hindu pilgrims, offered promise of an environment in which

---

11. Ibid., p. 23.

12. N. H. Palkar, *Shri Ma Sa Golwalkar*, published by N. H. Palkar, Mumbai, 1956, p. 5.

these hapless priests could eke out a living. The evidence about the emigrants' circumstances after their arrival in Pandharpur is sketchy, as they were now separated from the group that, by returning to Golwali, kept what oral history survives.

At some point around the middle of the nineteenth century, Golwalkar's great-grandfather, Sakharam Golwalkar, decided to break away and look for fresh pastures. He started a second chain of journey as he found a job as a priest in Paithan, another Hindu pilgrimage town about 250 km north of Pandharpur.[13] His son, Bal Krishna Golwalkar, was an enterprising man. He gave up the family's traditional priestly profession and travelled almost 800 km east to work in the court of the Kawardha princely state in central India. But his journey ended in disaster. One day, while on an administrative tour, he was riding a horse and following his boss, a British judge of the Kawardha court, through a dense forest when his head hit the branch of a tree full of wasp nests. As he fell down, frenzied wasps swarmed over him. He died on the spot.[14]

At the time Sadashiv, Bal Krishna Golwalkar's elder son, was a 15-year-old. He had not yet completed his matriculation and had just been married to a nine-year-old girl, Laxmibai of Kamthi, a suburb of Nagpur, the capital of the Central Provinces and Berar. Burdened with family responsibilities, Sadashiv had to leave school and take up a lowly paid job that had been offered to him on compassionate grounds in the Kawardha court.[15] Soon, however, he seemed to feel the need to provide himself with security and

---

13. Ranga Hari, *The Incomparable Guru Golwalkar*, Prabhat Paperbacks, New Delhi, 2018, p. 10.

14. N. H. Palkar, *Shri Ma Sa Golwalkar*, published by N. H. Palkar, Mumbai, 1956, p. 6.

15. Ranga Hari, *The Incomparable Guru Golwalkar*, Prabhat Paperbacks, New Delhi, 2018, p. 12.

a firm footing. So he resumed his studies while continuing at the job. Sadashiv passed his matriculation examination in 1893.[16] Eight years later, in 1901, he entered the postal department in the Central Provinces and Berar and was posted as a clerk at Kamthi, where he cleared his Intermediate examination in 1903.[17] Though the new post did not fetch him any significant increase in salary, it provided the security of a government job and brought him to the place where Laxmibai's male cousin, Balkrishna Raikar, a relative the couple had always relied on for support at the time of crisis, lived. In fact, it was at Raikar's home in Kamthi that Laxmibai gave birth to Madhav Sadashiv Golwalkar in 1906.

Golwalkar was the fourth child born to his parents. Of the three older children, two had died young and only one, Amrit, had survived; of the five younger ones, all had passed away in infancy. Unstable and poor though his family was, Golwalkar was to be given a chance that most did not get in those days—he was going to be properly educated. In no way, however, did this point towards his future. There was nothing at the time of his birth to foretell his destiny. Golwalkar's upbringing, too, lacked any definite signs to predetermine the career he would ultimately opt for. A lot more had to happen before he would settle for a specific sphere of activity, and this included his particular experiences, varied nostalgias, anxieties and resentments as well as events in the wider world.

The evidence about Golwalkar's earliest years is thin. He was two years old when his father left the job in the postal department and took up a teacher's post in a newly started government school at Saraipali, a remote subdivision of Raipur district in the Central

---

16. Shri Gangadhar Indurkar, *Guruji: Rashtriya Swayamsevak Sangh ke Sarsanghchalak Shri Madhav Sadashiv Golwalkar ka Jeevan Charitra*, Sangh Vastu Bhandar, Delhi, 1949, p. 2.

17. Ibid.

Provinces. Sadashiv joined the new service on 1 October 1908. According to most accounts, his stay at Saraipali was not for long. In fact, his two decades of service as a teacher was marked by frequent transfers, leading to shifts of his residence to different parts of the Central Provinces. Golwalkar, known to everyone by the diminutive Madhu, was three years old when his father was transferred to Durg, about 200 km west of Saraipali.[18] From there, at frequent intervals, the family moved to Raipur and then to Khandwa, Bhandara, Balaghat, Narsinghpur, Hoshangabad and Chanda.[19]

IV

In a series of biographies, all written by his aides, Golwalkar is portrayed as a wunderkind who started going to school when he was not even three and was instantly recognized for his brilliance. A few recollections about his childhood, all in keeping with the precocity of genius, tend to leap out in these accounts of his life. 'Guruji had an amazing capacity to memorize anything by reading it or hearing it once,' writes Indurkar, 'That is why people used to call him *ekpathi* (or one with amazing capacity to memorize).'[20] Palkar told a story to drive home the point:

> At the time when Madhav was still learning his first letters, Bhauji [his father] turned his attention to memorization. When Madhav turned six, Bhauji bought for him a booklet of *Shri Ramraksha Stotra* [a 38-verse ancient Sanskrit hymn dedicated to Lord Rama]. But Madhav was stumped by compound letters

18. Ranga Hari, *The Incomparable Guru Golwalkar*, Prabhat Paperbacks, New Delhi, 2018, p. 13.

19. Ibid.

20. Shri Gangadhar Indurkar, *Guruji: Rashtriya Swayamsevak Sangh ke Sarsanghchalak Shri Madhav Sadashiv Golwalkar ka Jeevan Charitra*, Sangh Vastu Bhandar, Delhi, 1949, p. 4.

> in Sanskrit in the verses and he couldn't read them. 'I much prefer if you read out the *Ramraksha* to me,' Madhav told his father, 'I will learn it by listening to you.' In clear tones Bhauji read out the verses to Madhav a few times and based on this recitation Madhav memorized the *Ramraksha* in its entirety. This uncommon accomplishment earned the boy some praise. He soon came to be known as the child who had unusual powers of retention.[21]

Indurkar has other descriptions of his prowess. In school, no sooner would a teacher finish describing a problem than he would furnish the solution, leaving little room for other boys to take part in the classroom exercise. He was, therefore, instructed by his admiring teacher to follow restraint in the classroom and write down the answer on his palm, instead of speaking it out, to show it to him separately.[22] On one occasion, when a mathematics teacher in a higher class could not solve a problem despite repeated attempts, Golwalkar was summoned for help. After that, boys of even senior classes started seeking help from him in solving problems of mathematics.[23]

How much of this is true is now impossible to say. Nor is it possible to disentangle the facts from the legends that seem to have been created with his own permission, if not by his own imagination. In any event, the cloak of legend the biographers throw over Golwalkar's childhood contrasts strongly with the reality. The evidence available about his primary-school education suggests that it was not very smooth. He passed his fourth standard

---

21. N. H. Palkar, *Shri Ma Sa Golwalkar*, published by N. H. Palkar, Mumbai, 1956, pp. 10-11.

22. Shri Gangadhar Indurkar, *Guruji: Rashtriya Swayamsevak Sangh ke Sarsanghchalak Shri Madhav Sadashiv Golwalkar ka Jeevan Charitra*, Sangh Vastu Bhandar, Delhi, 1949, p. 5.

23. Ibid.

in 1915, six years after he apparently joined the first standard which in those days used to be the lowest class in government schools.[24] This could have been due to a complex of reasons. One significant factor must have been the frequent transfer of his father. Also, in 1913, he suffered from a mysterious fever that became chronic and continued in varying degree for most of his student life.[25] Yet another tragedy marred these years when in 1918, Amrit, Golwalkar's elder brother, was fatally struck down by influenza.

After Golwalkar passed the matriculation examination with a second class in 1922, his parents sent him to Pune's Fergusson College, an elite institution for higher studies. But no sooner did he take admission in the Intermediate of Science than he had to leave the college due to an unexpected Bombay Presidency regulation reserving all educational institutions of the province for local students.[26] The regulation was withdrawn a few months later, but not before forcing Golwalkar to shift to another, equally famous educational institution, Hislop College of Nagpur.[27]

Here, surprisingly, he proved a total failure. His father wanted to steer him into the medical profession after Intermediate.[28] In those days, admission to a medical college was gained on the basis of marks obtained in the Intermediate examination. But Golwalkar's studies were undermined by his incapacity to

---

24. N. H. Palkar, *Shri Ma Sa Golwalkar*, published by N. H. Palkar, Mumbai, 1956, p. 12.

25. Shri Gangadhar Indurkar, *Guruji: Rashtriya Swayamsevak Sangh ke Sarsanghchalak Shri Madhav Sadashiv Golwalkar ka Jeevan Charitra*, Sangh Vastu Bhandar, Delhi, 1949, p. 10.

26. N. H. Palkar, *Shri Ma Sa Golwalkar*, published by N. H. Palkar, Mumbai, 1956, pp. 14-15.

27. Ibid., p. 15.

28. Shri Gangadhar Indurkar, *Guruji: Rashtriya Swayamsevak Sangh ke Sarsanghchalak Shri Madhav Sadashiv Golwalkar ka Jeevan Charitra*, Sangh Vastu Bhandar, Delhi, 1949, p. 12.

concentrate on his course. The pattern that appeared at Hislop College survived for the rest of his student life.

In later years, Golwalkar's biographers sought to explain away his deviation from studies by references to his artistic vocation and his willingness to spend time in helping his classmates so that none would fall behind. However, it seems plausible that the shift away from Chanda, where his schoolteacher father was posted at the time, was merely the fulfillment of his desire for freedom. Suddenly, he didn't have to continually run into the powerful figure of his father, who, according to most accounts, insisted on discipline and who translated his pride as a strict teacher into inflexible demands for obedience. Liberated from the stringent rules of the household, Golwalkar appeared inclined to follow his own bent. Rather than concentrating on his studies, his life at Nagpur, where he lived under the guardianship of his uncle Balkrishna Raikar, rolled along in leisure with friends.

Aesthetic matters gave him extraordinary pleasure. In fact, we must assume that his father paid little attention to his son's artistic aspirations. Certainly, he seemed to be guided by his own dream to see his son be a doctor one day and did not insist upon knowing why his grades in matriculation were not satisfactory or what bent of mind he actually possessed. That is apparent, if only because Golwalkar's dedication to his studies was never even remotely close to that which he displayed to the learning of the flute after he met Nagpur's famous blind flutist, the maestro Sawlaram, during his days at Hislop College.[29] In his two years at Nagpur, he spent a considerable amount of time with his flute and learned quite a bit.

Time passed and the exams approached. In the absence of adequate preparation, his grades continued to be unsatisfactory.

29. N. H. Palkar, *Shri Ma Sa Golwalkar*, published by N. H. Palkar, Mumbai, 1956, p. 15.

He passed the exams with a second class in 1924.[30] He excelled in English but not in the science papers, which were critical for admission to a medical college.[31]

Golwalkar still tried his luck, pressurized, as he apparently was, by the social ambition that drove his father. He applied for admission in a medical college in Lucknow, the capital of the United Provinces, but could not succeed.[32] However, freedom from the demands of his father's dream did not automatically lead him to a vocation that would suit his temperament. He moved to Banaras Hindu University and enrolled for the Bachelor of Sciences in the Department of Zoology. Here, too, the decision was not entirely his own; it was prompted and facilitated by Balkrishna Raikar.

V

Though founded in 1915, much of the construction work of the BHU was yet to be completed when Golwalkar arrived there in 1924. Yet, it was already seen as a respectable institution of higher education operating in a traditional Hindu religious atmosphere. Its location in Varanasi, a quintessential Hindu holy city, added to its aura. At the end of the first quarter of the twentieth century, the BHU prided itself on blending Hinduism with modern curriculum. In 1924, its Zoology department, though barely three years old, had already acquired considerable repute.

Like Golwalkar, most BHU students were boarders; they lived in the newly constructed hostels, as did most of the university teaching staff. University regulations served to keep the campus

30. Shri Gangadhar Indurkar, *Guruji: Rashtriya Swayamsevak Sangh ke Sarsanghchalak Shri Madhav Sadashiv Golwalkar ka Jeevan Charitra*, Sangh Vastu Bhandar, Delhi, 1949, p. 12.

31. N. H. Palkar, *Shri Ma Sa Golwalkar*, published by N. H. Palkar, Mumbai, 1956, p. 16.

32. Ibid., p. 17.

distinctly Hindu. Smoking and drinking alcohol, considered imported western vices, were forbidden and a vegetarian diet was enforced upon all the students in the hostels, though exceptions were made for the few Europeans who lived in a separate hostel at the end of the campus.[33]

When Golwalkar entered the BHU, he stood out because of his reticent personality. He sat long hours, sometimes for whole nights, by the Ganga, watching the waves that washed the eastern edge of Varanasi.[34] Though he seemed a little afraid of making mistakes, he was not shy. He was lanky, pallid, thoughtful, and always dressed with extreme care. Usually, he sported a starched white dhoti and kurta and shaved every day. His moustaches were well trimmed and his fine, thick hair neatly parted from the middle. His large, dark eyes were bright and communicative, but his manner was reserved.

Throughout his life, he was to remember his days of youth in the BHU with pleasure and pride, speak of his eagerness to help other boys and his love for books. His biographers, too, have tended to depict him as a voracious reader 'who read almost all important books in the BHU library'.[35] The books that he read were mostly related to Hindu religion and spiritualism.[36] It would seem that as he became immersed in exploring texts on religion, his preparation for the final B.Sc. examination suffered. He now wrote to his father requesting that he be allowed to skip the examination for a year so he could get extra time to prepare.[37]

---

33. Leah Renold, *A Hindu Education: Early Years of the Banaras Hindu University*, Oxford University Press India, Delhi, 2006, pp. 148-151.

34. Ranga Hari, *The Incomparable Guru Golwalkar*, Prabhat Paperbacks, New Delhi, 2018, p. 27.

35. Shri Gangadhar Indurkar, *Guruji: Rashtriya Swayamsevak Sangh ke Sarsanghchalak Shri Madhav Sadashiv Golwalkar ka Jeevan Charitra*, Sangh Vastu Bhandar, Delhi, 1949, p. 15.

36. Jagat S. Bright, *Guruji Golwalkar & R.S.S.*, New India Publishing Co., Delhi, 1950, p. 22.

37. Ibid.

He was aided by the precarious equilibrium of his health. In the letter he pitched his illness as the main ground for his desire to skip the examination.

But there were limits to how much his father was prepared to tolerate. In 1926, when Golwalkar was to appear for his B.Sc. examination, his father was left with three years of service as a school teacher. An era was ending, and soon he would not be in a position to pay for his son's education and upkeep at the BHU. Perhaps, like any middle-class salaried person, he wanted his son to be on his feet before his own retirement. One early biography obliquely suggests this mood of tension between father and son that sprang from his failure to concentrate on his regular courses and from the father's realization that his son was misusing his trust and testing his patience. 'Guruji wired his father asking his permission to take the examination next year,' writes Jagat S. Bright in his 1950 biography of Golwalkar. 'His father delayed the reply. He understood that his father was displeased with him and he did not want to displease his father.'[38] With his father cracking the whip, Golwalkar instantly dropped the idea of extending the B.Sc.

In later years, biographers told a vivid story about how for a short while just before the examination, he plunged himself into his course material day and night; he studied practically twenty-four hours a day. He was stung by a scorpion once. The pain surged, but he did not stop. When friends asked him to take a break, he smiled: 'The scorpion has stung my foot, not my head. It need not, therefore, interfere with my reading.'[39] Golwalkar passed the B.Sc. examination with a second class in 1926.[40]

---

38. Ibid.

39, Ibid., pp. 22-23.

40. Shri Gangadhar Indurkar, *Guruji: Rashtriya Swayamsevak Sangh ke Sarsanghchalak Shri Madhav Sadashiv Golwalkar ka Jeevan Charitra*, Sangh Vastu Bhandar, Delhi, 1949, p. 15.

VI

At twenty, Golwalkar was distinctly passionate about matters of religion. Years later, while speaking at Ajmer in 1963, he said, 'When I was in Benaras, one of my teachers was a volunteer of Arya Samaj. He used to do *yagna* every week. I also used to take part in it.'[41] Initiated in the late nineteenth century as a movement to reform Hinduism, the Arya Samaj had by now transformed itself into a hardliner Hindu community. Soon, it would become a breeding ground for Hindu communal organizations.

Yet, what stirred Golwalkar the most were the teachings of Theosophy.[42] In that period in the BHU, largely because of the impact of Annie Besant, a member of the Theosophical Society and an active advocate of Hinduism, it was common to be a Theosophist. Founded in the late nineteenth century, the Theosophical Society was a movement in favour of esotericism and embraced what it regarded as the more spiritual traditions of the ancient East, particularly Hinduism and Buddhism.[43] Besant, a European woman who had come to India under the auspices of the Theosophical Society in 1893, quickly made this country her chosen homeland and championed Hinduism and Indian nationalism. She spoke against the westernizing of India and highlighted what she considered the glory and greatness of ancient Indian thought.[44] She regarded western education as vital for Indians but also supported the learning of Hindu culture and

41. *Shri Guruji Samagra*, Vol. 5, Suruchi Prakashan, Delhi, p. 35.

42. N. H. Palkar, *Shri Ma Sa Golwalkar*, published by N. H. Palkar, Mumbai, 1956, p. 29.

43. Leah Renold, *A Hindu Education: Early Years of the Banaras Hindu University*, Oxford University Press India, Delhi, 2006, p. 16.

44. Raj Kumar, *Annie Besant's Rise to Power in Indian Politics 1914-1917*, Concept Publishing House, Delhi, 1981, p. 41.

traditions.[45] In order to put her ideas into practice, she founded Central Hindu School at Varanasi in 1898. Later, it became Central Hindu College and formed the kernel of the BHU.

In the early years of the BHU, Hindu students in large numbers were attracted to the Theosophical Society. They responded to its critique of orthodoxy in Christianity and its praise of their own religion and cultural traditions. Its credo fit in with known Brahminical impulses. It appeared to strengthen Hindu conservatives as well as their attempts to revive orthodoxy. There is no specific evidence to suggest that Golwalkar ever formally became a Theosophist. It seems most likely that his connection to the Theosophical Society was through a man who was an expert in teachings of Theosophy. This man, mentioned as 'Shri Desai' in Golwalkar's letters and biographies, lived outside the BHU campus in Varanasi.[46] Soon, as the two became very good friends, he moved into Golwalkar's hostel room, and they started living together. Desai guided him enthusiastically into Theosophical literature and introduced him to his Theosophist friends. For a short while, Golwalkar was so impressed by this man that he even started wearing the outfit of a Theosophist—a long, loose white kurta with a single button to fasten its collar-less neck.[47]

Quite how he dealt with the M.Sc. examination in the midst of all this is unclear. The accounts are generally silent or extremely vague. He passed the exam in 1928 with a grade good enough to encourage the idea of a future in academics. He moved to Madras, chasing an aspiration to enroll for a doctorate degree.

---

45. Leah Renold, *A Hindu Education: Early Years of the Banaras Hindu University*, Oxford University Press India, Delhi, 2006, p. 15.

46. N. H. Palkar, *Shri Ma Sa Golwalkar*, published by N. H. Palkar, Mumbai, 1956, p. 29.

47. Ibid., p. 30.

Job-hunting

Golwalkar came to Madras with the idea of securing from a local benefactor the financial aid that he would need to pursue his research. Sources are silent about the name of this benefactor except that he was an extremely wealthy man and a philanthropist. It is also not clear who recommended Golwalkar to him.

In Madras, Golwalkar became engaged in some kind of research in a marine aquarium while waiting for an appointment with the philanthropist. In the bustling metropolis where he spent the next three quarters of a year, from August 1928 to April 1929, Golwalkar faced a culture shock much more intense than in Varanasi. Constrained by language for having no knowledge of Tamil, he developed a pronounced tendency to keep to himself. All his time was spent at work in the marine aquarium located close to the famous Marina beach.

He lived on the fifty rupees his father sent him every month.[1] He cooked for himself and stayed in a squalid rented room in Triplicane about half a mile away from the aquarium. He was at the aquarium most of the day, and when at home, he was usually

---

1. N. H. Palkar, *Shri Ma Sa Golwalkar*, published by N. H. Palkar, Mumbai, 1956, p. 18.

cooking, reading or writing letters, mainly to his friend Baburao Tailang, a resident of Nagpur who at the time was studying at the BHU. Sometimes he would break off suddenly and pick up his flute. Perhaps, it eased his nerves.

He started smoking, and he did so perhaps the way he played the flute—to ease his nerves. In a letter to Tailang, he talked of an 'inner conflict' lasting several days in the course of which his emotions of being a young man sought to resist the inexorable commands of his reason that tried to pull him towards the Hindu religious philosophy of Vedanta. 'On the one side there were powerful waves of youthful energies and on the other unmovable mountains of Vedanta—the conflict was so intense that my heart was shaken badly,' he wrote. 'I was deeply upset, and this situation continued for several days. It led to high fever and severe headache. [...] To comfort my heart, I started smoking.'[2]

In a very discriminatory manner, he admired everything related to Hinduism. 'It [Hinduism] is unique in the entire world,' he wrote to Tailang on 9 February 1929. 'Western civilizations are excessively materialistic. Islam is still guided by brutal instincts. Only Hinduism makes it possible to achieve spiritual progress. This trait of Hinduism has survived for thousands of years. But in recent times, we are getting dazzled by western materialism. This has affected our spiritualism, too. Can we let this continue? We should ponder over it.'[3]

So drawn was he to that appeal of tradition that he even found merit in its *chaturvarnya* system, or the caste system.[4] In 1928, Madras had already become a socially restive city, prevalently in favour of the 'Self-Respect Movement' founded in 1925 by 'Periyar' E. V. Ramaswami Naicker. The city was witnessing the burning of

2. *Shri Guruji Samagra*, Vol. 6, Suruchi Prakashan, Delhi, p. 179.

3. Ibid., pp. 196-197.

4. Ibid., p. 180.

Manusmriti, the ancient text that describes and ranks the castes, in public demonstrations. The upsurge was everywhere, with forcible temple-entry and the outright promotion of atheism by non-Brahmins.[5] 'I have not found even a small basis of untouchability in Manusmriti,' he wrote to Tailang on 9 February 1929.[6]

In a milieu that was marked by the growing radicalization of the anti-caste movement, the views held by Golwalkar regarding *Manusmriti* were not unusual for an orthodox Brahmin. Madras as well as the Marathi linguistic districts of Bombay Presidency and the Central Provinces, which included Nagpur, were emerging as major focal points of a growing rift between Brahmins and non-Brahmins. In late 1927, B. R. Ambedkar had publicly condemned *Manusmriti* for scripturally justifying caste discrimination and untouchability and led thousands of followers to burn its copies.[7]

Golwalkar returned frequently to the growing conflict between Brahmins and non-Brahmins in the letters he wrote from Madras. In a vein that would be familiar to latter-day adherents of conservative arguments, he described the miserable conditions to which Brahmins had been consigned due to the conflict: 'The result [of this conflict] is that Hindu Brahmins are dying of starvation whereas Christians and Muslims are having food to their fill.'[8] In another letter, he wrote, 'The conflict between Brahmins and non-Brahmins will result in total destruction of our country.'[9]

---

5. Ibid., pp. 243-244.

6. Ibid., p. 197.

7. Sumit Sarkar, *Modern India: 1885-1947*, Macmillan Publishers India Ltd, Delhi, 2013, p. 243.

8. *Shri Guruji Samagra*, Vol. 6, Suruchi Prakashan, Delhi, p. 187.

9. Ibid., p. 197.

II

Virtually since his arrival in Madras in August 1928, Golwalkar had been waiting for an appointment with the philanthropist-sponsor. This man had been constantly travelling and Golwalkar had waited for him all these months. Around the beginning of March 1929, the would-be benefactor returned to Madras but apparently showed little interest in financing Golwalkar's research. 'The man who was to give me a scholarship had come back in March,' Golwalkar wrote to Tailang on 23 March 1929. 'He had been holidaying in America, Europe and other places. On his return, he stayed in Madras for about fifteen days. I could not succeed in getting an appointment with him. So, I did not get the scholarship from him.'[10]

It was a cruel shock. 'I can obtain the degree of doctorate only if I go to England and stay there for two years or if I produce a thesis after researching for four-five years in a big Indian university,' he wrote. 'Now, all the possibilities of doing a doctorate have ended.'[11]

He described this experience as a blow that made him leave everything 'in the hands of god'.[12] He had been so confident about getting the financial support that it never occurred to him to try working toward an alternative plan. He could not produce so much as a research article from his time at the aquarium.[13] Instead, he seemed to have mostly used the labours of his intellect in exploring English fiction.

Among the authors he admired most was a British thriller writer, Edgar Wallace. A most prolific writer of the early twentieth

---

10. Ibid., pp. 234-235.

11. Ibid., p. 235.

12. Ibid.

13. Ibid.

century, Wallace mainly wrote crime stories wherein a Scotland Yard official would always act as the central figure solving problems, not on the basis of his superb intellect and his ability to chase clues or deductions but often on the basis of some incredible coincidences and some unexplained leads. Wallace, therefore, was also known as a mystery novel writer. Golwalkar was so deeply impressed that he once wrote to Tailang: 'If Edgar Wallace is left out, there won't be any good novelist.'[14] Golwalkar also claimed to have read *Uncle Tom's Cabin*, the famous anti-slavery novel by American author Harriet Beecher Stowe. In his letter to Tailang, however, he mistakenly named a 'Mrs. Margaret Stowe' as its author.[15]

The new situation gave rise to an acute anxiety. So far afforded a carefree and untrammeled existence, he became depressed. 'It is a baseless speculation that I would get a job of a teacher here,' he wrote to Tailang on 23 March 1929. 'As it is, the locals [people of Madras] are themselves not being able to obtain employment and are migrating to other parts of the country in search of livelihood. In such a situation, I am surprised, how anyone could imagine that I would get a job here.'[16]

It would seem that his longing for a stable life intensified. He craved to go back to Varanasi, but his father's retirement meant an abrupt end to his freedom of movement. 'Perhaps there would be some opening for me in Benaras. Let's see. I am trying, but I don't have any answer at the moment,' he wrote.[17]

Golwalkar was at a loose end. He returned to Nagpur in April 1929.[18]

---

14. Ibid., p. 217.

15. Ibid., p. 216.

16. Ibid., p. 235.

17. Ibid.

18. N. H. Palkar, *Shri Ma Sa Golwalkar*, published by N. H. Palkar, Mumbai, 1956, p. 24.

III

One time, while in Madras, Golwalkar had shown enthusiasm for the nationalist cause in a letter to Tailang. A murder was committed on 17 December 1928 in Lahore, the capital of Punjab, by the revolutionaries Bhagat Singh and Shivaram Rajguru, who mistook their victim John Saunders for another police officer, James Scott, whom they held responsible for the death of nationalist leader Lala Lajpat Rai. 'News of Saunders' murder soothed my heart, and instantaneously, I shouted—bravo-bravo,' Golwalkar wrote. 'The revenge, even if partial, had no doubt been taken. Had I been in that situation, I would also have committed the same secret act.'[19]

Then he got to know that Tailang had shared his views on Saunders' assassination with other friends at the BHU. 'I never thought that you would share my views regarding the revenge of Lala Lajpat Rai's murder with other people,' Golwalkar wrote in his next letter to Tailang, dated 24 January 1929. Pointing out that some of the students at the BHU worked for the intelligence department, he said he could be arrested if the government got to know that 'Golwalkar, who always talks of world harmony, holds this view'.[20]

In the non-violent movement for independence led by Mohandas Karamchand Gandhi, or the Mahatma, he seemed to discern the debasement of sublimity, the presence of something that was repugnant to him. Characteristically, therefore, he sought to ridicule Gandhi and his non-violent movement in his letter to Tailang. 'No one can question the honesty of Gandhi even if his politics is full of weaknesses,' he wrote on 20 March 1929. 'It is this honesty that makes him believe that independence can be won on the basis of non-violence, non-cooperation and charkha

---

19. *Shri Guruji Samagra*, Vol. 6, Suruchi Prakashan, Delhi, p. 178.
20. Ibid., p. 183.

[domestic spinning wheel]. That is why he always talks of this. Even if people laugh, he remains unaffected.'[21]

Golwalkar's biographers would have it that he refrained from joining the struggle for India's independence because he remained completely occupied with his studies and spiritualism. But it would be more accurate to say that he was filled with inchoate emotions of pride in orthodox Hinduism and an aching desire to be treated as an intellectual in some way. His interest in public affairs at the time was excessively subjective, and he grasped what was happening in the world around him more by instinct than by reason.

Nagpur was one of the centres of foment against British imperialism when Golwalkar came back. Yet, this sensitive young man, for whom music and literature had been among the great liberating experiences of his youth, seemed unaffected by the nationalist movement now raging in the country. No reverberations of the call given on 19 December 1929 by the Indian National Congress to all Indians to fight for complete independence from British rule seemed to reach his ears. Nor was he stirred by the sensations of the Civil Disobedience Movement, by far the most widespread anti-British struggle, which began on 6 April 1930 when Mahatma Gandhi entered the sea at Dandi village in Gujarat and broke the salt laws by picking up lumps of natural salt lying in a small pit. Similar peaceful breaches of law started taking place everywhere, provoking a vigorous and open movement for political freedom. The nation started ringing with denunciations of the British Raj, but Golwalkar didn't seem to have felt part of the nationalistic opposition.

The series of ideas he seemed attracted to were precisely the same that would come to the fore repeatedly on more diverse planes in later years.

---

21. Ibid., p. 218.

IV

In the beginning of August 1931, Golwalkar received a telegram from the BHU. A temporary job had become available against a leave vacancy. For the last two years after his return from Madras, he had been living with his uncle Balkrishna Raikar in Nagpur and assisting him in the running of his coaching centre, Raikar Coaching Classes.[22] He had tried to find a teaching job in Nagpur. All the while, he had maintained regular contact with his friends at the BHU, including Desai, the man who had introduced him to the Theosophical Society. The role of Desai in getting Golwalkar the job at the BHU should not be overlooked or underemphasized, for it was his friend V. L. Pawar who had gone on leave, causing the vacancy.

At the time, the Zoology department of the BHU had four permanent teachers and two lab assistants or demonstrators. The teachers included Dr. A. B. Mishra, Chandra Bal, Kedar Nath Gupta and Ram Chandra Saksena. Pawar was one of the two permanent demonstrators, the other being Shashadhar Chatterjee.[23]

On 16 August 1931, Golwalkar reached Varanasi. The decision was made so abruptly as to startle his family and friends. 'I had to immediately come here after I received the university office's telegram in Nagpur,' he wrote to a friend on 2 September 1931. 'I am working as a demonstrator in the Department of Zoology here [BHU]. This is a temporary post caused by a leave vacancy. So, I can't tell you when I will become unemployed once again.'[24]

Not only in getting the job but also in arranging for accommodation, he received help from his friends in Varanasi.

---

22. Ranga Hari, *The Incomparable Guru Golwalkar*, Prabhat Paperbacks, New Delhi, 2018, p. 38.

23. Benares Hindu University, Calendar for 1930-31, p. 940.

24. *Shri Guruji Samagra*, Vol. 6, Suruchi Prakashan, Delhi, p. 243.

His monthly salary of Rs 100 seemed enough to take care of his expenses.

'I don't have any complaints regarding my salary; it is the uncertain nature of the job that makes me impatient,' he wrote on 6 October.[25] At any rate, Golwalkar remained deeply unsettled. The recurring fever had not given him much respite, and the fear of an uncertain future seemed to weigh upon him oppressively. He was five feet and six inches but looked considerably tall as he had become very thin, weighing merely 48 kg at the age of twenty-five.[26]

As a demonstrator, Golwalkar's duty was to assist students in the use of laboratory equipment and to oversee them carrying out experiments. Although there was no scope of a demonstrator ever getting promoted to the post of a professor, or even a lecturer, the job of assisting serious students in the laboratory satisfied Golwalkar's self-image. He began to use his leisure time after his duty hours to run a free study circle for students. This sometimes led him to study the textbooks of subjects like English, mathematics, economics and philosophy so that he could teach boys of even those courses.[27] At the time in the BHU, it was common to find Maharashtrian students, many of whom belonged to the Brahmin caste and had come from Nagpur. Golwalkar's study group mostly comprised students from this stock.

Golwalkar lived outside the BHU, though not far from it, in a private accomodation called Gajanand Lodge.[28] The after-college study sessions took place in his room in the lodge; students would

25. Ibid., pp. 243-244.

26. Ibid., p. 244.

27. N. H. Palkar, *Shri Ma Sa Golwalkar*, published by N. H. Palkar, Mumbai, 1956, pp. 26-27.

28. Ranga Hari, *The Incomparable Guru Golwalkar*, Prabhat Paperbacks, New Dehi, 2018, p. 44.

sometimes crack jokes but he would mostly remain serious. Anna Pandharipande, a BHU student from Nagpur and a member of the study circle, remembered Golwalkar's room as a 'jungle' of books.

'In the corners, on the table, on tripod—there were books all around, piles of books. One would wonder if a library was being shifted here. If my colleague Raghuvir Dhongdi, who became a *sanyasi* later, spoke about these books, Guruji would carry on with his subject without responding to his query,' Anna wrote in his reminiscences.[29]

The members of this study circle were the first to call Golwalkar Guruji, or Teacher.[30] Golwalkar revelled in the attention but the arrangement did not last long. In January 1933, sixteen months into his stint, Pawar resumed his duties. Relieved from his job, Golwalkar returned to Nagpur in February.[31]

V

There is no evidence from any source—no document, no interview—to suggest that Golwalkar ever met Keshav Baliram Hedgewar, the head of the Rashtriya Swayamsevak Sangh (RSS), until he returned from the BHU in 1933. The only RSS man of any significance whom he is known to have befriended while in Varanasi—apart, perhaps, from his interactions with Sadgopal, a young member of the Sangh from Nagpur and a student of the BHU—was Prabhakar Balwant Dani, or Bhaiyaji Dani, an associate of Hedgewar. On 24 March 1929, while still in Madras, he had scolded his friend Baburao Tailang for not reining in his

29. *Annaji Pandhripande Smritiyan*, as cited in Ranga Hari, *The Incomparable Guru Golwalkar*, Prabhat Paperbacks, New Delhi, 2018, p. 44.

30. N. H. Palkar, *Shri Ma Sa Golwalkar*, published by N. H. Palkar, Mumbai, 1956, p. 27.

31. Ranga Hari, *The Incomparable Guru Golwalkar*, Prabhat Paperbacks, New Delhi, 2018, p. 45.

younger brother who had joined the RSS and been ignoring his studies.

'It is foolish to do Sangh work at the cost of one's studies,' he wrote to Tailang, whose brother had flunked his matriculation examination, apparently due to spending too much of his time with the RSS. 'One should not forget that passing examinations with good marks is always more commendable than spending one's time in the Sangh.'[32] By the time Golwalkar returned from the BHU in 1933, he was no longer wary of the RSS.

To the extent it formally existed at all, the RSS at this stage was a private militia of Hindu men of the Brahmin caste. It had arisen from within this community at Nagpur in 1925. All its 'seven-eight' founders, including B. S. Moonje, Ganesh Damodar Savarkar, K. B. Hedgewar and L. V. Paranjpe, belonged to this caste.[33] So did its members, called swayamsevaks. The RSS kept itself away from the nationalist struggle for independence. Its leaders claimed to train its members for an eventual fight against 'internal enemies'—Muslims—whom Hedgewar referred to as 'snakes'.[34]

Until 1931, when Golwalkar joined the BHU as a demonstrator, the RSS was purely a local affair centred in Nagpur and neighbouring areas of the Central Provinces. Its members dressed themselves in a uniform similar to that of the colonial police force—khaki shorts and khaki shirt—and wore a black cap. They spent much of their time in pseudo-martial behaviour: farcical parades and marches, physical exercises, drills and manoeuvres, weapons training and ideological classes. They engaged in an elaborate paraphernalia of hoisting a flag, taking an oath and reciting a prayer in Marathi. They were also capable of more sinister things: they intimidated Muslims and broke up meetings and rallies that deplored the

32. *Shri Guruji Samagra*, Vol. 6, Suruchi Prakashan, Delhi, pp. 236-237.

33. Dr. Laxman Vasudev Paranjpe, *Kesari*, 5 July 1940, p. 5.

34. M. J. Akbar, *India: The Siege Within*, Penguin Books, New Delhi, 1985, p. 306.

RSS.[35]

Shaped without a constitution, the RSS did not openly define its aims and objects. Yet it was widely perceived as an organization through which these Maharashtrian Brahmin men dreamt of reviving the glory of Peshwa rule—a euphemism for the rule of Brahmins—after the British withdrew from India. The RSS adopted the bhagwa (saffron) flag of the erstwhile Peshwas as its own flag. Non-Brahmins despised the RSS and sometimes even attacked its members.[36]

Ideologically, the RSS was rooted in a monograph of 1923 by Vinayak Damodar Savarkar, a difficult personality, deeply embittered and rigid in his principles. In the past, while pursuing a Barrister-at-Law in London, he had been fiercely anti-British. He was arrested in a murder case, sentenced to life and sent to Cellular Jail in Andaman and Nicobar Islands. But a little over a decade later he made his way out by writing a series of mercy petitions to British authorities, making abject appeals and promising loyalty, obedience and good behaviour in return for clemency.[37] In 1921, he was moved to a jail on the mainland, and in 1923, about a year before his release from prison, he penned a monograph, *Hindutva: Who is a Hindu?*, in which he claimed the whole of India for Hindus by virtue of the fact that they alone, and not Muslims or Christians, considered its territory sacred.

'All Hindus claim to have in their veins the blood of the mighty race incorporated with and descended from the Vedic fathers, the Sindhus,' Savarkar wrote.[38] 'We [Hindus] are one because we are a nation, a race and own a common Sanskriti.'[39]

---

35. Bhaiya Ghatate, *Shri Babasaheb Ghatate Yanche Atmakathan*, Shri Babasaheb Apte Smarak Samiti, Nagpur, 1997, p. 46.

36. S. H. Deshpande, 'My Days in the RSS', *Quest*, July-August 1975, p. 20.

37. *Frontline*, 17 January 2020, Vol. 37, Number 01, p. 97.

38. V. D. Savarkar, *Hindutva: Who is a Hindu?*, Hindi Sahitya Sadan, New Delhi, 2005, p. 85.

39. Ibid, p. 92.

The text defined the term 'Hindutva'—literally meaning Hinduness—as a politically conscious Hinduism that sought to organize Hindus as a nationality. India's Muslims and other religious minorities did not constitute a part of this vision of the nation. The text also conspicuously echoed Savarkar's call for action against enemies of the faith, particularly Muslims, for he specified that 'a conflict of life and death' ensued after Mahmud of Ghazni crossed the Indus to invade India in the eleventh century.[40]

'In this prolonged furious conflict our people became intensely conscious of ourselves as Hindus and were welded into a nation to an extent unknown in our history,' he wrote.[41]

By carrying Hindus into a state of opposition, Savarkar's book sought to channel the dominant anti-British sentiment of Hindus into anti-Muslim action—a shift that fitted into the British strategic policy of divide and rule. In January 1924, he was released from jail on the condition that he would not participate in politics and would not leave Ratnagiri district without prior permission.

Golwalkar admired Savarkar for more than his 1923 book on Hindutva. He had read *Gomantak*, a novel that Savarkar had written in Marathi. The novel had so impressed him that he sent Savarkar a personal letter commending him and seeking some clarifications.

'I received his [Savarkar's] reply day before yesterday,' Golwalkar wrote to Tailang on 16 March 1929 from Madras, thrilled. 'I am in double mind whether I should write to him now or after reading *Gomantak* again. Perhaps, I should first read his book before writing another letter to him.'[42]

His early interest in Savarkar was as fleeting as his indifference towards the RSS at the time. In a few short years, while he worked

40. Ibid, p. 42.

41. Ibid, p. 44.

42. *Shri Guruji Samagra*, Vol. 6, Suruchi Prakashan, Delhi, p. 212.

as a demonstrator and ran his study circle, the BHU became something of a hotbed of debate on the RSS and Hindutva, albeit within the limits of the university's dull political culture with its emphasis on promoting a Hindu religious atmosphere.

In 1932, when Golwalkar was in the BHU, the Hindu Mahasabha started working vigorously to help widen the Sangh's area of operation outside the Central Provinces.[43] Established in 1915, the Hindu Mahasabha initially considered itself more of a socio-cultural group than a proper political party and operated as an adjunct of the Congress. By the late 1920s, it transformed its image to a hardline organization, marginalizing the moderate Hindu leadership from within and directing its activities against Muslims. Nevertheless, it remained, at least nominally, allied to the Congress. After the Congress and Gandhi supported separate electorates for Muslims in 1932, the Mahasabha started drifting away from its parent party. It severely condemned the decision and increasingly grew estranged, accusing the Congress and Gandhi of Muslim appeasement.

Although all the founders of the RSS belonged to the Hindu Mahasabha, the one Mahasabha leader who seems clearly to have had a sense of himself as the guardian of the Sangh was B. S. Moonje. He mentored Hedgewar in Nagpur and sent him to Calcutta to study at National Medical College.[44] A British intelligence report ascribed to Moonje the responsibility of the reorganization of the RSS in the Marathi-speaking districts of the Central Provinces during the early 1930s.[45] On his trip to Italy,

43. Government of India, Home Department, File No. 28/5/46—Pol (I), p. 30, NAI, New Delhi.

44. B. V. Deshpande and S. R. Ramaswamy, *Dr Hedgewar: the Epoch-Maker*, Sahitya Sindhu, Bangalore, 1981, pp. 14-32.

45. Government of India, Home Department (Political), File No. 88/33, 1933, p. 28, NAI, New Delhi.

he met Benito Mussolini and visited the Balilla and Avanguardisti organizations—the keystones of the fascist system of indoctrination of youths—in March 1931. Thereafter, Moonje played a decisive role in moulding the RSS.[46] Noted an intelligence report of 1933: 'It is perhaps no exaggeration to assert that the Sangh hopes to be in future India what the "Fascisti" are to Italy and the "Nazis" to Germany.'[47]

In its Delhi session in 1932, the Mahasabha passed a resolution according official recognition to the RSS and commending its activities.[48] Later that year, Mahasabha leader Bhai Parmanand called an all-India Hindu youth conference—Hindu Yuvak Parishad—in Karachi where another resolution was adopted: 'Sangh work should be expanded all over the country.'[49] Ganesh Damodar Savarkar or Babarao, V. D. Savarkar's elder brother, and Moonje opened new avenues for the RSS in north and western India. Hedgewar, who was taken to attend the Karachi conference by Ganesh Savarkar, stayed there for six days, discussing organizational issues with various Mahasabha leaders and youths who had gathered from Sind and Punjab provinces.[50]

The BHU, with its significant presence of Maharashtrian Brahmins, was far from isolated. Its founder vice-chancellor, Pandit Madan Mohan Malviya, a former president of the Mahasabha, was overtly promoting Hindu ethos on the campus. When Golwalkar was still in Varanasi, a group of RSS men, including Bhaiyaji Dani

---

46. Marzia Casolari, 'Hindutva's Foreign Tie-up in the 1930s: Archival Evidence', *Economic and Political Weekly*, 22 January 2000, pp. 219-220.

47. Government of India, Home Department (Political), File No. 88/33, 1933, p. 28, NAI, New Delhi.

48. Government of India, Home Department (Political), File No. 220-P/42 (Sec), 1942, p. 1, NAI, New Delhi.

49. D. R. Goyal, *Rashtriya Swayamsevak Sangh*, Radhakrishna Prakashan, Delhi, 1979, p. 83.

50. Ibid.

and Sadgopal, started RSS activities at the BHU, and the university seemed set to become one of the nuclei for the expansion of the organization in north India.

VI

From his subsequent letters, from his behaviour, his attitude and actions, it is clear that Golwalkar first met Hedgewar after his return from the BHU, prompted apparently by Bhaiyyaji Dani and Sadgopal, and that he now associated himself with the Sangh's views. For a short while, Golwalkar was seized by excitement. He openly adopted the styles and convictions of an enthusiastic swayamsevak, and increasingly, he lectured Sadgopal about activities related to the RSS. On occasion, he even conducted himself as a self-appointed emissary of Hedgewar.

'What talks have you had with Babasaheb [about Sadgopal persuading him to become Varanasi RSS chief]?' he wrote to Sadgopal on 22 July 1933. In the letter, he asked Sadgopal to quickly identify someone for the slot in Varanasi so that the person 'may be sent a formal letter of appointment by the Chief Sangh Chalak [Hedgewar]'.[51]

On another occasion, Golwalkar became high-strung when Sadgopal did not share with him information on the talks he had had with the person who was to be the chief guest for the RSS's Vijayadashami, or Dasehra, event at Nagpur—an annual practice ever since the formation of the organization on the day of Dasehra in 1925. Hedgewar had asked Sadgopal to persuade a BHU professor, Dr. M. V. Godbole, to be the chief guest for the event that year.

'Is Dr. Godbole coming here at all?' Golwalkar asked Sadgopal in a letter dated 17 September 1933.[52] The BHU professor did

51. Golwalkar Papers, Microfilm Section, NMML, New Delhi, pp. 5-6.

52. Ibid., p. 7.

indeed visit Nagpur and attend the Sangh's meeting on Dasehra, which fell on 28 September that year. A month later, on 28 October, Golwalkar, as a way of informing Sadgopal, wrote: 'Dr. Godbole had been here & honoured in Dasehra by Sangh.'[53]

There is no evidence to suggest that Hedgewar showed any special interest in Golwalkar at the time nor any indication that the latter's enthusiastic volunteerism was recognized by the top leadership of the RSS. In none of Hedgewar's letters to his associates written around this time did Golwalkar figure.[54]

Golwalkar was twenty-seven years old and once again at a crossroads. For long he had cherished hopes of a career in academics but could not succeed in making this a reality. Even a permanent job of lab assistant in the BHU seemed a far-fetched idea. He tried to immerse himself in the RSS, acted with excessive enthusiasm and remained deferential to Hedgewar. Perhaps, the situation that he faced here worried him into an alternative line of action and led him to take admission into a law college at Nagpur.

At least some part of Golwalkar's decision to go into the legal profession was played by Vamanrao Wadegaonkar, another blind teacher of music, whom he had met in 1930 when he was living an idler's life in Nagpur following his return from Madras. This meeting, and the relationship that developed, were to be among his most influential experiences of the time.[55] Vamanrao ran a school for visually impaired children that had been set up by his father, Nagpur's District and Sessions Judge Narayanrao Wadegaonkar. Perhaps Golwalkar thought that with the help of Vamanrao's father he would comfortably establish himself in the legal profession.[56]

---

53. Ibid., p. 10.

54. See N. H. Palkar, *Dr. Hedgewar: Patraroop-Vyaktidarshan*, Archana Prakashan, Indore, 1989.

55. Golwalkar Papers, Microfilm Section, NMML, New Delhi, pp. 1 4.

56. N. H. Palkar, *Shri Ma Sa Golwalkar*, published by N. H. Palkar, Mumbai, 1956, p. 39.

But he was still incapable of pursuing a course systematically. And, he was also troubled by recurring fever. 'I do not accept defeat at the hands of chance,' he wrote to Sadgopal on 19 November 1934. 'Still I must say that this year is much worse than any I had till now. [...] Studies are out of question. Digestion is bad. Fever [has caused] a general weakness which keeps me confined to my room almost all day.'[57]

Golwalkar passed the L.L.B. examination in 1935. He registered as a lawyer and opened an office, but within months he realized that alone he wouldn't be able to earn a livelihood from the legal profession. He started working together with his advocate friend Dattatreya Deshpande.[58] The joint effort yielded results and he started earning from his practice.[59]

The contradiction between intent and temperament began to show up by the middle of 1936. As the professional growth did not match his expectations, his interest in the legal practice started plummeting. In later life Golwalkar did not like to recall the years he spent in studying for the L.L.B. and trying to establish himself as a lawyer, although his efforts at the time were strenuous. These efforts obviously cast a doubt upon the claim his biographers made in later years that he was aware from the beginning that he was not suited to the legal profession.

Disenchanted, he now flirted with a new idea and would soon embrace it.

---

57. Golwalkar Papers, Microfilm Section, NMML, New Delhi, pp. 11-12.

58. N. H. Palkar, *Shri Ma Sa Golwalkar*, published by N. H. Palkar, Mumbai, 1956, p. 40.

59. Ibid., p. 40.

Diksha and Devotion

Golwalkar now decided that he wanted to become a monk. This choice was prompted equally by his obsessive leaning toward Hindu orthodoxy and the rather florid notion a caste elite unable to cope with the changing tides must have had of the free and untrammeled monk's life. Never in the past did he reveal any sign of a passion for monkhood; he always focused on securing a definite job that could provide him a livelihood as well as social respectability. To be sure, such a decision can be explained as a way of using spiritualism to escape the uncertainties of the material world, to soar instead into realms of the ideal. However, the manic fervour with which he threw himself into his efforts to get ordained as a monk of Ramakrishna Mission, a Hindu religious and spiritual organization, in 1936, forgetting and rejecting everything else, shows that inside he was, during this period, a loner. The sudden eruption of this passion also meant that in a concentrated and obstinate manner, he lived only for himself. It would seem that Golwalkar sought elevation through monkhood in a social sense as well. He had so far been driven by an overpowering social ambition but had ultimately achieved what he seemed to regard as a paltry career—a fact borne out by his visible retreat from the legal practice within a year of joining it. Either he was still incapable of any systematic work or his own goals were pitched far higher.

His new passion was related to his notion that in the orthodox Hindu society, monkhood was a pursuit of something 'higher'.[1] As he looked for new stimuli and new goals, the monkhood seemed to satisfy his imagination of his self.

Golwalkar's connections to Ramakrishna Mission ran through Raghuvir Dhongdi, his one-time chum from his days in the BHU.[2] Founded by Ramakrishna Paramahansa's chief disciple, Swami Vivekananda, in 1897 and supported by Ramakrishna's widow, Sarada Devi, the Mission had established a network of mathas and ashrams to propagate Hindu spiritual philosophy and carry out educational and philanthropic work. In Nagpur, the Ramakrishna Matha was established in 1928. In 1934, a hostel for poor students was added to it.[3] Raghuvir, a native of Nasik district of Bombay province, was one of the residents of this hostel.[4]

Like Golwalkar, Raghuvir had, after his days in the BHU, completed LLB. In 1935, when the two entered the legal profession, their acquaintanceship deepened into friendship. Raghuvir shared Golwalkar's sentimental passion for spiritualism, and the two regularly met at the hostel. Here Golwalkar sat idly around, apparently depressed by the uncertainty of his future. Raghuvir had decided to become a monk. At the time he was preparing to shift to Sargachhi in Bengal's Murshidabad district where Swami Akhandananda, the head of Ramakrishna Mission, lived.

Golwalkar's true attitude toward monkhood—until Raghuvir made up his mind—is difficult to discern. But as he kept visiting

1. *Shri Guruji Samagra*, Vol. 6, Suruchi Prakashan, Delhi, pp. 269-280.

2. Ranga Hari, *The Incomparable Guru Golwalkar*, Prabhat Paperbacks, New Delhi, 2018, p. 56.

3. Swami Amurtanand, *Swami Akhandanand Smriti Charan*, in 'Swami Akhandanand Smorone', Ramakrishna Mission Ashram, Sargachhi, Murshidabad, 2020, p. 655.

4. Ranga Hari, *The Incomparable Guru Golwalkar*, Prabhat Paperbacks, New Delhi, 2018, p. 56.

Ramakrishna Math, Golwalkar's inclination to spiritualism, which had so far been tempered by a sense of material ambition, seemed to stir suddenly. Swami Amurtananda, the monk who headed Ramakrishna Math at Nagpur, felt that a similar passion to become a monk was overtaking Golwalkar.[5] Before leaving for Sargachhi, Raghuvir had introduced him to the hostel warden, Swami Bhaskareshwarananda. Golwalkar continued to spend time with Bhaskareshwarananda, discussing Hindu philosophy, spiritualism and renunciation. When he seemed determined to go to Sargachhi and become a disciple of Akhandananda, Bhaskareshwarananda asked him to speak with Amurtananda.[6]

According to Amurtananda, Golwalkar asked him for permission to visit Sargachhi and be the disciple of Akhandananda. He looked up at him and said, 'For that you will have to leave everything—your name, your prestige, your family, everything. Are you ready for that?'[7] Golwalkar replied in the affirmative. Amurtananda, thereafter, wrote to Swami Akhandananda, seeking his permission to send a new guest to Sargachhi ashram. 'Eight days later the reply came, and it was decided that Madhu [Golwalkar] would go to Sargachhi,' Amurtananda wrote in his reminiscence. 'I told him not to waste any time and go straight to Sargachhi without giving a halt at Calcutta or Belur Math [the headquarters of Ramakrishna Mission]. That very day Madhu started his journey and reached Sargachhi three days later.'[8]

Golwalkar left Nagpur on 6 November 1936. The evidence suggests that he did not reveal his plans to his parents before leaving for Sargachhi. Instead, he handed over a letter addressed

---

5. Swami Amurtanand, *Swami Akhandanand Smriti Charan*, in 'Swami Akhandanand Smorone', Ramakrishna Mission Ashram, Sargachhi, Murshidabad, 2020, p. 655.

6. Ibid.

7. Ibid.

8. Ibid., p. 656.

to his father to his advocate friend, Dattatreya Deshpande, with the instruction that it be posted after his departure from Nagpur.[9]

With a stubborn attitude, but without a coherent plan, he quietly passed into a new life of voluntary exile.

II

On 9 November 1936, four days before the festival of Diwali (Kali Puja), which fell that year on 13 November, he entered the Sargachhi ashram of Ramakrishna Mission. Golwalkar was received with open arms as he carried a recommendation letter from Amurtananda, who was known in the ashram as Amitabh and considered a most trusted and favoured disciple of Akhandananda. Raghuvir, who had already arrived, led Golwalkar to Swami Akhandananda, whom everyone called Baba.[10] 'You must evaluate me thoroughly since you want to make me your guru,' Akhandanand told him. 'Likewise, I will also assess you thoroughly since you want me to make you my disciple.'[11]

Candidates for diksha, or initiation, had to first serve in the Ashram, and Golwalkar was kept in the personal service of Akhandananda. He was assigned a corner of the kitchen-cum-store as his resting place.[12] He started growing his beard and hair.[13]

In the beginning, by his own accounts, he faltered. 'I fell down and broke a cup which was Baba's favourite,' Golwalkar

---

9. Ranga Hari, *The Incomparable Guru Golwalkar*, Prabhat Paperbacks, New Delhi, 2018, p. 57.

10. Ibid.

11. Swami Amurtanand, *Swami Akhandanand Smriti Charan*, in 'Swami Akhandanand Smorone', Ramakrishna Mission Ashram, Sargachhi, Murshidabad, 2020, p. 656.

12. *Shri Guruji Samagra*, Vol. 6, Suruchi Prakashan, Delhi, p. 275.

13. N. H. Palkar, *Shri Ma Sa Golwalkar*, published by N. H. Palkar, Mumbai, 1956, p. 48.

wrote in his diary. Instead of showing anger, Akhandananda asked, 'Did you hurt yourself?'[14] Golwalkar felt relieved and grateful. A few days later, he lost his balance as he hurriedly tried to enter the kitchen and fell down. 'That time Shri Baba was taking lunch in the kitchen,' he wrote.[15] Again, Akhandananda responded in a manner that soothed him. In fact, on no such occasion would Akhandananda ever get angry, anger and harshness being antithetical to the credo of the Ramakrishna Mission.

In December 1936, Akhandananda's health deteriorated, and he asked his favourite disciples, including Amurtananda, to return and be with him at the ashram. 'I rushed to Sargachhi,' Amurtananda recalled. 'After reaching the ashram, I prostrated before Baba. Madhu, who stood nearby, became happy to see me. Baba said your Golkar [Akhandananda could never pronounce Golwalkar and called him Golkar] is fine here. I said that is because of your mercy.'[16]

Later that day, Amurtananda spoke with Golwalkar separately. 'After talking to him, I got to know that the tough life of Sargachhi ashram didn't have any adverse impact on Madhu's body and soul and that he was happy. Madhu told me that he could stay there for whole life if the situation remained as it was. I asked him whether he received diksha. He said he had not received it yet. I realized that Baba was still assessing Madhu through his activities and behavioural patterns. His examination was still on.'[17]

In later years, Golwalkar's biographers romanticized every aspect of his three-month stay at Sargachhi. They particularly

---

14. *Shri Guruji Samagra*, Vol. 6, Suruchi Prakashan, Delhi, pp. 271-272.

15. Ibid., p. 272.

16. Swami Amurtanand, *Swami Akhandanand Smriti Charan*, in 'Swami Akhandanand Smorone', Ramakrishna Mission Ashram, Sargachhi, Murshidabad, 2020, p. 656.

17. Ibid.

exaggerated Akhandananda's fondness for him. 'Because of the utmost similarities in their nature and inclination, the two [Golwalkar and Akhandananda] got together like the blue sky and the blue sea,' writes Palkar. 'Guruji always used to be with Swamiji [Akhandananda] like shadow as if they were inseparable, he being the most genuine disciple and Swamiji his most authentic guru.'[18]

No doubt, Golwalkar was devout. His own diary, which has entries from 13 December 1936 to 24 January 1937, is a testimony of his complete devotion to Akhandananda. 'His [Akhandananda's] body was soft and my palms were rough,' Golwalkar noted in his diary on 19 December 1936. 'Yesterday I started massaging his feet. The skin of my palms was hard and it hurt him when I massaged him. [...] Then Jagdish [another inmate] took my place. Still I massaged him in the evening.'[19]

Such entries as well as other contemporary sources of Sargachhi ashram suggest that Golwalkar was one of many attendants who served Akhandananda in a manner that often marks the beginning of renunciation. The guru, in such relationships, is seen as a pivot in a novice's life, the route to his spiritual awakening and to his monkhood.

Yet, Golwalkar finds no place in the diary of Swami Niramayananda, who lived with Akhanadananda at Sargachhi and made detailed daily entries from 28 January 1935 to 5 February 1937.[20] A second diary maintained by another disciple, Satyendra Mohan Roy, who lived in Sargachhi ashram between 13 March 1936 and 8 January 1937, refers to Golwalkar once as one of the attendants. In his last diary entry on 8 January, Roy notes the sudden deterioration in Akhandananda's health. 'Baba took a deep

---

18. N. H. Palkar, *Shri Ma Sa Golwalkar*, published by N. H. Palkar, Mumbai, 1956, p. 47.

19. *Shri Guruji Samagra*, Vol. 6, Suruchi Prakashan, Delhi, p. 273.

20. Swami Niramayanand, *Swami Akhandanand Ke Sannidhya Mein*, Ramakrishna Math, Nagpur, 2015.

breath and asked me to hold him for support. I embraced him and laid him on the bed,' Roy reminisced. 'He then asked for some water. I called Brahmachari Golwalkar who brought water and I gave it to Baba.'[21]

By all means, therefore, Golwalkar was serving Akhandananda earnestly, as if aware that surrendering to the guru was a precondition for obtaining real knowledge. 'Until the late hours of the night, he served the guru and got up by four in the morning,' Amurtananda wrote about Golwalkar. 'Before the guru could leave the bed and put his foot on the ground, he again stood there holding the guru's *khadau* [clogs] in his hands. A rigorous test of the disciple was on.'[22]

But Golwalkar was getting restless.[23] Two months had passed and he was yet to get diksha. Perhaps both Akhandananda and Amurtananda knew about his restlessness—the reason why neither of them seemed to believe that Golwalkar was suited for an ascetic life.

'One day in the first week of January [1937], I told Baba that it would be better to give diksha to Madhu and then ask him to go back to Nagpur. He would do some work there and serve his parents,' Amurtananda recounted. 'Baba said the time has not come yet to give diksha to him. [...] He should go back to Nagpur and get engaged in some work there, but who can tell this to him?'[24]

---

21. *Swami Akhandanand Smorone*, Ramakrishna Mission Ashram, Sargachhi, Murshidabad, 2020, p. 644.

22. Swami Amurtanand, *Swami Akhandanand Smriti Charan*, in 'Swami Akhandanand Smorone', Ramakrishna Mission Ashram, Sargachhi, Murshidabad, 2020, p. 657.

23. *Shri Guruji Samagra*, Vol. 6, Suruchi Prakashan, Delhi, p. 275.

24. Swami Amurtanand, *Swami Akhandanand Smriti Charan*, in 'Swami Akhandanand Smorone', Ramakrishna Mission Ashram, Sargachhi, Murshidabad, 2020, p. 657.

A few days later, Akhandananda resolved the issue himself.

'On the morning of 13 January, on the day of makar-sankranti [an auspicious day for Hindus], while I was worshipping Thakur [Ramakrishna Paramahansa], Madhu came and stood by me,' Amurtananda wrote later. 'He looked cheerful and sought to touch my feet. I understood that Madhu had got diksha. I told Madhu that one should not touch the feet of anybody in front of Thakur.'[25]

After finishing his prayers, Amurtananda went to see Akhandananda. 'He [Baba] said as per the mercy of Thakur diksha has been given to him. But don't keep him in ashram; let him work outside ashram. If required, you may give him suggestions from time to time.'[26]

But before Amurtananda could speak with Golwalkar, Akhandananda's health deteriorated again. He was taken to Calcutta by Amurtananda and some others for his medical check-up. From there he was moved to Belur Math, the Mission's headquarters, located across the Hooghly. At Belur, his health continued to worsen, and on 7 February 1937, he died. On hearing the news, most of the inmates of Sargachhi ashram, including Golwalkar, rushed to Belur Math.

'I took Madhu aside and told him that as per the decision he could no longer stay in Ramakrishna ashram,' Amurtananda noted. 'Madhu was shocked and agitated. He asked me whether I was serious and how I could get to know [about the decision]. I then told him in detail the conversation that I had with Shrimat Baba about him.'[27]

25. Ibid., p. 658.

26. Ibid.

27. Ibid.

III

Golwalkar retreated temporarily and resumed his legal practice. But there is some indication that he wanted to avoid staying in the legal profession. 'Today, I am in a queer fix,' he wrote to Sadgopal on 2 April 1937, two months after returning home. 'Ever since I left Nagpur, my practice is at a standstill [...]. Hence I am face to face with the most unpleasant situation.'[28]

He hoped to find new occupation that could promise new stimuli. But it may also be that this constant search reflected the aimlessness of his life. He looked pale, with sunken cheeks, hair brushed low over his neck merging with an overgrown, unkempt beard. The chronic fever that had troubled him in the past seemed to have vanished after three months of the disciplined life at Sargachhi, but the uncertainty caused by the lack of a coherent plan for his life nevertheless depressed him.

He lived with his parents at Nagoba Lane in the Mahal locality of Nagpur—where they had moved after his father's retirement—and frequently visited Ramakrishna Mission's local ashram. Despite the Mission disallowing him to stay in the ashram, he still felt he belonged to it by inclination and initiation. In 1937, shortly after his return, he volunteered to translate into Marathi Swami Vivekananda's famous speech on Hindu philosophy, delivered in English at the World's Parliament of Religions at Chicago in 1893.[29] It seems that his response to his rejection by Ramakrishna Mission was not a rebellious gesture but an intensified longing for acceptance and recognition.

The multi-linguality that he employed in translating Vivekananda's speech soon brought another translation offer. This

28. Golwalkar Papers, Microfilm Section, NMML, New Delhi, p. 35.

29. N. H. Palkar, *Shri Ma Sa Golwalkar*, published by N. H. Palkar, Mumbai, 1956, p. 53.

is the one that would help him emerge from the anonymity that had so long dampened his spirits.

The offer came sometime in the beginning of 1938. Babarao Savarkar was looking for an English translator for his book, *Rashtra Mimansa Wa Hindusthanchen Rashtraswaroop*, published in Marathi under the pen name 'Durgatanaya'. Rooted in the theoretical premise set forth in 1923 by Vinayak Savarkar in *Hindutva: Who is a Hindu?*, which was in English, Babarao's Marathi book, published in 1934, sought to further lengthen how India belonged to Hindus because of its specific racial, religious, cultural and geographical characteristics and how Muslims being 'a foreign race' should have no claim over it.[30]

Babarao wanted it to be translated by someone who could be trusted not just for his proficiency in the English language but also with his ability to see the issue through the right ideological prism. He bestowed upon Vishwanathrao Kelkar, a relative and close associate, the responsibility of identifying a suitable translator and supervising the translation of the book.[31] Bhaiyaji Dani was Kelkar's friend. He arranged the introductory meeting with Golwalkar.[32] 'He [Kelkar] called him [Golwalkar] to his residence and asked whether he would be able to do the translation,' wrote Palkar. 'Guruji gave his assent. He then took the book [*Rashtra Mimansa*] and the blank sheets of paper and returned home.'[33]

By this account, Golwalkar completed the translation of the 109-page book in one day. 'Guruji again went to Shri Kelkar's residence a day later,' Palkar wrote in a heroic vein. He continued:

---

30. See for detail, 'Durgatanaya' [Pseudonym of Ganesh Damodar Savarkar], *Rashtra Mimansa Wa Hindusthanchen Rashtraswaroop*, published by Vaidyaratna Vishnu Ganesh Kelkar, Nasik, 1934.

31. N. H. Palkar, *Shri Ma Sa Golwalkar*, published by N. H. Palkar, Mumbai, 1956, p. 61.

32. Ibid.

33. Ibid., pp. 61-62.

> On seeing him with the book and a bundle of papers the very next day, Kelkar thought that perhaps for some reason he did not want to do the translation job and had come to return them. But he was surprised when he found that the papers were no longer blank and that the entire book had been translated. He became even more amazed after reading the translated version of the book because the translation was of very high quality. Translating a 109-page book into an alien language in one day would have astonished anyone.[34]

The English translation of *Rashtra Mimansa* stayed with Kelkar and for whatever reason was never published.[35] In the preface of his own book, *We or Our Nationhood Defined*, which was published in 1939, Golwalkar expressed his belief that his English translation of *Rashtra Mimansa* was 'due to be shortly out'.[36] *Rashtra Mimansa* made a strong impression upon Golwalkar. His involvement in its translation marked the beginning of his integration into the elite circle of Hindutva politics.

That was the time when Hindutva politics was under the aegis of four men. V. D. Savarkar, of course, was the ideological fountainhead and the supreme leader. But in that peculiarly iridescent area where Hindu communal politics and the political ambitions of a section of Maharashtrian Brahmins coalesced—that fringe of contemporary politics which so significantly determined Golwalkar's future career—Babarao, Moonje and Hedgewar were other overwhelmingly dominant figures. Ideologically, these four were the key personalities of his formative years.

Of these, the ideological impact of Babarao, one of the most eloquent spokesmen of the Savarkarite opposition directed chiefly

---

34. Ibid., p. 62.

35. Ibid.

36. M. S. Golwalkar, *We or Our Nationhood Defined*, Bharat Publication, Nagpur, 1939, p. 4.

against the anti-British nationalists and one who contributed significantly to the deteriorating communal atmosphere, cannot be overemphasized. No specific evidence suggests that Golwalkar had until then read the younger Savarkar's treatise. Babarao's *Rashtra Mimansa* might well have been the first to teach Golwalkar how to twist his Hindu feeling—hitherto mostly religious in its motivations—into formal anti-Muslim ideology with a political, social and, above all, racial basis. The lesson would eventually convert him into a demagogue with a keen sense for the effectiveness of primitive emotions. Yet, one might say that Golwalkar at the time did not so much absorb Babarao's ideology as catch the infection that underlay it.

IV

Vishwanathrao Kelkar, who was close not just to Babarao but also to Hedgewar, had been associated with the RSS since its inception. It was at his residence in the Mahal locality of Nagpur that the process which culminated in the formation of the RSS began. 'Sometime towards the end of 1924 Babarao came to Nagpur and started living at the residence of Shri VV Kelkar,' D. N. Gokhale, Babarao's biographer, wrote.

> After arriving in Nagpur, he began to hold meetings with youths every day in the morning, afternoon and the evening. [...] Dr. Hedgewar also used to attend these meetings of young Hindu men. He neither spoke nor asked a question but sat quietly for hours and listened to the discussion attentively. [...] Soon, under the leadership of Baba, there emerged in Nagpur a group of youth dedicated to the cause of Hindutva. Later, when came the time for Baba to leave Nagpur, there arose a question of who would take his work forward and lead the group of these young men. Shriyut Babarao discussed the issue with Kelkar, and it was felt that Dr. Hedgewar would be best suited for this

> job and that he alone could keep the group together and carry the work forward. Thus, before leaving Nagpur, Babarao handed over the responsibility of this small group of Hindu youths to Dr. Hedgewar.[37]

Some months later when the RSS was formed in September 1925, this group acted as its nucleus.[38] Kelkar, quite naturally, was among the first to join the RSS. By the time Golwalkar came close to him by way of translating Babarao's *Rashtra Mimansa*, Kelkar had long become a close associate of Hedgewar. The senior men seemed to have noted Golwalkar's abilities. Continual displays of loyalty to the RSS brass aside, Golwalkar's facility with languages proved critical and now he was considered best suited to coordinate the first ever multi-lingual, multi-state RSS training camp—called Officers' Training Camp or OTC—which was held at Nagpur in the summer of 1938.[39] He had good grasp of at least four languages—English, Hindi, Marathi and Bengali—and was fluent in Sanskrit.

In the role of 'sarvadhikari', or officer-in-charge, of this RSS camp, Golwalkar was eager. As far as is known, there was no talk of fighting British colonizers in their camp, even though India was passing through the most crucial phase of its independence struggle. Swayamsevaks prayed before the bhagwa flag of the erstwhile Peshwas, went through military-style drills and fostered the notion of sacrificing one's life in order to establish a Hindu Rashtra. Military-style bands performed martial tunes and the bivouac, under the nimbus of military patriotism, was transformed into a site of brutish soldiery. The ideological classes—which were

---

37. D. N. Gokhale, *Krantiveer Babarao Savarkar*, Mangal Sahitya Prakashan, Pune, 1947, p. 350.

38. Ibid., p. 351.

39. Ranga Hari, *The Incomparable Guru Golwalkar*, Prabhat Paperbacks, New Delhi, 2018, p. 73.

called 'boudhik'—were profusely illustrated with stories from a long-ago past and Hindu scriptures. Savarkar's *Hindutva: Who is a Hindu?* was the most important text that the swayamsevaks studied. Swayamsevaks attending the camp flaunted their religious identity and felt themselves part of a Hindu opposition directed chiefly at the so-called conspiracies of Muslims.

For the duration of 40 days, Golwalkar intervened in the issues that cropped up in the camp in a manner which showed his intelligence, remaining fervently committed to the well-being of every swayamsevak attending the camp.

'Hundreds of swayamsevaks from different parts of the country had come to attend the camp,' writes Indurkar. 'Ten to twenty of them were always unwell. There were doctors to look after them. But Guruji himself took care of these swayamsevaks. Such care was especially required during the night, when swayamsevaks retreated for rest after the whole day's hectic programmes. No one could know when Guruji used to sleep in the night.'[40]

When the camp wound up in June, Golwalkar had transformed fully into a dedicated RSS man. His lawyer's nameplate still hung at his office on Walkar Road (later renamed Ruikar Road) in Nagpur, but his energy and all the drive of his growing ambition were thrown into Hindutva politics and into the RSS.

Since the early years of this decade, the RSS had started expanding out of the Marathi-speaking districts of Bombay Presidency and the Central Provinces. While still an organization serving the cravings of Maharashtrian Brahmins for the restoration of a bygone era, it had developed bases among Maharashtrian Brahmins living in Karachi, Lahore, Varanasi, Delhi and other isolated pockets in northern India. Now Golwalkar was rarely at home. In Nagpur, he was often seen strolling the streets on his

---

40. Shri Gangadhar Indurkar, *Guruji: Rashtriya Swayamsevak Sangh ke Sarsanghchalak Shri Madhav Sadashiv Golwalkar ka Jeevan Charitra*, Sangh Vastu Bhandar, Delhi, 1949, pp. 33-34.

way to meetings of the RSS. Fast emerging as a good speaker, his multi-linguality, his provocative and vigorous gestures, his gift for dramatic phrases and for enigmatic allusions drawn from Hindu religious mythologies seemed to fascinate RSS men.

In August 1938, shortly after the OTC at Nagpur, another RSS camp was planned at Lahore. This was to be the first such camp in north India. Golwalkar's name came up as one of the two lieutenants who would accompany Hedgewar to Lahore, the other being Babasaheb Apte, a senior man in the RSS.[41]

The Lahore camp proved to be of profound significance. Hedgewar remained unwell with a recurring backache, and Golwalkar, with the RSS chief's approval, practically ran the show. Discussions, conversations and debates traversing the vast spectrum of the idea of a Hindu Rashtra and the militarization of Hindus abounded, and Golwalkar led them all.

'The Officers' Training Camp at Lahore continued till August 27,' Golwalkar wrote to Abaji Hedgewar, Dr. Hedgewar's uncle, considered a father figure in the RSS, on 31 August.

> It was decided to honour Param Pujya [His Holiness] Doctor [as Hedgewar was fondly referred to by his associates] on August 27. Several pro-Hindutva invitees attended that event in the evening. A large number of swayamsevaks from Lahore and Sialkot regions [of Punjab] had gathered. At 6.15 pm, Param Pujya Doctor reached the campsite. Immediately, he was given guard of honour in military style. Thereafter, he unfurled the RSS flag and was honoured with garlands. [...] At the end, he gave a brief speech, in which he talked about organizational and working style of the Sangh. He said that the Sangh is the only real way of protecting Hindu religion, Hindu culture, Hindu society and Hindu nation.[42]

---

41. Ranga Hari, *The Incomparable Guru Golwalkar*, Prabhat Paperbacks, New Delh, 2018, p. 74.

42. Golwalkar Papers, Roll No. 12269, Microfilm Section, NMML, New Delhi, pp. 37-40.

Now, with round-the-clock involvement in the organizational works of the RSS, Golwalkar experienced a surge of political consciousness—not of the kind that drove the majority of Indians to fight for independence but of the variety that rested on the obsessive desire of a section of upper caste Hindus to secure Brahmin ascendency in politics like the one that the Peshwas had established in western and central India before the British conquest. From the limbo in which he lived previously, Golwalkar abruptly found himself caught up in events that aroused in him passions and hopes. In a burst of rapture, he suddenly saw a way out of a life of despair and found prospects for a future in the RSS.

V

Golwalkar's ambitions were swelling, but his ego was not immediately gratified by Hedgewar, who had someone else in mind for a leadership role. The RSS chief had a favourite, Gopal Mukund Huddar, also known as Balaji Huddar, a Brahmin who had grown up in Nagpur. He went to Morris College and completed his graduation in 1924. He was part of the group of young Hindu men who formed the nucleus of the RSS in 1925. Like Hedgewar and other RSS men of the time, he was an active participant in the activities of the Hindu Mahasabha, and was considered a favourite of Moonje, too.[43]

Young though he was, his radiant energy produced such an impression of absolute reliability that Hedgewar made him the first sarkaryavah, or general secretary, of the RSS.[44] In particular, Hedgewar admired his ability to deliver enigmatic speeches which

---

43. File No. PF710182, Gopal Mukund Huddar, 'Identity Sheet', National Archives, UK.

44. Bhaiya Ghatate, *Shri Babasaheb Ghatate Yanche Atmakathan*, Shri Babasaheb Apte Smarak Samiti, Nagpur, 1997, p. 45.

awoke enthusiasm and delight in the listener. Ordinarily, he would always show up to listen to Huddar's speeches. In August 1929, a visit to Indore kept him from a speech Huddar delivered at Nagpur.

'I regret I was not there to listen to Balaji Huddar's speech,' Hedgewar wrote in a letter to two of his associates. 'No matter how many times you listen to him, his speeches are so delightful that you feel like listening to them again and again.'[45]

In 1931, Huddar was arrested for his role in an armed robbery at Balaghat in the Central Provinces. He was tried and sentenced to five years in jail.[46] He lost his job as a teacher in a girls' school. He was released on 1 November 1935.[47] Initially jobless, Huddar started working for *Sawadhan* (Warning), a journal that was edited by his friend Ramchandra Balaji Maokar, a local Hindu Mahasabha leader. Not long after, in September 1936, with the encouragement and financial support of friends, he left for London to study journalism.[48]

Six months later, he was attending rallies and meetings addressed by communist and progressive speakers and witnessing the powerful international solidarity for the Left-leaning Spanish Republic's fight against fascist forces of General Francisco Franco.[49] It drew in many individual volunteers from England, who were moved by the Spanish resistance against the tide of 'Hitler, Mussolini, Franco' (including, famously, George Orwell, who wrote about the trenches in *Homage to Catalonia*, and his

45. N. H. Palkar, *Dr. Hedgewar: Patraroop-Vyaktidarshan*, Archana Prakashan, Indore, 1989, p. 17.

46. File No. PF710182, Gopal Mukund Huddar, 'Identity Sheet', National Archives, UK.

47. Ibid.

48. *The Times of India*, 23 November 1938.

49. File No. PF710182, Gopal Mukund Huddar, British intelligence letter dated 23 June 1937, National Archives, UK.

wife Eileen). Largely because of the influence of communists in London, Huddar's conversion into an enthusiastic supporter of the fight against fascism was quick and smooth. The ease with which he crossed from one worldview to another betrays the fact that he had not properly understood the world he had grown in.

A British intelligence letter noted that after 5 October 1937, 'there was no trace of him in London'.[50] As per an article published in *The Volunteer*, a journal founded by veterans of the International Brigades, Huddar arrived in Albacete, a Spanish town that served as the headquarters of the International Brigades, on 17 October 1937 and was assigned as a member of the Saklatvala Battalion, a British battalion named after Sapurji Saklatvala, a prominent Indian communist in England who had died in 1936. On 3 April 1938, while taking part in the battle of Gandesa, he was captured by Franco's forces and imprisoned with other members of the International Brigades in San Pedro de Cardena. Later that year, he was released under a prisoner swap arranged by Britain.[51]

All the while, before leaving London to take part in the Spanish Civil War, Huddar had been in regular contact with Hedgewar. The latter also reciprocated in equal measure. Their separation seemed to have brought them even closer to each other. Sample the letter Hedgewar sent Huddar on 11 March 1937. 'I received your letter dated February 4 on February 20. Your letter made me elated but simultaneously I became sad to know that we won't be able to meet for one year.' He further wrote:

> But whatever it takes, we have to wait till then. [...] The work of the Sangh is going well. It is true that my health is not as good as it should be. But the problem is not with my health. Keeping in account the pressure of work and the efforts it

---

50. Ibid.

51. https://albavolunteer.org/2016/08/gopal-mukund-huddar-an-indian-volunteer-in-the-ibs/ (Accessed on 20 April 2023)

> requires, the kind of health I am maintaining is not bad. For last four months I was travelling for the Sangh work. During this period, every day was spent at a new place, and it was not possible to sleep before 2 am during any of these nights. [...] But I will remember your suggestion that I should take care of my health, and I will definitely do efforts to that end.[52]

Huddar's association with communists in London had influenced him but it had not shaped him yet. On 1 October 1937, five days before he left London to take part in the Spanish Civil War, he wrote to W. W. Fadnavis, the new editor of *Sawadhan*, detailing his future plans. The Intelligence Bureau intercepted the letter. In its report, Huddar was quoted revealing to Fadnavis that 'after furious thinking for last three months he has decided to work in the R.S.S.S. after his return to India'.[53] Along with his letter, Huddar also sent a message to swayamsevaks with an instruction that it be read out in that year's annual Dassehra celebration which marked the foundation day of the RSS. 'In addition to his letter the writer has enclosed a very inspiring message in Marathi for the R.S.S.S. volunteers giving Maratta History and urging every one of them to spread R.S.S.S. movement throughout Asia. This message is meant for the celebration of "Dasera" by the R.S.S.S. Nagpur,' said the IB report.[54]

By the time he came out of Franco's prison, Huddar had relinquished many of his old ideas. He displayed a worldview completely different from that of the RSS, even though he continued to remain deferential to Hedgewar and maintained

52. N. H. Palkar, *Dr. Hedgewar: Patraroop-Vyaktidarshan*, Archana Prakashan, Indore, 1989, pp. 77-78.

53. File No. PF710182, Gopal Mukund Huddar, 'Brief summary of an airmail letter dated 1-10-37 from Bala Huddar, London, to W.W. Fadnavis, Nagpur', National Archives, UK.

54. Ibid.

a personal relationship with him. On 12 November 1938, days after his release, he was given a public reception by the Indian Swaraj League, a communist-dominated body, in London. Rajani Palme Dutt, a prominent leader of the Communist Party of Great Britain (CPGB), chaired the meeting, which was also addressed by Benjamin Bradley, another distinguished leader of the CPGB.

'Receiving a great ovation when he rose to speak, Huddar said that he had returned from Spain a new man. He was very proud to have fought with the Battalion of British anti-Fascists,' reported a London-based newspaper, *The Daily Worker*. It also quoted Huddar saying that when the battle for India's freedom would commence 'this great anti-Fascist body of men have assured me that they will fight side by side with the Indian peoples'.[55]

Huddar returned to India on 18 December 1938.[56] According to *The Volunteer*, addressing a public meeting organized by several Bombay unions and the Bombay Congress Socialist Party, Huddar said: 'The honour you have done me is really the honour to the cause of democracy and freedom which Spanish workers and peasants are defending with their lives. [...] The fight for democracy is in India just as it is in Spain. The very same British Imperialism which helps Franco and Mussolini in their attempt to destroy Spain is holding us down. We have to fight against it. We have to build the unity of the workers, peasants and the middle classes just as the Spanish people have done.'[57]

It was obvious that Huddar had absorbed the complex notions that gave this period its mood and absorbed them with that heightened sensitivity which had led progressives all over the

55. File No. PF710182, Gopal Mukund Huddar, 'Fighters' Pledge to India', National Archives, UK.

56. *The Times of India*, 19 December 1938.

57. https://albavolunteer.org/2016/08/gopal-mukund-huddar-an-indian-volunteer-in-the-ibs/ (Accessed on 20 April 2023)

world to come out in solidarity with the Spanish people's fight for democracy. Along with the values of anti-imperialism and democracy, the period passed on to him the nationalistic missionary faith in building the unity of workers, peasants and the middle class.

These notions were the obverse of Hedgewar's dreams, a rebuke to a narrow politics of crude preoccupations.

Mentor and protégé met a few days into Huddar's return from London, in December 1938. They had changed beyond recognition. While Hedgewar had become even more servile to the colonial regime, Huddar had progressed to become hardcore anti-British in his thought and action. Perhaps, neither was completely aware of the transformation the other had undergone—this may well have been due to their separation for such a long period and a complete absence of communication for over a year.

Huddar was no longer blind to the motivations that fuelled the RSS or naïve about the mechanisms by which it sought to achieve its objectives. Yet, he believed that through persuasive arguments he would bring Hedgewar to a change of heart and make him align the RSS with the anti-imperialist cause.

'I brought it to his [Hedgewar's] notice that the RSS remained a static organisation and that it did not develop into a dynamic movement, while we know that it was the dynamism of a movement alone that made an organisation powerful—otherwise it degenerated into a *samsthan*,' Huddar recounted. 'The RSS had to guard against this danger which helped the growth of complacency and self-righteousness. My words fell on deaf ears and all my efforts to woo the Sarsanghchalak came to a naught.'[58]

The meeting was an effort to tell Hedgewar indirectly that the RSS could develop into a dynamic body only if it changed

58. Balaji Huddar, 'The RSS and Netaji', *Illustrated Weekly of India*, 7 October 1979.

its course and joined the nationalist mainstream. But since what he was proposing was altogether alien to the RSS chief, he was unable to arouse Hedgewar's interest in it. After the meeting, the two seemed to start distancing themselves from each other; certainly, Hedgewar must have become wary of Huddar's penchant for fighting against the British regime.

Hedgewar and Huddar had forged a bond because they had compatible values and political outlook when the latter had left for London over two years back. That was the reason why Hedgewar eagerly waited for Huddar's return to the RSS. The values and political outlook they shared now, however, were notably different—a difference that would prompt Hedgewar's turn to Golwalkar.

We or Our Nationhood Defied

By the end of 1938, Golwalkar had begun to increasingly distinguish himself in the RSS. Reports spoke of his enthusiasm in travelling from place to place to conduct RSS camps and expand the organization, his extraordinary affability and friendliness with leaders and cadres, his capacity to inspire trust in everybody, his expertise at acting as intermediary and resolving issues with his infectious smile. His command over multiple languages was often described as a big asset that could be employed for expanding the RSS into non-Marathi linguistic regions of the country. He could also be trusted for providing intellectual leadership to cadres.

As might be expected, in many things he was orthodox and conservative. He had a pervasive self-awareness of his own caste. He was a Brahmin, and always conscious, even if only subliminally, of being one. For him, being a Brahmin was not merely an exalted social status, but a basic premise of his existence. However, he was highly educated and attached no intrinsic value to something simply because it happened to be old and hallowed. When required, he could also display passionate support for the new and untested.

Like most leaders of the RSS and Hindu Mahasabha, Golwalkar had stayed out of an anti-British stance or activity, and any membership of a party that vowed to fight the colonial regime. It is questionable whether Golwalkar would ever have belonged to such a party anyway. Like most members of the RSS, he found it difficult to muster any great enthusiasm for the rapidly growing debates and movements for national independence. Revolutionary ideas held no attraction for him. Strictly speaking, these views on British rule placed Golwalkar in total harmony with Hedgewar, whose temper was that of a loyalist. For example, Hedgewar described the British rule as 'an act of providence' on 7 October 1935, during the tenth-anniversary celebrations of the RSS. A *Times of India* report quoted Hedgewar saying that 'the British Raj afforded them a lesson in organisation, and he looked upon it as an act of providence that the Britishers were ruling over them'.[1]

Golwalkar's experiences and circumstances during 1938 made his dreams ambitious and helped him arrive at that political philosophy which became the central core of his view of India. Evidently, Babarao's *Rashtra Mimansa* had made a deep impression upon him. But as he got involved in the activities of the RSS he must also have read Savarkar's *Hindutva: Who is a Hindu?*—the source text for the ideological training of swayamsevaks—as well as pro-Hindutva articles and pamphlets. Views that Golwalkar found expressed by the literature did not constitute, by any means, the negation of his values, and he did not have to abandon any of the ideas that had helped him achieve his initial orientation. New ideas he was encountering now seemed only a progression of what he had picked up earlier, and they merely opened for him an entrance into the political circle he wanted to belong to.

The need to consolidate his position in the new political circle also underlay his efforts at this stage to give a concrete ideological shape to the ideas he had acquired in the last few months. That also seemed to satisfy his intensified egotism, which made him constantly self-conscious about his conversion experience and aware that in some sense he was special. These efforts culminated

1. *The Times of India*, 10 October 1935, p. 10.

in November 1938, when he finished the manuscript of his maiden book, *We or Our Nationhood Defined*.[2] In the book, he took over the prejudices, anxieties and desires of the Hindutva leaders. He described and prescribed a solution for the so-called minority problem in India based on the Nazi's treatment of Jews in the Third Reich. Among the elements in the book were both anti-minority and master-race theories that sought to counter the secularist vision being championed by nationalist leaders in India. These were in accordance with the mood of the votaries of a Hindu Rashtra, and by incorporating them in the Hindutva ideology he attempted to raise himself in the eyes of this class.

Starting from the late 1920s, orthodox Brahmins of Maharashtra—the Marathi-speaking areas of Bombay Presidency and the Central Provinces—were getting seduced by at least certain aspects of Nazism and fascism. Their belief that they occupied the apex of Hindu society and polity and that the majority of their coreligionists were theologically duty bound to accept their servile position meant that they were inherently susceptible, and vulnerable, to exploitation by right-wing totalitarianism. Naturally, therefore, a fascination with Nazism and fascism was common to both the RSS and the Hindu Mahasabha—a fact that must have inspired Moonje's trip to Italy where he met Mussolini in 1931.

As pointed out by Italian scholar Marzia Casolari, beginning with the 1920s, Hindu militant organizations 'seemed to uneasily oscillate between a conciliatory attitude towards the British and a sympathy for the dictators'.[3] The RSS and the Hindu Mahasabha saw the European dictatorships as an example of conservative revolution, a concept that was being discussed widely by the pro-

---

2. M. S. Golwalkar, *We or Our Nationhood Defined*, Bharat Publications, Nagpur, 1939, p. 4.

3. Marzia Casolari, 'Hindutva's Foreign Tie-up in the 1930s: Archival Evidence', *Economic and Political Weekly*, 22 January 2000, pp. 218-219.

Hindutva section of the Marathi press.[4] Further, all the Marathi newspapers and pamphlets, eulogizing these regimes, belonged to Brahmins. *Kesari*, which published a series of editorials on the subject, was the most prominent among them.

Cherished ambitions of continuing the anti-Mughal exploits of Shivaji and the Peshwas found fertile soil in the fascist emphasis on discipline and respect for traditional values. They marveled at the martial traditions of Maharashtrian Brahmins of yore and considered the fascist advocacy for a militarized society a natural choice and pathway to revive the glories of the Peshwa Raj. That's why the aspects of fascism that seemed to appeal to the Hindu organizations most were both its stress on militarization of society and the figure of a strong leader controlling a highly centralized organization.[5]

Moreover, a decidedly pro-Nazi temper marked many of the speeches that V. D. Savarkar was delivering after the restrictions on him were removed and he became the president of the Hindu Mahasabha in 1937. For instance, he said on 1 August 1938: 'Germany has every right to resort to Nazism and Italy to Fascism and events have justified that those isms and forms of governments were imperative and beneficial to them under the conditions that obtained there.'[6] This speech was made before a crowd of 20,000 in Pune.

That year when Congress leader Jawaharlal Nehru spoke against Nazism in Germany and Fascism in Italy, Savarkar offered a riposte: 'Who are we to dictate to Germany, Japan or Russia or Italy to choose a particular form of policy of government simply because we woo it out of academical attraction?' he asked. 'Surely, Hitler

4. Ibid., p. 219.

5. Ibid., p. 221.

6. Savarkar Papers, m 23, part 2, Miscellaneous Correspondence, January 1938-May 1939, Microfilm Section, NMML, New Delhi.

knows better than Pandit Nehru does what suits Germany best. The very fact that Germany or Italy has so wonderfully recovered and grown so powerful as never before at the touch of Nazi or Fascist magical wand is enough to prove that those political "isms" were the most congenial tonics their health demanded.'[7]

Defending Germany on its claim over Czechoslovakia and Austria, Savarkar said, '[...] as far as Czechoslovakia question was concerned the Hindu Sanghatanists in India hold that Germany was perfectly justified in uniting the Austrian and Sudetan Germans under the German flag. Democracy itself demanded that the will of the people must prevail in choosing their own government. Germany demanded plebiscite, the Germans under the Czechs wanted to join their kith and kin in Germany. It was the Czechs who were acting against the principle of democracy in holding the Germans under a foreign sway against their will.'[8]

In a more guarded manner, Savarkar also sought to augment his anti-Muslim rhetoric by supporting Hitler's anti-Jewish policy. On 14 October 1938, hinting heavily, Savarkar said: 'A nation is formed by a majority living therein. What did the Jews do in Germany? They being in minority were driven out from Germany.'[9] In December that year, when the Congress expressed its resolution against Germany, Savarkar stated that 'in Germany the movement of the Germans is the national movement but that of the Jews is a communal one'.[10]

---

7. Savarkar Papers, m 1, part 2, May 1937-May 1938, Microfilm Section, NMML, New Delhi.

8. Ibid.

9. 'Translation of the verbatim speech made by VD Savarkar at Malegaon on October 14, 1938', 60 D(g), Part III, 1938, Home Special Department, Maharashtra State Archives, Mumbai.

10. 'A report on the meeting held on December 11, 1938', 60 D(g), Part III, 1938, Home Special Department, Maharashtra State Archives, Mumbai.

II

Though indirectly, Savarkar was the first to defend the Nazi's treatment of Jews in the Third Reich. Golwalkar, with his own keen sense for the effectiveness of primitive emotions, quickly went ahead of the Hindutva ideologue by pushing this line of thinking to extremes. In *We or Our Nationhood Defined*, Golwalkar attempted to deal with his repugnance for Muslims and took Hindutva's prevalent attraction for European dictatorships to a new level. The virulent idea fuelling the RSS—which demanded that Hindus must be granted the exclusive right to define India's national identity—was in nebulous form in Savarkar's treatise on Hindutva. His speeches in support of European dictators and their policies, too, were largely guarded. Golwalkar argued his views sharply and consistently and added considerable details to the idea of Hindutva. Without any ambiguity, he presented the Nazi treatment of Jews as a model to be applied on Indian minorities, especially Muslims, and thus provided the core of the Sangh's credo.

'To keep up the purity of the Race and its culture, Germany shocked the world by her purging the country of the semitic Races—the Jews,' Golwalkar wrote. 'Race pride at its highest has been manifested here. Germany has also shown how well nigh impossible it is for Races and cultures, having differences going to the root, to be assimilated into one united whole, a good lesson for us in Hindusthan to learn and profit by.'[11]

With Nazi experiment of cleansing of Jews in mind, Golwalkar—having declared Muslims and Christians as foreign races—prescribed a formula for India:

> From this standpoint, sanctioned by the experience of shrewd old nations, the foreign races in Hindusthan must either adopt

11. M. S. Golwalkar, *We or Our Nationhood Defined*, Bharat Publications, Nagpur, 1939, p. 35.

> the Hindu culture and language, must learn to respect and hold in reverence Hindu religion, must entertain no idea but those of the glorification of the Hindu race and culture, i.e., of the Hindu nation and must lose their separate existence to merge in the Hindu race, or may stay in the country, wholly subordinated to the Hindu Nation, claiming nothing, deserving no privileges, far less any preferential treatment—not even citizen's rights. There is, at least should be, no other course for them to adopt. We are an old nation; let us deal as old nations ought to and do deal, with the foreign races, who have chosen to live in our country.[12]

Evidently, German theoreticians, especially Swiss jurist Johann Kaspar Bluntschli, had made a deep impression on him. In the book, he made continuous references to them—though he misspelled Bluntschli as 'Blunstley'—as he set out to radically reject the idea of India being a multi-religious nation. 'Most of the books mentioned by Golwalkar are illustrative of the German ethnic definition of nationalism,' writes French political scientist Christophe Jaffrelot. 'He paid little attention to the English authors from whom the Congress leaders drew their idea of the nation in universalistic terms, such as the role of individual will and the social contract.'[13]

Golwalkar's growing hatred for a multi-religious nation made him hostile to the idea of secular democracy. He despised the word 'Indian' and called it 'the outlandish name' which was coined to strengthen 'wrong notions of democracy' by promoting unity among people of different religions, particularly Hindus and Muslims. 'The result of this poison is too well known,' he wrote. 'We have allowed ourselves to be duped into believing our foes to be our friends and with our own hands are undermining true

12. Ibid., pp. 47-48.

13. Christophe Jaffrelot, *The Hindu Nationalist Movement and Indian Politics, 1925 to 1990s*, Hurst & Company, London, 1996, p. 54.

nationality. That is the real danger of the day, our self-forgetfulness, our believing our old and bitter enemies to be our friends.'[14]

In *We or Our Nationhood Defined*, Golwalkar sought to bring communal cruelty to the history of India as an inescapable part of nation-building. He imagined a long period of 'unflinching war' through which the 'Hindu nation' struggled for existence and protection of its 'swa' or identity. 'Ever since that evil day, when Moslems first landed in Hindusthan, right upto the present moment, the Hindu Nation has been gallantly fighting on to shake off the despoilers,' he wrote. 'It is the fortune of war, the tide turns now to this side, now to that, but the war goes on and has not been decided yet. Nor is there any fear of its being decided to our detriment. The Race Spirit has been awakening.'[15]

Concluding what he called 'the History of Hindusthan', he sought to carry Hindus into a state of constant opposition toward Muslims:

> In short our history is the story of our flourishing Hindu National life for thousands of years and then of a long unflinching war continuing for the last ten centuries, which has not yet come to a decisive close. And when we understand our history, thus rightly, we find ourselves not the degenerate, downtrodden, uncivilized slaves that we are taught to believe we are today, but a nation, a free nation of illustrious heroes fighting the forces of destruction for the last thousand years and determined to carry on the struggle to the bitter end with ever-increasing zeal and unflagging national ardour. And Race Spirit calls. National consciousness blazes forth and we Hindus rally to the Hindu Standard, the Bhagawa Dhwaja, set our teeth in grim determination to wipe out the opposing forces.[16]

---

14. M. S. Golwalkar, *We or Our Nationhood Defined*, Bharat Publications, Nagpur, 1939, p. 14.

15. Ibid., p. 12.

16. Ibid., p. 13.

Nevertheless, the component of the communal theory of history in Golwalkar's thought cannot be attributed solely to him. He was really reflecting the imagination of India's past as presented by Savarkar. In *Hindutva: Who is a Hindu?*, Savarkar had written that 'a conflict of life and death' ensued 'after Mohammad of Gazni crossed the Indus' and invaded India: 'In this prolonged furious conflict our people became intensely conscious of ourselves as Hindus and were welded into a nation to an extent unknown in our history.'[17]

Golwalkar carried Savarkarite imagination of India's past further. He took the idea, developed it, turned it into an actionable programme and made it part of a blueprint meant to achieve their common goal—the Hindu Rashtra.

III

The book increased Golwalkar's credibility in the RSS. In fact, most of the Sangh office-bearers and swayamsevaks—excepting Hedgewar and a few others at the top—came to know him first as the author of this book.[18] Within months of the completion of the manuscript in November 1938 he could look back upon some impressive successes. Hedgewar, apparently disappointed with Balaji Huddar's changed outlook, was just as happy to let Golwalkar run the show. Among other things, this meant helping Golwalkar adapt more thoroughly in the Sangh's work culture and discipline and enabling him to expand Sangh work in non-Marathi linguistic zones.

In February 1939, some two months before the book was published in April, Hedgewar called a special ten-day-long

17. V. D. Savarkar, *Hindutva: Who is a Hindu?*, Hindi Sahitya Sadan, New Delhi, 2005, p. 44.

18. D. R. Goyal, *Rashtriya Swayamsewak Sangh*, Radhakrishna Prakashan (P) Ltd., New Delhi, 2000, p. 93.

meeting of select RSS leaders at Sindi village near Nagpur to review the Sangh's working and organizational issues. Golwalkar's biographers maintained that he was among the star participants here even though he was still an 'outsider' as he had no formal position in the RSS. 'All the participants noted Guruji's highly analytical intellect, logical approach, sharp focus, strong ideological clarity,' wrote Ranga Hari, for example.[19] Among the many organizational changes the Sindi meet would introduce was the adoption of a Sanskrit prayer to be recited by RSS cadres.[20] The prayer in Marathi that had been used by swayamsevaks until then naturally seemed quite inadequate to cater to the requirements of an organization that had set its sights on non-Marathi regions.

At the time, Hedgewar was fifty. He was a full-faced man, about the same height as Golwalkar, but hefty, quiet and watchful. His white hair had started thinning on the scalp and his face was dominated by his lush white moustache. He seemed enterprising and had a ready smile on his face. From the point of view of RSS men, his persona exuded confidence and an irrepressible charm. His large eyes were bright and communicative, but his manner was reserved.

His growing interest in Golwalkar was visible. It was apparent not only at the Sindi meet, but also in letters he wrote to regional satraps of the RSS during this period. In fact, reading and writing letters was one of the most important activities in Hedgewar's daily routine, a way to take stock of the RSS work in different areas.

He wrote to his colleagues Dadarao Parmarth and Janardan Chinchalkar on 24 March 1939: 'After your departure [from Nagpur], Shri Golwalkar and Shri Patki [...] left for Calcutta for

---

19. Ranga Hari, *The Incomparable Guru Golwalkar*, Prabhat Paperbacks, New Delhi, 2018, p. 76.

20. Ibid.

starting Sangh activities.'[21] This was the first time Golwalkar popped up in such correspondence. It was Golwalkar's first independent organizational assignment. His task was to help Vitthalrao Patki, who was designated as the Sangh's in-charge of Bengal, in finding volunteers for RSS activities. Around mid-April they succeeded in starting a shakha in Maniktola locality of Calcutta. Shortly afterwards, Golwalkar returned to supervise the annual summer camp of the RSS in Nagpur, leaving Patki to continue the Sangh work in Bengal.[22]

Perhaps, the scheduled release of his book sometime around the end of April also mandated his sudden return from Calcutta.[23] There is no known record of the manner in which Golwalkar's book was released, but there appears to be a reliable indicator to show that Hedgewar played a key role in its publication. It was primarily due to his efforts that M. S. Aney, a well-known Congress conservative, Maharashtrian Brahmin and a close friend of Hedgewar, wrote a foreword to *We or Our Nationhood Defined.* His choice of Aney was understandable. Despite being a Congress leader, Aney was seldom wholly united with the Gandhians on ideological issues. Instead, he was sympathetic to the idea of a Hindu Rashtra, though without any express hatred of Muslims. In his foreword, Aney tried to distance himself from Golwalkar's prescription of Hitler's anti-Semitism as the role model to deal with Muslims in India. Yet, the fact that he wrote the foreword added considerable weight to Golwalkar's book, and that was exactly what Hedgewar seemed to have desired.

Now onwards, Golwalkar stayed close to Hedgewar. He was

21. N. H. Palkar, *Dr. Hedgewar: Patraroop-Vyaktidarshan*, Archana Prakashan, Indore, 1989, pp. 99-100.

22. N. H. Palkar, *Shri Ma Sa Golwalkar*, published by N. H. Palkar, Mumbai, 1956, p. 63.

23. Ibid.

approaching his mid-thirties and seemed bent on making it to the top—not just as a leader of the RSS but also as its exponent. At the RSS office in Nagpur, he was the rising star; at the Officers' Training Camp, he was the boss; on visits to supervise outstation meetings of swayamsevaks, he was the chief orator-cum-organizer; and in a general gathering of Hindutva men, he was an ideologue. For the first time in his life, his area of operation demanded no qualifications other than those he naturally possessed: passion, imagination, organizational talent and demagogic gifts. His success was due in considerable part to his having unlimited time at his disposal for Hedgewar, the sarsanghchalak. While other RSS leaders preferred to work for the organization during the time they took out from their routine work, Golwalkar put himself forward as a devout follower, treating Hedgewar as the pivot of his life.

Hedgewar seemed to like it. When, in an RSS meeting at Poona around the middle of June 1939, he praised Golwalkar's oratorical skill in Hindi and invited him to say something to demonstrate it, the latter obliged by delivering a eulogy about Hedgewar, as the topic he spoke on was 'sarsanghchalak'![24]

IV

From Poona, Hedgewar went to Deolali, a small hill station on the outskirts of Nasik, on the invitation of M. N. Ghatate, a rich swyamsevak of Nagpur. Ghatate was the scion of an extremely wealthy family that owned large tracts of land in Nagpur and ran a moneylending business. He was a friend of Balaji Huddar and a die-hard supporter of Moonje. In the past, he had donated liberally to the RSS at the behest of Huddar, but he became a member of this organization only in March 1939 when Hedgewar personally

---

24. Ranga Hari, *The Incomparable Guru Golwalkar*, Prabhat Paperbacks, New Delhi, 2018, p. 77.

approached him.[25] He also had properties in Deolali, including a large farm house.

Ghatate was in Deolali when Hedgewar visited Poona along with Golwalkar to attend the RSS meet in June 1939. As Hedgewar was not keeping well, Ghatate invited him to Deolali where he could stay for some time in order to escape the fierce Nagpur summer.[26] On the evening of 20 June, Hedgewar, along with Golwalkar and three other associates, reached Deolali.[27] Ghatate received them and took them to his place. The trip was meant for two weeks, but it was prolonged to almost one and a half months as Hedgewar fell ill due to an attack of pneumonia.

During their stay here, Golwalkar conducted himself as an exceptionally caring man. He served the RSS chief with energy and dedication. He got up early, arranged for Hedgewar's puja, accompanied him on walks, travelled to Nasik to procure his medicines and wrote letters indefatigably at his instructions to Abaji Hedgewar, the RSS chief's uncle, and Krishnarao Mohril, the in-charge of the RSS headquarters at Nagpur, conveying through them instructions to provincial heads of the organization. He also eagerly noted every unfamiliar face that turned up to meet Hedgewar. Thus, when Huddar visited Hedgewar on 7 July, Golwalkar duly reported it to Abaji in his letter dated 11 July 1939.[28]

Huddar had visited Hedgewar as an emissary of Subhash Chandra Bose, the Congress president who had to resign from the post due to his differences with Mahatma Gandhi on various

25. Bhaiya Ghatate, *Shri Babasaheb Ghatate Yanche Atmakathan*, Shri Babasaheb Apte Smarak Samiti, Nagpur, 1997, p. 54.

26. Ibid.

27. Golwalkar Papers, Roll No. 12269, Microfilm Section, NMML, New Delhi, p. 43.

28. Ibid., pp. 53-56.

ideological issues, including the method of fighting the British regime. At the time, Bose, having formed the All India Forward Bloc as a faction within the Congress, had been exploring new options to continue his anti-British struggle independent of Gandhi. By Huddar's account, Bose had heard of the RSS and thought he could bring it into the anti-British struggle. The former Congress president, therefore, contacted Huddar, whom he knew as 'a soldier in the International Brigade and of [his] very personal and long-standing relationship' with Hedgewar. 'One evening, he [Bose] called me to his place in Bombay,' Huddar wrote later. 'One Mr. Shah, with whom I was not acquainted, was with him. Netaji asked me if I would be his emissary to Dr. Hedgewar, with whom he would like to have a talk. He asked me to go to Nasik where Dr. Hedgewar was spending the summer with Babasaheb Ghatate […]. Mr. Shah was to accompany me.'[29]

Huddar readily agreed. 'In Nasik, Babasaheb greeted me warmly and enquired about our mission. I told him that we had come to see Doctorsaheb. Mr. Shah waited outside and I was ushered into the room where Doctorsaheb was joking and laughing with some youngsters—all volunteers of the RSS,' Huddar recounted.

After the volunteers left the room on his request, Huddar told Hedgewar that Bose eagerly wanted to have a meeting with him. 'Doctorsaheb protested that he had been in Nasik as he was ill and was suffering from some unknown malady,' Huddar wrote. 'I entreated him not to give up this chance of an interview with a great leader of the Congress and the nationalist force in India, but he would not pay heed to me. He protested all through that he was too ill to have a talk.'[30]

Huddar then said that it would only be fair for Hedgewar

29. Balaji Huddar, 'The RSS and Netaji', *Illustrated Weekly of India*, 7 October 1979.

30. Ibid.

to inform Mr Shah, who had accompanied him and was waiting outside the room, about 'his genuine difficulty which, after all, was only physical illness of a kind'. Otherwise, he feared, Bose might suspect that Huddar had sabotaged the mission.

'Shrewd as he was,' Huddar wrote, Hedgewar 'took the hint and stretched himself out on the bed, saying, "Balaji, I am really very ill and cannot stand even the strain of a short interview. Please don't."' Huddar understood that there was no point in pursuing the matter. Hedgewar would not fight the British for India's freedom. 'As I left the room,' he recounted, 'the RSS volunteers entered and laughter broke out again.'[31]

In later years, pro-RSS writers quietly circulated a completely opposite version of Hedgewar's conversation with Huddar, apparently to show that the Sangh chief never spurned the call to join the freedom struggle. In *Builders of Modern India: Dr. Keshav Baliram Hedgewar*, RSS ideologue Rakesh Sinha claimed—without referring to a document or an interview—that during his conversation with Huddar, Hedgewar actually agreed to meet Bose. 'After resigning as the Congress president, Bose began making contact with Dr. Hedgewar. A former Sarkaryavah (general secretary) of the RSS, Huddar (Balaji) came to Nagpur to meet Hedgewar in July 1939 as Bose's emissary along with another individual by the name of Shah. Hedgewar was then convalescing after a bout of pneumonia. He accepted the invitation to meet Bose immediately even as his health was actually continuously failing,' Sinha wrote.[32]

This is a clear case of myth-making. It fits in with the Sangh's desire to show its association with the Indian freedom movement. Sinha obviously did not see Huddar's own account of his visit to

---

31. Ibid.

32. Rakesh Sinha, *Builders of Modern India: Dr. Keshav Baliram Hedgewar*, Publications Division, Government of India, New Delhi, 2015, p. 167.

Hedgewar. He even goofed up on the location of the meeting, mistakenly writing that it took place in Nagpur.

V

Exactly a week after Hedgewar returned to Nagpur from Deolali, Golwalkar was made sarkaryavah of the RSS—they returned on 6 August[33] and Golwalkar was anointed sarkaryavah on 13 August.[34] The speed with which the decision was taken gives rise to a number of questions. Did Hedgewar consider the disavowal of the nationalist cause a crucial prerequisite for choosing his number two in the RSS? Did Huddar's elimination on this ground clear the way for Golwalkar? And was Golwalkar's own dispassionate attitude towards the nationalist cause part of the reason for his elevation?

We can probably no longer plumb a satisfactory answer to all these questions. Yet it is evident that Golwalkar was the biggest gainer post the stint in Deolali. No one in the RSS was now as close to Hedgewar, or seen as such by the members of the organization. The Sangh's office-bearers considered him—some with skeptical tolerance and others with unequivocal admiration—as the organization's remarkably committed leader, while Hedgewar looked at him as his most reliable lieutenant. Soon after his elevation, Golwalkar set out for Lahore to supervise the successful conclusion of the OTC. Lahore had become the hub of RSS activities in north-western India. From this bastion, the RSS work had begun to start in Rawalpindi, Sialkot, Amritsar, Multan and Ambala. Along with senior RSS member Babasaheb Apte, he travelled to all these places after the completion of the Lahore camp on 8 September 1939. From there, he traveled eastward,

---

33. Golwalkar Papers, Roll No. 12269, Microfilm Section, NMML, New Delhi, p. 61.

34. N. H. Palkar, *Dr. Hedgewar: Patraroop-Vyaktidarshan*, Archana Prakashan, Indore, 1989, pp. 100-101.

supervising RSS activities and clearing up local issues, if any. During this itinerary of two months, he covered Delhi, Varanasi, Patna and Calcutta, besides Lahore and neighbouring towns.[35]

By the time his initial travels ended, Golwalkar, in his devotion to the RSS and in his dedication to its expansion and consolidation, had come to model his life on that of the RSS chief. He was at ease even in linguistic climates far removed from Marathi-speaking areas. Under Hedgewar, he had learned to work hard and to concentrate on results, but since he was a newcomer, he lacked natural control over many of the colleagues who were senior to him in the RSS, especially in Bombay Presidency. As almost anyone would, Golwalkar suffered by comparison to Hedgewar. Yet he seemed to have genuinely admired Hedgewar, and as he explored his new circumstances, Golwalkar tried to live in some ways as Hedgewar had done. Like Hedgewar, he tried to work in close cooperation with all the senior RSS functionaries and evolved into something of a workaholic.

Hedgewar's constantly deteriorating health burdened Golwalkar with leadership responsibilities, but it also freed his considerable ambition. With growing self-assurance, he seemed to think of following in the footsteps of Hedgewar, who apart from being the sarsanghchalak of the RSS had also remained a national office-bearer of the Hindu Mahasabha. Golwalkar did not have to wait long. In December 1939, the Mahasabha held a session in Calcutta where it decided to conduct its first organizational election. Golwalkar fought for the position of the Hindu Mahasabha's secretary (karyavah). Acharya Balarao Savarkar, the personal secretary of V. D. Savarkar, gave a vivid description of the organizational election. 'Earlier, there used to be no election for president or any other post,' he wrote, adding:

35. Golwalkar Papers, Roll No. 12269, Microfilm Section, NMML, New Delhi, pp. 63-67.

> However, elections for various posts were fought keenly in Calcutta session. Savarkar could not remain present at the time of election as he was ill. But he had informed the executive president, Dr. Moonje, that office-bearers must be selected on the basis of proper election. Of these elections, the one that was held for the post of karyavah [secretary] was most keenly contested. There were three candidates in the fray—Indra Prakash, Jyotishankar Dixit and MS Golwalkar Guruji, who later became sarsanghchalak of the RSS. But Guruji lost the election. He got 40 votes, while his opponent Dixit got two votes and Indra Prakash got 80 votes.[36]

Balarao's account of the election—based on Indra Prakash's testimony—also suggests at some tension and confusion in the Hindu Mahasabha and hints at the hidden aspects of Golwalkar's expanding political life.

'According to Indra Prakash, Golwalkar had the backing of [Jugal Kishore] Birla faction. He was also supported by Babarao Savarkar, who had very good relationship with the Sangh. Still, he lost the election,' Balarao wrote.[37] Jugal Kishore Birla, a prominent businessman, was an important leader of the Hindu Mahasabha. He headed one of the factions of the Mahasabha in north India, the other being led by Bhai Parmanand, another important party leader who backed the candidature of Indra Prakash in that election.

Golwalkar's ties with Babarao Savarkar had only grown since he first met him regarding the translation of *Rashtra Mimansa*. A well read and shrewd Hindu Mahasabha leader who possessed extensive knowledge consonant with his prejudices, Babarao had opened many doors to Golwalkar. He seems to have wielded the

---

36. Acharya Balarao Savarkar, *Swatantryaveer Savarkar: Hindu Mahasabha Parva*, Vol. II, Swatantryaveer Savarkar Rashtriya Smarak, Mumbai, 2020, p. 360.

37. Ibid.

most lasting ideological influence upon Golwalkar during his early period in the RSS. That was perhaps the reason why Golwalkar, while on his way to Lahore after becoming sarkaryavah, had broken his journey in Delhi where he had first visited Hindu Mahasabha Bhawan, the national headquarters of the party, to pay obeisance to Babarao before meeting office-bearers and members of the RSS.[38]

VI

The setback that Golwalkar received in the Calcutta session of the Hindu Mahasabha was scarcely of much significance. There is hardly any evidence to suggest that it affected his position in the RSS in any way. On the contrary, the events around this time forced Golwalkar to play an even more central role in the functioning of the RSS than ever before. On 31 January 1940, Hedgewar, whose health had deteriorated even more, went on a two-and-a-half month vacation to Bihar's hilly town of Rajgir, where taking regular baths in its hot-water springs was believed to cure all kinds of diseases.[39] Among other things, this meant Golwalkar practically ran the organization during this period even though he kept writing to Hedgewar on a regular basis in order to inform him about the RSS's activities and to seek his approval for major organizational decisions.

Generally, at this stage Golwalkar worked collectively with important leaders of the RSS in Nagpur and neighbouring areas. He consulted them for every decision that he took and made them feel involved in the running of the RSS. He also made it a point

38. Golwalkar Papers, Roll No. 12269, Microfilm Section, NMML, New Delhi, p. 63.

39. Ranga Hari, *The Incomparable Guru Golwalkar*, Prabhat Paperbacks, New Delhi, 2018, p. 79.

to read Hedgewar's letters in their presence.[40] They responded to him positively. M. N. Kale, a senior RSS member, helped him in writing letters to regional office-bearers, which now became an important part of Golwalkar's daily routine.

'As per your instruction, all letters have been dispatched. Only the letter to Shridev Phule brothers is yet to be sent. Besides, I am also writing and mailing important letters on daily basis. Shri M.N. Kale is helping me write these letters every day at my place from 7 to 9.15 in the morning,' he wrote to Hedgewar on 8 February 1940.[41]

While writing to regional heads, however, his tone would become firm and he politely exhibited his authority. This becomes obvious in his letter to Delhi RSS chief Vasantrao Oak on 3 February 1940. 'Nagpur sanghchalak Babasaheb Ghatate is going to Delhi to attend the working committee meeting of Hindu Mahasabha. He will reach Delhi on February 9. Please be with him and show him shakhas in Delhi,' he wrote.[42] This was Golwalkar's instinctive balancing tactic, and it also reflected his embryonic love for the position of power.

Hedgewar returned to Nagpur on 20 April 1940.[43] A week later, on 27 April, both he and Golwalkar went to attend the summer camp of the RSS at Poona.[44] The camp was the biggest ever in Poona. It was followed by a meeting on 11 May of RSS organizers from various districts of Bombay Presidency as well as state-level office-bearers. State sanghchalak Kashinath Bhaskar

40. Golwalkar Papers, Roll No. 12269, Microfilm Section, NMML, New Delhi, p. 84.

41. Ibid., p. 86.

42. Ibid., p. 83.

43. Ranga Hari, *The Incomparable Guru Golwalkar*, Prabhat Paperbacks, New Delhi, 2018, p. 79.

44. Ibid.

Limaye was there. As was Nathuram Vinayak Godse. At the time, he was one of the RSS organizers of Poona. Less than a decade would pass before Godse killed Mahatma Gandhi. 'In one file the details of Bombay Provincial RSSS[45] meeting held in 1940 were available,' an investigation report, based on documents seized from the RSS headquarters after the assassination, said.

> In this file the name of N.V. Godse, tailor, has been noted on page 8 in the list of RSSS organizers of Poona, who had attended the meeting. The organizers' meeting was held on 11-5-40. In this meeting Tatyarao Savarkar [as VD Savarkar was fondly referred to], Kashinath Pant Limaya [Limaye], the Provincial Organizer of Bombay Province, Berar Provincial RSSS Organizer Appaji Joshi, Wardha District Organizer of the RSSS and others from Nasik, Poona, Satara, Ratnagiri, Bombay, East Khandesh, etc. were present. The name of Godse was third from the top.[46]

As per Limaye's biographer D. S. Harshe, who witnessed its proceedings, the meeting was held in a large conference hall of NM Vidyalaya, a school run by RSS men in Poona, and was conducted by 'three most prominent men of the Sangh' at that time—Hedgewar, Golwalkar and Limaye. 'Veer Savarkar attended part of the meeting. He also addressed it before leaving the venue,' Harshe wrote.[47]

By all accounts, this was the first occasion when Godse, who ran a tailoring shop in Poona, was seen in the company of Golwalkar. Nothing is known about what happened between the

45. In archival sources the acronym RSSS is occasionally used for this organization, whereas nowadays the shorter form RSS is more common. The meaning, however, is in both cases the same.

46. D. P. Mishra Papers, I & II Inst., Sub File No. 18, p. 137, Records Section, NMML, New Delhi.

47. D. S. Harshe, *Adarsh Hindu Sanghatak: Ka. Bha. Limaye*, published by Sudha Dattatreya Harshe, Satara, 1981, pp. 5-6.

two. Golwalkar, on completion of the Poona meeting, rushed to Nagpur where another summer camp of RSS men was due to begin. Hedgewar followed suit and reached Nagpur on 15 May. He was seriously ill, and for almost a month remained confined to his room and could not even attend the Nagpur camp. With the shadow of his mentor withdrawing, Golwalkar had to work round the clock on two fronts—looking after Hedgewar and ensuring smooth and successful completion of the camp. He remained careful, taking earnest care of both.

The RSS camp ended on 8 June. Hedgewar managed to briefly attend the valedictory function on the morning of 9 June before returning to his bed. His condition kept deteriorating. On 20 June, doctors tried to remove fluid from his spine. On the morning of 21 June 1940, Hedgewar passed away.

Sarsanghchalak

Hedgewar had been responsible in many important respects for Golwalkar's rise in the RSS. He publicized Golwalkar's multi-lingual abilities, helped him gain his standing as a scholar, contributed to his exposure to almost all units of the RSS across India, promoted him to the position of number two by making him sarkaryavah and handed him the opportunity to practically run the organization during the last five months of his life. With Hedgewar's abrupt death, Golwalkar lost his patron. Hedgewar was the guarantor of Golwalkar's special status and his rapid rise in the RSS; without that guarantee, he was vulnerable against the ambitions of any senior man bold enough to grab the top slot in the organization.

In these hours when they were plunged in grief and despair, Golwalkar claimed that Hedgewar had handed him the reins the day before his death.

'Now you take up the job' were the words, according to a Hedgewar biography, which appeared later in 1940.[1] It was written by a Golwalkar loyalist, Damodar Trayambak Sabnis. The narrative doesn't mention the presence of a third person at the

1. Damodar Trayambak Sabnis, *Swargiya Ke. Ba. Hedgewar: Ojharte Darshan*, Arvind Prakashan, Nagpur, 1940, p. 29.

time.[2]

Hedgewar did not discuss the succession even with Moonje, who last met him that very day before his death.[3] Nor is it in any publicly available record that he discussed it with his uncle Abaji Hedgewar or other associates of the RSS. Was Golwalkar's claim then a scene he contrived to create?

Thirteen days later, on 3 July 1940, Hedgewar's friends and local RSS men gathered for his *shradh,* a Hindu funeral rite, at the RSS headquarters in Nagpur.

'On this occasion, prantsanghchalak [chief of the Central Provinces] Babasaheb Padhye announced that, as per the wishes of Doctor Hedgewar, Madhavrao Golwalkar or Guruji would now work as our new sarsanghchalak,' wrote Sabnis.[4]

With the departed soul sent along on its last journey, Golwalkar was straightaway declared the new sarsanghchalak.

About a year back, Padhye had relinquished his position as sarkaryavah in order to let Golwalkar become number two in the RSS, and now he was instrumental in bringing the overwhelming moment to him. In contemporary accounts, there is no evidence of debate or deliberation within the RSS before Golwalkar's anointment as the sarsanghchalak.

In later years, after Golwalkar had established his complete hold over the RSS over a period of nearly a decade, the Indurkar biography introduced a meeting at Hedgewar's behest. 'During his last illness, Doctor sahib understood that he was left with only a few days of his life,' writes Indurkar, Golwalkar's first biographer.

> Fluid had accumulated in his body. Doctors suggested lumbar puncture for the removal of fluid from his spine. Before lumbar puncture could be carried out, Doctor saheb called all important

---

2. Ibid.

3. Ibid.

4. Ibid., p. 31.

> workers in his room and said in serious tone: 'I want to say something to you. Now my body would be handed over to doctors. I can't say what will happen afterward. I have a feeling that I may not be able to speak with you later. After me, you all will have to carry forward the activities of the Sangh under the leadership of Guruji.' At the same time, he told Guruji—'Now the Sangh-Parivar's responsibility is on you.' Guruji exclaimed in deep grief, 'Doctor saheb, what are you saying? You will be alright very soon.' Doctor saheb smiled on hearing this and said, 'That is alright. But do remember what I have told you.' After that, lumbar puncture was carried out. He lost his consciousness and never regained it.[5]

Following this, sixteen years after Golwalkar's coronation, Palkar wrote:

> On the tenth day of Doctor-ji's death, a meeting of select workers was held at Akola to discuss the question of new sarsanghchalak. Among those present were Nagpur city sanghchalak Babasaheb Ghatate, Vardhasanghchalak Appaji Joshi, Berar sanghchalak Bapusaheb Sohoni, Maharashtra sanghchalak Kashinathrao Limaye and [Central Provinces] sanghchalak Babasaheb Padhye. Taking into consideration the last wish of the founder sarsanghchalak, these functionaries unanimously decided that Guruji should be the new sarsanghchalak.[6]

This was the first talk of such a meeting. No previous account says a word about it. In fact, Sabnis, writing immediately after Hedgewar's death, would definitely have talked about the Akola meeting had there been one.

---

5. Shri Gangadhar Indurkar, *Guruji: Rashtriya Swayamsevak Sangh ke Sarsanghchalak Shri Madhav Sadashiv Golwalkar ka Jeevan Charitra*, Sangh Vastu Bhandar, Delhi, 1949, pp. 37-38.

6. N. H. Palkar, *Shri Ma Sa Golwalkar*, published by N. H. Palkar, Mumbai, 1956, p. 78.

In the persisting elements of the legend that Golwalkar's biographers later constructed over the carefully obscured trail of his past life, even the details of the conversation he claimed to have had with Hedgewar a day before the latter's death underwent a drastic facelift. While Sabnis does not talk of the presence of any third person when Hedgewar asked Golwalkar to 'take up the job', later accounts insert—without citing a document or a testimony—a conversation that supposedly took place in front of several RSS men in the room. In these accounts, new details were added and Hedgewar's one line in the original account grew with time and turned into a long discussion between Hedgewar and Golwalkar.

In the most recent retelling, by Ranga Hari, published in Hindi in 2012 and in English translation in 2018, the author went further than others before, naming two RSS men while marking their presence in the room with Hedgewar in those so-called eventful moments of 1940—once again without citing any record. Senior RSS members Krishnarao Mohril and Yadavrao Joshi were named among the men present who, in this new version, later conveyed the entire episode to the core group that supposedly met at Akola on 30 June to decide on a new sarsanghchalak.[7] By the time Ranga Hari's book was written, both were long dead. Mohril died in 1982, Yadavrao Joshi in 1992.

Did Golwalkar consider the possibility of a section of RSS leaders ganging up to deprive him of what he aspired to the most? In a secretive society like the RSS, it would be far more exceptional if he did not. Perhaps the same concern was also felt by some of the key Hedgewar associates in the Central Provinces who adored Golwalkar. They seemed to have no choice but to go with the claim about their dear departed leader's last wish. Waiting

7. Ranga Hari, *The Incomparable Guru Golwalkar*, Prabhat Paperbacks, New Delhi, 2018, p. 82.

for a wider consultation for selecting the new RSS chief may have yielded new claimants and caused dissension in the organization.

II

'Doctor's death was a big shock for Babarao,' wrote D. N. Gokhale, the elder Savarkar's biographer, in his 1947 book. Babarao Savarkar, himself ailing at the time, died five years after Hedgewar's death.

> After serious contemplation he prepared on urgent basis a contingency plan for the management of the Sangh and conveyed it to Advocate VV Kelkar of Nagpur. He proposed that for the time being full control of the Sangh should be vested in the hands of Madhavrao Golwalkar. Simultaneously, he also suggested that a committee, consisting of Ghatate, Padhye, Baburao Kelkar [VV Kelkar] and a few others, should be formed for advising Golwalkar and that Kakaji Hedgewar [Abaji] should be the president of this panel. Kakaji even forwarded these suggestions [to concerned people in the RSS]. But things developed differently in Nagpur. The position of sarsanghchalak fell on Golwalkar and the proposed committee could not come into existence.[8]

There were many in the RSS who did not see merit in the claims of Golwalkar, or in his hasty elevation, and they continued with their opposition to the decision taken on 3 July. A rumour did the rounds about Ghatate, who was with the RSS sarsanghchalak in his last few days, that he might well have fabricated Hedgewar's choice.[9]

---

8. D. N. Gokhale, *Krantiveer Babarao Savarkar*, Mangal Sahitya Prakashan, Pune, 1947, p. 359.

9. Walter K. Andersen and Shridhar D. Damle, *The Brotherhood in Saffron: The Rashtriya Swayamsevak Sangh and Hindu Revivalism*, Westview Press, Boulder and London, 1987, Notes 85, pp. 63-64.

In later years, Balasaheb Deoras, who had joined the RSS before Golwalkar did and who succeeded him in 1973 as sarsanghchalak, spoke of the dissension that followed Hedgewar's death: 'Possibly some of us may have thought at that time, that Guruji Golwalkar was new to the Sangh, and not experienced enough. So we might have been doubtful about how he would discharge his responsibility.'[10]

As per K. K. Javadekar, whose son Prakash Javadekar became a minister in the Modi government, the panel was actually formed but it was derailed by the sudden announcement of Golwalkar as the new sarsanghchalak on 3 July.[11] At the time the drama was unfolding, K. K. Javadekar was in Nagpur as an active member of the Hindu Mahasabha. He joined the RSS soon after Hedgewar's death in 1940 and remained active in both the organizations for the next several years.[12]

Even Ranga Hari hints of discord that cropped up at the time of Golwalkar's succession: 'For nearly a month after the demise of the Sangh founder, there had been a feeling of uncertainty, especially in Maharashtra. Conflicting reports floated around.'[13]

In this season of disputation, Golwalkar responded by digging in his heels and preparing for a showdown, which many feared could happen on 21 July, when important RSS men from across the country would gather in Nagpur to take part in the first monthly anniversary of Hedgewar's death. The developments of the last few months seemed to have given Golwalkar a sense of worth. The opposition that sprang suddenly hardened this touchy and sentimental man. Caught up in the succession dispute, he learned toughness, self-discipline and the uses of solidarity. The

---

10. *Organiser*, 14 July 1973.

11. K. K. Javadekar, *Sakal*, 23 April 2003.

12. Ibid.

13. Ranga Hari, *The Incomparable Guru Golwalkar*, Prabhat Paperbacks, New Delhi, 2018, p. 85.

dispute was at times baffling and annoying, at times intrusive and insulting, but it was now an inexorable part of his newly acquired status. Managing his nerves would be essential to overcome the crisis that he faced.

Golwalkar continued the practice started by Hedgewar and spent several hours every day writing letters to regional office-bearers. But since he had a deep-seated fear of his detractors, he used these hours writing to his loyalists in the RSS, asking them to definitely be present in Nagpur to attend the 21 July event. For support, he seemed to rely primarily on RSS men working in non-Marathi regions as the dispute had arisen in Maharashtra. 'This is just to remind you about July 21,' he wrote to Vasantrao Oak, the regional head of Delhi, on 7 July. 'I have also written to [another Delhi leader] Prof. Ram Singh. [...] The programme will start at sharp 5 in the evening. Keeping that in mind, try to come slightly before that. Shakhas of Delhi and Ambala divisions will have to organize military salute on the lines of Nagpur [on that day]. Make necessary arrangements for that before July 21. It would be better if one more important person of [Ambala] division attends the programme in Nagpur. If necessary, bring him along with yourself.'[14]

In a similar letter to Sadgopal on 9 July, he wrote:

> The Centre has decided to offer homage in military fashion to the hallowed memory of our Revered Doctorsaheb on the 21st. I have invited prominent Sanghchalaks and workers from all over the country to attend in their respective uniforms. [...] May I request you to make it a point to attend this function? It will indeed be to me a matter of personal gratification to have you in our midst on that day. This day particularly has been fixed because it is the first monthly anniversary. The function shall

14. Golwalkar Papers, Roll No. 12269, Microfilm Section, NMML, New Delhi, p. 112.

> begin at 5 pm sharp. At night there will be meeting of important workers and office-bearers. [...] Rest is alright, although under the new circumstances I feel too much responsibility has been put upon me by Revered Doctorsaheb by directing me to take up the whole job. However, by the Grace of God, things will go on well, I hope.[15]

Golwalkar also reached out to Savarkar, the supreme ideologue who enjoyed utmost respect in the RSS. Although his access to Savarkar had so far not been much more than most other associates of Hedgewar, Golwalkar wrote an earnest letter, requesting him to attend the first monthly anniversary of Hedgewar's death. In his reply dated 13 July, Savarkar expressed his confidence in Golwalkar as the new sarsanghchalak, while conveying his inability to attend the event personally because of his appointment with Viceroy Lord Linlithgow 'on or about the same date' at Simla. 'The kind thoughts you have expressed in your letter have deeply touched me,' Savarkar wrote.

> To pay our homage to and perform the funeral solemnities in connection with the passing away of one whom we deeply love or adore is the last, the saddest and yet the most sacred duty one has to perform; and yet it is painful to me that I have to fail to do that on this particular occasion owing to the necessity of attending to a still more pressing public engagement which is simply unavoidable in consideration of the fact that I as the President of the Hindu Maha Sabha cannot shift on any other shoulder the responsibility of going to Simla once more on or about the same date to interview the Viceroy in connection with the negotiations dealing with the future constitution of India and the present political situation. [...] Even in the life time of Dr. Hedgewar I always used to advice the Sangha meetings hundreds of which I had to attend throughout India, that so

15. Ibid., pp. 113-114.

> far the Sangha was concerned, it is Dr. Hedgewar alone who must have the last word on any question and that I had full confidence in his discretion on that matter. Now that the mantle and the responsibility have fallen on your shoulders as the Sar Sangha Chalak of the R.S.S. and that was just the choice [...] Dr. Hedgewar's heart, I feel no hesitation in placing the same confidence in you and the council of the chosen few who are to advice you.[16]

The turbulence that Golwalkar feared was nowhere in sight at the memorial meeting on 21 July 1940. If anything, the meeting solidified his position within the RSS. Sabnis, who witnessed the event, described it in detail. By his account, Ghatate gave the inaugural speech in which he expressed full confidence in Golwalkar as the new sarsanghchalak.[17] Then Kashinath Bhaskar Limaye got up to speak. Most voices of dissent had come from the province he was in charge of. 'Doctorsahib has put the responsibility of our organisation on Madhavrao-ji, who will work with so much commitment and enthusiasm that you will not notice Doctor's absence and instead feel that he is alive in the form of the new sarsanghchalak,' Limaye said.[18] It was a clear indication that the detractors didn't have majority support even in Maharashtra. M. S. Aney, Hedgewar's friend who had written the foreword for Golwalkar's book, also spoke on the occasion and endorsed the new RSS leadership. 'In this dark hour, your new leader will guide the Sangh and the nation forward,' he said.[19] Moonje was the most prominent Hindu Mahasabha leader who

---

16. Dr. Shrirang Arvind Godbole (ed.), *Yugpravartak Dr. Hedgewar*, Sanskritik Jagaran Mandal, Pune, 2014, p. 220.

17. Damodar Trayambak Sabnis, *Swargiya Ke. Ba. Hedgewar: Ojharte Darshan*, Arvind Prakashan, Nagpur, 1940, p. 39.

18. Ibid., p. 40.

19. Ibid., p. 41.

spoke on the occasion. He talked only about his relationship with Hedgewar and nothing about the new leadership of the RSS.[20]

Golwalkar, who spoke at the end, kept his focus on emphasizing his relationship with Hedgewar. 'I am occupying this position only because of Doctor Hedgewar's wish and order,' he said. 'The RSS is immortal. Despite the death of its founder, the organisation will keep moving forward. Other organisations have so far been individual-centric but our organisation is devoted to a cause. [...] I don't know why Doctor has placed me in this great position, but I can say this much that he had enormous love for me. This love cannot be compared even with that between father and son or teacher and disciple.'[21]

According to K. K. Javadekar, the discontentment continued to simmer even after 21 July.[22] But the shift in power relations had taken place. With Golwalkar firmly in control and with his loyalists in the RSS moving boldly into the organization, it was difficult for any dissident to imagine what might threaten the existing set up.

III

This fracture in the RSS coincided with Golwalkar's rising tension, during August 1940, over a government order putting restrictions on the functioning of quasi military organizations. The order was part of the British Indian government's efforts to help Britain in the Second World War. Accordingly on 29 September 1939, weeks after the war broke out, the Defence of India Act was passed, empowering the Viceroy to make rules for promoting the British government's war efforts and to provide for punishments in case

20. Ibid., p. 42.

21. Ibid., p. 43.

22. K. K. Javadekar, *Sakal*, 23 April 2003.

of any contraventions. It was under this Act that the government's communiqué ordering restrictions on quasi military organizations was issued on 5 August 1940, fifteen days after Golwalkar's anointment as sarsanghchalak was affirmed in the July event.[23]

The new order banned parade ground activities, including the performance of drills of military nature and the wearing of uniform that fully or partly resembled those of military or police forces.[24] Military-style drills in military-style uniform of khaki shorts and khaki shirts produced a charged atmosphere and served as the main attraction for the youth who joined the RSS. The organization's prospects depended too entirely, too exclusively, too absolutely on the parade ground activities. In their absence, the organization would falter and stall, and its determined approach would disintegrate into uncertainty, panic, hysteria and inertia.

The communiqué, however, did not mention any organization by name, thus leaving enough room for rumours. Unprepared politically and psychologically, Golwalkar remained deeply unsettled for some time about the scope of the order or the extent of the government's seriousness in enforcing it. 'The government is conducting its enquiry, and people are worried,' he wrote to an associate on 21 August 1940. 'But swayamsevaks are fearless, and so there is no reason for any anxiety. There are suggestions that, if required, we should do away with *ganavesh* [RSS uniform] and military department's training programmes and continue our work as usual. These changes have already been done in some areas.'[25]

---

23. Government of India, Home Department (Political), File No. 190-P (S), 1943, p. 26, NAI, New Delhi.

24. The Defence of India Act, 1939 and The Rules Made Thereunder, Manager of Publications, Government of India Press, New Delhi, 1943, p. 106.

25. Golwalkar Papers, Roll No. 12269, Microfilm Section, NMML, New Delhi, p. 122.

On 27 August, Golwalkar wrote to Vasantrao Oak in Delhi that he was convinced the restrictions were applicable only on such organizations that had political or casteist objectives and that the RSS would certainly not fall in any of these categories. 'You should not be apprehensive about what will happen in the new environment,' he wrote.

> The government order doesn't really apply to organizations like us because we have no relations with any political or casteist party. We never get into any political or casteist controversy, nor are our aims meant to create fear in anyone's heart. That is why we should not get affected by this. Still, if there is some effect because of local factors, we can stop the training programmes by our military department at some places and continue our ideological classes and physical exercises as usual. The decision about what should be done has to be taken on the basis of local conditions in respective areas. As far as possible, all the programmes should continue as usual.[26]

It was not long before the confusion and perplexity of initial weeks passed. As there was penal provision for the violation of the order, the functioning of the RSS slipped into difficulty in many areas where the local Sangh units were forced to stop parade ground activities. S. H. Deshpande, an active member of the RSS in Poona from 1938 to 1946, noted that in the city, where the ban was taken seriously, drills stopped and swayamsevaks mostly occupied themselves with lecture courses designed to make them 'tough and brave'.[27]

Ram Rakha Mal, a senior member of the RSS in Punjab, also recounted that 'due to the restrictions on quasi military activities imposed by the Government' the RSS had to discard 'lathi fighting and squad drill' in many areas. 'Now the Sewaks

26. Ibid., pp. 123-124.

27. S. H. Deshpande, 'My Days in the RSS', *Quest*, July-August 1975, p. 22.

are only made to do physical exercises including races, kabaddi, tug of war, long jump and flag salutation, etc,' he said.[28] One of the lasting impacts these restrictions had on the RSS was a change in swayamsevaks' uniform. Earlier, their uniform was designed to resemble that of the colonial police force; now, with the RSS's situation becoming increasingly desperate, a new uniform was designed to make swayamsevaks look different from the police. 'Before the restrictions, the volunteers used to wear Khaki uniform but now black cap, white shirt, khaki short, grey socks and fleet foot-wear are worn by Sevaks as official uniform,' Ram Rakha Mal pointed out.[29]

Before long, the impact of the 1940 ban order on the RSS was visible. In a detailed impact assessment prepared in 1942, the Intelligence Bureau Director, E. J. Beveridge, wrote: 'The ban struck at the very core of the Sangh's existence by seeking to suppress those features of the organization which were its chief attractions in the eyes of its youthful recruits, viz., its uniform and its parade-ground activities.'[30] Regarding the observance of the ban by the RSS, he pointed out:

> While the official attitude of the Sangh to this ban is one of compliance with Government orders, there have been a number of instances of failure to comply either with the spirit or letter of the ban. Such cases have occurred repeatedly in Central Provinces and occasionally in Delhi, Bombay, Madras, Sind, the Punjab and the United Provinces. Information on record shows that in only three cases have officers of the Sangh been persecuted (in Bombay, Madras and the Punjab). The Punjab

28. Government of India, Home Department (Political), File No. 190-P (S), 1943, pp. 7-8, NAI, New Delhi.

29. Ibid., p. 8.

30. Government of India, Home Department (Political), File No. 220-P/42 (Sec), 1942, p. 5, NAI, New Delhi.

> case was under the Arms Act for unlawful possession of a store of swords and daggers.[31]

There is no evidence that Golwalkar was burdened by pangs of conscience over his apolitical posturing for the RSS. Perhaps he thought it fit to rely on the same rationale that his predecessor had used. Hedgewar, too, had declared the organization apolitical in 1932 when the Central Provinces government had called it a communal and political body and debarred state employees from joining or taking part in its activities.[32] Golwalkar was, therefore, very careful to avoid any dispute with the government. His views were nuanced, changeable and laced with contradictions—reason enough for the British authorities not to take them seriously.

IV

Golwalkar's move to portray the RSS as an apolitical body did not present much of a complication for Hindutva organizations. Despite the founders of the RSS laying out its growth chart alongside the Hindu Mahasabha, there was hardly any structural arrangement that could make it a wing of the political party. Yet, the divorce that Golwalkar sought to demonstrate did not hold steady for most of 1940s—until the events that followed the assassination of Mahatma Gandhi in 1948 shattered the very rationale that sustained the unity.

For the whole of the period till 1948, the two organizations showed a notable tendency towards close cooperation. Not only was the Sangh's ideology rooted in the same source that fuelled the Hindu Mahasabha, the two organizations also remained intertwined

---

31. Ibid.

32. Government of India, Home Department (Political), File No. 88/33, 1933, p. 14, NAI, New Delhi.

with fluid and overlapping memberships.[33] For example, Golwalkar's close aide M. N. Ghatate, who was sanghchalak of Nagpur and acted as the organization's bagman, handling its cash deposits, also remained the treasurer of the Hindu Mahasabha till the late 1940s. That the practice continued for most of 1940s was confirmed also by a report prepared by the Intelligence Department of Bombay Police in September 1947 on the membership pattern of the two organizations. The report said that 'although not affiliated, most of its [RSS's] prominent organizers and workers are either members of the Hindu Mahasabha or sponsors of the Hindu Mahasabha ideology'.[34]

With equal hatred for Muslims and similarity in the background of their members, the two organizations hardly differed in their ideology and orientation. Overtly, the RSS and the Hindu Mahasabha vowed to make India a Hindu Rashtra after termination of British rule and sought to articulate it as a Hindu search for self-esteem. Covertly, for the Maharashtrian Brahmins, both promised to reinstate the hegemony of the traditional caste elites.[35]

What distinguished the RSS from the Hindu Mahasabha were the secretive nature of its organization and the military discipline of its cadres. While the Hindu Mahasabha was a political party duly recognized by government authorities, the RSS was a communal militarist organization without any legal recognition and with violent tendencies. Unlike the Hindu Mahasabha, the RSS maintained utmost secrecy about its organizational proceedings

---

33. Dhirendra K. Jha, 'The Apostle of Hate', *The Caravan*, Volume 12, Issue 1, January 2020, pp. 28-49.

34. Justice J. L. Kapur, Report of Commission of Inquiry into Conspiracy to Murder Mahatma Gandhi, Part II, New Delhi, Government of India, 1969, p. 61.

35. Ashis Nandy, *At the Edge of Psychology: Essays in Politics and Culture*, Oxford University Press, Delhi, 1980, p. 81.

and did not keep any membership register. The tramp of marching feet in RSS shakhas attested to the belief of swayamsevaks in the militaristic models offering a solution to socio-political problems. Drawn to these shakhas were mostly young Brahmin men, school-going boys of the caste being the most enthusiastic elements of the RSS's membership.

Savarkar, the Hindu Mahasabha president, was indispensible to the RSS. He remained something of a supreme ideologue and the fundamental source of inspiration for both the organizations. The notion that Savarkar acted as the motive force for the RSS was beyond contestation those days, wrote Javadekar. 'I worked for both the Hindu Mahasabha and the RSS. My main job in the RSS was to take ideological classes in shakhas across Maharashtra,' he recounted. 'While teaching the history of the RSS, I used to tell swayamsevaks that Dr. Hedgewar established the Sangh after meeting Swatantryaveer Savarkar in 1924 and taking guidance from him.'[36]

S. H. Deshpande recalled emphatically that Savarkar was held in the highest esteem by RSS men. 'The intellectual food of the RSS volunteers has been the speeches and writings of Savarkar,' he wrote. 'How very dependent they were on Savarkar can be gauged from the fact that the day he was to address a meeting in Poona, it would be announced at the various shakhas of the town that the evening's proceedings stood cancelled and that the volunteers could "go home" (i.e. to Savarkar's meeting! This was never officially mentioned). This concession was not granted on any other occasion.'[37]

In fact, as a leader, Savarkar attracted a following both in the Hindu Mahasabha and the RSS. He was very proud of the reputation he enjoyed among swayamsevaks and left no opportunity to visit shakhas or address them whenever he went on

36. K. K. Javadekar, *Sakal*, 23 April 2003.

37. S. H. Deshpande, 'My Days in the RSS', *Quest*, July-August 1975, p. 21.

tour. The book compilation of Savarkar's diary entries, speeches, articles and notes—*Whirlwind Propaganda: Extracts from President's Diary of His Propagandist Tours, Interviews from December 1937 to October 1941*—shows that meeting RSS volunteers constituted an important part of his itineraries during this period.[38] On several occasions after Savarkar became the president of the Hindu Mahasabha, the RSS regularly collected huge sums of money and presented it to him as a mark of respect—a fact that the British intelligence agencies recorded repeatedly during the period spanning the late 1930s and most of 1940s.[39]

Nor was there any evidence—barring those meant to help the RSS circumvent the 1940 restrictions—that Golwalkar was actually willing to snap the Sangh's ties with the Hindu Mahasabha. His true attitude toward the Hindu Mahasabha was difficult to discern from what he was doing to make the RSS adjust in the new environment. In the closed-door meetings of the RSS, he remained as reverential to Savarkar and the Hindu Mahasabha as he had been before the 1940 order. An Intelligence Bureau report stated that Golwalkar, while addressing a meeting of swayamsevaks in Bombay in November 1940, propounded 'the pan-Hindu theory of one undivided India under the Hindu rule of the Mahasabha'.[40] Analysing the Sangh's relationship with the Hindu Mahasabha, the report said,

> The policy of the Sangh is influenced to a considerable extent by its association with the Hindu Mahasabha. Exactly how

---

38. For detail see A. S. Bhide (ed.), *Whirlwind Propaganda: Extracts from President's Diary of His Propagandist Tours, Interviews from December 1937 to October 1941*, All India Hindu Mahasabha, Bombay, 1941.

39. Marzia Casolari, 'Hindutva's Foreign Tie-up in the 1930s: Archival Evidence', *Economic and Political Weekly*, 22 January 2000, p. 228.

40. Government of India, Home Department (Political), File No. 220-P/42 (Sec), 1942, p. 3, NAI, New Delhi.

> closely the Sangh is connected with the Hindu Mahasabha is not known, as no public reference to its association is ever made by the leaders of other organisation. That it is close, however, is clear from the respect with which Hindu Mahasabha leaders such as V.D Savarkar and Dr. B.S. Moonje are treated by the Sangh and the authority with which they make public pronouncements regarding the Sangh. [...] It is, therefore, necessary to bear in mind that any radical change in the declared policy of the Hindu Mahasabha will probably affect the policy of the Sangh.[41]

Savarkar's leadership and the Hindu Mahasabha's strategy of accommodating the RSS kept the Hindutva organizations integrated. The eyes of both the outfits remained fixed on the same star that had guided them during the time of Hedgewar.

V

Golwalkar's own vision of a politically conscious Hinduism echoed Savarkar's call for action against enemies of the faith. His idea of replicating the Nazi anti-Semitic model to deal with minorities in India was consistent with Savarkar's insistence on Hindus treating Muslims, rather than the British, as the main opposition.

Shortly before Golwalkar became the RSS chief, the Muslim League had on 23 March 1940 adopted a resolution demanding a separate state of Pakistan. The Pakistan resolution brought the League face to face with Hindu supremacist organizations, the Hindu Mahasabha and the RSS. It was clear to all that the British government's policy of divide and rule had worked exceptionally well. Communalists among both Hindus and Muslims now hated each other even more than they hated the British.

For Savarkar and the Mahasabha, the Pakistan resolution brought a sense of confidence they had never experienced before.

41. Ibid., p. 4.

Savarkar had already declared that Hindus and Muslims constituted two nations in India. 'Hindustan Hinduon Ka' (Hindustan belongs to Hindus) had already become the main slogan of the Hindu Mahasabha and the RSS. But Savarkar's campaigns had little appeal until the Muslim League adopted the Pakistan resolution. The ground now seemed set for refashioning the Mahasabha into a mass party. The RSS under the leadership of Golwalkar readily identified with it. The new situation threatened to stir up trouble, and a civil war seemed in the offing. But at a time when promoting war efforts was uppermost in the minds of colonial rulers, a civil war was the last thing they wanted on their hands—the reason why in August 1940 a notification was issued to ban the military activities of all private militias.

Golwalkar agonized and tricked, but eventually gave in. It was a demoralizing time. New recruits dried up, and the expansion of the RSS halted in British Indian provinces. Before long, many in the RSS started fearing that they were destined not to control the country but to be recorded as one of the most spectacular failures in recent history. Yet, Golwalkar found ways to keep the organization alive. In fact, his ability to find new ways to keep afloat in the face of difficulties would always remain a particular source of his strength.

As the RSS's problems compounded, Golwalkar tried desperately to expand the organization's activities in states ruled by Hindu princes. In the face of restrictions in British provinces, this was the only way he could have kept the RSS alive. The Intelligence Bureau, which was keeping a close eye on RSS activities, noted this shift. Detailing the activities of the RSS following the 1940 order, an IB report of June 1943 said that 'the Rashtriya Swayam Sevak Sangh, in its anxiety to avoid any action which would draw the attention of the authorities in British India to its activities, is endeavouring more and more to entrench itself in the Hindu States where, according to one report, it hopes to perfect its organization and training unhindered'.[42]

Of all such states, the ones where the RSS succeeded the most were those in the Deccan zone or Marathi linguistic region. The RSS leader with the most embedded life in these princely states was Bombay sanghchalak Kashinath Bhaskar Limaye, a tall and handsome Maharashtrian Brahmin who had a passion for physical fitness and for the possession of a hard, strong body. He had received his primary education in Sangli, a princely state over 200 km south of Poona, and attended high-school in Kolhapur, a neighbouring state.[43] After completing his matriculation, he got himself enrolled in Poona's elite Fergusson College, but because of his family's financial constraints he could not continue his education.[44] In 1916, shortly after his return from Poona, he took up the job of a teacher in a high school that was run by the princely court of Sangli state.[45] Two years later, Limaye left the job and formed a private firm, Deccan Commercial Company, an agency to sell swadeshi goods. In Sangli, however, he continued to be known as 'Limaye Master'.[46] He joined the RSS at the behest of Babarao Savarkar in 1932 and was made the sanghchalak of Bombay province in 1934. Since then, he had been the pivot of the RSS's activities in Bombay province.

Limaye was forty-seven when Golwalkar met him in 1940, but his energy was still indefatigable. Restless, impatient and vibrant, he seemed never tired and never relaxed. Though Poona acted as the headquarters of RSS activities in Bombay province, Limaye

42. Government of India, Home Department (Political), File No. 190-P (S), 1943, P.51, NAI, New Delhi.

43. D. S. Harshe, *Adarsh Hindu Sanghatak: Ka. Bha. Limaye*, published by Sudha Dattatreya Harshe, Satara, 1981, p. 1.

44. Ibid.

45. Ibid.

46. Ibid., p. 2.

operated mostly from Sangli, where he had gathered around him a band of highly motivated disciples who imitated him in his contempt for Muslims and glorification of Brahminism.[47] Among the states in the Marathi linguistic region, Sangli was one where the RSS—due primarily to Limaye's efforts—already had a strong base when the 1940 ban order came. With Sangli acting as the RSS bastion in the region, Limaye oversaw the expansion of the Sangh's activities in the neighbouring princely states of Kolhapur, Ichalkaranji, Jamkhandi, Miraj, Kurundwad, Budhgaon, Aundh, Kirloskarwadi, Kundal, Phalton, Bhor and Akalkot.

Within a year, his hard work started showing results and the RSS base expanded in the princely states of Maharashtra beyond Golwalkar's imagining. Such, in fact, was the transformation that a senior British official found in early 1943 that 'the Rashtriya Swayam Sewak Sangh has a strong following in many of the Deccan states'. In his letter to the Viceroy's Secretary, Sir Kenneth Fitze, he further noted: 'In Kolhapur and several of the Deccan states the Rashtriya Swyam Sewak Sangh is openly patronized and helped by the Rulers. For example, the Maharani Regent of Kolhapur opened their camp at Kolhapur in December 1942. I should be grateful to know whether it is considered advisable that I should give any personal hint to Rulers of States to try to avoid giving their patronage to activities of the Sangh.'[48]

Around this time, the Intelligence Bureau was also recording the growing activities of the RSS and its synergy with Hindu Mahasabha in different princely states of the Deccan region.

> The Rashtriya Swayamsevak Sangh has succeeded fairly well in consolidating its strength in almost all the Hindu states. The members or volunteers of the Sangh are not allowed to take part

47. Ibid.

48. Government of India, Home Department (Political), File No. 190-P (S), 1943, p. 42, NAI, New Delhi.

> in any kind of activities of other political bodies. The trained volunteers and the officers from the Training Class give the volunteers semi military training in drill etc., hold study circles and political training classes. The volunteers are taught to obey implicitly their High Command and their officers. Political training on the lines of the Hindu Mahasabha is given to all the volunteers.[49]

For all of Golwalkar's handicaps in British-ruled provinces, his strategy in the princely states of the Deccan had produced striking results. Under the new strategy, Limaye was assigned the responsibility to oversee the expansion of the RSS. This sounded fairly clear-cut, but the inner workings of the RSS in these states remained idiosyncratic. In many of these states, the RSS was started with changed names aimed at flattering the rulers. Thus, in Kolhapur, the RSS unit was named as 'Rajaram Swayam Sevak Sangh' after the name of the state's former ruler, and in Bhor, the Sangh unit was called 'Raghurathrao Swayam Sevak Sangh' after the incumbent ruler.[50] In fact, the RSS units Limaye oversaw in the Deccan states remained utterly dependent on the respective royal houses, habitually secretive, compartmented, and at times confusing, particularly for outsiders who happened to know the RSS through its activities and character in British-ruled areas.

During this period, Golwalkar also tried to expand the RSS in some other Hindu-ruled states outside Maharashtra. But in the absence of patronage from local rulers, there was no major progress. In Kashmir, the first unit of the RSS was started at Jammu in December 1940 by Golwalkar's associate Babasaheb Apte, according to a report sent by the Kashmir Resident to the Viceroy in early 1944. 'Its purpose, [Apte] said, was to improve the health of Hindus by physical exercise,' the report noted.

49. Ibid., p. 45.

50. Ibid., p. 107.

> Three days after the inauguration ceremony about 50 volunteers of the Sangh dressed in white clothes and carrying batons (Dandas) paraded inside one of Jammu's temples. At subsequent meetings held in December 1940 and January 1941 (the latter attracted an audience of 700 Hindus under the chairmanship of a retired Sessions Judge) speakers said that the Sangh aimed at uniting Hindus, making them physically fit and saving them from oppression by following in the footsteps of Guru Gobind Singh and [Shivaji Maharaj]. During 1941 and 1942 no particular activities came to notice except that the Sangh held meetings on important Hindu festivals and increased its membership to about 200 of whom about 125 paraded regularly.[51]

Nor did the RSS at the time succeed in making any significant headway in the princely states of Punjab and Rajputana.[52] A shared antipathy to Muslims was yet to bind these states to the RSS.

Yet the connections that Golwalkar developed in the Hindu princely states, particularly in the Deccan, and the contributions he received from them offered him a way to offset the reverses the RSS received due to the 1940 order in British provinces. In deepening his contacts with the princely elites, he was able to construct, subtly but unmistakably, an alternative basis to deal with future challenges. The more trouble the British Indian government caused, the more Golwalkar searched for ways to garner help from new friends.

51. Ibid., pp. 109-110.

52. Ibid., pp. 85-86, 98-99.

The Guru Grows His Footprint

The swift and overwhelming success of the RSS in the princely states of the Deccan infused Golwalkar with relief and confidence. He looked upon states ruled by Hindu princes as natural hubs for the politics of the Hindu Right—even more than they had previously been. On the British India front, Golwalkar seemed to have a divided mind; he thought suspension of parade ground activities might assuage the British government and allay the fear of a clampdown, but he also sought to ensure that these steps did not lead to general apathy among young swayamsevaks towards the RSS.

Encouraged by successes in princely states, Golwalkar proceeded to devise alternate means to keep swayamsevaks in British Indian provinces involved and active. Instead of focusing on shakhas, the new framework he was exploring was to be centred on regular camps of swayamsevaks dominated by ideological classes rather than military-style drills. Any move to continue usual military drills in shakhas, it must have been recognized, would attract the government's attention as the 1940 order essentially pertained to such activities. But frequent camps could become a new means to keep swayamsevaks charged and motivated. All the available testimony shows that in the new atmosphere, imparting of military training gave way to teaching of courses designed to make swayamsevaks 'tough and brave'.[1]

To change the nature of training of swayamsevaks in British India, Golwalkar himself led the way in infusing new spirit into the organization in Nagpur as well as in provinces. The new emphasis on camps shaped the style and methods of all he did. His own energy seemed inexhaustible, and he spent most of his time travelling. His principle was: an interaction with a group of cadre almost every day. The increasingly rapid tempo of his meetings with swayamsevaks and heads of local units in different parts of the country reflects the growing intensity of his affair with his organization. With his efforts, Golwalkar gradually succeeded in providing the RSS with a new method to operate in British India.

Until 1940, the RSS had been organizing two annual OTC camps—one each at Nagpur and Poona—plus an additional localized camp once a year in Lahore. After 1940, camps started proliferating. Old camps continued, and new ones, often shorter in duration, were added, sometimes for get-togethers of swayamsevaks and on other occasions for holding ideological classes.[2] At the same time, there was a gradual increase in the number of places for organizing OTC camps. In all this, Golwalkar's own contribution consisted not just of the original idea but of the constant efforts to make his subordinates implement it promptly. So rapid was his success that on 16 April 1943, he informed Tej Narain, the RSS leader in Lucknow, that 'the OTC will be organized at more than ten places this year'.[3]

To all those who had doubted his leadership, especially in the aftermath of the 1940 restrictions, he offered an unmistakable

1. S. H. Deshpande, 'My Days in the RSS', *Quest*, July-August 1975, p. 22.

2. Golwalkar Papers, Roll No. 12269, Microfilm Section, Part IV, pp. 8-70. NMML, New Delhi.

3. Ibid., p. 69.

message: we are back with a vengeance. Maneuvering restrictions, Golwalkar, to a virtually unprecedented degree, reshaped in a short while the entire organization by his own efforts and was himself everything at once: the chief architect of the RSS, its supreme teacher, author of its ideology, master tactician and its demagogic leader.

Encouraged by this growing success, Golwalkar became increasingly intemperate. He became more and more clamorous against Muslims. In his speeches, which he delivered in the ideological classes—baudhiks—during the OTC camp at Poona, he openly advocated the efficacy of violence. The camp was organized in April-May 1942, and its proceedings were recorded in detail by the Intelligence Bureau. 'This country belonged to the Hindus whose forefathers spilt their blood for its sake,' he said in his speech on 26 April, as per an IB report. He continued:

> The Sangh was meant for the whole of India and was therefore termed 'National'; but the Hindus alone had so far proved loyal to the country; therefore they alone were eligible for enrolment to the Sangh. Whoever, forgetting his traditions, joins hands with the enemies should be killed even if he were their own brother, because only he who follows and sticks to their principles would be regarded as their real brother. The mental apathy of the Hindus should be removed and a feeling of hatred towards the men of other religions, who were getting high-handed, should be created in them. The Sangh was doing this work.[4]

The OTC at Poona that year was attended by 1,100 volunteers and it continued for 35 days. Golwalkar addressed swayamsevaks on seven separate occasions, the IB report said, adding that in his speech on 3 May, he 'clearly revealed the communal and

4. Government of India, Home Department (Political), File No. 220-P/42 (Sec), 1942, p. 8, NAI, New Delhi.

Fascist nature of the organisation. He said that the Sangh had been started not only for combating Muslim aggression but for completely extirpating that disease; it was therefore necessary to have proper men at the helm whose attention should be focused on the achievement of their goal.'[5]

In the RSS camp, it was common to find Sangh teachers openly glorifying Nazism and fascism. Yadavrao Joshi, an intimate companion of Golwalkar, emphasized 'the importance of the mental training classes and asked the Sangh volunteers to give up all ideas of individuality, quoting the example of Japan and Germany, where every individual has identified himself with the ambitions of his nation.'[6] Dr. P. G. Sahasrabuddhe, one of the most prominent members of the ideological division of the RSS, was the most outspoken in his support for European dictatorships. A teacher of Marathi literature in the RSS-run NMV High School of Poona, Sahasrabuddhe was known for using his lectures in the camps for promoting a pro-authoritarian mindset among swayamsevaks. Referring to a series of lectures he gave in this OTC, the IB report said:

> On 4.5.42 he [Sahasrabuddhe] announced that the Sangh followed the principle of dictatorship. Denouncing democratic government as an unsatisfactory form of government, he quoted France as a typical bad example and, praising dictatorship, he pointed to Japan, Russia and Germany. He particularly praised the Fuehrer principle of Germany. On 21.5.42 he drew attention to the value of propaganda, quoting Russia and Germany as examples, and again extolled the virtues of the Leader principle, citing Mussolini's success as a further example.[7]

5. Ibid., p. 9.
6. Ibid., p. 8.
7. Ibid., p. 9.

These teachings in the camps proved important to the RSS. They brought a sense of confidence the organization had never experienced before. They ensured that Nazism wielded the most lasting ideological influence upon swayamsevaks. Evidently they also made Golwalkar aware of his own exalted status. After a short period of extreme uncertainty, he now seems clearly to have had a sense of himself as a cult leader and a dictator in chrysalis.

II

The tenets of the curriculum devised for swayamsevaks attending the Poona OTC were inseparable from German Nazi ideology. Sahasrabuddhe's speeches or the one by Yadavrao Joshi were not exceptions; they were conspicuous examples of Golwalkar's programme of training swayamsevaks to fight for the supremacy of Hindus by 'extirpating' Muslims just as Hitler was trying to establish the supremacy of German race by annihilating Jews. That was also the reason why the RSS volunteers attending the OTC were asked to read the biographies of Hitler and Mussolini along with those of Hedgewar, Savarkar and the Maratha king Shivaji.[8]

His own book, *We or Our Nationhood Defined*, was not the only pro-Nazi text included in the curriculum for the OTC. The list of suggested readings, as recorded by the Intelligence Bureau, also had an unusual entry—*Caution to Hindus* by a mystical admirer of Hitler and a devotee of his Aryan myth, Savitri Devi.[9] The echo of Golwalkar's repugnance for Muslims, which is so evident in *We or Our Nationhood Defined*, can easily be detected in Savitri Devi's book.

In actuality titled *A Warning to the Hindus*, the book was published by Hindu Mission in 1939 in English as well as in six

---

8. Ibid., p. 12.

9. Ibid.

Indian languages, including Marathi, Hindi and Bengali.[10] Possibly, the IB man covering the Poona OTC saw the Marathi edition and committed a mistake while translating its title into English.

Savitri Devi was a French woman originally named Maximiani Portas, who was born to an English mother and Greek-Italian father in Lyon in 1905.[11] From an early age she was obsessed by the myth of Aryan supremacy. Though not a German, she became an admirer of Hitler because of his desire to eradicate Europe's Jews and restore the Aryan race to its 'rightful' position of power.[12] In the early 1930s, hoping to find the cradle of the Aryan race, she sailed for India, where she was convinced that the caste system had preserved pure Aryans by forbidding intermarriage.[13] Until the end of the Second World War, she stayed in India in expectation of a global Axis victory. She learned Bengali and Hindi, joined Hindu Mission, a Brahminical Hindu religious organization headquartered in Calcutta, adopted the Hindu name Savitri Devi, married a Bengali Brahmin, A. K. Mukherji, and settled down in Calcutta.[14] She forged an elaborate synthesis of Hindu mythology and German Nazi ideology, in which Hitler was given the status of an incarnation of Lord Vishnu.

Her ideas were actually representative of a small section of Bengal's Hindu caste elites who hated the colonial regime and were impressed by Hitler's dramatic challenge of British imperial power.[15] Some of them were also fascinated by Nazism because of

---

10. Ibid., p. 52.

11. Nicholas Goodrick-Clarke, *Hitler's Priestess*, New York University Press, New York and London, 1998, p. 4.

12. Ibid.

13. https://www.bbc.com/news/magazine-41757047

14. Ibid.

15. Nicholas Goodrick-Clarke, *Hitler's Priestess*, New York University Press, New York and London, 1998, p. 4.

its use of the swastika—a holy Hindu symbol—and its emphasis on restoring Aryan supremacy. Indian intelligence agencies kept a close watch on the activities of this group and the movement of German propaganda material directed to them. Thus, on the declaration of the Second World War, Calcutta police conducted a search operation on German nationals and other known Nazi sympathizers, seized a large number of propaganda literature and destroyed them.[16] Similarly, on 8 January 1940, the Home Department of the Central government wrote to Bengal Chief Secretary H. G. Twynam to be watchful about a set of fourteen German propaganda films that had been dispatched from Romania to India. Twynam, on his part, instantly alerted the departments concerned in the state.[17]

Savitri Devi, much more devoted to Hitler than most of the local Nazi sympathizers in Calcutta, worked as a teacher for Hindu Mission. Its director, Swami Satyanand, shared her admiration for Hitler and allowed her to mix Nazi propaganda with her talks on Hinduism and Hindu identity. Through Hindu Mission she came into contact with the Hindu supremacist leaders of Maharashtra, including Moonje, whom she regarded as the man behind the formation of the RSS, V. D. Savarkar and other leaders of the Hindu Mahasabha.[18] It is possible that through these men she learnt about the Hindutva ideology and got inspired to write her book, *A Warning to the Hindus.*

In the book's first chapter, 'Indian Nationalism and Hindu Consciousness', Savitri Devi echoes Savarkar's Hindutva and argues that Hinduism is the national religion of India and that there is no real India besides Hindu India. 'And the only civilization for all

16. Government of Bengal, File No. W-602/40, Home (Poll) Department, pp. 2-6, West Bengal State Archives, Kolkata.

17. Government of Bengal, File No. 21/40, Home (Poll) Department Confidential, pp. 2-5, West Bengal State Archives, Kolkata.

18. Ibid., p. 45.

India is Hindu civilization. The only culture for all India is Hindu culture. Indian national consciousness is nothing else but Hindu national consciousness, strengthened, enlightened, broadened,' she wrote.[19]

In the preface of the book, Savitri Devi thanked V. D. Savarkar and Moonje. But she seemed bound more firmly to Ganesh Savarkar than any other Hindu Mahasabha leader. In fact, Ganesh Savarkar even wrote a foreword for her book in which he profusely praised her efforts and said: 'This highly inspiring and thought-provoking book will make the Hindus realize where they stand, and what dangers are threatening their very existence as a nation; it will put them on the right turn of national thinking.'[20]

Interestingly, this was the same period when Ganesh Savarkar was also propelling Golwalkar into the RSS. He even backed him for the post of secretary of the Hindu Mahasabha. Although Golwalkar visited Calcutta many times during the late 1930s and early 1940s, no one knows whether he ever met Savitri Devi. It is far more likely that he had no actual encounter with her, even though they had too many commonalities. Both were united in their loyalty to Babarao Savarkar. Both were equally seduced by Hitler and his treatment of Jews. Golwalkar's admiration for Nazism was unequivocal in his book, which, like *A Warning to the Hindus*, was published in 1939. And both were deeply influenced by Swiss jurist Johann Kaspar Bluntschli's concept of German ethnic nationalism.

In 1945, devastated by Hitler's defeat, Savitri Devi returned to Europe, where she pursued a long and busy career as a neo-Nazi apologist and ideologue.[21] Among swayamsevaks, she continued

---

19. Savitri Devi, *A Warning to the Hindus*, Hindu Mission, Calcutta, 1939, p. 7.

20. Savitri Devi, *A Warning to the Hindus*, Hindu Mission, Calcutta, 1939, p. ix.

21. Nicholas Goodrick-Clarke, *Hitler's Priestess*, New York University Press, New York and London, 1998, p. 4.

to remain popular because the synthesis of Hindutva and Nazi ideologies that she had called for was consistent with all that Golwalkar was sermonizing in the baudhik classes of the RSS.

III

Whatever his association with Savitri Devi, Golwalkar was not blind to the mechanisms whereby he had succeeded in establishing his grip over the RSS. He had already learnt the advantages of having a useful clique of RSS leaders around whom he could build a powerful following of men ready to regard him as their supremo. In 1942, while everyone was distracted by the maneuverings required to survive the 1940 restriction order, Golwalkar undertook to effect a more serious and consequential restructuring of the organization, creating an institutional mechanism for a new set of young RSS men who would take a pledge of celibacy, dedicate their lives for a Hindu Rashtra, fan out in different parts of the country as his emissaries and follow him blindly as their cult leader.

These new RSS leaders were called pracharaks, or preacher-cum-organizers. They were Golwalkar's all-powerful lieutenants whose goals included the imposition throughout India of Hindu values that would prevent the nationalist forces from turning the country into a secular, democratic nation after Independence. Golwalkar typically recruited the members of the new group from relatively better educated young swayamsevaks, who were nostalgic about the Hindu Rashtra and were ready to remain bachelors and forego the life of a householder. Partly this reflected Golwalkar's millenarian beliefs, but partly it was an organizational strategy crafted on the basis of Brahminism's teacher-disciple relationship by a loyalty-conscious leader eager to appropriate both temporal and religious authorities.

The plan had a slow beginning. Encouraging response came primarily from the Marathi-speaking districts of Bombay and the Central Provinces after Golwalkar started the recruitment of pracharaks in the beginning of June 1942.[22] But he persisted. In recruiting pracharaks, he appealed to swayamsevaks across India. In some cases, he himself had to convince the parents of swayamsevaks to allow their sons to become pracharaks. Bhaiyaji Dani, one of his old associates, was among the first to become a pracharak, and he could do so only after Golwalkar, following hours of persuasion, prevailed upon his father and made him support his son's decision.[23]

On 26 June 1942, Golwalkar revealed his thoughts on how the plan was progressing and what kind of challenges it faced. In a letter to his associate Annasaheb Goregaonkar of Bombay, he said: 'At present, I am sending pracharaks to various states. After completing this task in next eight to ten days, I will go to Poona to get a sense of how the pracharak recruitment plan is working on the ground and to explore whether there are new ways to convince more men to become pracharak.'[24]

Nominally at least, the plan had begun. In course of time, the number of these full-time soldiers of Golwalkar increased, and they began changing the sociological face of the RSS. The contemplative groups of the old-generation RSS leaders were infiltrated by dedicated men who followed army-like discipline and vowed to do anything necessary to achieve the ultimate objectives of the organization and its leader. Here was the new structure that offered a haven for young Brahmin men unable to cope with the changing tides and frightened of being declassed. Within its framework they could satisfy their craving for reviving—through

22. N. H. Palkar, *Shri Ma Sa Golwalkar*, published by N. H. Palkar, Mumbai, 1956, p. 82.

23. Ibid.

24. Golwalkar Papers, Roll No. 12269, Microfilm Section, Part IV, pp. 55-56, NMML, New Delhi.

the Hindu Rashtra—a feudal structure dominated by Hindu caste elites.

With the aid of these pracharaks accustomed to subordination, discipline and devotion, Golwalkar gradually succeeded in providing the RSS with a firm inner structure.

IV

For a section of swayamsevaks in Maharashtra, however, ideological lectures in the RSS camps were no match for military drills. These drills had attracted them to the RSS and generated in them a notion of virility and masculinity. Although communally explicit and tactlessly assertive, the military drills embodied the qualities associated with youth—energy and idealism—and appeared alluringly dynamic. Their suspension in the aftermath of the 1940 order had meant the end of exuberance. These testosterone-driven young swayamsevaks, who at one blow found themselves deprived of the thrill and glamour of the potential soldier's life, found the early 1940s grim. The government order, quite aside from dampening their morale, had minimized their role in the RSS. In the absence of parade-ground activities, they had ended up becoming mere spectators and listeners of speeches of their leaders in camps. Such lives seemed to them wretched and utterly unworthy of them. The number of such swayamsevaks was quite large in Maharashtra. They were too impatient to wait for the promised, and a more systematic, future action.

Finding a suitable avenue for them to exert their energies was a challenge that the RSS leadership could not ignore. Quietly, discreetly, virtually unnoticed by the government, the RSS in the Marathi-speaking districts of the Bombay province embarked on a process of forming a new outfit, the Hindu Rashtra Dal. This took place under the auspices of Limaye, Golwalkar's lieutenant with deep connections in Maharashtra and the Deccan's princely states.

The new outfit was born in the summer of 1942, around the

time the Poona OTC of the RSS concluded. It was a hybrid, at times curious, political entity, a covert joint venture of the RSS and the Hindu Mahasabha. Nathuram Godse, the RSS hothead of Poona and a protégé of Limaye, and Narayan Dattatreya Apte, a Hindu Mahasabha member and a Savarkar loyalist, acted as the outfit's chief organizers. While the planning seems to have come from the Hindu Mahasabha, much of the new outfit's energy was channeled from the RSS. Though in later years the RSS refused to admit this and asserted instead that the Hindu Rashtra Dal was some kind of an informal wing of the Hindu Mahasabha, contemporary sources suggest that the Sangh was perfectly integrated into the new venture.

In fact, amidst growing despondency in the aftermath of the 1940 order, increasing numbers of RSS volunteers in Maharashtra joined the eighteen-day-long foundation camp of the Hindu Rashtra Dal in 1942. 'The first camp of the Dal was organised in Poona from May 1 to 18. A total of 160 swayamsevaks and sympathizers took part in it,' Godse revealed years later.[25] According to Laxman Ganesh Thatte, a Hindu Mahasabha member who, as a close friend of Godse, had actively participated in the formation of the new outfit, 'The Hindu Rashtra Dal was formed out of trusted R.S.S. men.'[26] Vasudev Balwant Gogate, a Savarkar loyalist and one of the organizers of the Poona camp, wrote in his memoir: 'Apart from a large number of swayamsevaks of Poona, those from Miraj, Sangli and Satara also attended the camp. I was in charge of ideological classes. Godse acted as the host, looking after the arrangements and conduct of classes and training programmes in the camp.'[27]

25. Mahatma Gandhi Murder Case, Statement of Accused in Original, File No. 23, p. 20, NAI, New Delhi.

26. Mahatma Gandhi Murder Trial Papers, Special Branch, CID, Bombay, File No. 5, Crime Report No. 2, pp. 9-10, NAI, New Delhi.

27. Vasudev Balwant Gogate, *Hotson-Gogate: Atmavritta*, published by Anil Vasudev Gogate, Pune, 2006, p. 94.

The Hindu Rashtra Dal worked in harmony with the RSS. The lines between the two organizations were not always easy to discern. No swayamsevak was expelled for joining it, nor was there any official announcement by the top leadership of the RSS asking its members to stay away from the new outfit—an indication that swayamsevaks attending the meeting of the new outfit enjoyed some kind of an official sanction. Moreover, right since its inception, Limaye, who at the time was the sanghchalak of the Maharashtra unit of the RSS, acted simultaneously as the prantpramukh—state chief—of the Hindu Rashtra Dal. As such, he was its most important decision maker—a fact that, more than anything else, signified the close association of the RSS with the HRD. 'Shri Kashinath Limaye started working as prantpramukh [of Hindu Rashtra Dal],' Godse recounted.[28] The revelation is at odds with the commonly accepted opinion that the HRD had nothing to do with the RSS and was essentially, though not formally, a Hindu Mahasabha offshoot consisting of hardcore Savarkar loyalists.

The association of the RSS with the Hindu Rashtra Dal became more elaborate and complex during the latter's second annual camp organized at Ahmednagar in May 1943. Held for fifteen days, the Ahmednagar camp was attended by around a hundred swayamsevaks.[29] This camp was much more organized than the previous one. Each swayamsevak attending the camp was told in advance to bring a set of khaki shorts and white shirt—the uniform of an RSS member—along with a saffron cap.[30] Changing the

28. Mahatma Gandhi Murder Case, Statement of Accused in Original, File No. 23, p. 20, NAI, New Delhi.

29. Mahatma Gandhi Murder Case, Statement of Accused in Original, File No. 23, p. 21, NAI, New Delhi.

30. B. S. Moonje Papers, Sub File No. 75, p. 68, Records Section, NMML, New Delhi.

colour of the cap from black to saffron was probably a deliberate move to make two sets of swayamsevaks look different from each other. They were also asked specifically to wear the saffron cap, along with khaki shorts and white shirt, only on special occasions in the camp.[31] Every morning the swayamsevaks would assemble in rows for a military-style call to order, followed by exhaustive physical exercises. The camp's curriculum included training in the handling of air guns and theoretical instructions—baudhikvarg—delivered by teachers from the RSS and the Hindu Mahasabha. It is likely that the HRD camp—like the camps of the RSS—did not attract the government's attention as the 1940 order exempted camps and prohibited only military drill and the wearing of dress resembling military uniform. For theoretical classes in the Ahmednagar camp, the RSS sent two of its best teachers—Dr. P. G. Sahasrabuddhe and D. V. Gokhale.[32] In the ideological classes of the RSS, Sahasrabuddhe used to sermonize on subjects like capitalism, socialism, fascism and social and political philosophy.[33] In the Ahmednagar camp of the HRD, he delivered lectures on the subject of 'socialism and the Hindu Rashtra'.[34] Gokhale, the other RSS man who addressed the HRD members attending the Ahmednagar camp, was considered the Sangh's most prominent rising star in Poona. He was among the youngest swayamsevaks who, responding to Golwalkar's call, had become a pracharak in 1942. At the time he was nineteen and had just passed the Intermediate exams from Poona's SP College. Gokhale was a strict disciplinarian and was considered in the RSS circle an expert

31. Ibid.

32. Ibid.

33. Based on interview with 93-year-old RSS member Shrinivas D. Acharya, who has been living in Poona since 1941, on 11 October 2019.

34. B. S. Moonje Papers, Sub File No. 75, p. 67, Records Section, NMML, New Delhi.

on war-related issues.[35] In the HRD camp at Ahmednagar, he spoke on the subject of 'current war [Second World War] and Hindusthan'.[36]

Heading it all as leader, star speaker and organizer during the Ahmednagar camp was Limaye himself. This fact was widely advertised by Godse and Apte, who sent a jointly signed and printed advisory to participants ahead of the camp: 'Rashtriya Swayamsevak Sangh's prantsanghchalak KB Limaye will stay in the camp for two to three days. You will, therefore, get an opportunity to listen to his precious thoughts.'[37]

On the whole, the training seemed to draw on the tested practices of the RSS and was meant to prepare the Hindu Rashtra Dal cadres for specific political purposes. It could be that the Hindu Mahasabha also provided teachers for the Ahmednagar camp, but it was the imprint of the RSS that was most visible. The Hindu Rashtra Dal had sinister motives. The ostensibly non-political organization was actually meant to carry out secret and violent operations—those which the RSS and the Hindu Mahasabha would not undertake themselves.[38] The combination of promised violence and conspiratorial ideology must have exerted a strong allure for that section of swayamsevaks who sought an outlet for their violent instincts. In the Hindu Rashtra Dal, the RSS seemed to have found a way to keep even despondent swayamsevaks, for whom the Sangh had started to lose its charm in the absence of parade ground activities, involved for the cause it cherished.

---

35. Neela Vasant Upadhye (ed.), *DV Gokhale: Vyaktitvava Krititva*, Navachaitanya Prakashan, Mumbai, 2013, p. x.

36. B. S. Moonje Papers, Sub File No. 75, p. 67, Records Section, NMML, New Delhi.

37. B. S. Moonje Papers, Sub File No. 75, p. 67, Records Section, NMML, New Delhi.

38. Mahatma Gandhi Murder Trial Papers, Special Branch, CID, Bombay, File No. 5, p. 228, NAI, New Delhi.

If we are to believe the available accounts, the Hindu Rashtra Dal was the Sangh's first attempt under the leadership of Golwalkar to create a buffer organization, which was bent on making an impression of being a different outfit but was actually working equivocally for the parent body. It was an experiment that would assume a pattern after the assassination of Mahatma Gandhi when, due to changed political circumstances, the RSS would develop into a hydra-like network defined by the same equivocation. Whether Golwalkar sanctioned the formation of the Dal remains a mystery. There is no specific evidence to suggest that he ever took part in any of its meetings or that he ever discussed the issues of the Hindu Rashtra Dal with Limaye. Yet, the fact that he had no qualms about letting Limaye and a large number of RSS men form the Hindu Rashtra Dal without leaving the parent organization only shows that he was not averse to the initiative.

V

In a broad sense, then, Golwalkar had come a long way. A neutral onlooker would be astounded at the rapid progress he had made in just two years of becoming the RSS sarsanghchalak. With extraordinary boldness and coldness, he had very nearly attained the dream of his youth. He had taken in at a glance people, motivations, forces and ideas and bent them to his own aim—achieving respectability and enlarging his power. At any rate, he had proved capable of coping with whatever came his way—challenges from within the RSS or restrictions imposed by the government.

Inside, however, Golwalkar even now was perhaps no different from what he had been. His emotions, the fears and obsessions remained fixed. His views on the anti-British freedom movement, and even his personal preferences, remained what they had been in the days of his boyhood and youth. The framework he had put himself in seemed to make him even more conscious of keeping himself and his organization away from any resistance to the colonial masters. Thus, when India exploded in violent uprisings against the British rule in the summer of 1942, Golwalkar remained cordial with the government, watching the development indifferently.

The Quit India movement, as it was called, began on 9 August 1942, following the arrest of Mahatma Gandhi and other leaders of the Indian National Congress by the British government. A day before, on 8 August, the Congress had adopted the 'Quit India' resolution asking for an immediate end to British rule. The resolution declared that the Congress would 'no longer [be] justified in holding the nation back from endeavouring to assert its will' and, therefore, sanctioned 'a mass struggle on non-violent lines under the inevitable leadership of Gandhiji'.[39] As the news of the arrests spread, trouble erupted on a wide scale. Crowds vandalized local trains, cut telephone wires, damaged post-offices, street lamps, etc. Schools and colleges were closed, so were markets and bazaars in most parts of Bombay.

From Bombay, the trouble spread to the rest of India. There were Quit India hartals across the country, and many of them turned into anti-government riots. Security forces sought to suppress the movement brutally, causing a massive death toll. Though the official estimate of civilian loss of life was 1,028, Jawaharlal Nehru guessed the death toll at 10,000.[40] Bengal, like Bombay, emerged as another major flashpoint of intense protests, witnessing hundreds of incidents of cutting of telegraph wires and burning of mail bags and letter boxes as well as attempts to force village headmen and petty officials to resign.[41]

39. Jawaharlal Nehru, *The Discovery of India*, Penguin India, New Delhi, 2008, p. 454.

40. Ibid., pp. 460-464.

41. Ramachandra Guha, *Gandhi: The Years that Changed the World, 1914-1948*, Penguin Random House India, Gurgaon, 2018, p. 684.

The imprisonment of Congress leaders created an empty space in politics and gave the Muslim separatist and Hindu supremacist organizations their chance to rush in. Jinnah declared that it was not in the interests of Muslims for the British to abandon them in a potentially hostile swamp of Hinduism.[42] His logical position was, therefore, to keep the British in India—at least for as long as it took to convince them of the case for Pakistan.

The Hindu Mahasabha, on its part, stuck to its line of cooperation with the government. Savarkar described the Congress-led movement as nothing but a 'ridiculous jail seeking programme' and asked Hindus to boycott it.[43] In fact, in Bengal, where the mobilization of almost all sections of society was virtually complete in favour of Quit India movement, this line created an unusual confusion in the ranks of the Hindu Mahasabha. This was reflected in a letter Hindu Mahasabha leader N. C. Chatterjee wrote to Moonje on 14 August 1942. The 'present position in Bengal', Chatterjee wrote, 'is that the entire Hindu population is with Gandhiji and his movement and if anybody wants to oppose it, he will be absolutely finished and hounded out of public life. The unfortunate statement issued by Veer Savarkar [opposing Quit India movement] made our position rather difficult in Bengal. It is rather amusing to find that Mr. Jinnah wants the Mussalmans not to join the Congress movement and Mr. Savarkar wants the Hindus not to join the same.'[44]

Golwalkar toed the Mahasabha line. S. H. Deshpande, who

---

42. Akbar S. Ahmed, *Jinnah, Pakistan and Islamic Identity: The Search for Saladin*, Routledge, London & New York, 1997, p. 82.

43. Nandini Gondhalekar and Sanjoy Bhattacharya, 'The All India Hindu Mahasabha and the End of British Rule in India, 1937-1947', *Social Scientist*, July-August, 1999, Vol. 27, No. 7/8, p. 55.

44. N. C. Chatterjee to B. S. Moonje, 14 August 1942, cited in Ramachandra Guha, *Gandhi: The Years that Changed the World*, Penguin Random House India, Gurgaon, 2018, pp. 684-685.

was about to complete high school in Poona and was a very active member of the RSS at that time, was shocked to see the Sangh's approach to the movement since he had been given to believe that his organization had transformed itself into a 'truly revolutionary' one. 'However, when the Quit India movement gathered momentum the RSS remained a passive onlooker,' he wrote in his reminiscences. 'In one of the theory classes, this isolation was justified on the ground that neither the RSS nor the country was yet strong enough to overthrow the foreign yoke. The speaker [of the RSS] told us that all the blood that was being spilled in the firings was in vain!'[45]

According to Deshpande, the argument seemed convincing to him, and as such the Quit India movement left him unmoved. In fact, the school he was studying in, NMV High School, had a very strong RSS base, all its teachers being staunch supporters of the Sangh. 'I was now in the matriculation class and held a position of some importance and authority as a leader of my school-mates who were in the RSS.' He wrote:

> I could therefore see to it that not once during the days of the '42 movement did our school remain closed, although we had often to face Congress-sponsored picketing by students from the other city schools, who would stand outside our school gate and shout slogans. Once when a batch of demonstrators threatened to stop classes, we got together a small band of RSS volunteers outside the gate, broke their cordon and forced them to beat a retreat.[46]

Not all in the school was as convinced by the RSS argument as Deshpande. Shrinivas D. Acharya, who was a 16-year-old member of the RSS at that time and a year junior to Deshpande in the

---

45. S. H. Deshpande, 'My Days in the RSS', *Quest*, July-August 1975, p. 23.
46. Ibid.

same school, found himself burdened by pangs of conscience over not being able to take the risk of violating the diktat of the Sangh and participate in the Quit India movement. 'On the whole, it was a mentality rather than a class of people which marked the members of the Sangh in those days,' Acharya recounted. 'It was an ostensibly revolutionary but actually a servile state of mind, and one that existed both inside and outside the Sangh. We as the RSS workers were given to believe that the Quit India movement was the movement of Congress and that we would have our own separate movement which would be much more decisive for setting up Hindu Rashtra. A small number of swayamsevaks could make out that such a movement would never happen, and they left the Sangh. I could not because I feared being left isolated in my group.'[47]

Acharya, in fact, never left the RSS. Until his death on 20 March 2021, he kept attending a local shakha in Poona.

47. Based on an interview with RSS member Shrinivas D. Acharya, who lived in Poona from 1941 until his death in 2021. The interview was done on 11 October 2019.

Stirring the Communal Pot

In keeping with the theory of focusing upon a single opponent, Golwalkar made Muslims the grotesque projection of all imaginable vices and dreads, the cause of tyranny in the past and a threat for Hindus in future. In *We or Our Nationhood Defined*, the most authentic treatise on a Hindu Rashtra, he expounded that all non-Hindus were 'either traitors or enemies to the national cause, or, to take a charitable view, idiots'.[1] Even when he sought to avoid the government's attention by abandoning the overtly militaristic aspects of the dress and ceremonials in RSS shakhas or decided to side with the British during the Quit India movement, Golwalkar never lost sight of the propaganda value of his anti-Muslim rhetoric.

In fact, the entire Hindutva politics was so highly aware of that aspect of things that one wonders how it would have survived if Muslims did not exist. To be sure, the form that the Muslim took in Golwalkar's own mind did not differ greatly from the diabolical propaganda image that the Hindutva organizations had created. 'I had been taught and tutored by the RSS to look upon every Muslim as a snake which must be killed,' writes Ram Lall

1. M. S. Golwalkar, *We or Our Nationhood Defined*, Bharat Publications, Nagpur, 1939, p. 44.

Dhooria, who joined the RSS in Montgomery district of Punjab just after the Quit India movement.[2] Within the RSS, therefore, the figure of the Muslim was the incarnation of everything it hated.

Certainly the thesis that Muslims were striving to divide India made good propaganda, but Golwalkar saw it as the key to all sorts of crisis. He clung more and more to this redeeming formula as he dealt with a section of swayamsevaks' apathy caused by the suspension of parade ground activities or when he sought to convince RSS men not to take part in the Quit India movement but to conserve their energy for their own 'decisive' struggle in the future. The veil of ambiguity regarding the future struggle was dropped in August 1943, when Babasaheb Apte, a close associate of Golwalkar, declared in an RSS camp at Allahabad that 'Hindus might have to fight Islam after the War [Second World War] and that it was, therefore, important to instill courage and spirit in volunteers'.[3]

Of special significance was Golwalkar's way of taking his beliefs and overlaying them with an aggressive and purposeful theory of action. This sometimes required an aggravation of his hate complex so that his anti-Muslim rhetoric would not just remain the ranting of a demagogue but would be part of a coherent system necessary to achieve the goal of a Hindu Rashtra. But along with the goal, Golwalkar also recognized the risk. The 1940 order seemed to have made him careful not to spell out openly the kind of politics he was fostering. He, therefore, pretended that his relentless views on Muslims had nothing to do with politics and that his organization was truly apolitical. Explaining his motivations, he told a group of RSS men in a closed-door meeting at Amraoti in 1943 that

---

2. Ram Lall Dhooria, *I Was A Swayamsewak*, Sampradayikta Virodhi Committee, New Delhi, 1976, p. 7.

3. Government of India, Home Department (Political), File No. 190-P(S), 1943, p. 22, NAI, New Delhi.

'any announcement of political aims would almost certainly invite controversy which may lead to the Sangh's early disintegration'.[4]

His strategy, therefore, also required finding new ways for maintaining utmost secrecy about the internal affairs of the RSS. To the extent it existed, the RSS's organizational structure had already been promoting an authoritarian institutional secrecy that concealed the internal workings of the organization and conflicts and discussions within it.[5] An Intelligence Bureau report of late 1943 noted fresh attempts at concealment. 'For the first time in the Sangh's history, a special censorship branch was opened at the Nagpur summer camp and all outward mail was scrutinized,' the report said. It added:

> At the Bombay headquarters, a system of Visitors' Passes has been organized. Lectures at the Officers' Training Camp at Meerut last May were held behind closed doors and only those with special passes were admitted. The same precautions were taken at the Officers' Training Camp at Benaras where students were also forbidden to reduce anything to writing. At a meeting in Rawalpindi on August 4th, L. Kundan Lal Kakar [a local RSS leader] advocated caution in enlisting members lest police informers should be able to find their way into the Sangh. [...] When important Berar organizers met in Akola last September to chalk out the Dussehra programme, special precautions were taken to safeguard the secrecy of their names and of the proceedings.[6]

Although Golwalkar was anxious to leave no room for doubt that he was unmistakably on the side of the colonial government, he

4. Ibid., p. 25.

5. Chetan Bhatt, *Hindu Nationalism: Origins, Ideologies and Modern Myths*, Oxford, New York, 2001, p. 116.

6. Government of India, Home Department (Political), File No. 190-P(S), 1943, pp. 22-23, NAI, New Delhi.

never seemed to be sure whether the British trusted him. Nor did he have any illusions about the fact that he would stand no chance of success in the absence of help—at least covertly—from within the government machinery. As direct support from the government was out of the question, Golwalkar instructed 'secret enrolment of reliable Government servants, teachers and clerks in order to spread the influence of the Sangh in official circles'.[7]

Before long, the results started showing, although at the time it was restricted primarily to the Central Provinces. 'A new feature of the Sangh activity in the Central Provinces is the establishment of branches in the Gun Carriage Factory, Jubbulpore, and the Ordnance Factory, Khamaria, while several employees in the Ordnance Factory at Katni are said to belong to the local branch of the Sangh,' noted an Intelligence Bureau report. 'The leaders of the branches in the first two installations (which are controlled by the Supply Department of the Government of India) have been warned to cease their activities but it is doubtful if the warning has had any real effect.'[8]

The Intelligence Bureau's analysis was that Golwalkar and his associates were travelling extensively to stimulate interest of swayamsevaks, impart secret instructions and strengthen the local units of the RSS. Referring to Golwalkar's itineraries in 1943, it said, 'Last April he was at Ahmedabad, in May at Amraoti and Poona, in June at Nasik and Benaras, in August at Chanda, in September again at Poona, in October in Madras and the Central Provinces and in November at Rawalpindi.'[9]

7. Ibid., p. 23.

8. Ibid.

9. Ibid.

II

There are credible accounts that Golwalkar was flirting with a vision of politics that would accord him a position similar to the German Fuehrer but was unable yet to openly embrace it. 'R.S.S.S. is aimed at bringing the Hindus of India under the control of a dictator (Guru Ji) and solidify their organisation for the ultimate purpose of capturing political power,' an important RSS man in Punjab, Ram Rakha Mal, told the Intelligence Bureau in 1943. 'A spirit of discipline, martial tendencies and developing healthy bodies by the Hindus is to be inculcated so that the Hindu nation may turn matchless in strength due to its overwhelming majority in India.'[10]

As Golwalkar's political thought became central to the Sangh's ideological training, the demand for *We or Our Nationhood Defined* increased phenomenally. The book was republished four times in the 1940s until the RSS was banned following the assassination of Mahatma Gandhi on 30 January 1948.[11] With his book as the guiding force and a new institutional mechanism of pracharaks in place, Golwalkar seemed on a mission to convert the RSS into a powerful instrument of attack and conquest, perhaps imagining himself as something akin to a Hindu Hitler.

Prompted by ideas borrowed from Nazism, he was coming to the belief that he must quietly wait for the British to leave the country before setting out to overthrow the present order and seize political power and that this the RSS must do under his own leadership. His extreme and violent views on politics find expression in a diary confiscated from the RSS headquarters in the aftermath of the assassination of Mahatma Gandhi. The diary

10. Ibid., p. 7.

11. Chetan Bhatt, *Hindu Nationalism: Origins, Ideologies and Modern Myths*, Oxford, New York, 2001, p. 126.

contained the minutes of a meeting of top RSS leaders held on 9 September 1945, in which deliberations were written by hand in a question-and-answer format.

The meeting was thought to have been a confidential affair meant to explain Golwalkar's oft repeated statement: 'We have no connection with present politics.'[12] The idea seems to have been to convey the RSS plan from the top leadership to prominent organizers and teachers, who would then—by virtue of being in regular touch with swayamsevaks—carry the secret message down the line. The meeting was attended by 'Balasaheb Deoras, PV Savarkar, Datta Vaidya, Anna Pandharipande, Baburao Savatker, Nandlal Verma, Nana Narale, [Pandurang] Kshirsagar, Madhukar Oak and Tatyaji [Tatyarao Telang]'.[13]

All the participants were close associates of Golwalkar. While Deoras was in charge of the organization's headquarters at Nagpur and considered the main executioner of Golwalkar's ideas, others were prominent organizers and teachers of the RSS. The diary details a discussion, in which Deoras responded while the RSS's organizers and teachers asked questions touching primarily upon the organization's approach to politics in independent India. The meeting had been convened by Deoras with the apparent purpose to ideologically equip 'RSS organizers and main teachers' with the nuances required to instill the Sangh's idea of politics in the ranks and files of the organization.[14]

'It is wrong to say that we have no connection with politics,' Deoras, according to the diary, remarked while responding to a question by P. V. Savarkar. 'Today our plan is to create a powerful body by organizing the Rashtriya Swayamsevak Sangh all over

12. D. P. Mishra Papers, I & II Inst., Sub. File No. 18, p. 199, Record Section, NMML, New Delhi

13. Ibid., p. 198.

14. Ibid.

India and thereby to effect an all India unity, and at an opportune moment to seize the power on receipt of an order from our Leader. Obviously, to achieve this power, it is necessary that it should not be utilized in any other sphere and our attention should not be diverted to any other thing.'[15]

In the meeting, Deoras tried to show that the new politics under Golwalkar was in no sense contradictory to the fundamental trend of Indian history and mythology. Arjun, one of the main characters of the ancient Hindu epic Mahabharat, and Shivaji, the Maratha king and the most revered political figure in Maharashtra, were shown to have followed the same political line. 'Arjun could see only an eye of the bird. Does this mean that Arjun was unaware of the fact that Dronacharya [his teacher] was standing by his side and that the bird was sitting on the tree? But with all this when the vision is directed towards a certain object it is necessary not to divert it towards anything else,' Deoras said.[16] Referring to Shivaji, he said:

> Did Shivaji overthrow the empire of Aurangzeb by utilising the present politics? The present politics has come into existence on account of the novel way of administration of the British. The British followed the Roman method of administration by avoiding its defects. As the sentiments of enslaved people are apt to rise they created an outlet for it and decided to do everything according to law. [...] The present politics is the creation of this system. The fruits achieved out of the present politics are also limited, e.g. an ordinary reduction in taxes or an achievement of some minor rights. [...] To think that there was any advantage in getting some reforms or some rights is a mistake. Britishers have done this for their own interest.[17]

15. Ibid., p. 199.
16. Ibid., pp. 199-200.
17. Ibid., p. 200.

Responding to a question by Anna Pandharipande, Deoras said, 'Our plan is of "surprise".' Then, in a nuanced way, he added: 'It is not that all the things are done according to the settled plan. Even if we think that we will do the work step by step, there is no guarantee that all the factors will remain till the last.'[18] Deoras also talked about the political role swayamsevaks should be playing till the RSS was organizationally ready to seize power:

> It is possible that we will be required to do anything. It is also possible that the Sangh might tell 5-10 persons to start their own political party. Everything is possible. This is our general plan. [...] We should bear this thing in mind that we would take a particular step suitable to the occasion. [...] It is said about the Imperial Guard of Napoleon that he used to feed it as much as possible till the approach of the suitable moment. At a proper moment it used to take the offensive.[19]

It was in this context that Deoras stated that the RSS would not formally take part in the upcoming elections to central and provincial legislatures in the winter of 1945-46 but that its cadre should vote. To a question about why swayamsevaks should vote at all, he said, 'There are several things of which we are not in favour but still we have to do those things. We are not in favour of slavery but still we are [in] it. The same will be the case with elections.'[20]

The conversation contained in the diary gave the gist of Golwalkar's political programme. His RSS, unlike the Hindu Mahasabha, did not pursue democratic political goals but worked instead for violent seizure of power. Despite the ambiguity being so fundamental to the political outlook of Golwalkar, intelligence

---

18. Ibid., p. 202.
19. Ibid., pp. 202-203.
20. Ibid., p. 203.

agencies could easily see that there was much more than what was apparent. According to an Intelligence Bureau report, Golwalkar, addressing a closed-door meeting of RSS office-bearers at Hoshangabad in March 1946, claimed that the total strength of swayamsevaks was around 250,000 and 'that his plan of direct action was held in readiness for disclosure at the psychological moment'.[21]

On 13 April 1946, the intelligence department of Delhi Police reported: 'Openly the Sangh professes to be working for the solidarity and organisation of the Hindus. Their ultimate aim, however, is to try to capture political power in India when chaotic conditions prevail.'[22] Similarly, on 19 May 1946, another intelligence report of Delhi Police noted that in a secret RSS meeting at Rohtak, one Dada Bhai of Nagpur said that 'the Sangh's struggle was not against the British but against the Muslims and that every Hindu should be ready to take part in this struggle when the time comes'.[23]

III

At any rate, it was not Golwalkar's extreme and violent views on politics which most disturbed the Hindu Mahasabha. Hindu supremacists in general had no compunction about taking an anti-democratic and authoritarian political position. The point about Golwalkar, however, was that while he expected the Hindu Mahasabha to be supportive all the time, he refrained from taking an open political position in support of the Hindutva

21. Government of India, Home Political (I), File No. NA-F-5-12, 1946, 'Note on Rashtriya Swaymsevak Sangh', pp. 12-13, NIA, New Delhi.

22. Delhi Police Records, VIII Inst., File No. 417, p. 4, Record Section, NMML, New Delhi.

23. Government of India, Home Political (I), File No. NA-F-5-12, 1946, 'Note on Rashtriya Swaymsevak Sangh', p. 13, NIA, New Delhi.

party. His somewhat unclear political posturing was especially apparent during the elections of 1945-46. The best evidence suggests that he genuinely wanted to help the Hindu Mahasabha in the elections but was ambivalent about changing his public posturing on electoral politics at a time when the Defence of India Act was still in force.

In November 1945, for example, Moonje, while campaigning for Hindu Mahasabha candidates in Bihar, watched with concern whether local RSS men were coming forth to back the party or not. He was relieved to know that they did. At Bhagalpur, his first halt in Bihar, the local head of the RSS, Bhaskar Zinzarde, met him on 27 November 1945 and assured the Sangh's support to the Hindu Mahasabha candidate.[24] While addressing a small gathering of about 300 people at Banka on 28 November, Moonje noticed that a group of RSS men who were conducting their evening shakha at a nearby place quickly wound up their programme and joined his meeting.[25] Such assurances were repeated at many other places in Bihar. On his return, Ghatate informed him that RSS men would support the Hindu Mahasabha candidate in Nagpur.[26] In at least one instance, Golwalkar himself came out to assure him about the support of local RSS men for a Mahasabha-backed candidate from Umred.[27]

In the elections, the Congress won in almost all general constituencies whereas the Muslim League captured an overwhelming majority of Muslim seats. The Hindu Mahasabha was virtually decimated.[28] Although Golwalkar's inability to give

24. B. S. Moonje Papers, Diary No. 6, p. 4, Record Section, NMML, New Delhi.

25. Ibid., pp. 5-6.

26. Ibid., p. 53.

27. Ibid., p. 79.

28. Sumit Sarkar, *Modern India: 1885-1947*, Macmillan India Ltd., Delhi, 2003, p. 426.

an open call to support the Hindu Mahasabha in the elections had been intensely irritating, there was little doubt on the question of their actual relationship. The two still remained intertwined. In some respects, their alignment deepened during the next two years until the assassination of Mahatma Gandhi turned it into a burden for Golwalkar.

The fact that they continued to work in tandem became apparent immediately after the elections when the Cabinet Mission arrived in India to develop a road map for the transfer of power from the British government to the Indian political leadership. The Mission, a three-member committee of the British Cabinet, consisted of Secretary of State for India Lord Pethick-Lawrence, Sir Stafford Cripps and A. V. Alexander. It was born in the aftermath of UK Prime Minister Clement Attlee's 15 March 1946 declaration promising India speedy and full freedom. The Cabinet Mission reached India on 24 March and instantly began to carry out long and often very tortuous negotiations with Indian leaders on issues such as forming an interim government and framing a new constitution.[29] The Viceroy of India, Lord Wavell, also participated in some of the discussions.

Within days of the arrival of the Cabinet Mission, all political parties got busy in firming up their views to be presented before the high-powered committee. In the Hindu Mahasabha, Moonje was given the task to prepare a draft statement to be submitted to the Cabinet Mission.[30] Besides consulting various leaders of the Mahasabha, Moonje also incorporated Golwalkar's opinion in the party's draft statement. On 1 April 1946, he asked Ghatate to fetch Golwalkar so that they could finalize the statement. 'About 12.30 noon [on April 2], came Ghatate and Guruji,' Moonje noted in

29. Ibid., p. 428.

30. B. S. Moonje Papers, Diary No. 6, p. 82, Record Section, NMML, New Delhi.

his diary. 'He has read over the statement. He thinks the portion that deals with our preparation to meet Civil War threat should be omitted. I did not agree with him. He then suggested that there must be a definite mention that if Hindu Mahasabha is not consulted, the Constitution will not be acceptable. I agreed.'[31]

Obviously, Golwalkar was still worried; he didn't want to invite any trouble by openly talking about a 'Civil War' in a statement meant for the British panel. But he seemed clearly to have had a sense of himself as part of the Hindutva brigade, for he identified with the Hindu Mahasabha's insistence to be regarded as a participant in any future settlement. On 14 April, Hindu Mahasabha leaders Shyama Prasad Mookerjee and L. B. Bhopatkar met the Cabinet Mission and presented the party's viewpoint. 'The Viceroy [Lord Wavell] and Lord Pethick-Lawrence were absent, being busy otherwise,' Moonje noted in his diary. 'Only Sir Stafford Cripps and Mr. Alexander were present. Our representatives put up their case freely and frankly and fearlessly. They told them their uncompromising opposition to Pakistan [...]. They were not afraid of the threat of Civil War by Mr. Jinnah.'[32]

As it happened, the negotiations with political parties led nowhere. Therefore, the Cabinet Mission on 16 May put forward its own plan that proposed a federal India, with a ten-year constitutional review that would allow Muslim provinces to leave the Indian union if they wished. Initially, both the Muslim League and the Congress accepted the plan, but soon differences regarding its interpretation cropped up.[33] Simultaneously, Lord Wavell was getting desperate to form an interim government but was halted by Jinnah's precondition that the Congress should not have the

31. Ibid., p. 89.

32. Ibid., p. 96.

33. Sumit Sarkar, *Modern India: 1885-1947*, Macmillan India Ltd., Delhi, 2003, p. 430.

right to include Muslims among its nominees—a demand that the Congress was not ready to accept. For a short while, Wavell, in his bid to appease Jinnah, tried to run the country through a caretaker government of officials alone.

But by now the country was a mess. Attlee's 15 March announcement had made British civil and military officers increasingly desperate to leave as there had emerged a growing hostility to their presence among Indians. Within a few weeks, Lord Wavell realized that for the interim government to be effective, the Congress would have to be on board, even if that meant the Muslim League staying out.[34] He, therefore, gave up his appeasement of Jinnah and started prodding the Congress to form the interim government and put the country in order.

It fell on Nehru, who informed Lord Wavell on 10 August that he was prepared to form a government. The change, of course, resulted in the Muslim League's mistrust of the Congress reaching a fever pitch. As soon as Nehru accepted the premiership of the interim government, Jinnah dropped his support for the Cabinet Mission plan and called for a Direct Action Day to force the partition of India.

IV

The Direct Action Day, which was observed on 16 August 1946, provoked widespread communal clashes in eastern and northern states. These clashes made the partition of India inevitable and gave the RSS a major organizational boost. It all started on the morning of 16 August when Calcutta was engulfed in a frenzy of violence. Groups of Muslims and Hindus attacked each other in the streets and ventured into different quarters of the city, killing, beating and raping anyone they could find. Within three

34. Ibid., pp. 430-431.

days, 4,000 of Calcutta's residents lay dead and over 10,000 were injured.[35] From Calcutta, the communal inferno quickly spread through Bengal and Assam and triggered copycat killings in Bihar, the United Provinces, Punjab and the North-West Frontier Province (NWFP).

These communal events gave a final shape to the polarity of the pre-Partition era. Many Hindus started believing that organizations such as the RSS would be in a position to defend their interests and save them from Muslim aggression.[36] This was the first of the two abrupt twists that the kaleidoscope of Golwalkar's life experienced around this time. The second was the withdrawal, in September 1946, of the government's restrictions on parade ground activities of private militias.[37] With the withdrawal of the order, the colonial government did practically nothing to stop the armament of the RSS and other private armies—the Muslim League National Guards, the volunteer outfit of the Muslim League, and the Akal Saina, a radical organization of Sikhs.

Shortly after the removal of these restrictions, the British authorities noted the revival of the RSS and other private armies: 'The lapse of the Defence of India Rules at the end of September 1946 and the restrictive orders passed under them was followed by the immediate revival of the wearing of uniforms, the carrying of weapons, parade and marching. These have added to the growth of communal tension, provoked anger, fear and suspicion.'[38]

By now India's situation was becoming increasingly desperate.

---

35. Ibid., p. 432.

36. Pralay Kanungo, *RSS's Tryst with Politcs: From Hedgewar to Sudarshan*, Manohar, New Delhi, 2002, p. 54.

37. Government of India, Home Department, File No. 28/5/46—Pol (I), P. 15, NAI, New Delhi.

38. Mountbatten Papers (Microfilm), Reel 13, File 117/13/1-6, 'Private Armies, Secretary, Governor, Central Provinces & Berar', 26 May 1947, NMML, New Delhi.

Partition seemed imminent, the only uncertainty about it being when it would take place. The RSS was racing, almost unimpeded now, towards an approaching confrontation, and the colonial government seemed paralyzed.

During this period, the RSS made massive inroads among Hindus, but also among state employees, including railwaymen and local police forces, especially in UP, Delhi and Punjab.[39] It did not only expand its network of shakhas in areas such as the NWFP, Sind, Punjab, Delhi, UP or Bihar, where it had been present before, but also made intrusions into regions such as Assam, where it had previously been unknown.[40]

In UP, the RSS had gradually been building up its forces even before the rioting in Calcutta in August 1946. In June, for example, the state intelligence noted that the RSS was growing rapidly: 'In Meerut, a well organized and disciplined camp of some 1200 members has been opened; in Benaras 1000 officers [trained swayamsevaks] have been trained; a new branch has been started at Harduaganj in the Aligarh district; and further enlistments are reported in Muttra [Mathura].'[41] In July, according to another intelligence report, 'The RSS has been carrying on their usual routine activities in many districts of the province. At Hathras instructors are being trained who will be expected to go in the countryside and train new volunteers.'[42]

---

39. William Gould, *Religion and Conflict in Modern South Asia*, Cambridge University Press, New York, 2012, pp. 180-181.

40. Government of India, Home Department (Political), File No. 22/3/1947-Poll. (I), Express Letter, Home Department to the Chief Commissioners, 9 January 1947, NAI, New Delhi.

41. Government of India, Home Department (Political), Extracts from Fortnightly Report for the United Provinces for the first half of June 1946, File No. 18/6/46, NAI, New Delhi.

42. Government of United Provinces, Extracts from Weekly Report No. 27, 5 July 1946, CID Records, UP State Acrhives, Lucknow.

In the aftermath of the Calcutta killings, the RSS in UP escalated its activities, often creating panic in an attempt to entice Hindus to join its ranks against Muslims. On 18 August 1946, the RSS organized a massive rally in Aligarh.[43] There were reports suggesting that daily meetings of hundreds of swayamsevaks now started taking place even in the state's central and eastern districts like Kanpur, Etah and Gorakhpur, and at Mathura, the local RSS deliberately organized meetings in Muslim residential areas.[44]

In November, the province was shaken by a massive communal riot that competed with Calcutta in its carnage. It started during a local religious fair near Garhmukteshwar, a small market town in an area of UP dominated by fierce Hindu Jats. The next day, the killings continued in the Muslim quarters of Garhmukteshwar town. Muslim casualties ran into hundreds. Witnesses suggested that RSS men were at the core of this riot.[45] As pointed out by historian Willliam Gould, the involvement of the RSS allowed attacks to be carefully planned.[46]

V

No other province in India was so shaken by the events and emotions generated in the run-up to Partition as Punjab. Embittered by heightened polarization, the province seemed readying itself for such horrific ordeals and brutal massacres that would keep reverberating for ages. Quietly, discreetly, virtually unnoticed by

43. William Gould, *Hindu Nationalism and the Language of Politics in Late Colonial India*, Cambridge University Press, New York, 2004, p. 257.

44. Ibid.

45. AICC Papers, File No. 20/1946, 'Statement of Major General Shah Nawaz Khan', Manuscript Section, NMML, New Delhi; O. P. Singal, 'What happened at Garhmukteshwar', *People's Age*, 22 December 1946.

46. William Gould, *Religion and Conflict in Modern South Asia*, Cambridge University Press, New York, 2012, p. 181.

the rest of the country, the RSS as well as the private armies of Sikhs and Muslims embarked—even before the Muslim League's call for Direct Action Day—on hoarding arms and ammunitions in almost every part of the province. There are indications that the colonial authorities did not comprehensively collect rifles and guns from former soldiers of the Indian Army returning from the Second World War and even sold to civilians empty bombshells and chemicals used later in the riots before and after Partition.[47]

At the time, Golwalkar's close associate Madhavrao Muley was the Sangh's prantpracharak, the organization's chief, in Punjab. Evidence suggests that Muley was personally involved in the collection of arms by RSS men in the state. Balvir Sharma, an RSS worker at Montgomery in Punjab, claimed in an interview that Muley 'entrusted him with two jobs—to bring arms from Bikaner via Abohar and take them to Lahore, and to train workers in their use'.[48] Sharma also spoke of the accidental killing of a senior RSS man, Hansraj Kamboj, during the training in 'capped' rifle firing. 'In capped rifles you have to fill the barrel with gunpowder, so a bag of gunpowder was kept nearby,' he recounted. He added:

> Hansraj was firing shots at a target one after the other. Thrice in a row nothing happened, but when he pressed the trigger the fourth time a spark from the gun fell on the bag of gunpowder. With a big bang the powder exploded, Hansraj's clothes caught fire, and he suffered fatal burns. [...] In his dying declaration, he told the police that he was scorched by a gas lamp that had exploded, so the matter ended there.[49]

---

47. Clemens Six, *Secularism, Decolonisation, and the Cold War in South and Southeast Asia*, Routledge, London and New York, 2018, p. 93.

48. Manik Chandra Vajpayee & Shridhar Paradkar, *Partition-Days: The Fiery Saga of RSS*, Suruchi Prakashan, Delhi, 2002, p. 162.

49. Ibid.

Such accidents were not uncommon, especially during the making of bombs. In one instance, two senior office-bearers of the RSS—Tehsil pracharak Vishwanath and Nagar karyavah Madanlal—were seriously injured while making a bomb in a factory owned by the organization's Nagar sanghchalak at Pakpattan in Punjab. The explosion was so powerful that it created panic in the town. The case could be hushed up only with the support of RSS sympathizers in the local police.[50]

There are credible accounts that the RSS in Punjab had found definite ways to obtain firearms and impart training in their use to their swayamsevaks. Places in the NWFP, especially Peshawar, 'where weapons were plentifully available', constituted one of the important sources of firearms, while Montgomery's district pracharak Ramdutt was considered an expert in preparing a 'plan' for safe procurement of the consignment.[51] According to Om Prakash Dutt Vaidya, a prominent RSS man in Lahore and the in-charge of 40 shakhas, 'Training in bombs and pistols was given in the pits on the banks of the Ravi [river] and in the fields. Shooting tests were also carried out here. The centres were changed from time to time. The whole operation was carried out so systematically that none knew about it.'[52]

Vaidya also revealed that the RSS had a separate intelligence wing in Punjab, and its operatives wore Muslim dresses. 'They were well-versed in Muslim customs,' he recounted. 'Some had even got *Sunnat* [circumcision] done. These people posed as Muslim League workers, gained the confidence of the League leaders, and relayed information about their plans to Sangh leaders.'[53]

In Punjab, the RSS was only one of several volunteer

50. Ibid., pp. 172-173.

51. Ibid., p. 171.

52. Ibid., pp. 80-81.

53. Ibid., p. 81.

organizations that amassed arms and ammunitions. The Muslim League's volunteer wing, Muslim National Guards, was also in the same spree. So were several extremist Sikh groups, including the Akal Saina. The RSS found in the Sikh groups—who were ripe with grievances on the prospects of Partition—a readymade ally and cooperated closely with them. In January 1947, the colonial provincial government in Punjab banned the RSS and some other radical organizations as it was revealed that they were stockpiling weapons.[54] But the ban remained in place for less than a week. The government authorities lifted it in response to widespread protests not only by RSS members but also by a large number of supporters who considered the Hindutva outfit vital for local Hindu communities.[55]

VI

Around the time when Madhavrao Muley was guiding the RSS in stockpiling pistols and bombs in Punjab, another of Golwalkar's lieutenants, Vasantrao Oak, was quietly giving a sinister turn to the Sangh's activities in Delhi. On 23 November 1946, Oak held a meeting of more than two hundred prominent RSS workers in Delhi and decided to investigate the 'number of Muslim residents of the vicinity dominated by the Hindus' and also the 'number of Muslims able to take part in riots'.[56] They also resolved that 'all the Hindus of Delhi and surrounding places should be armed' and supplied with knives and daggers.[57] Sikhs were called upon to keep their kirpans (swords) ready and Hindus were asked to

54. Clemens Six, *Secularism, Decolonisation, and the Cold War in South and Southeast Asia*, Routledge, London and New York, 2018, p. 94.

55. Ibid.

56. Delhi Police Records, File No—409, p. 34, Manuscript Section, NMML, New Delhi.

57. Ibid.

store all available firearms in local temples, ready for the 'times of emergency'.[58]

Golwalkar, who was in Punjab around the middle of November, wanted to visit Delhi ahead of this meeting, but, as he wrote to his associate Babasaheb Apte, he dropped the idea due to 'some prohibitory orders' in the national capital and went instead to Kanpur in UP.[59] It is not clear what kind of prohibitory orders were in place those days in Delhi, but it was definite that Golwalkar was closely monitoring the Sangh's activities in the national capital as well as in its neighbouring areas—Punjab and UP.

As in Punjab, the Sangh's close cooperation with radical Sikhs helped it in Delhi, too. According to an intelligence report of Delhi Police, 'Some Sikh members of the Sangh are reported to be taking prominent part in supplying the members of the Sangh with lethal weapons including daggers, kirpans, etc., which they succeed in procuring from Gurdwara Sis Gunj and the shops adjoining it.'[60] Another intelligence report suggests that in the beginning of 1947, Jugal Kishore Birla, a big industrialist who was among the main donors of the RSS, bought a large number of steel helmets for swayamsevaks.[61] For undeclared reasons, months before Independence, the RSS added the steel helmet to the uniform of its swayamsevaks[62]—a fact that lent encouragement to theories that the Sangh was gearing up for an impending showdown.

---

58. Ibid.

59. M. S. Golwalkar Papers, Roll No—12269, Golwalkar's letter to Babasaheb Apte dated 21 November 1946, Part V, p. 22, Microfilm Section, NMML, New Delhi.

60. Delhi Police Record, File No. 405, p. 25, Manuscript Section, NMML, New Delhi.

61. Delhi Police Records, V Inst., File No. 137, p. 43, Manuscript Section, NMML, New Delhi.

62. Ibid., p. 46.

In fact, so emboldened did the RSS feel in Delhi that it planned a three-day rally in the city from 25 to 27 January 1947, for an anticipated 40,000 volunteers.[63] The first two days were strictly to be a gathering of volunteers, but on the third day, the RSS planned to welcome the general public.[64] To this end, the RSS booked practically every dharamshala (religious guest house) available in Delhi and organized 125 horses to be used during the rally.[65] As the preparations gained momentum, Delhi Police banned the rally on 20 January.[66] The RSS and the Hindu Mahasabha responded to this order with organized public protests and asked Hindus in Delhi to keep their shops shut for one day. As per a Delhi Police Intelligence report, 'The Hindu Mahasabha and the R.S.S.S. succeeded in bringing about a complete hartal of Hindu shopkeepers in the city on the 25th January. In the evening a meeting was held by the Hindu Sabha attended by about 23,000 persons to protest against the ban imposed on the R.S.S.S. rally in Delhi.'[67]

It is striking how the colonial authorities rarely got beyond crisis management when it came to dealing with the RSS. There were not only frequent reports of the outfit growing menacingly in the national capital but also occasional instances of arrests of RSS men on specific charges of attack on minorities. On 4 and 5 November 1946, for example, nine members of the RSS were arrested for demolishing 'a Pir's tomb' in Delhi's Nangloi locality.[68]

---

63. Delhi Police Record, File No. 413, p. 12, Manuscript Section, NMML, New Delhi.

64. Ibid.

65 Ibid.

66. Ibid., p. 41.

67. Ibid., p. 27.

68. Delhi Police Record, File No. 409, p. 16, Manuscript Section, NMML, New Delhi.

But the authorities never tried to act firmly. If they failed, it was certainly not for the lack of their ability to control private armies; it had much more to do with their intention. This was what many Congress leaders generally felt. As reported by the intelligence department of Delhi Police, at a meeting of workers of the Delhi Congress held on 11 November 1946, 'Mrs. Asaf Ali said that the present disturbances in the country were being engineered by the British with the help of reactionary parties such as the Muslim League, the Hindu Mahasabha and the Rashtriya Swayam Sewak Sangh with the object of discrediting the Congress and proving to the outside world that Indians were not fit to rule themselves.'[69]

At any rate, the Sangh's growing presence in Delhi and its neighbourhood created a springboard which would soon help Golwalkar start the work on his political fantasia in full swing.

69. Ibid., p. 23.

Guruji and Guns

By the beginning of 1947, Golwalkar's political climb was complete. In establishing his hold over the RSS and in spreading it across major parts of the country, he had made important progress. Despite all odds, he could preserve, over the long haul, the Sangh's hopes, its conception of its aims and his own image of the chosen leader. By his exceptional capacity to evoke loyalty, he demonstrated, in his own way, his talent for leadership. He liked to be called Guruji—an expression that accorded sacred nature to his authority and invested him with messianic qualities. This not only raised his status as someone more exalted than ordinary people but also gave him the nimbus of a godly man entrusted with accomplishing a task of divine significance. Members and supporters of the RSS seemed to believe that their punctiliousness in their respect for Golwalkar would tantamount to their devotion to the idea of a Hindu Rashtra.

Golwalkar himself soaked up this basic change in his status. He dressed in silk kurta and white cotton dhoti and sported wire-rimmed glasses, and his travels—which were unusually frequent now—became expensive. Around the beginning of 1947 he seemed to stop travelling by train and started spending increasing amounts on flight tickets. On 19 January 1947, for example, he wrote to Oak from Calcutta that he would reach Delhi on 24 January by plane and, after staying there for four days, he would take the morning flight on 28 January for Nagpur.[1] Such descriptions of his flight details now became a regular feature of his letters. Golwalkar's lavish expenditures indicate a sudden transformation in the financial health of the RSS. The organization had suffered from a chronic shortage of funds during the early years. Even as late as in the middle of the 1940s, Golwalkar could not afford to travel by plane or even in the first class compartment of a train. But as Partition started seeming imminent and the RSS's feverish activities brought it more into the forefront, the organization's financial predicament began to improve.

There is no doubt that the RSS still derived its basic income from its members' contributions—called guru dakshina or offering to the guru—once a year and small donations from Hindu shop-owners on special occasions. Henceforth, the RSS could also count on a wide circle of financial benefactors and supporters who belonged to rich, and sometimes super rich, classes and seemed ready to support any group that promised to fight for establishing a Hindu Rashtra. A report of the intelligence department of Delhi Police listed six such big business benefactors of the RSS in the national capital itself—Seth Laxmi Narain Gadodia, a business magnet of Delhi; Lala Hans Raj Gupta, Ghasi Ram Lohia, Pratap Singh Lohia and Chiman Lal Lohia, all iron merchants of Delhi's Chaori Bazar; and industrialist Jugal Kishore Birla.[2]

Around the time, Golwalkar also managed to find ways to get patronage from many of the Hindu princes of north India. He owed a considerable part of the Sangh's entry into these principalities to the Hindu Mahasabha, which seemed to have

1. Golwalkar Papers, Roll No. 12269, pp. 34-35, 'Golwalkar to Basantrao Oak', Microfilm Section, NMML, New Delhi.

2. Delhi Police Records, File No. 417, pp. 30-31, Manuscript Section, NMML, New Delhi.

entered into an understanding with Hindu princes by promising to use its influence to support their efforts to preserve their autonomy. In fact, if the time was critical for the country, it was desperate for the princes, many of whom were toying with a variety of plans to avoid territorial merger with India or at least to preserve as much of their independence as possible after the British withdrawal. According to a report published in *The Times of India* on 24 April 1945, Savarkar, the supreme leader of the Hindu Mahasabha, had called Hindu princes 'the bedrock of Hindu Power' and advised his supporters 'not to take part in any subversive movements aimed at destroying' them. 'That [does] not mean [...] that they [members of Mahasabha] should not demand responsible government, but under the cover of demanding their rights, they should not undermine the power of the Princes, who are the bedrock of Hindu power,' it said, quoting Savarkar. 'Mr. Savarkar disagreed with those who said that the States were pillars of British imperialism and that they should be completely eliminated.'[3]

In consonance with this line, the Hindu Mahasabha acted as a robust advocate for Hindu princes, arguing strongly in public forums and in representations to the government in New Delhi that states should be allowed to remain in existence as internally autonomous entities within a loose-knit federal structure.[4] Because of this political position, most Hindu states opened their doors to Mahasabha leaders. The RSS also benefited handsomely from this alliance. Not only was the RSS allowed to work inside Hindu kingdoms openly without any official interference, but it was also extended all kinds of support from the princes and their subordinates.

3. *The Times of India*, 24 April 1945, p. 7.

4. Ian Copland, State, *Community and Neighbourhood in Princely North India, c. 1900–1950*, Palgrave Macmillan, New York, 2005, p. 112.

Golwalkar seemed to believe that his personal fate as well as the future of his political vision depended on the success of the Sangh's outreach to the national capital and the adjoining British provinces on the one hand and the Hindu principalities of north India on the other. He had to, therefore, strengthen the RSS in Delhi and its neighbourhood as well as win the trust of Hindu princes of the region. That is, he had to appear simultaneously as the leader determined to convert India into a Hindu Rashtra and as the defender of the rights of Hindu princes. He had to both threaten the system and play the part of its preserver in a manner that convinced his supporters in British-ruled provinces as well as the rulers of Hindu principalities. Golwalkar never seemed to have articulated this paradoxical strategy, and yet realizing these paradoxes remained the sole objective of almost everything that he did now.

II

The RSS pracharak with the deepest connections in the princely states of Rajputana was Ramraj Vyas, who worked under the direct supervision of Oak, the chief of the Sangh's Delhi Prant.[5] From the point of view of the Sangh, Delhi Prant included, apart from the national capital, the whole of Rajputana, the Ambala division of Punjab and western districts of the United Provinces. Vyas earlier headed the Jodhpur division of the RSS and was given charge of the Ajmer division in 1945.[6] Carrying the message of Golwalkar, he toured across Rajputana, contacted princes and, whenever required, arranged their meetings with Oak.[7]

5. Manik Chandra Vajpayee & Shridhar Paradkar, *Partition-Days: The Fiery Saga of RSS*, Suruchi Prakashan, Delhi, 2002, pp. 432-433

6. Ibid., p. 433.

7. Ibid.

One of the biggest successes for the RSS in the princely states came from principalities which were in the vicinity of Delhi—Alwar and Bharatpur. The two states had witnessed a considerable increase in the activities of the Hindu Mahasabha during the period after the Second World War. According to Mahavir Prasad Sharma, a swayamsevak based in Alwar, 'Sangh workers had a good relationship with the Maharaja [Tej Singh]. Swarupchand Mehta [a district pracharak in Alwar] had taken him [Maharaja] to a Sangh programme held in Delhi in 1946. He was greatly impressed with it, and became an admirer of Vasantrao Oke [sic.]'[8] The RSS profited even further after Hindu Mahasabha leader N. B. Khare became the prime minister of Alwar in April 1947.[9] Khare belonged to Nagpur and was a personal friend of Golwalkar. In a short while after assuming the charge, Khare made Alwar the training ground for a large number of RSS men with a definite plan that they would act as the nucleus of a movement for setting up of the Hindu Rashtra.[10]

With his encouragement, the RSS ran several training camps in the state. One of them, which was organized at Alwar town in May 1947 and attended by swayamsevaks from different parts of Rajputana, was addressed by Golwalkar himself. 'That year three training camps were held for Delhi Province (which till then included Rajasthan),' recounted Mahavir Prasad Sharma. 'The Alwar camp was attended by 1,300 trainees. Shri Guruji visited it and addressed its public valedictory function. The then [prime minister] of the state Dr. N.B. Khare and his entire Cabinet were present at the function.'[11]

8. Ibid., pp. 445-446.

9. Ian Copland, *State, Community and Neighbourhood in Princely North India, c. 1900–1950*, Palgrave Macmillan, New York, 2005, p. 119.

10. J. N. Sahni, *Fifty Years of Indian Politics: 1921-1971*, Allied Publishers, New Delhi, 1971, p. 303.

11. Manik Chandra Vajpayee & Shridhar Paradkar, *Partition-Days: The Fiery Saga of RSS*, Suruchi Prakashan, Delhi, 2002, p. 447.

On 8 July 1947, five weeks before Independence, Khare sent out a circular having Tej Singh's signature to Hindu leaders and friendly rulers of different principalities, inviting them to attend a convention in Delhi.[12] The two-day 'All India Hindus Convention', which was held on 9-10 August 1947, called for the establishment of a Hindu Rashtra 'to be officially called Hindusthan, with Sanskrit-based Hindi written in Devnagari script as the official language, with its flag saffron-coloured and Vande Mataram as its national anthem'.[13]

M. M. L. Hooja, the Assistant Director of the IB who closely monitored RSS activities in Alwar on the eve of Independence, claimed that the royal court did everything for the Sangh to help it raise a militia of armed Hindu men ready to turn any area into a hot battle zone. 'There were considerable evidence of patronage and aid to the R.S.S.,' he asserted. 'Full facilities were provided for the training camp and rally organized in May-June 1947 of R.S.S. officers. This was given under the direct orders of the Prime Minister [Khare] and the Home Minister [Raghuvir Singh] apparently with the knowledge of the ruler. Both Prime Minister and the Home Minister took prominent part in R.S.S. activities and the Prime Minister was in constant touch with all local activities and extended fullest patronage.'[14]

The state's patronage of the RSS was visible in the past too. Hooja remembered how Alwar provided military training to three batches of swayamsevaks belonging to Delhi, the United Provinces and other parts of the country between November 1946 and

12. Ian Copland, *State, Community and Neighbourhood in Princely North India, c. 1900–1950*, Palgrave Macmillan, New York, 2005, pp. 143-144.

13. AICC Papers, File No. G-7/1946-48, Roll No. 8668, p. 133, Microfilm Section, NMML, New Delh.

14. Report of the Commission of Inquiry into Conspiracy to Murder Mahatma Gandhi, Part I, p. 242, Government of India, 1970.

February 1947. 'The whole scheme was well organized,' he said. 'The R.S.S. volunteers were put up in the Old Pratap Paltan lines but they made their own food arrangements. The training of volunteers included physical training, bayonet exercises, drill and rifle exercises. They also did firing practice with muzzle-loaders. Some were given secret training in rifle and revolver practice. Part of the expenses [was] borne by the Home Minister [Raghuvir Singh] either from the secret funds of the state or from the non-official subscriptions raised by him.'[15]

By the time India gained independence, Alwar had in place proper supply lines to help the RSS organize its camps and rallies. 'It was in the form of supply of petrol, furniture, accommodation, essential and controlled articles, electricity, etc. which were given under the orders of the Prime Minister and the Home Minister with the knowledge of the Ruler,' Hooja recounted. 'Dr. Khare also attended the functions of the R.S.S. and its rallies at Rajgarh. Besides some Ministers and high officials, the Ruler also attended a R.S.S. function at Bansur 34 miles away from Alwar.'[16]

Prompted by an identity crisis similar to Alwar's, and equally seeking post-Independence autonomous status, Bharatpur, a neighbouring princely state, was experiencing the same developments. A comparable version of rapport between the royal court and the RSS emerged in Bharatpur. In the state, the RSS activities had begun in 1942, and by 1946, Golwalkar had developed good relations with the ruler, Brijendra Singh.[17] In fact, Brijendra Singh even called an all-India conference of RSS sanghchalaks in 1946. The conference was organized at the military headquarters at Kanjoli Line in Bharatpur, and it was presided

15. Ibid.

16. Ibid., p. 243.

17. Shail Mayaram, *Resisting Regimes: Myth, Memory and the Shaping of a Muslim Identity*, Oxford University Press, Delhi, 1997, pp. 171-172.

over by Golwalkar.[18]

Bharatpur was a Jat-dominated principality. In the mid-1940s, its ruler harboured the notion of an independent state of Jats and believed that Jats in Bharatpur as well as in Delhi and other neighbouring areas were with him in creating a separate state of 'Jatistan'. Ahead of Independence, Brijendra Singh even got a map of this putative state drawn along with its 'borders'.[19] It seems that the Hindutva organizations' advocacy of a strong Hindu militia to be able to fight successfully for the domination of Hindus in India made their worldview cohere with the Bharatpur ruler's own ambitions, and this turned him into 'a very staunch and a determined patron of the Hindu Mahasabha movement and the Rashtriya Swayam Sevak Sangh'.[20]

Bachchu Singh, the ambitious and impetuous younger brother of Brijendra Singh, found in this transitional period of political change a good opportunity of building Bharatpur into virtually a mini-Hindu Rashtra. There were allegations that the king and his brother had a direct hand in some brutal attacks against Muslims and the looting of their property in Bharatpur.[21] Bachchu Singh was also instrumental in building up a powerful RSS cell in the state.[22] Bharatpur's police and military supported the RSS, while the royal court provided it with all kinds of assistance, financial and otherwise.[23] The RSS used the exhibition grounds of Bharatpur

18. Ibid.

19. Ian Copland, *State, Community and Neighbourhood in Princely North India, c. 1900–1950*, Palgrave Macmillan, New York, 2005, pp. 135-136.

20. Shail Mayaram, *Resisting Regimes: Myth, Memory and the Shaping of a Muslim Identity*, Oxford University Press, Delhi, 1997, p. 172.

21. J. N. Sahni, *Fifty Years of Indian Politics: 1921-1971*, Allied Publishers, New Delhi, 1971, p. 304.

22. Ibid.

23. Shail Mayaram, *Resisting Regimes: Myth, Memory and the Shaping of a Muslim Identity*, Oxford University Press, Delhi, 1997, p. 171.

for the parades of its swayamsevaks and the state's forests for its weekend camps; Golwalkar himself took salute in one such camp in July 1947.[24] Bharatpur also covertly set up a factory for the production of weapons and munitions. Much of this weaponry would end up in the hands of rogue militias linked to the RSS.[25]

In a broad sense, then, Golwalkar had come to enjoy deep relations with darbars of Bharatpur and Alwar. By the time of Independence and Partition, the two states had become areas of increasing strategic importance for the RSS as they acted as significant bases for military and political training of swayamsevaks. Trainees, both local as well as those from outside, were rushed through intensive courses before being sent back to their respective locations in Delhi and its neighbourhood.

III

At least some part in helping the RSS establish its bases in the princely states of north India was played by the religious heads—dharma gurus—of the rulers. This aspect of the Sangh's expansion in princely states of north India was to be among the experiences that would shape Golwalkar's attitudes towards sadhus in later years. According to intelligence reports, two dharma gurus who proved to be of particular importance for the RSS at this juncture were Swami Madhavanand in Rajputana and Swami Sant Dev in Jammu and Kashmir.

Swami Madhavanand's reputation at the time was ambiguous. He was regarded by Rajput princes as a scholar of Sanskrit, and he had the habit of calling everyone 'my son'. At the same time, he had an exalted sense of his own mission. He was the president of the All India States' Hindu Mahasabha, the name of the Hindu

---

24. Ibid.

25. Ian Copland, *State, Community and Neighbourhood in Princely North India, c. 1900–1950*, Palgrave Macmillan, New York, 2005, p. 143

Mahasabha wing that worked in princely states. He considered that Rajputs, by virtue of being a martial caste, were the only 'capable class' to rule. As such, one of his main concerns was 'conversion of Muslims and Hindus to Rajputs' in order to ensure 'protection of the country'.[26]

Swami Madhavanand was the guru of the young Maharaja of Jodhpur. He had followings in multiple states of Rajputana but operated mainly from Jodhpur. Intelligence officers believed that he exercised control over almost every aspect of Jodhpur state, from the transfers and postings of the state's officials to the marriage relations in the ruling household.[27] 'This Swami, who has been exploiting the Maharani of Jodhpur for his selfish ends, lives in Jodhpur in a palatial building specially constructed for him,' said an intelligence report. 'He professes to possess many spiritual qualities of an extraordinary nature and is known as "Shri Bhagwan" among thousands of his admirers. He is anti-Congress and pro-Rajput and is responsible for organizing the Rajputs under the auspices of the "Rajasthan Kshatriya Sabha" of which he is the virtual dictator. He has been instrumental in strengthening the RSS in the Rajputana states.'[28]

Swami Madhavanand had the habit of getting his 'miracles' published in local newspapers. He also had his own 'propaganda machinery' which publicized all his activities. He moved between palaces and was known to carry 'princely intrigues' from state to state. According to an intelligence report, 'Hindu Sabha, R.S.S. and communalist leaders' were always found with him. 'He is their brain trust [sic.] and financer in the sense he orders princes to help them.'[29]

---

26. Government of India, Ministry of States, File No. 74-p/48, Vol I (Secret), 1948, p. 165A, NAI, New Delhi.

27. Ibid.

28. Ibid., p. 153.

29. Ibid., p. 165A.

In Jammu and Kashmir, Golwalkar could muster even more weighty and dynamic support from the ruler's personal guru, Swami Sant Dev. In fact, it was Sant Dev who encouraged the RSS to open offices in Jammu city and several other provincial towns during the early 1940s.[30] 'During 1943 the activities of the Sangh definitely seem to have been on the increase in Jammu and to have spread to the rural areas of the Province,' noted an intelligence report prepared in February 1944. 'During 1943 and up to January 1944 four more branches were opened in Jammu itself, and new branches in the Udhampur, Mirpur, Riasi and Kathua Districts, mainly by members of the Jammu branch.'[31]

Having built a secure foundation under the protection of Sant Dev in Jammu, the RSS grew fast in the state after the talks of Partition began to polarize the society on religious lines. In time, as Independence approached, the king's personal insecurity also mounted, and he started looking at the RSS as a favourable ally. His insecurity even led him to facilitate the influx of swayamsevaks from neighbouring Punjab. In early 1947, for example, some 2,000 trained RSS cadres entered the state, apparently by arrangement with the darbar.[32]

An era was ending, and the shudder was being felt by most princes. The British rule had acted as a guarantee for their power and privilege, but it had begun to come apart. The increasingly well-organized praja mandals, the legitimate organizations of people living in princely states, had started to call for the end

---

30. Ian Copland, *State, Community and Neighbourhood in Princely North India, c. 1900–1950,* Palgrave Macmillan, New York, 2005, p. 119.

31. Government of India, Political Department ('P' Branch), File No. 190-P (S), 1943-44, p. 109, NAI, New Delhi.

32. Ian Copland, *State, Community and Neighbourhood in Princely North India, c. 1900–1950*, Palgrave Macmillan, New York, 2005, p. 119.

of monarchies. The RSS, on the other hand, promised loyalty to Hindu rulers. Many of these princes, therefore, seemed ready to provide their money and favour to ensure the expansion of the RSS in their states as it constituted a useful counterweight to praja mandals.

IV

Clearly, while Golwalkar kept whipping the RSS on, these successes were not entirely the result of his drive. Rather, the growing anxiety and insecurity of Hindus in the British provinces and the rulers of princely states in north India came to his aid. In the run-up to Partition, Hindus listened to horrifying stories of atrocities and the rulers stared at the prospect of losing their principalities and privileges. With remarkable instinct, Golwalkar grasped these feelings of panic, uncertainty and anxiety and became super active in order to reap the maximum dividend from what seemed to be an imminent catastrophe. To be sure, there was no change in the staples of his propaganda: the need for a Hindu Rashtra, retention of Hindu monarchies as the core of new India and, above all, the Muslim conspiracy to partition the country. But now each of these items could easily be linked with the crisis that an increasingly large number of people were getting conscious of.

In fact, Golwalkar surpassed all other Hindutva leaders in giving a political colour to his personal wishes and the despairs of a significant section of Hindu masses and feudal elites. The swift and overwhelming support the RSS received from them infused him with extraordinary confidence. Without any prior consultation or decision, a loose coalition of varied segments of the Hindu society was gradually emerging under his undeclared leadership.

How did Golwalkar himself regard his new status? The evidence is thin but it nonetheless makes plain that with his latest success he started spending more of his time in north India, with Delhi increasingly becoming the locus of his activities. His letters show that he flew into Delhi every now and then as if the national capital was moving more and more into the centre of some kind of his strategy.[33] He also travelled extensively to western districts of the United Provinces, Punjab and the princely states of Alwar and Bharatpur.

Oak, Golwalkar's chief aide in the region, proved to be a particular workhorse. He was exceptionally well organized and seemed to pride himself on putting in long hours in managing the RSS activities in a vast area that included Delhi, Rajputana, parts of Punjab and the western districts of UP. As the day of Independence on 15 August 1947 approached, intelligence officers started reporting that the RSS units under Oak accelerated the movement of large batches of swayamsevaks to western UP, Alwar and Bharatpur for training. 'About 1000 Swayam Sewaks and Adhikaris of the Delhi Sangh are going to attend a camp in Muttra which will start from 30th May,' they reported on 28 May 1947.[34] Another report filed on 29 May said Oak had also left to supervise the month-long camp.[35]

A growing effort to radicalize the RSS workers by its office-bearers was also noted in an intelligence report dated 31 May: 'During the month under report the "Adhikaris" [RSS office-bearers] have been exhorting the volunteers that the time was approaching when they would be required to undertake the work for which the Sangh was organized.'[36] Addressing a meeting of 'about 2000 volunteers and Adhikaris' in Delhi on

---

33. Golwalkar Papers, Roll No. 12269, Microfilm Section, NMML, New Delhi.

34. Delhi Police Records, File No. 416, p. 8, Manuscript Section, NMML, New Delhi.

35. Ibid., p. 13.

36. Ibid., p. 21.

the occasion of the Hindu festival of Guru Puja on 3 July 1947, Oak said:

> We hope that when we celebrate Guru Puja next year, we would be free, we would stand with a new life and the Hindu nation would plant its saffron coloured flag. Had the Hindus realised this essence, they would not have been in this sad plight. There is still time that the Hindus should change their views and establish the Hindu nation. [...] The time is not far off when the saffron flag of Hindus will fly throughout India.[37]

Under Oak, the RSS in the Delhi zone was not just indulging in normal drills or rhetorical speeches. He was also in regular contact with the two safe havens in Bharatpur and Alwar where training in arms and ammunition was being provided to swayamsevaks. 'Some workers [of the RSS] were invited by the Bharatpur State authorities to visit their State for training in the use of modern weapons,' noted an intelligence report filed on 31 July 1947, a fortnight before Independence. 'Volunteers from 20 to 25 years of age are being selected and it is believed that they are being sent outside for training.'[38]

These occasional reports by intelligence officers on the eve of Partition and Independence were usually overlooked. But there was little doubt that the RSS was up to something extremely violent. The signals were critical, though no one seemed to know what exactly was being devised quietly, almost secretly. The RSS swayamsevaks might have been a ragtag unit of volunteers in the past, but they were now 'very dangerous enemies of peace' in India, at least in the evaluation of Lieutenant General Sir Francis Tuker, who was the chief of the Indian army's eastern command

---

37. Delhi Police Records, File No. 414, pp. 13-15, Manuscript Section, NMML, New Delhi.

38. Ibid., p. 37.

from January 1946 to November 1947.[39]

Golwalkar was no longer just pushing the RSS into new areas; he was shaping the battlefield in the strategically important region of the national capital at the time of a massive communal escalation.

39. Sir Francis Tuker, *While Memory Serves*, Cassell and Company Ltd, London, 1950, pp. 281-282.

Riots and the RSS

For almost three weeks after India's Independence on 15 August 1947, Delhi was peaceful but there was panic. The violence in Punjab, one of the two provinces that were divided, was getting worse. At the end of August, even Calcutta, the capital of the other partitioned province of Bengal, detonated. And yet, the scale and awfulness of what was underway did not reach Delhi, despite a large influx of Hindu and Sikh refugees from Pakistan carrying—because of what they had to suffer—a strong anti-Muslim feeling.

But on 4 September, smoke started unfurling from Muslim residential quarters of Old Delhi.[1] Within the next twenty-four hours, the capital was in turmoil. Blood-chilling incidents of murder and loot started occurring on an hourly basis. A bomb exploded in Fatehpuri Masjid, a seventeenth-century mosque near Chandni Chowk in the heart of Old Delhi.[2] In Karol Bagh, between New and Old Delhi, a mob entered a local high school while an examination was on and 'called on the boys of one community to stand and they were butchered [outside the examination hall]',

---

1. G. D. Khosla Papers, Subject File No. 21, p. 8, Manuscript Section, NMML, New Delhi.

2. Ibid., p. 10.

the *News Chronicle* reported on 6 September.[3] The same day, a bomb was thrown into New Delhi's packed railway station, aimed at fleeing Muslims.[4] On 7 September, attacks on Muslims spread all across Delhi and happened so simultaneously and so brutally that many thought they must have been planned.[5] That day, an outburst of violence was noted for the first time in Connaught Place, the huge central market plaza of New Delhi, where Hindu and Sikh mobs began to loot Muslim-owned shops.[6]

On 7 and 8 September, the attacks spread to some of the best guarded areas of New Delhi. A Hindu mob of over 400 gathered outside the Willingdon Aerodrome and began attacking Muslim employees.[7] In Connaught Place, an enraged Prime Minister Nehru stopped his passing car, grabbed a baton from police personnel who were standing by idly, and personally dispersed some looters near Odeon cinema.[8] On 8 September, while touring disturbed localities, Nehru rescued two Muslim girls from one of the worst-affected areas in Old Delhi and gave them shelter in his own house.[9]

By the evening of 7 September, about 6,000 Muslims fled from their homes in the privileged Lodhi Colony area to Connaught Place's 'Pak Transfer Office', which was responsible for organizing

---

3. *News Chronicle* (6 September 1947), cited in Gyanendra Pandey, *Remembering Partition: Violence, Nationalism and History in India*, Cambridge University Press, 2001, p. 129.

4. Alex von Tunzelmann, *Indian Summer: The Secret History of the end of an Empire*, Simon & Schuster UK Ltd, London, 2007, p. 269.

5. Ibid., p. 270.

6. G. D. Khosla Papers, Subject File No. 21, p. 12, Manuscript Section, NMML, New Delhi.

7. Ibid., p. 13.

8. Gyanendra Pandey, *Remembering Partition: Violence, Nationalism and History in India*, Cambridge University Press, 2001, p. 130.

9. *The Times of India*, 9 September 1947.

the transport of Pakistani government officials and property to Pakistan.[10] The following day, the number of refugees in the 'Pak Transfer Office' increased to 12,000, and the place practically took the shape of a refugee camp.[11] By now, thousands of Muslims were in full flight from across Delhi, clustering in any part of the city that offered at least a modicum of security: Jama Masjid, Muslim graveyards, Mughal ruins, houses and gardens of well-known Muslims like union ministers Maulana Abul Kalam Azad and Rafi Ahmed Kidwai, the Pakistan High Commission and such other places which provided the idea of strength in numbers.[12] When these overflowed, refugees hurried into huge camps that had been set up by the government in Purana Quila and Humayun's Tomb.

Outside the camps, the situation kept worsening. Sabzimandi, where the local Muslims had already been subjected to several rounds of attacks, witnessed on 8 September a pitched battle between troops and rioters, leaving the 'roads littered with bodies' and the town 'burnt to ashes'.[13] On 9 September, Paharganj, a mixed locality north of Connaught Place, was reported to be 'like a battle-field with blazing houses, hordes of refugees, dead cattle and horses and the rattle' of machine-gun fire in the air.[14] On 10 September, the attack spread to Bara Hindu Rao, on the north side of Old Delhi, and more than 5,000 Muslim residents had to be evacuated the following morning. Trains were searched and Muslims were killed in cold blood. 'Before the arrival of

---

10. Gyanendra Pandey, *Remembering Partition: Violence, Nationalism and History in India*, Cambridge University Press, 2001, p. 123.

11. Ibid.

12. Ibid.

13. Sir Terence Shone to Secretary of State for Commonwealth Relations, 12 September 1947, TNA: PREM 8/584, cited in Alex von Tunzelmann, *Indian Summer: The Secret History of the end of an Empire*, Simon & Schuster UK Ltd, London, 2007, p. 271.

14. *Daily Mirror*, 9 September 1947.

Mahatmaji [on 9 September], I think, at least 8,000 to 10,000 Muslims were killed in Delhi alone,' recounted Jugal Kishore Khanna, a Special Magistrate who was posted in the Delhi railway station area and used to send daily reports to M. S. Randhawa, the Deputy Commissioner of Delhi.[15]

'Delhi became a prison for the Muslims,' wrote Ishtiaq Husain Qureshi, a professor of history in Delhi University, in an account of his family's and his escape from the university campus in September 1947. He continued:

> I lived on the campus of the university. In close proximity was Jawaharnagar which was a Rashtriya Svem Seva Sangh stronghold. The camps of the [Hindu and Sikh] refugees were also quite near. The arrival of the refugees naturally raised a wave of sympathy for them. I tried my best to accommodate and help refugee students because it would have been inhuman not to try to mitigate human suffering. The feelings of the Hindus and the Sikhs were greatly embittered for which no blame could attach to them. Soon after armed Sikhs and others were seen roaming in and around the campus. [...] My movements were watched throughout the day and [in] the night some agent of Rashtriya Svem Seva Sangh was posted at a vantage point to keep an eye on all those who came to see me. A student whom I knew to be a Rashtriya Svem Seva Sangh member came a little too often to see me. Some Muslim friends pointed it out to me that I was in a precarious situation, but there was little I could do. There was a small Muslim community on the campus and if I had left, their morale could have collapsed.
>
> At last the inevitable happened. The Muslim inhabitants of Timarpur, which was within a mile of the campus, were attacked. Stabbings around the campus became common. [One fine] morning the campus was attacked. There was no loss of

15. Shri Jugal Kishore Khanna, Oral History Transcripts, Oral History Project, pp. 133-134, Manuscript Section, NMML, New Delhi.

> life, but all Muslim houses were looted, one by one. Muslim students and teachers were evacuated with difficulty. We escaped in our car. Women hastily put on Hindu caste marks on their foreheads and put on Hindu clothes. I took them to Pakistan High Commission. The streets were littered with dead bodies. My nine year old son looked up and said simply, 'Father, are you afraid?' I said truthfully, 'No.' I had no emotion at that time. Our house was looted soon after.[16]

Qureshi put his family in the refugee camp of Purana Quila and joined the rescue work in the city along with some other members of the community. A few days later, as the siege of Muslims in Delhi continued, he and his family shifted to Pakistan.

II

More specifically, as far as Delhi was concerned, the siege of Muslims did not automatically follow the arrival of traumatized Hindu and Sikh refugees from Pakistan. It showed itself almost three weeks after Partition, thus indicating that Delhi's September turmoil was not solely the fallout of the anger of Hindus and Sikhs who had been ousted from Pakistan. As early as on 20 August 1947, merely five days after Partition, Alan Campbell-Johnson, the press attaché to Governor General Lord Mountbatten, made a diary entry about the seriousness the issue of Pakistani refugees had acquired in Delhi. 'The refugee problem,' he noted, 'is already assuming monstrous proportions.'[17] Hundreds of thousands of destitute refugees continued to pour into the city in the days to

---

16. I. H. Qureshi, 'A Case Study of the Social Relations between the Muslims and the Hindus, 1935-47', in C. H. Philips and Mary Doreen Wainwright (ed.), *The Partition of India: Policies and Perspectives*, George Allen and Unwin Ltd, London, 1970, p. 367-8.

17. Alan Campbell-Johnson, *Mission with Mountbatten*, Robert Hale Limited, London, 1951, p. 170.

come and yet, the situation, barring some isolated acts of violence, remained by and large under control.

No doubt, the creation of Pakistan as a homeland for Muslims and the subsequent flight of Hindus and Sikhs from that country led to a rise in intolerance among certain sections of refugees. But it did not on its own give way to the revolting events that shook Delhi during the first half of September. At least, that was the finding of intelligence officers and eye-witnesses. What they concluded was this: Partition and the increased intolerance among Hindu and Sikh refugees constituted a unique opportunity for RSS men to try to exterminate Muslims in Delhi and its neighbourhood in order to create panic and force the exodus of the entire minority community to Pakistan.

On 12 October, weeks after the September disturbances subsided, Golwalkar, in a meeting with the RSS office-bearers of Delhi, 'congratulated the Hindus' of Sabzimandi, Paharganj and Karol Bagh—the areas where Muslims suffered the most—and asked 'others to follow the example' set by them. 'The "Adhikaris" [office-bearers of the RSS] apprised "Guruji" of the happenings in Delhi,' said an intelligence report. It added:

> He blessed them and said that in future, also, they should save Hinduism in the same manner, and thus augment their strength. He warned them to keep alert always and never to trust Muslims. He added that they would have to put in one more effort to oust the Muslims from Delhi. Then, Delhi could be called 'Hindusthan'. He specially congratulated the Hindus of Sabzimandi, Paharganj & Karol Bagh areas for the work they had done in the disturbances and advised the others to follow the example set by them.[18]

18. Delhi Police Records, IX Inst., File No. 528, pp. 69-70, Manuscript Section, NMML, New Delhi.

The role of RSS men in the Delhi disturbances became even more evident in another report filed by the intelligence department of Delhi Police on 24 October. 'According to the Sangh volunteers, the R.S.S.S. stood for building the Hindus physically strong and for establishing Hindu rule in India,' said the report. 'In order to achieve their latter objective they would resort to warfare even but at present they were not allowed to enter into any open fighting against Muslims. So far the Sangh workers were acting in their individual capacity and were indulging in a sort of guerrilla warfare as was done by them in the recent disturbances in Delhi.'[19] Seen from the point of view of this report, the early September turmoil, which the intelligence official's dispatch referred to as 'recent disturbances in Delhi', was less a fallout of Partition than the first serious attempt by the RSS to set India in new ideological directions.

The fateful decisions secretly made, the intrigues, the treachery and the motives which led up to coordinated and massive attacks on Muslims—all this as well as the parts played by the principal actors behind the scenes have remained largely hidden from the outside world. It is also difficult to judge whether Golwalkar directly commanded the RSS men who took part in Delhi's disturbances. Even if he did not, these men, through the ideological classes during shakha training and by reading his book, *We or Our Nationhood Defined*, might still have known much of what Golwalkar was planning to achieve. In fact, practically all RSS members knew that their objective was to make India a Hindu Rashtra for which they needed to go all out to cleanse the country of Muslims.

That they did this quite faithfully was later found out by political scientist Thomas Blom Hansen. 'From my interviews with

19. Delhi Police Records, V Inst., File No. 138, p. 28, Manuscript Section, NMML, New Delhi.

older RSS men,' noted Hansen, 'it became clear that the communal carnage of Partition was seen as a kind of patriotic baptism, an initiation through blood and sacrifice to the nationalist cause, for the individuals involved as well as for the corporate RSS body.'[20]

At the time, however, many believed that the RSS men could not have succeeded in inflicting that much of damage in Delhi had they not received some kind of backing from M. S. Randhawa, the Sikh deputy commissioner of the city. 'The Muslims could not help noticing the coincidence that the Sikh deputy commissioner who was now always surrounded by the Rashtriya Svem Seva Sangh [sic.] would visit a village one day and the very next day its Muslim population would be exterminated,' recounted Ishtiaq Husain Qureshi. 'I had known him [Randhawa] earlier. He was sociable and had visited me in my house once or twice quite informally. He had admired my collection of Mughal miniatures. After my house had been looted, rumour has it that they found their way to his house.'[21]

III

Nehru was never uncertain as to who had been responsible for the Delhi disturbances. 'The information that has reached me from many sources indicates that the trouble in Delhi was caused by certain well organized bands, some Sikh and some Hindu,' he wrote to Sardar Vallabhbhai Patel, the Deputy Prime Minister and Home Minister. 'Probably most of the murders were committed by one or more organized and well-armed Sikh bands [...]. The

20. Thomas Blom Hansen, *The Saffron Wave: Democracy and Hindu Nationalism in Modern India*, Oxford University Press, New Delhi, 1999, p. 95.

21. I. H. Qureshi, 'A Case Study of the Social Relations between the Muslims and the Hindus, 1935-47', in C. H. Philips and Mary Doreen Wainwright (ed.), *The Partition of India: Policies and Perspectives*, George Allen and Unwin Ltd, London, 1970, p. 367.

Hindu bands seemed to owe allegiance to the RSS. It seems to me clear that the RSS have had a great deal to do with the present disturbances not only in Delhi but elsewhere.'[22]

Nor did Nehru have any doubt that what was happening in Delhi was inseparable from the ideology of Hindu Rashtra promoted by the RSS and the Hindu Mahasabha. He looked at the Delhi disturbances as something much more than a mere communal riot. To him, it was a very definite and 'a well-organised attempt of certain Sikh and Hindu fascist elements' to overturn the Government, or at least to break up its present character.[23]

At some point, shortly after the trouble began, Nehru went about the city to take stock of the situation and, during an informal interaction with some senior Delhi officials, including Chief Commissioner Khurshed Ahmed and Deputy Chief Commissioner Randhawa, he suggested that they trace and arrest the instigators of the disturbances. 'Randhawa seemed to think that the whole affair had been a spontaneous one and he could not think of any person who could be called an organizer or instigator,' Nehru wrote to Patel. 'This rather surprised me because it seemed pretty evident there was plenty of organisation behind the thing. Also it was stated definitely by some Delhi people that they were well-known persons who had organized and encouraged these disturbances.'[24]

During the interaction, Nehru also suggested to Randhawa that special police officers and magistrates might be appointed to help the administration in its efforts to control the situation and that the names could be finalized in consultation with 'the leading Congressmen' in Delhi. 'The next day, I think, or the day after, when I went to the Town Hall, I was informed that among the

---

22. *Sardar Patel's Correspondence, 1945-50*, Volume IV, Navajivan Publishing House, Ahmedabad, 1972, p. 297.

23. Ibid., p. 298.

24. Ibid., p. 296.

names of the special magistrates and special police were some persons whose names had been included in the list of principal organizers of the disturbances,' Nehru wrote, adding:

> The Chief Commissioner [Khurshed Ahmed] himself complained of this to me and further said that although this was his responsibility, he had been completely ignored in drawing up the list. I was very much surprised at this and I told Randhawa that it was very odd that persons charged with doing mischief should be included in the list of special magistrates. I knew nothing about these persons, but I suggested that any person who was supposed to be guilty by a number of others was hardly suitable to be appointed as special magistrate or a member of the special police. [...] I suggested to Randhawa that this was hardly a satisfactory way of drawing up lists when the reliability was the most important qualification and he might revise the list from this point of view and also keep the Chief Commissioner in the picture as the responsibility was his also.[25]

Later, Nehru even got to know that while 'the connection of the RSS with these disturbances [was] fairly well known, still noted members of the RSS were appointed as special magistrates and special police officers'. He was appalled, but preferred not to interfere in it at all after his first interaction with Randhawa.[26] Part of the reason why Nehru decided not to get into it was that Patel had taken personal offence to Nehru's interaction with Randhawa, asserting that it construed a direct interference in the area of his domain. As the Home Minister, Patel was in charge of Delhi and raised objection to Nehru issuing orders 'direct to the local authorities' in the matter of recruitment of special police officers. 'Finally, I should like to suggest,' Patel wrote to Nehru, 'that it is somewhat embarrassing both to me and to the local officials if

25. Ibid., pp. 296-297.

26. Ibid., pp. 297-298.

orders are issued to them direct by you in respect of matters which fall within my departmental responsibility.'[27]

Patel flitted evasively on the issue of the Sangh's role in the communal trouble in Delhi. He shared with Congress leader Rajendra Prasad on 5 September, a day after the disturbances began, that 'the attacks have been almost all one-sided and the aggressors have been Hindus and Sikhs'.[28] But he balked at the issue of the Sangh's involvement in these disturbances. The position that he took was rather strange, particularly because Delhi Police, which worked directly under his supervision, had sufficient information about the role of the RSS in the Delhi disturbances.[29] Moreover, the Delhi unit of the Congress, in a detailed note on the communal eruption in the city, identified the RSS as one of the main culprits. 'According to our information which we have received from various sources, there are organized forces and parties in the Indian Union that are working with the nefarious aim of undermining the National Govt.,' the note said. It continued:

> These are the forces: 1. A clique of Jat landlords and princes round Delhi. 2. The Akalis and the Sikh Premiers in the Punjab. 3. The Hindu Sabha and the R.S.S. aspiring to capture power and get a pure Hindu Govt. installed. 4. The High Command of R.S.S. working with some Maratha chiefs for a Maratha Confederacy. 5. A number of Rajput princes led by Maharaja of Alwar and helped by K.M. Munshi. 6. A section of the services, both civil and military, having close links with the R.S.S. and the Akali Party trying to sabotage peace measures of the Govt.[30]

27. Ibid., p. 294.

28. Ibid., p. 338.

29. Clemens Six, *Secularism, Decololisation, and the Cold War in South and Southeast Asia*, Routledge, New York, 2018, p. 105.

30. AICC Papers, File No. G-7/1946-48, Roll No. 8668, p. 191, Microfilm Section, NMML, New Delhi.

The Congress note also called upon the government to make a 'determined effort' to defeat these forces: 'The road to peace in the Indian Union is the road to war against these elements.'[31]

It is inconceivable that Patel might have been unaware of the findings of the party's Delhi unit or his own intelligence officers. And yet he seemed to be driven not by the actual facts but by his biases.

The most visible example of Patel's prejudice was his belief that Muslim officials were bound to be disloyal and should be dismissed.[32] He, like the RSS, looked at Indian Muslims as 'potential traitors' who would 'rise up in their hundreds of thousands and destroy India' if war broke out with Pakistan.[33] In terms of the working of his ministry, this meant a complete marginalization of Muslim officials, including the Chief Commissioner of Delhi, Khurshed Ahmed.

There could be one obvious explanation of Patel's stance: that he was working on a strategy which would have the RSS as an important component and which, therefore, led him to largely ignore, rather than counter, the Sangh's act of aggression. There was a second theory: that he didn't want the Congress to be upstaged by the RSS and the Hindu Mahasabha at a time when communalism was at its peak. 'It [the Congress] was obviously in some danger of breaking up, as it could no longer be held together solely by the anti-British appeal,' noted Alan Campbell-Johnson. 'He [Patel] had already largely deprived himself of the Princes as an alternative issue, and he must be under some pressure to substitute

31. Ibid.

32. Mushirul Hasan, 'Adjustment and Accommodation: Indian Muslims after Partition', in K. N. Panikkar (ed.), *Communalism in India: History, Politics and Culture*, Manohar Publications, New Delhi, 1991, p. 66.

33. Robert Payne, *The Life and Death of Mahatma Gandhi*, Rupa & Co., Calcutta, 1997, p. 550.

the Moslems, if only to avoid being trumped by the Mahasabha and the Rastrya Swam Sevak Sangh (R.S.S.S.).'[34]

Whatever the reasons, Patel's stance soured his relationship with Nehru. Trouble emanating from their respective positions was about to create a wide gulf between the two.

IV

When Delhi erupted on 4 September, Nehru was not alone in realizing what was at stake. Delhi was at the epicentre of the rage that had boiled up across Punjab—a fact that automatically converted a provincial crisis into a national one. Mountbatten, who was in Simla at the time, was summoned back by a peremptory telephonic message from Delhi. He arrived on the evening of 5 September and got down to work instantly. 'After Mountbatten had two or three hours to acquaint himself fully of the scale of the crisis, he proposed that an Emergency Committee should be set up,' noted Campbell-Johnson.

> This was at once agreed to by Nehru and Patel, and at their insistence Mountbatten accepted the chairmanship. [...] He said his objective was to convert the Emergency Committee into a daily staff meeting at which spokesmen from every department [...] could raise and answer questions. Out of these meetings priorities as between departments would be established. [...] He also resolved to resume his old war and map-room procedure to provide the Cabinet and himself with the maximum factual information by visual aid both with regard to the number of disturbances and the movement of refugees.[35]

34. Alan Campbell-Johnson, *Mission with Mountbatten*, Robert Hale Limited, London, 1951, p. 220.

35. Ibid., pp. 178-179.

It was decided that the committee should consist of essential cabinet ministers as well as the Commander-in-Chief, the Chief Commissioner of Delhi, the state police chief and heads of the civil aviation, the medical and the railways departments; everyone else would be co-opted as required. 'The general mood at the outset was of dazed bewilderment and aimlessness before the unknown,' recorded Alan Campbell-Johnson, who was present in the meeting as part of Mountbatten's team. 'Nehru, for whom all the horrors of the first month of Independence seemed to come as the crucifixion of his life-work, looked inexpressibly sad and resigned. Patel was clearly disturbed with deep anger and frustration. But for Mountbatten, weighed down by none of these inner misgivings, the occasion called forth all his powers of objective and dynamic decision, and he at once radiated confidence and a sense of purpose where none had existed before.'[36]

The Emergency Committee met for the first time at 5 p.m. on 6 September. By 8 p.m. the following evening, it had completed its third meeting, lasting a total of eight hours, in the course of which forty directives had been issued.[37] By Campbell-Johnson's account, in the first meeting, which cleared some twelve items, including setting up of a relief committee, there was an exhaustive discussion on the option of imposing martial law across disturbed areas, but this was shelved because of some practical difficulties and the focus shifted to stiffening of the existing acts in force.[38]

During the second meeting of the committee on the morning of 7 September, as Mountbatten raised the question of banning the carrying of all weapons, including *kirpans* (swords) worn by

---

36. Ibid., p. 180.

37. Philip Ziegler, *Mountbatten: The Official Biography*, Collins, London, 1985, p. 433.

38. Alan Campbell-Johnson, *Mission with Mountbatten*, Robert Hale Limited, London, 1951, p. 180.

Sikhs, the differences between Patel and Nehru suddenly stirred. 'Patel felt that any suggestion of banning *kirpans* would raise great difficulties, as they had been recognized by the Government as religious weapons for many years,' recounted Campbell-Johnson.[39] To this, Nehru suggested an ordinance making it an offence for anybody to be seen in public 'with an unsheathed weapon; or with any weapon of the category of firearms, explosives and bombs'.[40] Mountbatten, apparently aware of the strain in their relationship, quickly interjected. 'If we go down in Delhi,' he, according to Campbell-Johnson, warned, 'we are finished.'[41] Finally, the committee asked Patel 'to consult the Sikh leaders in Delhi with a view to their voluntarily inducing the Sikhs in Delhi not to carry *kirpans* except in a specified area'.[42]

The differences between Nehru and Patel again showed up on the question of hiring a cadre of special constables to reinforce the police. 'Patel was doubtful, but Nehru in favour,' noted Campbell-Johnson.[43] The committee, however, sided with Nehru, asking Patel 'to take steps to increase the subsidiary police force of volunteers in Delhi'.[44]

When the committee met again on the evening of 7 September, Nehru appeared standing firm about his position on *kirpans*, especially since Health Minister Rajkumari Amrit Kaur had told

39. Ibid., p. 181.

40. H. M. Patel, *Rites of Passage: A Civil Servant Remembers*, Rupa & Co., New Delhi, 2005, p. 282.

41. Alan Campbell-Johnson, *Mission with Mountbatten*, Robert Hale Limited, London, 1951, p. 181.

42. H. M. Patel, *Rites of Passage: A Civil Servant Remembers*, Rupa & Co., New Delhi, 2005, p. 283.

43. Alan Campbell-Johnson, *Mission with Mountbatten*, Robert Hale Limited, London, 1951, p. 181.

44. H. M. Patel, *Rites of Passage: A Civil Servant Remembers*, Rupa & Co., New Delhi, 2005, p. 284.

the panel that the majority of casualties in Delhi hospitals were victims of stabbing and slashing.[45] 'I am certain in my mind *kirpans* may have to be taken away,' Nehru said.[46] Patel seemed to be slightly relenting this time. He said an order had been issued during the day 'making it an offence to carry any arms in Delhi, including kirpans of greater length than nine inches; all kirpans under this length would have to be sheathed and concealed'.[47] However, a few days later, on 11 September, he again appeared to be changing his mind on the *kirpan* issue. 'There was quite a brisk exchange,' Campbell-Johnson noted, 'between the two strong men of the Government. "Murder," said Nehru, "is not to be justified in the name of religion." "This is not fair," Patel retorted. "There is no question of doing so, but the Government must respect all religions."'[48]

Nevertheless, in just two to three days, the Emergency Committee had launched a formidable administrative counter-offensive to the prevailing chaos. It had reorganized the relief work in refugee camps, made arrangements for smoothly transporting tens of thousands of Delhi-bound non-Muslim refugees to other provinces, arranged special trains with enhanced security for Muslims to go to Pakistan, organized special police officers and constables, arranged for harvesting crops from deserted lands, given orders for searching of passengers for arms on trains and for stiffening of punishments for delinquent military and police guards.[49] It put the government machinery in a mission mode,

45. Ibid., p. 282.

46. Alan Campbell-Johnson, *Mission with Mountbatten*, Robert Hale Limited, London, 1951, p. 182.

47. H. M. Patel, *Rites of Passage: A Civil Servant Remembers*, Rupa & Co., New Delhi, 2005, p. 291.

48. Alan Campbell-Johnson, *Mission with Mountbatten*, Robert Hale Limited, London, 1951, p. 186.

49. Ibid., p. 188.

An early portrait of M. S. Golwalkar.

The many images of Golwalkar.

Golwalkar's parents, Sadashiv and Laxmibai.

Anant Purushottam Padhye, a distant relative of Golwalkar, showing the remains of the Gurukul their ancestors ran before leaving Golwali village in modern Ratnagiri district, Maharashtra.

Bharat Publications: 1

We

OR

Our Nationhood defined

M. S. Golwalkar,
M. Sc., LL. B.
(SOMETIME PROFESSOR BENARES HINDU UNIVERSITY.)

With a foreword by
Loknayak M. S. Aney,
B. A., E. L., M. L. A. (CENTRAL)

1939 Re. 1-0-0

The title page of the first edition of Golwalkar's book, *We or Our Nationhood Defined.*

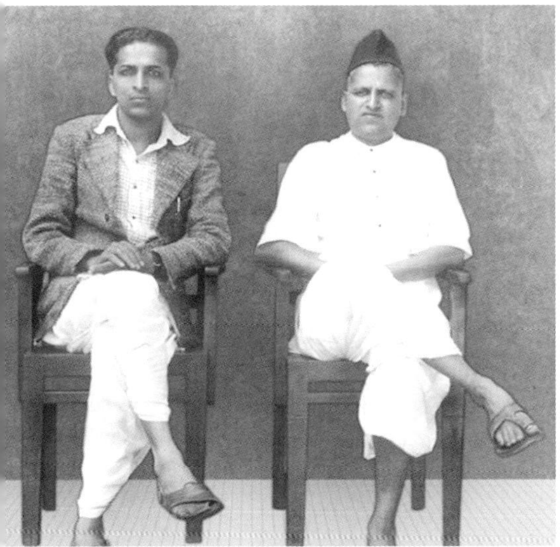

Mahatma Gandhi's killer Nathuram Godse right) along with co-conspirator N. D. Apte.

Following the ban on the RSS, Golwalkar called a meeting of RSS karyakartas at the residence of Delhi sanghchalak Hans Raj Gupta, 22 October 1948.

Golwalkar in Seoni jail in November 1948.

Golwalkar (centre) with Hindu Mahasabha leaders J. S. Karandikar (left), L. B. Bhopatkar and G. V. Ketkar (far right) at the *Kesari* office in Poona, 1949.

Golwalkar (left) with Kashinath Bhaskar Limaye (centre, seated) in Bombay, 1949.

Golwalkar's parents along with swayamsevaks welcome Golwalkar, 21 August 1949.

Golwalkar in a silk kurta along with businessman and Delhi sanghchalak Hans Raj Gupta.

Reception of Golwalkar with guard of honour at Amritsar, 27 August 1949.

Golwalkar addresses a public meeting at Hubli, Karnataka in 1949.
He is flanked by close aides Yadavrao Joshi (left) and Bhaiyyaji Dani.

Golwalkar addresses swayamsevaks at Calcutta, 8 September 1949.

Golwalkar hoisting the RSS flag in Hubli, Karnataka, 1949.

(From right) Golwalkar with Hindu Mahasabha leaders V. D. Savarkar and J. S. Karandikar in Pune.

Golwalkar with swayamsevaks in Calicut, Kerala, 1955.

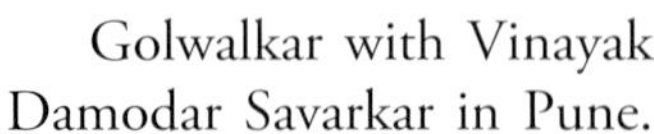

Golwalkar with Vinayak Damodar Savarkar in Pune.

Golwalkar performing puja on the occasion of his 50th birthday in Nagpur, 1956.

Swayamsevaks shower petals on Golwalkar during his birthday celebrations.

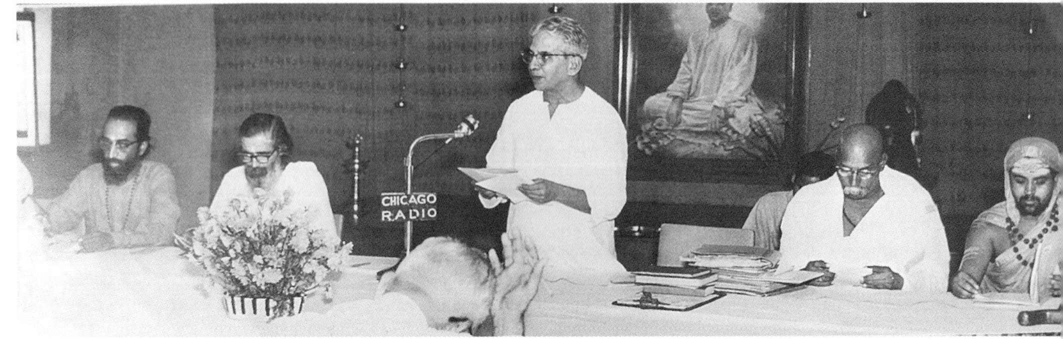

(From left) Swami Chinmayananda, Golwalkar, S. S. Apte and other religious leader on the occasion of the foundation of the VHP, Bombay, 28 August 1964.

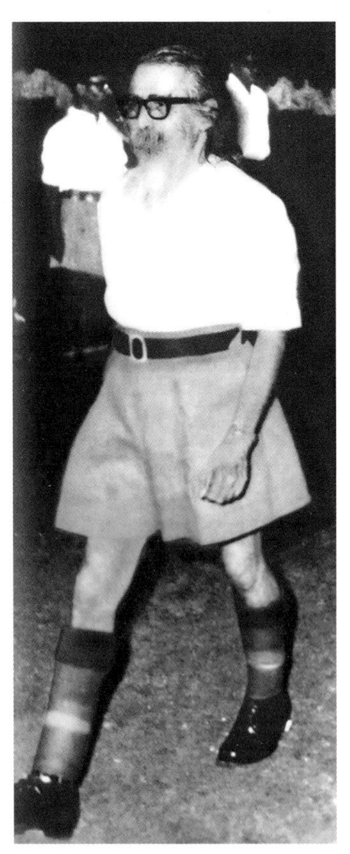

A rare photograph of Golwalkar in RSS uniform.

Golwalkar with Gen. Kariappa at a Vishwa Hindu Parishad meeting, Udipi, Karnataka, 1969.

Golwalkar with karyakartas at the RSS headquarters in Nagpur, 1970.

Golwalkar with Babasaheb Ghatate in Nagpur, 1970.

Golwalkar speaking at the Red Fort on the occasion of Sardar Vallabhbhai Patel's birth anniversary in 1964. Seen with him is President S. Radhakrishnan (in turban).

Golwalkar with Jana Sangh leader Rajmata Vijaya Raje Scindia and Swami Amurtananda from the Ramakrishna Mission's Nagpur ashram in Gwalior, 23 July 1972.

Golwalkar at a function with Atal Bihari Vajpayee.

Golwalkar in a procession with his followers.

Golwalkar with his followers.

Golwalkar in his last years after being diagnosed with cancer.

helped to keep going print and electronic media, strengthened the communication networks, arranged for guards for hospitals, for the movement of food and other essential items, for the disposal of corpses found in the streets, for large-scale cholera injections and for the broadcasting of daily official bulletins to the provinces.[50]

On 8 September, Delhi was declared 'a dangerously disturbed area' and the police and armed forces were instructed that any firing on the violent mobs should be shooting to kill.[51] On 9 September, the Emergency Committee set up a separate panel for Delhi and directed it to look into all the local complaints and issues, including 'measures to be taken in connection with the arrival that day of 100 R.S.S. young men, who were reported to have come by train from Amritsar with the object of creating further disturbances' in the capital.[52]

That day, Nehru also addressed the nation on All India Radio. 'I am speaking to you as the words come to me, without any script,' he said, and continued:

> During the last three weeks, I have wandered about the Punjab—West and East Punjab—and my mind has been filled with the horror of the things which I saw and heard. During the last few days in the Punjab and in Delhi I have supped up my fill of horror. It is the only feast left for us now. [...] I have seen horror enough and I have seen many people die. People will die of course, as they must some time or other. [...] But there are some things much worse than death that have taken place. I am ashamed of the acts that my people have done and I fear that the disgrace and the consequences of evil deeds will remain with us for a long time, for evil does not end by evil and you

---

50. Ibid., pp. 188-189.

51. *The Times of India*, 9 September 1947.

52. H. M. Patel, *Rites of Passage: A Civil Servant Remembers*, Rupa & Co., New Delhi, 2005, p. 307.

> cannot by murder put an end to murder. [...] So, I want you to consider this matter in all its seriousness, to consider where we are going, what kind of India we are going to leave to our children to live in. If this kind of thing continues, and if you are convinced, as I am, that this bad phase must be ended, then we must set about it with all the firmness at our command. [...] Whatever we may permit in peace time, now with a situation which is analogous to war we are going to deal with it on a war basis in every sense of the word.[53]

Nehru was in the lead, but inside he seemed distraught. His spirit was sinking. He devoted himself to his unending work with courage and diligence. Every day, as Delhi raged, he walked in the streets and listened to people's woes. 'Nehru has backed me to the hilt all through the past week,' Mountbatten wrote to British King George VI. 'I have also been able, I hope, to act as a source of consolation to him. He has come suddenly to see me alone on more than one occasion—simply and solely for company in his misery; to unburden his soul; and to obtain what comfort I have had to give. He has lately written me two or three letters indicating that he does not know why he is writing, except that he feels he must write to someone to get his troubles off his chest.'[54]

53. *Selected Works of Jawaharlal Nehru*, Second Series, Volume Four, Jawaharlal Nehru Memorial Fund, New Delhi, 1986, pp. 53-57.

54. Lord Mountbatten to King George VI, cited in Philip Ziegler, *Mountbatten: The Official Biography*, Collins, London, 1985, p. 433.

Gandhi and Golwalkar in Delhi

By the time Mahatma Gandhi returned to Delhi on 9 September 1947, his reputation was at a new high after his triumph in Calcutta. His three-day fast, which he had started on 2 September just when Calcutta had begun detonating around him, had produced miraculous results. The fast stirred people's conscience, and in a little more than 24 hours, the city calmed down and communal mobs vanished from streets. Massive crowds of all faiths turned up at his house as repentant masses, weeping and begging him to give up his fast and save his life. But he refused to yield and broke his fast only on the evening of 4 September, when the local leaders of all faiths and parties pledged that there would be no further communal trouble in Calcutta. 'My dear Gandhiji,' wrote Mountbatten, 'In the Punjab we have 55,000 soldiers and large scale rioting on our hands. In Bengal our forces consists of one man, and there is no rioting. As a serving officer, as well as an administrator, may I be allowed to pay my tribute to the One Man Boundary Force?'[1] On hearing the news that Hindus and Muslims by their thousands were mingling and embracing after the fast in Calcutta, Mountbatten told Campbell-Johnson that

1. Mountbatten to Gandhi, cited in Philip Ziegler, *Mountbatten: The Official Biography*, Collins, London, 1985, p. 436.

Gandhi had 'achieved by moral persuasion what four Divisions would have been hard pressed to have accomplished by force'.[2]

So, Gandhi's presence carried a remarkable sign of hope amidst the dark tales that emanated every now and then in Delhi. 'At the railway station, he was met by Sardar Patel, for the first time without his usual smile and apt pungent joke,' noted Pyarelal, Gandhi's personal secretary. 'Delhi had become the city of the dead. In the car the Sardar gave him the news. Since the 4th September communal riots had broken out in the capital.'[3]

As soon as the car reached Birla House—a grand New Delhi mansion, a wing of which had been refurbished to serve as a living apartment for Mahatma Gandhi—Nehru showed up. 'As he gave Gandhiji news, his face was pinched and furrowed by care, overstrain and lack of sleep,' recounted Pyarelal. 'A twenty-four hour curfew was in force in the city. The military had been called but firing and looting had not stopped altogether. The streets were littered with the dead. Pandit Nehru was indignant.'[4]

Quickly, a conference with the available leaders was organized for Gandhi. 'I find no one in Delhi who can accompany me and control the Muslims,' Gandhi, according to Pyarelal, told them. 'There is no such person amongst the Sikhs or among the Rashtriya Swayam-sevak Sangh either. I do not know what I shall be able to do here. But one thing is clear. *I cannot leave this place until Delhi is peaceful again.*'[5]

At noon, some local Muslims visited Gandhi. He quietly listened to their tragic stories and consoled them. Around that

---

2. Alan Campbell-Johnson, *Mission with Mountbatten*, Robert Hale Limited, London, 1951, p. 181.

3. Pyarelal, *Mahatma Gandhi: The Last Phase*, Volume X, Navajivan Publishing House, Ahmedabad, 1958, p. 431.

4. Ibid.

5. Ibid., p. 433.

time, someone brought the news that Muslim patients in the Tuberculosis Hospital opposite the Kingsway refugee camp in north Delhi were about to be attacked by a mob. At his instruction, Dr. Sushila Nayar, Pyarelal's sister who worked as Gandhi's personal physician, left for the hospital. 'On her way, she saw a mosque in flames,' recorded Pyarelal.

> She stopped to see if there was anyone inside. 'The flames prevented us exploring all the rooms. As I stood there, a shower of bullets came from the building opposite.' It was a stronghold of the Rashtriya Swayam-sevak Sangh. The bullets were evidently intended to kill the Muslims and any of their sympathisers prowling about the mosque.[6]

Gandhi was learning of the situation, and learning it fast. Delhi had become the focus of communal fury. 'When I left Calcutta on Sunday last,' Gandhi said in his press statement issued later in the day, 'I knew nothing about the sad state of things in Delhi. But since my arrival in the capital city, I have been listening the whole day long to the tale of woe that is Delhi today. I have seen several Muslim friends who have recited to me their pathetic story. I have heard enough to warn me that I must not leave Delhi for the Punjab until it has once again become its former peaceful self.'[7]

Thus, Gandhi outlined the tasks of his future battle. While leaving Calcutta, he had declared that he would stay in Delhi only briefly before heading for Punjab, the place where he was needed the most.[8] Once in Delhi, and after spending his first day in understanding the situation, he made his planned departure to Punjab conditional to the national capital's return to 'its former peaceful self'.

6. Ibid., 434.

7. Ibid., pp. 433-434.

8. *The Times of India*, 6 September 1947.

Gandhi had no illusions about the difficulties of the task he had taken upon himself. Having proved himself against communal adversaries in Calcutta, he was ready for a more serious and consequential confrontation. The whole of the communal poison that had entered society could not be cleansed from national existence overnight. But unlike other leaders of the time, he was not carried away by the events; he needed to study them with brutal patience.

From the next day onwards, therefore, he spent most of his time in visiting riot-affected parts of the city and various Muslim and Hindu-Sikh refugee camps. Never had he felt so dependent upon the masses as he did now. When he visited them, he would listen to their reactions with anxious concern and sympathy, but would often be blunt in his responses and suggestions. Over decades of working with the masses, he had developed the unusual ability to quickly know what was happening. So attached had he become of the Indian masses of all creeds and so perceptive had he been to their opinion that he could instantly read the debilitating factors that impeded them and analyse his own position with a great deal of accuracy.

On 12 September 1947, after having developed a fairly comprehensive view of the crisis, Gandhi met Golwalkar. As per the diary entries of Maniben Patel, daughter of Sardar Patel, Golwalkar visited Birla House twice that morning. He first arrived along with Hindu Mahasabha leader Shyama Prasad Mookerjee and an RSS colleague at 8 a.m.[9] But for some unknown reason the meeting could not take place. Golwalkar again called upon Gandhi two and a half hours later at 10.30 a.m.[10] By Maniben's account, Mookerjee was not with Golwalkar this time. Other

9. P. N. Chopra & Prabha Chopra (ed.), *Inside Story of Sardar Patel: The Diary of Maniben Patel (1936-50)*, Vision Books, New Delhi, 2001, p. 167.

10. Ibid.

accounts suggest that he was accompanied by some of his RSS colleagues. In the meeting, Gandhi told Golwalkar bluntly what he had been informed, 'that the hands of this organisation [RSS] too were steeped in blood'.[11] Golwalkar denied the allegation, claiming that the RSS was 'enemy to no man. It did not stand for killing of Muslims. All it wanted was to protect Hindustan to the best of his ability'.[12]

According to Pyarelal, Gandhi was not at all convinced by the reply, but, because of his faith in the 'redemptive power of truth', he 'felt he must give everybody a chance to make good his *bona fides*'.[13] Gandhi, therefore, urged Golwalkar to issue a public statement 'repudiating the allegations against them and openly condemn the killing and harassment of the Muslims that had taken place and that still was going on in the city'.[14] This was a proposal totally unacceptable to Golwalkar and his associates. Instead of making any public declaration on the issue, they said Gandhi could do that himself on their behalf on the strength of what they had told him. 'Gandhiji answered that he would certainly do that,' recounted Pyarelal, 'but if what they were saying was sincerely meant, it was better that the public should have it from their own lips.'[15]

Golwalkar's evasive replies did not seem to go unnoticed by Gandhi. When, after the meeting, a member of 'Gandhi's party' pointed out that the RSS men had done a 'fine job' at Wah refugee camp and that they had shown discipline, courage and

---

11. *The Collected Works of Mahatma Gandhi*, Volume: LXXXIX, The Publications Division, Government of India, 1983, p. 177.

12. Ibid.

13. Pyarelal, *Mahatma Gandhi: The Last Phase*, Volume X, Navajivan Publishing House, Ahmedabad, 1958, p. 439.

14. Ibid., p. 440.

15. Ibid.

capacity for hard work, his response was: 'But don't forget, even so had Hitler's Nazis and the Fascists under Mussolini.'[16] In fact, Golwalkar could not change Gandhi's understanding of the RSS: that it was a 'communal body with a totalitarian outlook'.[17] That evening, during the prayer meeting, Gandhi told the audience about the conversation he had had with the RSS chief, adding that the latter, instead of himself issuing a statement, had asked him 'to make his views public'.[18]

Four days later, on 16 September, Gandhi addressed a specially organized meeting of RSS workers at Valmiki Temple in New Delhi. Although the plan for the event had been finalized during Gandhi's interaction with Golwalkar,[19] the latter quietly skipped it. Being extremely aware of the unsparing manner of Gandhi's speeches, Golwalkar might just have decided to stay away from the event. Gandhi was, therefore, received at Valmiki Temple by Golwalkar's associate Vasantrao Oak.[20] In his welcome address, Oak described Gandhi as 'a great man' that Hinduism had produced. 'Gandhiji replying observed that while he was certainly proud of being a Hindu, his Hinduism was neither intolerant nor exclusive,' noted Pyarelal. Gandhi further said:

> If Hindus believe that in India there was no place for non-Hindus on equal and honourable terms and Muslims, if they wanted to live in India, must be content with an inferior status, or if the Muslims thought that in Pakistan Hindus could live only as a subject race on the sufferance of the Muslims, it would mean an eclipse of Hinduism and an eclipse of Islam. He was

---

16. Ibid.

17. Ibid.

18. *The Collected Works of Mahatma Gandhi*, Volume: LXXXIX, The Publications Division, Government of India, 1983, p. 177.

19. *Organiser*, 18 September 1947.

20. Ibid.

> glad, therefore, he said, to have their assurance that their policy was not of antagonism towards Islam. He warned them that if the charge against them that their organisation was behind the killing of the Muslims was correct, it would come to a bad end.[21]

Here again Gandhi displayed his fierce tenacity and concentration of will. In his own way, he hit out at the very premise of a Hindu Rashtra, expressed as it was in Golwalkar's *We or Our Nationhood Defined*, and warned that this vision would prove hollow at the first puff of reality. As events were shortly to show, these early encounters of Gandhi with Golwalkar and the RSS marked the beginning of a silent war—a war that became one of the most defining episodes of contemporary India.

II

Gandhi's return to Delhi coincided with Golwalkar's restlessness. From the meeting they had, Golwalkar was left with no doubt that Gandhi regarded him with some suspicion; certainly, he was wary of the communal attacks on Muslims. Despite the anger in a section of Hindu and Sikh refugees, Gandhi was still the most popular leader in the country. In the struggle for the hearts and minds of Hindu masses, so crucial for the successful implementation of Golwalkar's vision, much was to be gained in the absence of Gandhi rather than in his presence in Delhi. Determination, energy, resourcefulness, eloquence, charisma, an irresistible magnetic charm and moral strength—all the qualities Gandhi had previously employed in Calcutta could now be directed towards the RSS in Delhi. The only way to escape this was to let Delhi appear normal. An escalation in communal crisis would

21. Pyarelal, *Mahatma Gandhi: The Last Phase*, Volume X, Navajivan Publishing House, Ahmedabad, 1958, pp. 440-441.

make Gandhi stay put in Delhi; its subsidence would ensure his departure to Punjab, as he had already declared on several occasions. The RSS, it must have been felt, would then be no longer constrained by the presence of Gandhi; it would have open grounds on which to act.

Accordingly, as per an intelligence report filed on 29 September 1947, the RSS shakhas were instructed to maintain peace till Gandhi was in Delhi. 'The different "shakhas" of the R.S.S.S. have got instructions from "above" that rehabilitation of Muslims in Paharganj, Sabzimandi and Karol Bagh areas should on no account be tolerated,' said the report, outlining the general line the RSS men had to take.[22] In short term, however, the instruction, according to the report, was to maintain peace. 'At present the Muslims should not be stopped from coming back to their localities. They should be allowed to collect. Peace should be maintained for some days, i.e., as long as Mr. Gandhi is in Delhi.'[23] In the meantime, the instruction for RSS men was to continue their secret preparatory operations: 'Refugees should be well acquainted with the streets and roads of Delhi and the houses of Muslims should be pointed out to them. The Adhikaris [RSS office-bearers] should continuously change their circles. The volunteers should stick to their areas and keep alert to receive instructions.'[24]

On 12 October, Golwalkar himself held a meeting of RSS office-bearers in Delhi. Apart from telling them that 'they would have to put in one more effort to oust the Muslims from Delhi' and congratulating 'the Hindus of Sabzimandi, Paharganj & Karol Bagh for the work they had done in the disturbance', he also told

22. Delhi Police Records, IX Inst., File No. 528, p. 81, Manuscript Section, NMML, New Delhi.

23. Ibid.

24. Ibid.

the RSS men that 'the next step should be taken cautiously [...].'[25]

Another intelligence report, which was filed on 24 October 1947, revealed the RSS plan to affect 'total extermination' of Muslims in Delhi, thus creating panic strong enough to force the entire community to flee from India, after Gandhi's departure from the capital city as the Hindutva outfit considered him the biggest obstacle. 'According to the Sangh volunteers,' the report said, 'the Muslims would quit India only when another movement for their total extermination similar to the one which was started in Delhi sometime back would take place.'[26] The RSS men, it added, 'were waiting for the departure of Mahatma Gandhi from Delhi as they believed that so long as the Mahatma is in Delhi, they would not be able to precipitate their designs into action'.[27]

Tha Sangh's cautious moves in the face of Gandhi's firm resolve signaled Golwalkar's new direction—more pragmatic, supremely tactical, more nuanced. In the presence of Gandhi with all his hypnotic power, it was perhaps a realistic change for some from the volatility and peculiarity of the RSS men. But the forces fuelled by their nostalgia for a Hindu Rashtra were not destined to live placidly. Very soon, as Golwalkar's troubles deepened, these forces would confront problems and choices of extraordinary importance and complexity.

III

There are credible accounts that around the time the incidence of violence came down, a misinformation campaign aimed at inciting armed forces and defaming the government escalated. 'Concerted

25. Ibid., pp. 69-70.

26. Delhi Police Records, V Inst., File No. 138, p. 28, Nehru Memorial Museum and Library (NMML).

27. Ibid., p. 29.

attempts are being made to tamper with the loyalty of troops by the R.S.S. men by circulating faked pictures of naked women from Punjab,' said a report by a special magistrate who had started working in Delhi from 25 September.[28] Congress leader Govind Sahay, parliamentary secretary to UP premier Govind Ballabh Pant, told *The Leader*: 'Contempt for democracy (and thus for Congress leaders) and hatred against Muslims are the main political basis of their [RSS's] organisation and systematic attempts are being made to spread disloyalty amongst Government servants. A calculated effort is being made to prove the present Government weak and incompetent and the need for a militant organisation like theirs is thus sought to be established.'[29]

The campaign must have received a boost after the RSS purchased Delhi-based Latifi Press, which had been known for printing Muslim League publications, including its mouthpiece, *Dawn*, and which had been partly burnt during the September disturbances. 'In the course of talks with a few members of the R.S.S.S. it was understood that the Sangh had purchased the Latifi Press in Darya Ganj for 5 lakhs of rupees and they would now run it under the name of the "Bharat Parkashan Limited",' an intelligence report noted on 27 October 1947. 'Thus all the Muslim employees from the Press would be turned out and would be replaced by Hindu staff. One Raja Ram would be the Manager of the Press. The local "Organiser", weekly, and the Hindi Daily "Uthan" would now be printed at the press.'[30]

The Sangh's access to money was now unrivaled. The expansion in both its recruitment and fundraising networks was immense. It

28. AICC Papers, File No. G-7/1946-48, Roll No. 8668, p. 151, Microfilm Section, NMML, New Delhi.

29. *The Leader*, 7 December 1947.

30. Delhi Police Records, File No. 414, p. 63, Manuscript Section, Nehru Memorial Museum and Library, New Delhi.

now had considerable resources at its disposal, including its own publications, printing facilities and sophisticated communication strategies. Among other things, it even allowed Golwalkar to sometimes opt for big-budget journeys. His letters show that he was always on the move, quite often airborne and in one particular instance at the height of the September disturbances in Delhi, he even wrote to Madhavrao Muley, his lieutenant in Punjab, that in the absence of a regular flight, efforts were being made to arrange a chartered plane for him.[31]

Golwalkar, sure of his ground, his cadres organized in a dense network of shakhas in and around Delhi, waited coolly for a new opportunity that might emerge with the departure of Gandhi to Punjab. That would be the time when he could engage in a more serious and consequential confrontation. At last, after a long subterranean tussling to capture the hearts and minds of Hindus in India, he seemed intent on settling, once and for all, the vendetta with nationalists who were bent upon making the country a secular democracy. Quietly, discreetly, virtually unnoticed by the rest of the country, he had reached the final stages of achieving what he had been dreaming of for almost a decade—setting up of a Hindu Rashtra.

There is evidence that the period of wait was being used by Golwalkar and his men for entrenching themselves in western districts of UP, where the soil had started becoming fertile with the influx of a large number of Pakistani refugees who had been diverted from Delhi. The initial trend was noted in a cable by the British High Commission detailing the situation for the period from 18 to 26 September. 'Communal disturbances have also spread to western districts of province [UP] though so far on considerably smaller scale than those in Punjab and Delhi,' said the cable. 'Areas around Dehra Dun and Bharatpur State (near Agra)

31. Golwalkar Papers, Roll No. 12269, p. 49, 'Golwalkar to Madhavrao Mule', Microfilm Section, NMML, New Delhi.

have been worst affected and concentration of Muslim refugees are taking place in certain areas. Delhi riot photographs are reported to have been dispersed in villages to incite feeling.'[32]

B. B. L. Jaitley, the police chief of western UP, found Golwalkar flitting through these spheres of strife as communal instigator. 'When communal tension was still at fever-pitch, the Deputy Inspector-General of Police of the Western Range, a very seasoned and capable officer, B. B. L. Jaitley, arrived at my house in great secrecy,' recounted Rajeshwar Dayal, the home secretary of the United Provinces, in his memoir.

> He was accompanied by two of his officers who brought with them two large steel trunks securely locked. When the trunks were opened, they revealed incontrovertible evidence of a dastardly conspiracy to create a communal holocaust throughout the western districts of the province. The trunks were crammed with blueprints of great accuracy and professionalism of every town and village in that vast area, prominently marking out the Muslim localities and habitations. There were also detailed instructions regarding access to the various locations, and other matters which amply revealed their sinister purport.
>
> Greatly alarmed by those revelations, I immediately took the police party to the Premier's [Govind Ballabh Pant's] house. There, in a closed room, Jaitley gave a full report of his discovery, backed by all the evidence contained in the steel trunks. Timely raids conducted on the premises of the RSS (Rashtriya Swayam Sevak Sangh) had brought the massive conspiracy to light. The whole plot had been concerted under the direction and supervision of the Supremo of the organisation himself. Both Jaitley and I pressed for the immediate arrest of the prime accused, Shri Golwalkar, who was still in the area.[33]

32. Reference: DO 133/60, p. 258, Foreign Office Files for India, Pakistan and Afghanistan, 1947-1964, The National Archives, London, UK.

33. Rajeshwar Dayal, *A Life of Our Times*, Orient Longman, Hyderabad, 1998, p. 93.

However, Pant, despite accepting the evidence and expressing deep concern, prevaricated. Instead of seeking Golwalkar's immediate arrest, he asked for the matter to be placed for consideration in the Cabinet at its next meeting.[34] According to Dayal, this was a mistake because the Congress and even the UP Cabinet had RSS sympathizers, and the presiding officer of the state's Upper House, A. G. Kher, was an adherent and his sons active members of the Sangh.[35] 'At the Cabinet meeting there was the usual procrastination and much irrelevant talk,' Dayal wrote later. 'The fact that the police had unearthed a conspiracy which would have set the whole province in flames and that the officers concerned deserved warm commendation hardly seemed to figure in the discussion.'[36]

Finally, as per the Cabinet's decision, Pant issued a letter to Golwalkar detailing the evidence and asking for an explanation. 'Golwalkar, however, had been tipped off and he was nowhere to be found in the area,' Dayal recounted. 'He was tracked down southwards but he managed to elude the couriers in pursuit. This infructuous chase continued from place to place and weeks passed.'[37]

Years later, while deposing before the Kapur Commission, which probed the conspiracy angle of Gandhi's assassination, Jaitley confirmed Dayal's claims and said that the entire episode took place during October-November 1947.[38] He also added that at some point after Dayal and he met Pant, Patel called him and expressed his inability to ban the RSS 'because he thought that

34. Ibid., pp. 93-94.

35. Ibid., p. 94.

36. Ibid.

37. Ibid.

38. J. L. Kapur, Report of the Commission of Inquiry into Conspiracy to Murder Gandhi, GOI, 1970, Part II, p. 62.

the Muslims were already against them and he did not want the Hindu Public also to go against them'.[39]

IV

Patel's appeasement of the RSS, his insistence on winning over Hindus at the cost of Muslims, his treatment of Muslims as a governance problem and his repeated denial of the Sangh's role in anti-Muslim violence all contributed to a growing rift between him and Nehru. Patel himself seemed to find nothing wrong in his approach towards the RSS. To him, the RSS men were 'not thieves and dacoits. They are patriots who love their country. Only their trend of thought is diverted. They are to be won over by Congressmen by love'.[40] Apparently angered by the massacre of Hindus and Sikhs in Pakistan, he was nettled by what he seemed to feel was an undue solicitude on the part of Nehru for the Muslims in India. To Nehru, that was an outlandish allegation. On 15 October 1947, for example, Nehru wrote to the chief ministers of different states:

> I know there is certain amount of feeling in the country [...] that the Central Government has somehow or the other been weak and following a policy of appeasement towards Muslims. This, of course, is complete nonsense. There is no question of weakness or appeasement. We have a Muslim minority who are so large in numbers that they cannot, even if they want to, go anywhere else. They have got to live in India. That is a basic fact about which there can be no argument. Whatever the provocation from Pakistan and whatever the indignities and horrors inflicted on non-Muslims there, we have to deal with this minority in a civilized manner. We must give them security and the rights of citizens in a democratic state.[41]

---

39. Ibid.

40. *Bombay Chronicle*, 7 January 1948.

41. G. Parthasarathi (ed.), *Jawaharlal Nehru: Letters to Chief Ministers, 1947-1964*, Volume I, Jawaharlal Nehru Memorial Fund, New Delhi, 1985, p. 2.

Nehru and Patel were now far from a natural pair. Their differences deepened even after Gandhi's arrival in Delhi. 'I distinctly remember one occasion when the three of us [Patel, Nehru and Maulana Abul Kalam Azad] were sitting with Gandhiji,' Azad wrote in his memoir.

> Jawaharlal said with deep sorrow that he could not tolerate the situation in Delhi, where Muslim citizens were being killed like cats and dogs. He felt humiliated that he was helpless and could not save them. His conscience would not let him rest, for what answer could he give when people complained of these terrible happenings? [...]
>
> We were completely taken aback by Sardar Patel's reaction. At a time when Muslims were murdered in Delhi in open daylight, he calmly told Gandhiji that Jawaharlal's complaints were completely incomprehensible. There may have been some isolated incidents, but Government was doing everything possible to protect the life and property of Muslims and nothing more could be done. [...]
>
> Jawaharlal remained speechless for some moments and then turned to Gandhiji in despair. He said that if these were Sardar Patel's views, he had no comments to make.[42]

The signs of disaffection were certainly becoming more and more apparent. But Nehru, not one to get bogged down by differences in the government, kept pressing relentlessly. He retained strong convictions about secularism and democracy and seemed bent on using all available means to drive home his point. 'I would condemn those who advocate that all Muslims should be expelled from Delhi,' he said in a public meeting in Delhi on 29 September 1947. 'The great beauty of our country is that we have such a variety of cultures and religions. The demand for making India a

42. Maulana Abul Kalam Azad, *Indian Wins Freedom: An Autobiographical Narrative*, Orient Longman, Bombay, 1964, p. 214.

Hindu state is a virtual victory for the Muslim League, a victory compared with which achievement of Pakistan is of very little significance. You should not accept and follow the same principles that you have vehemently opposed in the past.'[43]

The next day, he told a gathering of mill workers and labourers of Delhi that the Muslim League and its supporters were not the only ones to betray the freedom struggle and that a large number of Hindus and Sikhs had also acted treacherously in the past. 'There were non-Muslims who had actively helped the British while they were suppressing the Indian patriots,' he said. 'What punishment would you suggest for them? The traitors are those who are disturbing the peace of the country and leading it to bankruptcy and ruin. [...] Your freedom is threatened today. If it is dear to you then work whole heartedly for the maintenance of law and order in the country. Your Government will be worth nothing if it is incapable of protecting the life of a loyal citizen simply because he happens to profess one particular faith.'[44]

The same day, Nehru also wrote to Patel cautioning him against any let-up. 'For the last four days I have been going into the city, addressing meetings, meeting groups of people, etc.,' he said. 'The impression I have got is that while there is an apparent improvement and incidents are few, this improvement is only on the surface. It is lull and preparations are going on for a fresh and organised attack. [...] Reports come to me from various sources to the effect that these preparations are proceeding. I hope the intelligence service is enquiring into this matter and that we shall not be caught unawares again.'[45]

Addressing Congress workers gathered to pay homage to Gandhi on his birth anniversary on 2 October, Nehru said: 'I

---

43. *Selected Works of Jawaharlal Nehru*, Second Series, Volume Four, Jawaharlal Nehru Memorial Fund, New Delhi, 1986, p. 105.

44. Ibid., pp. 107-109.

45. Ibid., p. 109.

strongly oppose the demand for making India a Hindu State. This is not only my personal view, but, it has the support of my Government and the entire Congress organisation. The demand for a Hindu State is not only stupid and medieval but also fascist in nature. Those who put forth such ideas will meet with the same fate as Hitler and Mussolini.'[46]

For his part, Patel had no choice but to appear to be adapting to Nehru's priorities and terms. At a time when Gandhi's shadow hung over everything, he, despite having established a firm control over the Congress organization, was in no position to publicly defend his conciliatory approach to the RSS and his drift away from the secular strand of the party.

V

Nehru disliked Golwalkar as much as Golwalkar disliked him when they first met, and the mutual antipathy survived for the rest of their lives. The exact date of the meeting is not known, except that it, according to Golwalkar's biographer Palkar, took place sometime in October 1947.[47] By this account, when Golwalkar explained the aims and objects of the RSS and argued why a powerful organization of this kind was necessary so that India could 'influence' the world, Nehru rebuked him, saying 'such a power should not be evil'.[48] Golwalkar then tried to convince Nehru that the RSS had no role in the communal disturbances, but Nehru was not interested in listening to his arguments. The meeting, according to Palker, was tense and lasted less than an hour.[49]

46. Ibid., p. 118.

47. N. H. Palkar, *Shri Ma Sa Golwalkar*, published by N. H. Palkar, Mumbai, 1956, p. 109.

48. Ibid.

49. Ibid., p. 110.

Nehru's own account of the meeting reflects, above everything else, an overwhelming revulsion. He referred to his meeting with Golwalkar in a letter to Dalip Singh, the central government's representative in the court of the Maharaja of Kashmir, Hari Singh, dated 21 November 1947. Perhaps, it was because of the revulsion that Nehru didn't even write Golwalkar's name in the letter. 'Their big boss saw me some time ago,' Nehru wrote without sharing details of when they met and what they discussed.[50]

Stating that 'the RSS people always say the same thing', he cautioned Dalip Singh not to trust them while dealing with the situation in Kashmir. 'Nevertheless the RSS is an injurious and dangerous organisation and fascist in the strictly technical sense of the word,' Nehru said in the letter. 'We have known about it for many years and some of our colleagues have been up against it for a long time. It is bad enough in Maharashtra where it originated. But the combination of the RSS and Punjab has produced something worse. I have little doubt that we have to stand up against this. [...] They are very well organized but extraordinarily narrow in their outlook and completely lacking in the appreciation of any basic problem.'[51]

In the letter, Nehru made no secret of his disgust over the Sangh's meddling in the Jammu region of Kashmir. At the time, Kashmir was passing through one of the most critical phases of its history. When India was partitioned, it was assumed that the princely state of Kashmir, with its predominantly Muslim population and its traditional lines of communications and trade running chiefly into Pakistan, would eventually go to the newly created country.[52] But Nehru held out hope that Kashmir would

---

50. JN (SG), File No. 4, p. 155, Manuscript Section, NMML, New Delhi.

51. Ibid.

52. Alex von Tunzelmann, *Indian Summer: The History of the End of an Empire*, Simon & Schuster UK Ltd., London, 2007, p. 285.

accede to India.[53] He, therefore, remained unperturbed when for some time after independence, Kashmir's Maharaja Hari Singh displayed his whimsical notion of remaining independent. Nehru continued to extend his passionate support to the Congress-aligned National Conference led by his friend Sheikh Abdullah that constituted the effective opposition to the Maharaja.[54]

Years later, RSS men quietly circulated stories suggesting that Golwalkar had played an important role in persuading the Maharaja to give up Kashmir's independent status and accede to India. It was claimed that Golwalkar met the Maharaja on the morning of 18 October 1947 and convinced him to sign the instrument of accession.[55] This looks clearly to be a case of myth-making. The notion that Golwakar played any role at all in Kashmir's accession to India is supported by virtually no specific evidence.

In fact, around the middle of October 1947, the Maharaja's Dogra-led troops carried out a campaign of sustained harassment, arson, physical violence and genocide against Muslim Kashmiris in Poonch and Jammu.[56] The precise number of casualties was difficult to assess, but by various accounts, the death toll ran into hundreds of thousands.[57] Soon a large number of Muslim refugees began to pour into Pakistan's Sialkot district. Using the massacre as a pretext, Pathan tribesmen of the NWFP, with tacit support from Pakistani authorities, swept down from the mountains in groups. On 22 October, they moved on, determined to capture Srinagar. The Maharaja panicked and deserted Srinagar for the

53. Ibid.

54. Alex von Tunzelmann, *Indian Summer: The History of the End of an Empire*, Simon & Schuster UK Ltd., London, 2007, pp. 285-286.

55. Manik Chandra Vajpayee and Sridhar Paradkar, *Partition-Days: The Fiery Saga of RSS*, Suruchi Prakashan, New Delhi, 2002, pp. 258-260.

56. Alex von Tunzelmann, *Indian Summer: The History of the End of an Empire*, Simon & Schuster UK Ltd., London, 2007, p. 286.

57. Ibid., pp. 286-287.

safer Jammu. On 27 October, the state acceded and India flew troops of its Sikh battalion into Srinagar. Three days later, on 30 October, Sheikh Abdullah, who had been virtually in control of the Kashmir valley, fighting the tribesmen with his National Conference militia consisting primarily of Muslims, was made the head of the Emergency Administration.

The development had been an overwhelming one for Nehru, full of satisfaction and vindications. But this was not yet his goal; it was only a stage along the way to defeat Pakistan-backed Pathan tribesmen and achieve a stable government in the state. But here, too, Nehru found the RSS, with the apparent backing of the royal court, trying to subvert the entire effort for establishing normalcy in Kashmir. Already, he had started getting reports of the RSS men conspiring to destabilize Sheikh Abdullah and launch a campaign against Muslims in the Jammu region. 'Information has reached me that RSS volunteers have been organised in East Punjab to be sent to Jammu for a campaign against the Muslims,' Nehru wrote to Patel on 30 October. 'It is stated that 500 were sent via Pathankot some days ago in special trucks. Further that a Special Recruiting Officer has been appointed by the Kashmir Government to go to Gurdaspur District and Kangra to recruit Sikhs, Dogras etc. This officer is especially in touch with the RSS.'[58]

In his letter to Patel, Nehru also expressed his fear of the Sangh's activities ending up in weakening India's case in Kashmir by lending credence to the Pakistani propaganda that 'the Indian Government has sent Sikh troops to exterminate the Muslims in Kashmir. Sheikh Abdullah is being attacked as being party to this'.[59] Referring to the Hindu Mahasabha resolution disapproving the appointment of Sheikh Abdullah, he wrote: 'A resolution does not much matter, but if the RSS carry on

58. JN (SG), File No. 4, p. 68, Manuscript Section, NMML, New Delhi

59. Ibid.

agitation on these lines and are supported by other elements, this would seriously hamper our work and would give a handle to the Pakistanis.'[60]

On 5 November 1947, while everyone's attention was distracted by the fighting with Pathan tribesmen in Kashmir, nearly five thousand Muslims of Jammu town were put in 120 trucks, which, they were told, would take them to the border of Pakistan, but instead drove into 'the interior', where the convoy halted, guards got out, and then, with machine guns and blades, massacred their charges, barring a few hundred who escaped by hiding in fields or canals.[61] The news of the massacre did not reach Delhi instantly, but when it did, Nehru was furious. The worst of his fears was coming true. By the time he wrote to Dalip Singh on 21 November, describing his meeting with Golwalkar and cautioning him against the RSS, he had already received considerable detail about the incident from 'impartial non-Muslim observers' who had indicated 'a great deal of trickery and very probably connivance by the State Dogra troops' in the massacre.[62] 'Gandhiji has also been greatly upset by these accounts,' Nehru wrote to Dalip Singh.

> He asked me to write to the Maharaja and to Mahajan [Kashmir's Prime Minister Meharchand Mahajan] about them and say that this matter must be cleared up and the guilty persons punished. I am not writing to either of them; but I suggest to you that you might speak to them and point out that this is a black stain on all of us and that it has injured our cause tremendously. I think you might suggest to the Maharaja that he should promise an enquiry. This need not be held immediately; but it should

60. Ibid., pp. 67-68.

61. Richard Symonds, *In the Margins of Independence: A Relief Worker in India and Pakistan (1942-1949)*, Oxford University Press, London, 2001, p. 68.

62. JN (SG), File No. 4, p. 155, Manuscript Section, NMML, New Delhi

> not be too long delayed either. You must remember that we are functioning on the world stage in Kashmir and it does not help to try to hide an unsavoury occurrence. UN observers or others might come and inquire themselves into the allegations made.[63]

Nehru also made it clear in the letter that the RSS would have no role in deciding the fate of the state. 'The fate of Kashmir is not going to be decided by the RSS, not even of Jammu, and the sooner this is appreciated the better,' he wrote. 'The only person in the State who, as an individual, will have the biggest say in the matter will be Sheikh Abdullah. If anyone can save Kashmir, it is he and not the RSS or anyone else. If by any chance the UNO intervenes, it is Sheikh Abdullah and his following that will impress them and show them that the people of Kashmir are fighting for their freedom against the raiders. The RSS will merely support Liaquat Ali Khan's case against us.'[64]

The emotional complexity of Nehru with regard to Kashmir can be easily imagined. His family's descent from Kashmir is the first thing he describes in his 1936 autobiography.[65] His love for the serene beauty of what is arguably the loveliest of the subcontinent's landscapes is also not a secret. But to restrict Nehru's attachment to Kashmir to his personal longing and love would mean overlooking the most vital fact: that the subject lay mainly in the realm of his secular imagination of India. Kashmir appeared to him as a powerful symbol of his belief that India could not become a Hindu Rashtra and that Muslims were no less Indians than Hindus. At a time when the country was witnessing all-out attacks on Muslims, it is not hard to see why such principles

---

63. Ibid., p. 154.

64. Ibid., p. 155.

65. Jawaharlal Nehru, *An Autobiography*, Oxford University Press, New Delhi, 1982, p. 1.

might have become an obsession with the secular Nehru. Even when these principles led him into direct confrontation with Patel, Nehru didn't relent. He remained firm and confident in his belief that these principles constituted the lifeblood of the newly independent nation.

Gandhi's Healing Touch

Gandhi presided over differences between Nehru and Patel in the style of a patriarch—authoritarian but eager to foster consensus and maintain balance. He held Patel as straightforward and a stalwart who could be trusted to make firm decisions even in the most difficult of situations, yet Nehru's commitment to secular and democratic ideals lay much closer to his own. Their confrontation on the question of the RSS, therefore, presented Gandhi with a problem of extreme complexity. Among the things that set this confrontation apart from other intra-party tussles was the fact that new sociopolitical concepts could be detected underlying it. Patel had no precedent of considering these concepts, not even a faint version of them, as the principal factor in his political calculations. Fundamentally, they belonged to people like Golwalkar whose sole concern was to take advantage of the communal mistrust caused by Partition and to impose Hindu principles over a nation that was being steered under the stewardship of Nehru towards secular democracy. The persecution of one segment of society solely on the basis of their religious belief ran counter not only to all civilized views of political conduct but specifically to the sociopolitical vision for which Gandhi had fought all his life. It was in this context that the confrontation between Nehru and Patel produced a grim image of what was going on in Delhi, and it must have led Gandhi to realize that to continue with his old balancing act would mean weakening Nehru and strengthening Golwalkar.

Perhaps the shift could not remain unnoticed. Hardly had he returned from Calcutta than the talks of a fracture in his alignment with Patel started doing the rounds. For example, K. M. Panikkar, the historian-diplomat who at the time was Dewan of Bikaner State, told Alan Campbell-Johnson that 'there was a definite clash between Patel and Gandhi when Gandhi arrived in Delhi [...]. Gandhi said then, "Vallabhbhai, I always thought you and I were one. I begin to see that we are two." Patel was in tears over his misunderstanding with Bapu [Gandhi].'[1] And yet in Panikkar's view, as he presented it to the press attaché of Mountbatten, Gandhi was trying to strengthen Nehru but didn't want to 'break Patel' in the process; his only objective was to 'bring him to the heel'.[2]

Although the tension in Patel's relationship with Gandhi was more whispered about than witnessed, its outlines were clear enough and became more so by the middle of November 1947 when the All India Congress Committee (AICC) meeting was held in Delhi. The speech that Gandhi delivered on the occasion and the resolutions that he helped adopt in the AICC left no one in doubt over what he was up to. Like a master strategist, Gandhi first escalated the stakes in order to get those Congressmen who seemed soft on the RSS to back down and then carefully made it clear that in this war against Golwalkar's project of a Hindu Rashtra, he was with Nehru, not with Patel. 'The Congress had never maintained that it worked for the interest of the Hindus only,' Gandhi said, addressing the AICC on 15 November. He continued:

1. Alan Campbell-Johnson, *Mission with Mountbatten*, Robert Hale Limited, London, 1951, pp. 268-269.

2. Ibid., p. 269.

> Must we now give up what we have claimed ever since the Congress was born and sing a different tune? Congress is of Indians, of all those who inhabit this land, whether they are Hindus, Muslims, Christians, Sikhs or Parsis. There have been Muslims, Christians and Parsis as Presidents of the Congress. But today we hear a different cry. Let me tell you that what we hear today is not the voice of the Congress. [...] It is the basic creed of the Congress that India is the home of Muslims no less than of Hindus.[3]

Without taking the name of any Congress leader, he said: 'If you think that they [Muslims] are all traitors and fifth-columnists, then shoot them down by all means, but to assume that they are all criminals because they are Muslims is wrong. If you bully them, beat them, threaten them, what can they do but run away to Pakistan? After all, life is dear to them. But it is unworthy of you to treat them so. Thereby you will degrade the Congress, degrade your religion and degrade the nation.'[4]

Among his intimates, Gandhi praised only Nehru. 'He [Nehru] is respected outside India as one of the world's greatest statesmen,' he said. 'Many Europeans have told me that the world has not known such a high-minded statesman. I have known Americans who hold Jawaharlal in higher esteem than they hold President Truman. Even those who have fabulous wealth, vast armies and the atom bomb respect the moral worth of Jawaharlal's leadership. We in India ought to have due appreciation for it.'[5]

More than any single speech Gandhi is known to have made around this time, this one seemed to carry an open subtext. Other

3. *The Collected Works of Mahatma Gandhi*, Vol. XC (11 November 1947–30 January 1948), The Publications Division, Government of India, New Delhi, 1984, pp. 38-40.

4. Ibid., p. 41.

5. Ibid.

aspects of the AICC session were no less significant from this point of view. The AICC continued for three days, from 15 to 17 November, during which several resolutions were adopted. One of them said: 'India is a land of many religions and many races and must remain so. Nevertheless, India has been and is a country with a fundamental unity and the aim of the Congress has been to develop this great country as a whole as a democratic, secular state where all citizens enjoy full rights and are equally entitled to the protection of the state, irrespective of the religion to which they belong.'[6]

Another resolution called upon the government and the people 'so to act as to enable all the Muslim evacuees, who had left their homes under pressure, to return and resume their original avocations'.[7]

Still another resolution described private armies including the RSS as a 'menace' to the hard-won freedom of India and asked central and state governments to take 'necessary steps' to curb their activities. 'The All India Congress Committee has noted with regret that there is a growing desire on the part of some organizations to build up private armies,' it said.

> Any such development is dangerous for the safety of the State and for the growth of corporate life in the nation. The State alone should have its defence forces or police or home guards or recognized armed volunteer force. The activities of the Muslim National Guard, the Rashtriya Swayam Sewak Sangh and the Akali Volunteers and such other organizations, in so far as they represent the endeavour to bring into being private armies, must be regarded as a menace to the hard-won freedom of the

---

6. *Selected Works of Jawaharlal Nehru*, Second Series, Volume Four, Jawaharlal Nehru Memorial Fund, New Delhi, 1986, 181.

7. Pyerelal, *Mahatma Gandhi: The Last Phase*, Voume X, Navajivan Publishing House, Ahmedabad, 1958, p. 519.

> country. The A.I.C.C. therefore appeals to all these organisations to discontinue such activities and the Central and Provincial Governments to take necessary steps in this behalf.[8]

Thus, the establishment of Nehru's psychological domination over Patel was accomplished by a combination of pressures and intoxicants—pressures of Gandhi's moral strength and the Congress's own legacy and intoxicants of the ideals of the freedom struggle. This compound had a special potency; after months of apparent paralysis caused by the growing rift between Nehru and Patel, Congressmen felt again that there was a firm hand at the helm of affairs. 'I see my battle has to be fought and won in Delhi itself,' Gandhi wrote to Pyarelal after the AICC session. 'There is a lot for me to do here.... The six resolutions of the All-India Congress Committee this time were practically mine.... It now remains to be seen how they are implemented.'[9]

In fact, by the time the AICC session was held, Gandhi, contrary to what is widely believed, had become a pervasive force in Delhi. Of course, he was seventy-eight and often during prayer meetings he complained that he was powerless and had no influence over men he had trained and appointed to high position.[10] 'People expect much from me,' he once said during one such meeting, 'but they must realise that I am not running the Government.'[11] Yet, as the British High Commission noted, ever since Gandhi arrived from Calcutta, Birla House had become

---

8. AICC Papers, File: G-30/1946 (Vol 1), p. 55, Manuscript Section, NMML, New Delhi.

9. *The Collected Works of Mahatma Gandhi*, Vol. XC (11 November 1947–30 January 1948), The Publications Division, Government of India, New Delhi, 1984, p. 145.

10. Robert Payne, *The Life and Death of Mahatma Gandhi*, Rupa & Co., Calcutta, 1997, p. 548.

11. Pyerelal, *Mahatma Gandhi: The Last Phase*, Voume X, Navajivan Publishing House, Ahmedabad, 1958, p. 692.

'the focal point' of political activities for all India. 'Through the constant stream of visitors he was able to keep in remarkably close touch with Indian opinion and continued to play a most important role as the principal advisor of the Indian Government on all major political issues. Scarcely any important decision was taken without his prior advice.'[12]

George E. Jones, a correspondent of *The New York Times*, saw Gandhi in Birla House and was impressed by his 'robust' appearance. 'His flesh seems firm and smooth, save for his wrinkled face,' he noted. 'He is short and spare in build, but no more than most Indians, and his tread is strong and unhesitating. His hair is closely cropped, almost shaved, and his rather large ears protrude boldly. Twinkling eyes behind steel rimmed glasses give him a genial look, except on the occasions when he becomes immersed in abstraction.'[13]

As the AICC session revealed, Gandhi, the most powerful voice in India, was not just firmly in charge but also perfectly serious about the challenge that the country faced. Through his shrewd strategy deployed to strengthen Nehru vis-à-vis Patel and the fantastic war waged to save the nation from the most ruthless attempt to convert it into a Hindu Rashtra, he made it clear that on his victory over the RSS rested the fate of his lifetime's struggle against the British.

II

As time passed and Gandhi consolidated his position, Golwalkar's nerves tensed. His plans rested on the hopes and expectations and the frustrations and disappointments of Hindu and Sikh refugees.

---

12. Foreign Office Files for India, Pakistan and Afghanistan, 1947-1964, Reference—FO 371/69729, p. 3, The National Archives, London, UK.

13. George E. Jones, *Tumult in India*, Dodd, Mead & Company, New York, 1948, p. 75.

The anti-Muslim climate that Partition had produced was critical to augment the efforts of his cadres for implementing his idea of a Hindu Rashtra. Golwalkar, therefore, not only had to worry about the morale of the RSS members, the mere passage of time also had its dangers—it threatened to evaporate the discontent of Hindu and Sikh refugees. Already, Gandhi's active presence in Delhi had started gradually bringing the situation back to normalcy. Even the strengthening of Nehru vis-à-vis Patel threatened to deprive Golwalkar of any profit that might have accrued from the top level differences in the government. It was obvious that the RSS men were a long way from finishing the task, and time was running out.

It would seem that by the beginning of December 1947, Golwalkar's cadres started becoming impatient. Intelligence officers of Delhi Police recorded a sense of desperation among RSS men during a secret meeting that was held on 1 December in the national capital. 'The [RSS] workers have alleged to have discussed the ways and means of capturing the seats in the Government,' an intelligence report said. 'It is also known that a meeting of delegates from all over India is to be held in Delhi on or about 8 December, 1947, and the future programmes would be chalked out. It is also alleged that one of its programmes would be to assassinate the leading persons of the Congress in order to terrorise the public and to get their hold over them.'[14]

There is evidence that Golwalkar at this point was formulating a strategy to counter the Congress government's campaign against the RSS, which had intensified following the AICC resolution on private armies. Simultaneously, he also seemed hard-pressed to offer his cadres, who had started becoming desperate because of Gandhi's pervasive presence in Delhi, an aggressive and purposeful theory of action.

14. Delhi Police Records, V Inst., File No. 138, p. 59, Manuscript Section, NMML, New Delhi.

The first objective was sought to be achieved by organizing a massive annual function of the Delhi RSS at Ramlila Maidan on 7 December 1947. 'About fifty thousand volunteers and about an equal number of visitors attended the function. Among the visitors were the Maharaja of Alwar, the Maharaja Kumar [younger brother of the ruler] of Idar, Dr. Gokul Chand Narang and Jugal Kishore Birla,' an intelligence report said.[15] Golwalkar appeared on the stage shortly after the function began. 'There had been scathing criticism of the organisation,' the intelligence report on Golwalkar's speech said. 'Perhaps people were expecting him to reply to such criticism but he was not going to do that. The founder of the Sangh [Hedgewar] had, likewise, declined to answer criticisms. The reason for this was that there was no intelligence in these criticisms, and, therefore, no clarification was called for. The Sangh is being called a militant body. It was a pity that the present Government was betraying the same ignorance as the British Bureaucracy.'[16]

The following afternoon, on 8 December, Golwalkar set about accomplishing his second goal. While fanning the flames with his own brand of rhetoric, he literally threatened that if Gandhi continued to protect Muslims he could even be 'silenced'. Golwalkar said this while addressing a crowd of 2,500 RSS men at Delhi's Rohtak Road camp where no outsider was allowed. Yet, an undercover agent, one of the finest spies on the rolls of the Criminal Investigation Department (CID) of Delhi Police, who filed his reports under the pseudonym 'Sevak', sneaked into the venue in plain clothes. His report of Golwalkar's speech revealed his sensational threat to Gandhi seven weeks before his assassination. 'He [Golwalkar] explained the principles of the Sangh and said that it was the duty of every individual to be prepared for facing

15. Ibid., p. 60.

16. Ibid.

the coming crisis with full force. Very soon they would be placing a complete scheme before them,' the report said.

> Referring to the Government he said that law could not meet force. We should be prepared for guerilla warfare on the lines of the tactics of Shivaji. [...] Referring to Muslims he said that no power on earth could keep them in Hindusthan. They shall have to quit this country. Mahatma Gandhi wanted to keep the Muslims in India so that the Congress may profit by their votes at the time of election. But, by that time, not a single Muslim will be left in India. If they were made to stay here, the responsibility would be Government's, and the Hindu community would not be responsible. Mahatma Gandhi could not mislead them any longer. We have the means whereby such men can be immediately silenced, but it is our tradition not to be inimical to Hindus. If we are compelled, we will have to resort to that course too.[17]

Partly because of these strong and threatening words of Golwalkar, the rumour of a coup swirled and became persistent. Years later, J. N. Sahni, who had been the editor of *Indian News Chronicle* in 1947, told the Kapur Commission, which probed the conspiracy angle of Gandhi's assassination, that 'it was being openly discussed in those days [...] that there was a secret organisation with about six lakh volunteers which would stage a *coup d'etat* and that organisation had secret cells in different parts of India including the Punjab, Maharashtra etc. It was then being rumoured that its leader was Golwalkar, Bhopatkar [Hindu Mahasabha leader] and Dr. Khare [prime minister of Alwar] and that its volunteers were being trained in Alwar, Bharatpur and some other places with the objective of overthrowing the Government after killing the top leaders and when Mahatma Gandhi was murdered it was

17. Ibid., p. 82.

considered to be a part of the plan [...].'[18]

Golwalkar's true attitude to the word on the street is difficult to discern. But those who had read *We or Our Nationhood Defined* or were aware of the arms training of RSS men at Alwar, Bharatpur and some other places and the Sangh's fascination for Nazism must have found it difficult to dismiss the rumour.

III

On 7 December 1947, while Golwalkar addressed the RSS rally in Delhi, Nehru occupied himself in writing a long letter to chief ministers across the country asking them to root out the Sangh. 'We have a great deal of evidence to show that the R.S.S. is an organisation which is in the nature of a private army and which is definitely proceeding on the strictest Nazi lines, even following the technique of organisation,' he wrote. 'It is not our desire to interfere with civil liberties. But training in arms of large numbers of persons with the obvious intention of using them is not something that can be encouraged. [...] The Nazy party brought Germany to ruin and I have little doubt that if these tendencies are allowed to spread and increase in India, they would do enormous injury to India. No doubt India would survive. But she would be grievously wounded and would take a long time to recover.'[19]

Nehru's fears were prescient. The situation in Delhi and some other areas was still tense and murky, and the future of India's democracy not yet secure. Along with the threat, he recognized the administrative lacunae in many provinces. The turn of events that followed Gandhi's arrival had gone against the RSS in Delhi.

---

18. J. L. Kapur, Report of the Commission of Inquiry into Conspiracy to Murder Gandhi, GOI, 1970, Part II, p. 62.

19. Jawaharlal Nehru, *Letters to Chief Ministers*, Volume 1, Jawaharlal Nehru Memorial Fund, New Delhi, 1985, pp. 33-34.

But the circumstances outside the national capital were still not working cohesively to uphold secular ideals and civil liberties. Nehru, therefore, made continuous efforts to make the system act against the RSS. 'You mentioned to me when we saw each other last about the steps you intended to take against the R.S.S.,' he wrote to UP premier Govind Ballabh Pant on 17 December 1947.

> Lal Bahadur [UP home minister] gave me some further details of the information you possess. He told me that probably you will take some action within a fortnight and the first step you intended taking was to inform the leader of the R.S.S. of the evidence you possess. I am glad you are moving in this matter as it is becoming very evident that the R.S.S. is a most objectionable and dangerous organisation and it has been responsible for a great deal of the trouble we have had. [...] I am sure we must not allow this mischief to continue. I hope you will move in this matter soon, if possible sooner than the fortnight.[20]

Nehru didn't leave it at that. In less than a fortnight, on 29 December, he followed up with another letter to Pant: 'You told me that you were going to take action against the R.S.S. When is this going to happen? I think the sooner something is done the better.'[21] Nehru's persistence might have annoyed Pant, as it had done Patel earlier, but ultimately, in an indirect fashion, his convictions kept the state government under huge pressure.

A more disturbing situation prevailed in Kashmir where Maharaja Hari Sigh, who operated from Jammu and was still technically the head of the government, was a man with strong anti-Muslim tendencies and appeared to be hobnobbing with the RSS. When Nehru came to know that arms being sent by the Centre to be used in battle against Pathan tribesmen were being distributed to RSS men, he wrote a strong letter to the Maharaja.

20. JN (SG), File No. 4, p. 261, Manuscript Section, NMML, New Delhi.
21. Ibid., p. 312.

'From the military point of view it is of exceeding importance that home guards and irregular forces should be built [to fight Pathan tribesmen],' Nehru wrote on 30 December 1947.

> Bakshi Ghulam Mohammad [Sheikh Abdullah's associate] has done a good job of work in building up the home guard, but he has been hampered by non-supply of rifles, bren-guns, sten-guns, etc, and yet our army authorities have sent a very large number of arms including mortars, bren-guns, sten-guns. Most of these have not even reached Bakshi Ghulam Mohammad for whom they were intended and we are inquiring into this matter. We are told that apart from some which has been distributed to the State Forces, which was right, others have been distributed to R.S.S. groups. [...] The R.S.S. in various parts of the country is at present engaged in active opposition to our government and has created any amount of trouble for us. We do not propose to tolerate this and we have taken action against them and may take stronger action in future. In the situation as it exists in Jammu and Kashmir State typical RSS activities are even more dangerous because they nullify to some extent the defence arrangements we have set up.[22]

Similarly, when Nehru was informed that the RSS was creating fear psychosis in Ajmer, forcing Muslims to migrate in large numbers, he unhesitatingly pledged his support to the minority community. 'I understand that about 10,000 out of 50,000 Muslims have been left in Ajmer and the exodus continues,' he wrote to Patel on 29 December 1947. 'I do not know how far these figures are correct. This indicates that while the situation is fully under control, there is fear among the Muslims of further attacks upon them. I do not know if this fear is justified. But we should try to remove it. The R.S.S. there and elsewhere is in aggressive mood and issues threats which frighten many people.'[23]

22. Ibid., pp. 318-319.

23. Ibid., p. 311.

Patel acted promptly on issues Nehru brought to his notice. Inside, however, he retained the same old biases for the RSS and against Muslims. Even Gandhi's overarching presence in Delhi could not wash away an undercurrent of mutual antipathy between the two. For a while it remained under check, and then it started growing again. During the first week of January, with Nehru and Patel taking divergent positions in public, it burst.

Addressing a public rally at Calcutta on 3 January 1948, Patel went so far as to say that even if Muslims declared their loyalty to India, the question would continue as to how those who 'helped' in the creation of Pakistan 'would change' overnight. 'The Muslims said they were loyal citizens, and therefore, why should anybody doubt their *bona fides*?' he proclaimed. 'To them we would say: "Why do you ask us? Search your own conscience."'[24] At this point, as Patel openly questioned the loyalty of Muslims, Nehru stiffenend his position on the RSS. On 5 January, two days after Patel's speech at Calcutta, Nehru mooted the idea of taking steps to completely 'check' the RSS. 'It is for you to judge whether you should ban the Muslim National Guards and the RSS,' he wrote to Dr. P. Subbarayan, the Minister of Police and Home in Madras Presidency. 'So far as I am concerned, I would certainly not object; indeed I think it is high time these communal organisations were completely checked.'[25] The same day, he wrote to chief ministers of various provinces: 'The R.S.S. has played an important part in recent developments and evidence has been collected to implicate it in certain very horrible happenings. It is openly stated by their leaders that the R.S.S. is not a political body but there can be no doubt that their policy and programme are political, intensely

24. *The Collected Works of Mahatma Gandhi*, Volume XC (11 November 1947–30 January 1948), The Publications Division, Government of India, New Delhi, p. 416, f.n. 2.

25. JN (SG), File No. 5, p. 10, Manuscript Section, NMML, New Delhi.

communal and based on violent activities. They have to be kept in check and we must not be misled by their pious professions which are completely at variance with their policy.'[26]

The very next day, on 6 January, Patel, in a public speech at Lucknow, took a diametrically opposite position on the RSS. According to a report published in the *Hindustan Times*, 'Sardar Patel said that they [RSS men] should leave the knife and danda [baton] and proceed more cautiously. Congressmen in office should deal with the R.S.S. in a different manner and not depend on their authority and ordinances. They were after all not working for selfish motives and they had their faults and it was Congressmen's duty to win them over and not to suppress them.'[27] With his characteristic bluntness, he also proclaimed that Muslims were not to be trusted unless they specifically declared their loyalty to India. 'It should not surprise Muslims if doubts were entertained about their loyalty,' he said, according to the report. 'They could not ride on two horses. Those who were disloyal could not remain in India for atmosphere would become too hot for them.'[28]

Besides causing a deep sense of hurt and alienation among Muslims, such statements of Patel tended to provide an enormous social respectability to the arguments of the RSS. Simultaneously, they also meant that Patel was indirectly bidding goodbye to Nehru. From now on, the political arrangement of the past could no longer work or generate any hope. Perhaps this explains why Nehru told Gandhi on 6 January 1947—the day Patel made his Lucknow speech—that he had reached an impasse and that either Patel had to go or he would.[29]

26. Ibid., p. 7.

27. *Hindustan Times*, 7 January 1948.

28. Ibid.

29. Alex Von Tunzelmann, *Indian Summer: The Secret History of the End of an Empire*, Simon and Schuster UK Ltd, London, 2007, p. 308.

IV

Gandhi was never interested in seeing just an end of communal riots in Delhi. He was at no time satisfied with it alone. Sheer absence of violent incidents would not suffice as explanation for his endeavour. He was fixated upon his mission of bringing back complete communal harmony, which would not be enforced by the police but upheld by people themselves. Unquestionably, Delhi had witnessed a spectacular improvement in situation since the time he had arrived from Calcutta. Violence had largely ended and attendance at Gandhi's prayer meetings had grown considerably. 'His audience at Birla House in the early days after his arrival were extremely small; perhaps not more than 40 or 50 attended,' said a report sent to London by the British High Commission on Gandhi's prayer meetings during those crucial months.

> And when he held a prayer meeting one evening in Old Delhi—the only one held outside Birla House during all these months—he was forced to abandon it because of Sikh opposition to his habitual practice of including recitations from the Koran in addition to other religious books. [...] As the weeks went by his congregations began to increase in size and included a number of Muslims who previously had not dared to leave their homes. There were prospects, very slight admittedly, that people were beginning to heed his exhortations.[30]

Yet, Delhi's situation remained dire and Gandhi disconsolate. Hindus, Sikhs and Muslims were still not ready to work together as instruments of peace. Properties of Muslims—mosques, mazars, houses, shops—were still under occupation of Hindus and Sikhs in many areas. For weeks at a time, there would be no incident, and then fresh trouble would break out. It was painfully apparent

30. Foreign Office Files for India, Pakistan and Afghanistan, 1947-1964, Foreign Office, File: FO 371/69729, p. 4, The National Archives, Kew, London.

that Delhi had not returned to complete normalcy in the real sense and that Muslims still lived in constant fear of fresh violence.

Gandhi was no less indignant at Patel's recent speeches at Calcutta and Lucknow.[31] They did not only threaten the collective camaraderie at the top level in the government but also seemed to indicate that Patel still looked at the RSS differently. Patel was the Home Minister and wielded massive clout over a large number of Congress leaders in different parts of the country. The smashing of the Hindu Rashtra project could not be imagined so long as he kept his biases for the RSS.

A rounding off of power positions already largely achieved since his arrival from Calcutta was, therefore, the only option left for Gandhi now. That alone would ensure a complete shattering of will of the RSS to resist the march of India's secular democracy and of Patel to covertly support this resistance. A whirlpool had to be created to suck the conspirators and their appeasers and collaborators. Hindu masses had to be stunned into shedding whatever thoughts they had been entertaining of making Golwalkar's idea of a Hindu Rashtra a success.

The first person to know of Gandhi's decision was Sushila Nayar. 'On the 12th January in the afternoon, Gandhiji was as usual sitting out on the sun-drenched spacious Birla House lawn,' wrote Pyarelal. 'As it was Monday, his duty of weekly silence, he was writing out his prayer address. As my sister [Sushila Nayar] looked through sheet after sheet that she was to translate and read out on the prayer congregation in the evening, she was dumb-founded. She came running to me with the news—Gandhiji had decided to launch on a fast unto death unless the madness in Delhi ceased.'[32]

31. Anis Kidwai, *In Freedom's Shade*, Penguin Books, New Delhi, 2011, p. 29.

32. Pyarelal, *Mahatma Gandhi: The Last Phase*, Vol. X, Navajivan Publishing House, Ahmedabad, 1997, p. 701.

Nehru and Patel, who had met Gandhi only a couple of hours ago, didn't even get an inkling of what was going on in his mind.[33] Nor did he share his decision with the members of his own entourage. Everyone, both his friends and foes, got the stunning news of Gandhi's decision to go on a fast unto death only when Sushila Nayar read out his prayer speech in the evening of 12 January.

At 11.55 a.m. on Tuesday, 13 January 1948, the aged Mahatma stretched out on a cot in the lawn of Birla House, vowing not to eat till the time all the seized Muslim establishments and mosques were returned to their rightful owners and total harmony among Hindus, Muslims and Sikhs was restored in the city.[34] 'Delhi is on trial,' Gandhi warned during the prayer meeting that evening. 'What I demand is that no amount of slaughter in India or Pakistan should deflect the people of Delhi from the path of duty.'[35] He also declared that he would break his fast only when conditions in Delhi permitted the withdrawal of the military and the police without any danger to peace. 'The police might remain but only to cope with anti-social elements, not for enforcing communal peace,' Gandhi, according to Pyarelal, said.[36]

The fast unto death immediately transported Gandhi from tumult to peace, but it left his countrymen with a mixture of confusion, consternation and even outright hostility. Health Minister Rajkumari Amrit Kaur confided to a member of the British High Commission's staff that she thought it would really

---

33. Ibid.

34. Pyarelal, *Mahatma Gandhi: The Last Phase*, Vol. X, Navajivan Publishing House, Ahmedabad, 1997, p. 705; Also see Larry Collins and Dominique Lapierre, *Freedom at Midnight*, Vikas Publishing House Pvt Ltd, Delhi, 1975, p. 376.

35. Larry Collins and Dominique Lapierre, *Freedom at Midnight*, Vikas Publishing House Pvt Ltd, Delhi, 1975, pp. 378-379.

36. Pyarelal, *Mahatma Gandhi: The Last Phase*, Vol. X, Navajivan Publishing House, Ahmedabad, 1997, p. 707.

be the fast unto death at last.[37] There were many who could not hold back tears, but there were those who responded with extreme hostility. When Nehru heard a crowd of demonstrators outside Birla House chanting, 'Let Gandhi die,' he ran to them and shouted: 'How dare you say that? Come and kill me first.' At this, the demonstrators dispersed.[38] At Connaught Circus, about 4 km away from Birla House, a group of RSS men in their khaki shorts, white shirts and black caps exercised vigorously, shouting at the top of their voices: '*Boodhe ko marne do* (Let the old man die).'[39]

The fast enhanced Nehru's admiration of Gandhi, but it outraged Patel. On 14 January, they both discussed the fast separately with Mountbatten. 'Their immediate reactions to Gandhi's decision are perhaps the best summary of the two men's divergence of opinion and outlook at this time,' recorded Alan Campbell-Johnson. 'Patel complained that the timing of the fast was hopelessly wrong, and that it was likely to have the opposite effect to what the Mahatma hoped from it, whereas Nehru could not conceal his pleasure and admiration at Gandhi's action.'[40]

Patel, in fact, was so upset that he decided not to change his tour plan despite Gandhi being on fast. On the morning of 16 January, he 'wrote a very pathetic letter' to Gandhi, according to the diary maintained by his daughter, Maniben Patel. He then left Delhi for Bhavnagar.[41]

---

37. Alex Von Tunzelmann, *Indian Summer: The Secret History of the End of an Empire*, Simon & Schuster UK Ltd, London, 2007, pp. 308-309.

38. Ibid., p. 309.

39. Ramachandra Guha, *Gandhi: The Years That Changed the World*, Penguin Random House India, Gurgaon, 2018, p. 869.

40. Alan Campbell-Johnson, *Mission with Mountbatten*, Robert Hale Limited, London, 1951, pp. 266-267.

41. P. N. Chopra & Prabha Chopra (ed.), *Inside Story of Sardar Patel: The Diary of Maniben Patel (1936-50)*, Vision Books, New Delhi, 2001, p. 182.

V

Gandhi's fast presented secularists of all hues—Congress, Communist and Socialist—with the opportunity to work together to reclaim Delhi, and they set out to seize it. 'The moment it was known that he had started his fast, not only the city but the whole of India was deeply stirred,' recounted Azad. 'In Delhi, the effect was electric.'[42] Soon after the fast began, a series of public meetings were planned in different parts of the city, to be addressed by Nehru, Azad and other top ranking Congress leaders.[43] Nehru, *The Statesman*'s former editor Arthur Moore and thousands of others, including a number of Hindu and Sikh refugees, decided to fast along with Gandhi.[44]

On 14 January, the Delhi unit of the All India Students Federation, the biggest students' organization led by Communists, organised a peace brigade to conduct communal amity campaigns in different parts of Delhi. 'Delhi Provincial Students' Federation has decided to run a city-wide campaign to restore complete peace in the city, and thereby bring Mahatma Gandhi's fast to a speedy end. The Federation has called upon all students to offer themselves as volunteers in the peace brigade,' said a report published in *The Leader* on 15 January. 'The students of Delhi are sending written pledges to Mahatma Gandhi, assuring him of their resolve to do their utmost in bringing about communal amity and peace in Delhi.'[45]

By 17 January, as Gandhi's health deteriorated, Delhi began to boil over. Bands of swayamsevaks who had appeared in the city

---

42. Maulana Abul Kalam Azad, *India Wins Freedom: An Autobiographical Narrative*, Orient Longman, Calcutta, 1959, p. 217.

43. *The Hitavada*, 15 January 1948.

44. Gyanendra Pandey, *Remembering Partition: Violence, Nationalism and History of India*, Cambridge University Press, Cambridge, 2001, pp. 143-144.

45. *The Leader*, 15 January 1948.

started vanishing from the streets, replaced by massive crowds of all faiths taking out processions and turning up at Birla House to persuade Gandhi to give up his fast. Representatives from across the city sent assurances to respect Muslim life, property and religion. 'Even refugees from West Punjab, the most embittered section of Delhi's population, whose sufferings have been successfully capitalized in the past by the riot-mongering vested interests, this time took their rightful place among the lakhs of people who joined the many unity processions and demonstrations which Delhi saw,' reported *People's Age*, the weekly organ of the Communist Party of India. 'On Jan 17, at the Urdu Park, near Jumma Masjid, a mammoth meeting of over one lakh people—Hindus, Muslims and Sikhs—saw striking expressions of the common people's anti-riot sentiment.'[46]

That day, a large number of Muslims returned to their homes in Sabzimandi, one of the worst affected areas, where a massive procession of Hindus, Muslims and Sikhs passed through the main streets of the locality 'shouting Hindu-Muslim unity slogans'.[47] Hundreds of telegrams arrived from different parts of India and Pakistan. Gandhi felt gratified but his written message that evening was still a warning: 'Neither the Rajas nor Maharajas nor the Hindus or Sikhs or any others will serve themselves or India as a whole if at this, what is to me sacred juncture, they mislead me with a view to terminating my fast.'[48]

Ever since Gandhi began his fast, committees representing various communities, refugee groups and organizations in Delhi had been continuously meeting in the house of Dr. Rajendra Prasad, the Congress president, in an effort to establish real

46. *People's Age*, 25 January 1948.

47. *The Hindustan Times*, 19 January 1948.

48. Louis Fischer, *The Life of Mahatma Gandhi*, HarperCollins Publishers, London, 2019, p. 618.

communal harmony and peace. They were all aware that it was not just a matter of obtaining signatures to a document; that would not satisfy Gandhi. They would have to make concrete pledges that they and their followers would carry out. Gandhi had been kept informed of the deliberations at Rajendra Prasad's house.[49]

By the night of 17 January, more than two lakh citizens of Delhi, including Hindu and Sikh refugees from various camps, signed a pledge vowing to 'do all in their power to promote a sense of security and inter-communal amity in Delhi'. The pledge read: 'We the Hindu, Sikh, Christian and other citizens of Delhi declare solemnly our conviction that Muslim citizens of Indian dominion should be as free as the rest of us to live in Delhi in peace and security and with self respect and to work for the good and well-being of the Indian Union.'[50] Delhi had reached its turning point, its moment of victory.

The next day, shortly after noon on 18 January, once the High Commissioner of Pakistan reiterated the appeal, followed by the representatives of the RSS, the Hindu Mahasabha, Delhi Muslims, the Sikhs and the Delhi administration, Gandhi gave up his fast and accepted a glass of lime juice from Maulana Azad.[51] Before breaking the fast, the Mahatma, in his brief address to the group, said that 'your guarantee is nothing worth and I will feel and you will one day realize that it was a great blunder for me to give up the fast if you hold yourself responsible for the communal peace of Delhi only.'[52] To the representatives of the RSS and the Hindu Mahasabha, he said if they were 'sincere about their professions'

49. Ibid., pp. 618-620.

50. *Hindustan Times*, 18 January 1948.

51. Maulana Abul Kalam Azad, *India Wins Freedom: An Autobiographical Narrative*, Orient Longman, Calcutta, 1959, p. 220.

52. Louis Fischer, *The Life of Mahatma Gandhi*, HarperCollins Publishers, London, 2019, p. 620.

they could not be 'indifferent to outbreaks of madness in places other than Delhi'.[53]

That was Gandhi's final blow. By the time it was delivered, the RSS was already in a miserably hopeless condition—time had run out and the groundswell in favour of Golwalkar's idea of a Hindu Rashtra had vanished. As the group dispersed, Nehru and Azad stayed back and took turns to feed the Mahatma fruit juice.[54]

53. Ibid.

54. Alex Von Tunzelmann, *Indian Summer: The Secret History of the End of an Empire*, Simon & Schuster UK Ltd, London, 2007, p. 310.

'Hey Ram!'

The final act of Golwalkar's conflict with Gandhi was played out by Nathuram Godse, the RSS hothead from Poona. At the time, Godse edited a local Marathi journal, *Hindu Rashtra*, just as his mentor, Kashinath Bhaskar Limaye, the chief of the Maharashtra unit of the RSS and one of the closest aides of Golwalkar, edited *Vikram*, another pro-Hindutva Marathi journal published from Sangli. N. D. Apte, a member of the Hindu Mahasabha, was the general manager of *Hindu Rashtra*. Limaye, Godse and Apte were also bound by their loyalty to V. D. Savarkar and had in the past organized the Hindu Rashtra Dal as a joint venture between the RSS and the Hindu Mahasabha. There is no specific evidence to suggest that Golwalkar, as the chief of the RSS, ever disapproved of the Hindu Rashtra Dal. The idea of a Hindu Rashtra, which Golwalkar pushed through his nationwide network of shakhas, was of profound significance to all three, but seems to have exercised a particularly strong hold over Godse.

While most of the RSS men shared Golwalkar's anger on Gandhi's determined bid to obstruct efforts to force Muslims to leave India, a few of them possessed Godse's intent to remove this stumbling block through violent means. In fact, it was only about three weeks after Golwalkar threatened to 'silence' Gandhi on 8 December 1947 that Godse set out to work on an assassination plan. Did Godse, an excessively enthusiastic RSS man, see in those threatening words of the sarsanghchalak some kind of a fatwa to kill Gandhi? Did he ever come to a secret understanding with Golwalkar? Or did he move in that direction on his own? There were theories, but, as there was no thorough investigation into the conspiracy angle in the immediate aftermath of Gandhi's murder, there could be no certainty or straightforward explanations.[1]

In any case, there were reasons for Godse wanting to kill Gandhi. As a passionate member of the RSS and the editor of *Hindu Rashtra*, he had been acting in close concert with the Hindutva movement and was obsessed, like any other member of the RSS and the Hindu Mahasabha, with the idea of making India a Hindu Rashtra. He was, therefore, part and parcel of a subterranean and organized Hindutva resistance to the Gandhian project of secular democracy—a resistance which had existed since before 1947, before the country was even thought to be partitioned. Through his nationalism and secularism, Gandhi had comprehensively countered the idea of a Hindu Rashtra, forcing its proponents—the RSS and the Hindu Mahasabha—to the margins of Indian politics. This made Gandhi the main target of attack not only by Golwalkar but also by individual members and leaders of the RSS and Hindu Mahasabha. Thus, if Godse, imagining himself as the deliverer of the idea of the Hindu Rashtra, set out to kill Gandhi, he seemed to have been resolving what might be described as a battle for the soul of India, an anxious and long-standing conflict to define the emerging nation state. The putative resolution posited by Godse can be seen a desperate attempt, but it was very much part of the struggle that Golwalkar had launched.

From childhood, Godse had been craving for a virile image. The artificiality of his existence that his desire of a masculine

1. For detail, see Dhirendra K. Jha, *Gandhi's Assassin: The Making of Nathuram Godse and His Idea of India*, Penguin India, New Delhi, 2021.

portrayal had triggered dominated his thinking since his early formative years and never allowed him to live a normal life.[2] This psychology got augmented by a consuming sense of mission towards the end of December 1947, when Godse entered into lengthy and reflective conversations with Apte and finalized the idea to kill Gandhi.[3]

The pace of events quickened when, on 2 January 1948, they held a closed-door meeting with Vishnu Ramkrishna Karkare at the latter's guest house in Ahmednagar.[4] When the issue of who would kill Gandhi was raised, Karkare resolved it quickly. He introduced them to Madanlal Pahwa, a young refugee from Pakistan who, having been cut off from his family, had been staying with him for the last couple of weeks and who would be 'ready to perform any daring act'.[5] At the time, however, Pahwa was not made privy to the plan. In a fortnight three more members—Godse's younger brother Gopal Godse, Pune-based arms peddler Digambar Badge and his assistant Shankar Kistaiya—joined the group. Necessary preparations were made and all of them set out for Delhi. Godse and Apte boarded a flight while others left separately by train.

On the afternoon of 18 January, hours after Gandhi broke his fast, Godse marched into Birla House along with Apte and Karkare for a preliminary survey of the prayer ground where the Mahatma was to be killed.[6] But things did not go entirely to plan. Late on 19 January, the day before the plan was to be executed, Pahwa, who had so far been kept out of the loop, refused to carry out the

---

2. Ibid., p. 6.

3. Mahatma Gandhi Murder Case, Statement of Accused in Original, File No. 23, p. 66, NAI, New Delhi.

4. Ibid., p. 138.

5. Ibid., p. 185.

6. Ibid., p. 146.

killing, thus blowing the plot to smithereens.[7] At the last minute, Apte tried to engineer the assassination and formed a new plan. According to it, Badge, who had been held in reserve, was now to carry out the assassination while others, including Pahwa, were to perform supporting roles.[8] It was decided that Pahwa would first ignite the guncotton slab at a spot almost outside the prayer ground far removed from Gandhi and his audience, and this would be followed by other members of the group throwing hand grenades from different directions, thus creating total chaos which would then be used by Badge to shoot Gandhi. On 20 January, after Gandhi's prayer meeting began, Pahwa did his part and blew the guncotton slab, but others abandoned him and fled in panic.

The urgency of the situation, however, took precedence over the fears of Godse, Apte and Karkare. By 24 January, Godse and Apte, following lengthy conversations, came up with a fresh plan. 'Instead of looking for a third person, I decided to go personally in front of Gandhi and empty the pistol in him,' Godse said later. 'It was also decided that Apte and Karkare would come along only to provide support to me.'[9] For the next couple of days, they managed the affairs in Bombay and Poona, and then on 27 January, a week after their retreat from Birla House, they flew to Delhi. Without any break, they took a train to Gwalior, and, after procuring a semi-automatic pistol, came back to Delhi on 29 January where Karkare also joined them.

On the evening of Friday, 30 January 1948, with Apte and Karkare watching from a distance, Godse positioned himself about

7. Mahatma Gandhi Murder Case, Statements of Accused, File No. 47, p. 79, NAI, New Delhi.

8. Mahatma Gandhi Murder Case, Statement of Accused in Original, File No. 23, pp. 115-116, NAI, New Delhi.

9. Mahatma Gandhi Murder Case, Statement of Accused in Original, File No. 23, p. 85, NAI, New Delhi.

8-10 feet away from the main entrance, right along the path in the prayer ground of Birla House that Gandhi would take to reach the wooden podium from which he led his prayer meetings. At about 5.15 p.m., Gandhi entered the lawn. He walked quickly towards the podium, the crowd opening to enable him to pass through. As he came close, Godse pushed his way roughly past Manu, one of his grand-nieces.[10] And then, in one furious movement, Godse stepped in front of Gandhi, his hands folded over his pistol. He fired a total of three shots in quick succession at almost point-blank range, at the end of which Gandhi collapsed, uttering his last cry: 'Hey Ram!'[11]

II

Golwalkar was in Madras when the news of Gandhi's assassination reached him. He immediately cancelled all his programmes and telegraphed condolence messages to Nehru, Patel and Mahatma Gandhi's son Devdas Gandhi: 'I am deeply shocked to hear about the tragic murder of a divine soul because of a cruel fatal attack. In these difficult times, this has caused an immeasurable loss to the nation. May God give you the strength to fill the vacuum caused by the passing away of an incomparable organiser.'[12] Promptly, he also wrote a one-line instruction to all sanghchalaks: 'To express our grief due to the sad demise of respected Mahatmaji, shakhas will observe a mourning for 13 days and all daily programmes will be put on hold.'[13]

---

10. Manuben Gandhi, *Last Glimpses of Bapu*, Shiva Lal Agarwala& Co. (P) Ltd., Agra, 1962, pp. 308-309.

11. D. G. Tendulkar, *Mahatma: Life of Mohandas Karamchand Gandhi*, Volume Eight, The Publications Division, New Delhi, 1963, p. 288.

12. *Shri Guruji Samagra*, Volume 10, Suruchi Prakashan, New Delhi, p. 5.

13. Ibid.

Early on 31 January, he flew to Nagpur. For some time after his arrival, he remained occupied by writing again to Nehru and Patel—this time more elaborate condolence letters. In the meantime, a firestorm set off by Gandhi's assassination was already under way in several parts of Bombay province. The vast multitude that spent the night of 30 January in grief and anguish was suddenly seized by a blind fury against the supporters of a Hindu Rashtra. The attacks were not limited to the members of the RSS and the Hindu Mahasabha, but were directed at Maharashtrian Brahmins in general. 'Bapu's assassination had created violent storm against Brahmins in Maharashtra as Godse was a Konkanastha [another name for Chitpawan] Brahmin,' Morarji Desai, the home minister of Bombay province, noted in his memoir. 'Tension between Brahmins and non-Brahmins in Maharashtra, and the violent anger against the Brahmins in general was a result of this terrible incident. In several places like Poona, Satara and Sangli, several Brahmins were attacked, and their property destroyed.'[14]

In Bombay, about a thousand people stormed Savarkar's residence and ransacked it.[15] Mobs attacked offices of the RSS and the Hindu Mahasabha across the province and in some other parts of the country. Many RSS members were stabbed in the streets of Bombay.[16] Limaye, the Maharashtra RSS chief, fled when his house at Sangli was set on fire by a mob of non-Brahmins.[17] Poona, the heart of Maharashtrian Brahmins and the centre of Godse's activities, was the worst hit. 'Everywhere people

14. Morarji Desai, *The Story of My Life*, Vol. One, Macmillan India, Delhi, 1974, p. 248.

15. Tapan Ghosh, *The Gandhi Murder Trial*, Asia Publishing House, Bombay, 1974, p. 47.

16. Ibid.

17. Narhari N. Kirkire, *Sangliche Diwas (1937-1945)*, N. N. Kirkire (publisher), Satara, 2008, p. 64.

started getting mobilized against Brahmins,' noted M. S. Dixit, an active member of the Hindu Mahasabha in Poona at that time. 'Announcements were made that Brahmins should be ostracized. Stone pelting began on their houses and properties. Mobs started roaming around shouting anti-Brahmin slogans.'[18]

In twenty-four hours, the RSS had fallen apart, its members scattered or at odds. It seemed as though Golwalkar's period of ascent was over. With the assassination of Gandhi, all hopes for his project of a Hindu Rashtra collapsed. Prior to the assassination, Golwalkar and his cadres had been riding a tide of anti-Partition, anti-Pakistan and anti-Muslim feelings. No doubt, Gandhi's fast had weakened the tide, but it had not vanished completely—sections of Hindu and Sikh refugees and those under the spell of the RSS and the Hindu Mahasabha still carried the hatred against Muslims. The assassination shook India to normalcy. Rapidly, almost instantaneously, the tide turned. In one stroke, public opinion took a great swing away from the champions of a Hindu Rashtra. Coming soon after Gandhi's painful fast, the murder appeared to be an act of reactionary conspirators desperate to set India in new ideological directions.

What the events would mean ultimately for the RSS was difficult to predict, but within twenty-four hours of the assassination, Golwalkar was searching for ways to save the organization from ruin and to salvage some of its standing. The grief of the multitude was unendurable, and people seemed to have lost their minds. On Sunday, 1 February, Golwalkar issued a statement to the press. 'In the presence of this appalling tragedy I hope people will learn the lesson and practice the doctrine of love and service,' it said. 'Believing in this doctrine, I direct all my brother swayamsevaks to maintain a loving attitude towards all, even if there be any sort of provocation born out of misunderstanding and to remember that

18. M. S. Dixit, *Mi Ma Shri*, Utkarsh Prakashan, Pune, 2004, pp. 63-64.

even this misplaced frenzy is an expression of unbounded love and reverence, in which the whole country held the great Mahatma, the man who made the name of our motherland great in the world. Our salutation to the revered departed one.'[19]

This was not the usual language for the RSS to use about Gandhi. When he was alive, it had spread venom against him and had even wished his death when he sat on fast a fortnight ago. Golwalkar's own view of Gandhi, as he explained it to RSS men on 8 December 1947 in Delhi, was that the Mahatma had gone off the deep end and become disloyal to Hindus by blocking efforts to cleanse India of Muslims, the reason why he had threatened to 'silence' him. Now, panicked at people's fury, Golwalkar espoused a new line, abandoning—at least publicly—his plan of undertaking ethnic cleansing of Muslims and establishing a Hindu Rashtra. What he claimed instead was that he believed in the 'doctrine' of Gandhi.

In actual fact, Golwalkar no longer had a choice. There was not much he could do except to desperately look for a way out. Making new pledges could not be an issue at a time when hesitation seemed fatal. This also explains why the RSS leadership did not take time to abandon Godse, even though he had served the organization for fourteen years.[20] Golwalkar's statement, for example, placed the responsibility for the assassination in a generalized context and made no particular reference to Godse. Another statement, which was also issued on 1 February, by the 'Sangha Chalak of Rashtriya Swayam Sevak Sangh, Bombay' said that 'the alleged assassin of Mahatma Gandhi was never connected in any way' with the Sangh. 'We have already condemned the dastardly and

19. Craig Baxter, *The Jana Sangh: A Biography of an Indian Political Party*, University of Pennsylvania Press, Philadelphia, 1969, p. 43.

20. For detail, see Dhirendra K. Jha, *Gandhi's Assassin: The Making of Nathuram Godse and His Idea of India*, Penguin India, New Delhi, 2021.

cowardly attack on Mahatma Gandhi's life and we mourn this national calamity. We are observing national mourning by closing our centres for 13 days,' the statement said.[21]

III

Later on 1 February 1948, after Golwalkar had issued the press statement, an angry mob gathered around the RSS headquarters. At the time, Golwalkar was holed up in it with over three dozen RSS men. In the heart of Nagpur, the RSS headquarters, Hedgewar Bhawan, was not an elaborate structure. It was a dilapidated, old, one-story building situated in the Mahal locality of the city. A large verandah in the centre was flanked by three rooms in a row on both sides. A tiny room on the right corner of the building served as the unifom shop for swayamsevaks. On its left, towards the verandah, was the sarsanghchalak's room—a modest twelve by twelve chamber with a bed, a wooden table, a few chairs and a flat wooden park-bench. Other rooms served as dormitories for the RSS men living at the headquarters, as well as visitors.

Quickly, the crowd swelled, and there began talks of setting the RSS headquarters on fire.[22] 'The inspector-general of police rushed to my residence and said that if nothing was done to prevent the intended incendiarism, about forty people inside the building would be burnt alive,' D. P. Mishra, Home Minister of the Central Provinces, reminisced. 'I asked the IGP whether the mob would be pacified in case Golwalkar and his friends were arrested. He said that in all likelihood the arrests would pacify the crowd but added that as the RSS was still a lawful organisation wholesale arrests of its executive committee could not be justified.

21. *Hindustan Times*, 2 February 1948.

22. D. P. Mishra, *The Nehru Epoch: From Democracy to Monocracy*, Vikas Publishing House Pvt Ltd, New Delhi, 1978, p. 57.

However, as the IGP failed to suggest any alternative, I ordered him to effect the arrests and treat them as of a protective nature.'[23]

By the time Golwalkar was taken into protective custody, about 10,000 persons had gathered around the RSS headquarters.[24] 'The police dispersed the crowd and took the R.S.S. members in the building into custody,' reported the *Hindustan Times*.[25] Ghatate and Deoras were among other important RSS leaders who were also picked up from the Mahal office. 'Hardly had Golwalkar and his associates been taken to the local jail in protective custody when I received a telephone call from L.V. Paranjpe [...], asking me to save him from a violent crowd which was on its way to attack his house,' recounted Mishra. Paranjpe was a Hindu Mahasabha leader and one of the founders of the RSS. 'To him also I had to suggest that the safest place for him in the prevailing situation was the Nagpur central jail but that I would order his arrest after he had given his consent. The doctor [Paranjpe] readily gave his consent and he too was made safe in prison.'[26]

On 2 February 1948, the union cabinet resolved to 'root out the forces of hate and violence'.[27] Accordingly, the government banned the RSS on 4 February. 'It has been found that in several parts of the country individual members of Rashtriya Swayamsevak Sangh have indulged in acts of violence involving arson, robbery, dacoity, and murder and have collected illicit arms and ammunition,' said the government communiqué.

---

23. Ibid.

24. *Hindustan Times*, 4 February 1948.

25. Ibid.

26. D. P. Mishra, *The Nehru Epoch: From Democracy to Monocracy*, Vikas Publishing House Pvt Ltd, New Delhi, 1978, pp. 57-58.

27. 'Text of Government communique dated February 4, 1948', cited in D. R. Goyal, *Rashtriya Swayamsewak Sangh*, Radhakrishna Prakashan (P) Ltd., New Delhi, 1979, p. 250.

> They have been found circulating leaflets exhorting people to resort to terrorist methods, to collect fire arms, to create disaffection against the government and suborn the police and the military. These activities have been carried on under a cloak of secrecy, and the government have considered from time to time how far these activities rendered it incumbent on them to deal with the Sangh in its corporate capacity. The occasion when the government defined this attitude was when the Premiers and Home Ministers of provinces met in Dehi in conference towards the end of November.
>
> It was then unanimously agreed that the stage when the Sangh should be dealt with as an association had not yet arrived and that individuals should continue to be dealt with sternly as hitherto. The objectionable and harmful activities of the Sangh have, however, continued unabated and the cult of violence sponsored and inspired by the activities of the Sangh has claimed many victims. The latest and the most precious to fall was Gandhiji himself.
>
> In these circumstances it is the bounden duty of the government to take effective measures to curb this reappearance of violence in a virulent form and as a first step to this end, they have decided to declare the Sangh as an unlawful association.[28]

The ban order resulted in the rounding up of RSS men across the country under public safety acts of various provinces. Golwalkar and his colleagues, who had already been taken into protective custody, were now formally arrested. Within six months, however, most of the RSS men were released.[29] On 6 August 1948, Golwalkar also came out of jail, although some restrictions were imposed on him, including his movement outside Nagpur. 'Many of these people have been released from detention,' Nehru wrote to

---

28. Ibid., pp. 251-252.

29. D. P. Mishra, *The Nehru Epoch: From Democracy to Monocracy*, Vikas Publishing House Pvt Ltd, New Delhi, 1978, p. 59.

the Indian High Commissioner in London, V. K. Krishna Menon, on 12 August. 'Some were released because they were unimportant, students and the like. Some have been released because their period of detention was over—six months. They could not be detained longer under the present law. It would have been necessary to issue an ordinance or amend the law. Thus, even the chief of the R.S.S., Golwalkar, was released a few days ago in Nagpur because his six months were up. Immediately on release, orders were served on him restricting his movements and activities. In case there is breach of any order, he can be arrested and sentenced.'[30]

IV

Within a week of his release, Golwalkar, in pursuit of his complete freedom, embarked on writing letters to Nehru and Patel. First he tried to ingratiate himself with the government. In his letter to Nehru dated 11 August 1948, he mentioned that despite his detention he retained 'the same love, respect and spirit of honourable cooperation' and that because of restrictions imposed on him he was not being able to spread 'this message of love' among all the members of the RSS. 'Also I would have really appreciated,' he added, 'if, instead of being placed under such unwarranted restrictions, I would have been given the chance to clear my position and to convince you of my feelings of love and real cooperation with the Government in these crucial times.'[31] The same day, he wrote a similar letter in Hindi to Patel.[32]

Nehru did not reply. Patel's response was cordial, but it took time to reach him. On 24 September, before receiving Patel's

30. J.N. (S.G.)–Post-Independence, File No. 12 (Part I), p. 196, Manuscript Section, NMML, New Delhi.

31. Ibid., p. 189.

32. *Shri Guruji Samagra*, Volume 10, Suruchi Prakashan, New Delhi, pp. 12-13.

reply, Golwalkar wrote a second set of letters to Nehru and Patel. This time, apart from claiming that all the allegations against the RSS were found to be baseless, he tried to impress upon Nehru and Patel as to why the unbanning of the RSS was the only way to deal with the growing presence of communists in the country as his organization alone could stop 'the intelligent youth' from 'falling into the snares of Communism'.[33] This was a shrewd tactical move of Golwalkar to convince the top government leaders about the transformation he had undergone with regard to the Sangh's objectives. Perhaps he hoped that the ban would be lifted if the Sangh's effectiveness was bound up with what many in the government saw in the communist movement a rising national threat.

In fact, this was also the central argument of a memorandum the RSS had submitted around the middle of September to Nehru, with copies marked to Patel, Governor General of India C. Rajagopalachari and Congress president Rajendra Prasad. The memorandum, making a point-by-point case for lifting of the ban, was signed by Delhi sanghchalak Hans Raj Gupta, Delhi organizer Vasantrao Oak, Punjab RSS secretary Dharam Vir and UP sanghchalak Narinderjit Singh. 'We do not think that the Communists can be beaten by any political or economic programme and propaganda for they can easily mislead the masses by holding out to them extravagant promises of a debasing nature,' it said, and then declared in italics: '*Rashtriya Swayamsevak Sangh is the only way to meet the challenge of Communism and its' is the only ideology which can harmonise and integrate the interests of different groups and classes and thus successfully avoid any class war.*'[34]

Nehru felt the sting of Golwalkar's condescension. Despite

33. Ibid., pp. 15-18.

34. Delhi Police Records, File No. 519, pp. 36-52, Manuscript Section, NMML, New Delhi.

being opposed to the violent means often professed by communists, he had closely identified with the progressive and secular trends. He had also monitored the RSS too closely to get carried away by any of the arguments put forth by Golwalkar in his letter. In a reply dated 27 September, the Prime Minister's Office informed Golwalkar that Nehru did not consider the RSS a harmless body and that the governments of several provinces had collected considerable evidence against its anti-national and illegal activities. 'Just before the banning of the R.S.S. he [Nehru] is informed that the U.P. Government sent you a note on some of the evidence they had collected about such activities of the R.S.S. in U.P.,' said the PMO's reply. 'Other provinces have also such evidence in their possession. Even after the ban we have received information about the undesirable activities of old members of the R.S.S. [...] It is Government's policy to root out communalism from this country and, therefore, not to encourage any movement which aims at the encouragement of the communal outlook. The approach of the R.S.S. as well as their activities have been definitely communal. What sometimes their leaders say is not borne out by what is done and there is a great disparity between outward precept and real practice.'[35]

By contrast, Patel's response was conciliatory. In his letter dated 26 September 1948, which was delivered to Golwalkar through Central Provinces chief minister Ravi Shankar Shukla, Patel made no categorical remarks on his assertions, but suggested that the RSS needed to adopt 'a new culture and a new policy' and that this 'could only be in accordance with the rules of the Congress'. Moreover, Patel added that he had written to Shukla to see how Golwalkar's visit to Delhi could be facilitated.[36]

This disagreement marked the beginning of a fresh tussle

35. *Shri Guruji Samagra*, Volume 10, Suruchi Prakashan, New Delhi, pp. 20-21.

36. Ibid., pp. 19-20.

between Nehru and Patel. They, however, appeared reluctant to openly confront each other this time. Yet, Patel, while maintaining restraint, seemed determined to pursue his plans. Thus, on 17 October 1948, while Nehru was out on an official tour to Europe, Golwalkar was quietly brought to Delhi.[37] This was despite Shukla writing to Patel on 30 September that he 'should not see Shri Golwalkar' till the trial of Godse in the Gandhi murder case was over. 'As a matter of fact, he has reconciled himself to this position and seems to be prepared to wait,' Shukla wrote. He added:

> The R.S.S. problem has two aspects. The first is the question about the removal of the ban. This can be done as despite our greatest opposition to the Communists we have not imposed a ban on their party. But Shri Golwalkar goes further and asserts that his R.S.S. will give unflinching support to the present Government. This is the second aspect of the problem. It is being explained to Shri Golwalkar through a third party that his mere promise to support the Government cannot inspire confidence. During the War, the Communists supported the British Government while keeping their entity separate. [...] The R.S.S. may follow the same policy simply to rehabilitate itself in the eyes of the people and stab the Indian democracy in the back when a favourable opportunity arises. Some common friends have asked Shri Golwalkar whether he was prepared to order the members of the R.S.S. to join the Congress enbloc. We are awaiting his reply. Friends who are discussing the matter with him have taken care to see that the Government is not brought into these negotiations. Under these circumstances, it is my view that his seeing you at present will not be of much use.[38]

37. D. P. Mishra, *The Nehru Epoch: From Democracy to Monocracy*, Vikas Publishing House Pvt Ltd, New Delhi, 1978, p. 59.

38. Ravi Shankar Shukla to Sardar Patel, Digitised Private Papers, Sardar Patel, p. 186, NAI, New Delhi.

There is more than a hint of a secret strategy in the way Patel overruled Shukla's suggestions and tried to befriend Golwalkar while Nehru was in London. The trial in the Gandhi murder case was still on and Godse was yet to make his statement in the court. Patel held a two-hour-long discussion with Golwalkar on the afternoon of 17 October, the day he reached Delhi.[39] On 19 October, he wrote a carefully drafted letter to Nehru, suggesting that Golwalkar and his RSS had undergone the required transformation, and, therefore, the ban should be lifted. 'I had talks with Golwalkar the day before yesterday when he was here to see me,' wrote Patel.

> They seemed to be in a chastened mood and their sense of discipline is still very strong. I had made it quite clear that if he came to Delhi there should be no demonstrations. To receive him at the station, there were three to four thousand people who received him in silence. Nobody said a word and no demonstration was made. [...] I am beginning to think as to how long under a democratic set-up we can justify restrictions on this organisation if their unlawful activities are abjured by them. I have made my views quite clear to Golwalkar, viz. that the Sangh will have to change its entire outlook and its programme before provincial governments could be satisfied that these activities would cease to be a menace to the peace and tranquility of India. I also drew his attention to the reports which we are receiving regarding the secret activities of RSS men.[40]

Nehru, however, made such a show of decisiveness as to overwhelm all skepticism. 'Regarding the R.S.S., there is a widespread impression

39. P. N. Chopra & Prabha Chopra (ed.), *Inside Story of Sardar Patel: The Diary of Maniben Patel (1936-50)*, Vision Books, New Delhi, 2001, p. 227.

40. Patel to Nehru, cited in D. P. Mishra, *The Nehru Epoch: From Democracy to Monocracy*, Vikas Publishing House Pvt Ltd, New Delhi, 1978, pp. 59-60.

in England that they are Fascist, communal-minded people and any action we take in regard to them will be considered from this point of view,' he responded to Patel on 27 October 1948. 'The R.S.S. have a definite ideology which is entirely opposed to that of the Government and the Congress. They oppose definitely the idea of a secular State. In fact, their ideology strikes at the root of our Constitution, present and future. If they continue to hold their ideology, their activities are definitely unconstitutional. The least they could do is to make clear publicly that they renounce their ideology and all activities to further it.'[41]

These observations involving the nature and perception of the RSS were hardly new to Patel, but then Nehru made them irrefutable by stating in the letter that Mahatma Gandhi had 'expressed a very strong opinion against Golwalkar and the R.S.S. and said that it was impossible to rely upon their word'. Pointing out that he also had the same impression, Nehru concluded: 'I suggest therefore that we should be very careful in taking any new step about the R.S.S. at the present juncture.'[42]

V

Patel seemed fairly sure that Golwalkar could be relied on for his plans to give a rightward shift to the Congress. But Golwalkar saw himself presented with unexpected opportunities once he arrived from Nagpur and met Patel on 17 October. In Delhi, he stayed with state sanghchalak Hans Raj Gupta at his 20, Barakhamba Road residence. Golwalkar's presence in Delhi galvanized the RSS men in the region. The intelligence department of Delhi Police noted that hundreds of RSS workers from Delhi and outside

41. *Selected Works of Jawaharlal Nehru*, Second Series, Volume VIII, Jawaharlal Nehru Memorial Fund, New Delhi, 1989, pp. 287-288.

42. Ibid., p. 288.

started paying daily visits to him. On 20 October, for example, about 500 RSS members visited him.[43] The intelligence officers also reported that during this period the Sangh workers 'under the garb of Jan Adhikar Samiti' started a signature campaign to 'enroll support in demanding the government to lift the ban' on the RSS.[44]

Coming to an agreement with Golwalkar was, therefore, proving to be difficult for Patel. Despite all his promises, Golwalkar didn't appear to be ready to give up the independent identity of the RSS, nor to change its ideological orientation. Patel, on the other hand, was aware that all his efforts to facilitate Golwalkar's visit to Delhi or to get the ban lifted from the Sangh presupposed an unambiguous commitment from the RSS chief to withdraw from politics and to direct his men to join the Congress—a condition made evident by Ravi Shankar Shukla's 30 September letter.

On 22 October, they met again, but Patel's hopes remained unfulfilled. 'Mr Golwalkar's stand was one of protest against the attacks made on the RSS without any justification and of his desires to introduce changes, provided the ban was withdrawn,' said a Home Ministry note sent to Ravi Shankar Shukla and D. P. Mishra on the same day. 'He [Patel] told Mr Golwalkar that it might be possible to review the position if he could publish the constitution of the Sangh and give a definite idea of their objectives, programme and constitution, abjure secrecy of their organisation and express a determination to confirm to constitutional methods. Mr Golwalkar conceded the necessity of a reorientation of the Sangh's activities on these lines, but felt that the removal of the ban would strengthen his hands; otherwise, things might go beyond his control. HM [Home Minister] has asked Mr Golwalkar to think

43. Delhi Police Records, File No. 519, p. 96, Manuscript Section, NMML, New Delhi.

44. Ibid., p. 61.

over the suggestions which he has made and for the time being to return to Nagpur. After he has thought over the matters, it might be possible to renew this contact.'[45]

Instead of returning to Nagpur, Golwalkar stayed on in Delhi to make preparations for a campaign to force the government to lift the ban. 'Uptil 3-11-48 when an order under section 4(1) Punjab Public Safety Act was served on the Sangh Guru prohibiting him from meeting large number of people or addressing them, the Sangh workers were under impression that soon the ban on the organisation would be lifted,' noted an intelligence report. 'After that day the position changed and the organ of the R.S.S.S. (*Organiser*, Delhi) in its issue dated 3rd November 1948 declared the failure of talks between the Government and the Sangh Guru.'[46]

Perhaps the many encouragements he received from Patel tended to support Golwalkar in his boldest expectations. In the past, too, the internal contradictions and antagonisms of the government had afforded Golwalkar almost unlimited freedom to manoeuvre. Apparently, it was in this context that, on finding Patel unyielding, Golwalkar turned to Nehru, who was soon to return from abroad. On 3 and 8 November, he wrote two consecutive letters to him. In the first, which was written with reference to the PMO's reply to him on 27 September, Golwalkar claimed that he never received any note containing charges against him from the government of the United Provinces. 'Long before the R.S.S. was banned, I too had heard much about a "charge-sheet" the U.P. Government was preparing against us. But months rolled by and it was not forthcoming,' he wrote and ended the letter by appealing to Nehru's sense of justice.

---

45. D. P. Mishra, *The Nehru Epoch: From Democracy to Monocracy*, Vikas Publishing House Pvt Ltd, New Delhi, 1978, p. 60.

46. Delhi Police Records, File No. 407, p. 19, Manuscript Section, NMML, New Delhi.

> It is unfair for a civilised Government that ours is, to charge any person or body of persons with crimes of a serious character, without laying sufficient weighty evidence on the table and giving the accused a chance to vindicate his innocence. In the case of the R.S.S. I am constrained to state that it is most unfair to continue to level charges against us, allow private individuals and parties to carry on a campaign of vilification against us under cover of the Government ban and at the same time gag us by use of Emergency Legislations like the Public Safety Acts. I fail to see how this course is calculated to do credit to the Government which we want to love and hold in esteem.[47]

On 8 November, on Nehru's return from Europe, he wrote: 'When in October, 1947, I had the happiness of meeting you I had said I would come again. But my ceaseless wanderings made it impossible. Now I hope the chance has been offered to me and I shall be very grateful if you will kindly communicate to me the date and time when I may have the interview and be given the chance of reiterating my assurance of last October, 1947, of unstinting support to the Government in these delicate times.'[48]

On 10 November, Nehru replied, reiterating the charges against the RSS and telling him categorically that a meeting would serve no purpose as it was the Home Ministry which was looking into the matter. 'In course of the last year both the Central Government and the Provincial Governments have received a mass of information in regard to the objectives and activities of the R.S.S.,' he wrote.

> This information does not fit in with what has been stated by you in this behalf. Indeed it would appear that the declared objectives have little to do with the real ones and with the activities carried

47. *Panchjanya*, 3 Margshirsh Krishna, Issue supplementary 26, Vikram Samvat 2005, Year 1.

48. Ibid.

> on in various forms and ways by people associated with the R.S.S. These real objectives appear to be completely opposed to the decisions of the Indian Parliament and the provisions for the proposed Constitution of India. The activities, according to our information, are anti-national and often subversive and violent. You would appreciate therefore that mere assertions to the contrary do not help very much.[49]

Golwalkar had once more worked himself into an almost hopeless position. To be sure, his bid to derive benefit from differences between Nehru and Patel only showed up the weakness of his sense of reality. He now had only one choice—to back down on the whole issue. But, true to his character, he refused to concede. Instead, he started working on a plan to launch a satyagraha campaign against the continuing ban on the RSS. On 15 November, he was picked up and sent back to Nagpur, where he was kept in a local jail before being shifted to the prison in neighbouring Seoni.[50]

---

49. J.N. (S.G.)–Post-Independence, File No. 15 (Part I), p. 57, NMML, New Delhi.

50. D. P. Mishra, *The Nehru Epoch: From Democracy to Monocracy*, Vikas Publishing House Pvt Ltd, New Delhi, 1978, pp. 60-61.

Jail-time

The theory that Golwalkar had despised all his life—the Gandhian concept of a determined but non-violent resistance—now appeared to him as the only way to save himself and his organization. Satyagraha, or civil disobedience, as evolved and practised by Gandhi, rested on soul force rather than brute force and contained the best of human civilizations filtered through the long struggle of India's independence—moral strength, courage, confidence, sagacity, forbearance. These concepts and values as part of a political theory had been alien to Golwalkar and his men. They never believed in their effectiveness and promoted, instead, the concept of communally-driven political theory as a legitimate tool to achieve their objectives. A trace of irony was, therefore, glaringly evident when Golwalkar decided to use the Gandhian weapon of satyagraha to force the government to revoke its ban on the RSS and release him from jail.

The debate over satyagraha had broken out during Golwalkar's stay in Delhi. After his arrest, the situation of the RSS became desperate. RSS men 'started considering the question of civil disoberience' as the sole means to bring the government under pressure.[1] They mustered all their energy and began to prepare

1. Delhi Police Records, File No. 407, p. 20, Manuscript Section, NMML, New Delhi.

plans for mobilizing volunteers who would demonstrate and court arrest. There was a sense of imminent victory among cadres as they were given to believe by their leaders that 'in 1942 only 80,000 Congressmen went to jail and achieved independence but now 80,000 Sangh workers were prepared to go to jail from one province alone'.[2] They also expected enthusiastic support from masses as they 'felt that the public hatred against the organisation [that followed Gandhi's murder] was gradually waning'.[3]

Nehru was quick to notice the irony, as well as the threat, in the much talked-about plan of Golwalkar and his cadres. 'For sometime past intelligence reports have stated that large scale arrangements are being made by the R.S.S. to challenge the authority of Government by satyagraha and other means,' he said in a note to the Home Ministry dated 5 December 1948. 'They have no conception of what satyagraha means and no intention of following the spirit of satyagraha conceived by Mahatma Gandhi or the Congress. It is in fact a mere cloak for other activities. R.S.S. is essentially a body which functions secretly. What it does or says in public has no relation to what it carries on in secret. Therefore, an open satyagraha movement will only be a cloak for other activities which may be very dangerous.'[4]

The RSS started the agitation on 9 December 1948. The intelligence officers noted that 'messengers were sent from Nagpur to all zonal headquarters in India to start Civil Disobedience on 9th December'.[5] Golwalkar's clarion call for satyagraha came four days later, on 13 December: 'We have been forced into this only

2. Ibid., IX Inst, File No. 527, p. 15.

3. Ibid.

4. *Selected Works of Jawaharlal Nehru*, Second Series, Volume VIII, Jawaharlal Nehru Memorial Fund, New Delhi, 1989, pp. 128-129.

5. Delhi Police Records, File No. 407, p. 36, Manuscript Section, NMML, New Delhi.

course by the narrow mindedness of the government, their greed for perpetration of party domination and their intolerance of the existence of every other form of thought and action.'[6]

It was a peaceful agitation in which the RSS workers and supporters, acting as satyagrahis, courted arrest in groups. In many cases, police resorted to the house arrest of potential satyagrahis.[7] Intelligence officers of Delhi, however, were amused to find most of the prominent RSS men and organizers behaving strangely. Contrary to the principles of Gandhian satyagraha known for the display of moral strength and courage of the participants, the local RSS leaders, instead of leading their groups of satyagrahis to court arrest, just went underground and started hiding from police. 'They have changed their dress,' said a report, 'and now are wearing European dress.'[8]

Satyagrahis who seemed most undeterred were students organized under the banner of the Akhil Bharatiya Vidyarthi Parishad (ABVP), a student body formed in July 1948 as an alternative outfit of young RSS men following the ban on their parent organization. 'Members of Parishad, an allying body of R.S.S., are organising Satyagraha very vigorously and they are sending students to participate in it,' said an intelligence report.[9] In fact, it was during the satyagraha that the ABVP consolidated itself as an important student body in Delhi and some other areas.

Another RSS-affiliated organization that took shape in the wake of satyagraha was a news agency, Hindustan Samachar. 'Further side-light into the R.S.S.S. drama of lawlessness reveals that

---

6. Government of Inida, Ministry of States–Political Branch, File No. 74(1)–P/48, pp. 44-47, NAI, New Delhi.

7. Delhi Police Records, File No. 404, p. 10, Manuscript Section, NMML, New Delhi

8. Ibid.

9. Ibid.

sometimes before the commencement of their Civil Disobedience movement, the R.S.S.S. set up its own news agencies with a view to disseminate all information regarding the activities of the R.S.S.S. at different places in the country,' noted an intelligence report. 'One such agency known as "Hindustan Samachar Delhi" is reported with its office somewhere near India Gate. It issues daily bulletins to the vernacular dailies of Delhi and the bulletins mostly contain information about the day to day activities of the R.S.S.S. at different places in the country. R.S.S.S. workers are then entrusted with the task of delivering typed copies of the bulletins issued by the "Hindustan Samachar Delhi" in the office of the daily newspapers of Delhi. The R.S.S.S. workers instead of making personal delivery of these bulletins, manage to throw the same in the boxes (meant for receipt of mails) of the newspapers.'[10]

Nevertheless, the satyagraha remained far less popular than it was made out to be by the RSS leaders. According to an Intelligence Bureau report, a total of 36,180 satyagrahis were arrested up to 30 December 1948 in the whole of India, including the princely states. Of these, the Bombay province recorded the maximum arrests of 9,050 satyagrahis, followed by UP with 7,029 arrests and the Central Provinces with 5,672 arrests. Delhi recorded a total arrest of 1,517 satyagrahis, while in East Punjab 2,550 RSS men were held. In princely states, including Alwar and Bharatpur, a total of 4,887 men courted arrest during this period.[11]

The report also pointed out that the agitation received a cool reception from the masses and that the RSS men were facing 'great difficulty in finding satyagrahis' for demonstrations and court arrests. 'Students in large number were sent in as satyagrahis without the consent of their parents and in the C.P. as well as in E. Punjab, many volunteers were hired to offer satyagraha on

10. Ibid., p. 2.

11. Delhi Police Records, IX Inst., File No. 518, p. 95, NMML, New Delhi.

the promise of payment of money,' it said. 'Due to the paucity of volunteers satyagraha was confined to the provincial headquarters in West Bengal, U.P. and Bihar. It was also restricted in other provinces. [...] The public in general remained indifferent and criticised the R.S.S. movement as being inopportune.'[12]

As the satyagraha waned, talks of Golwalkar going on hunger strike from 15 January 1949 started doing the rounds.[13] 'This tactics,' said an intelligence report, 'would have two objectives in view i.e. to put pressure on the Govt; and to incite his followers.'[14] But Golwalkar never seemed serious about starting a hunger strike. He rather appeared perturbed in his mind because of the worsening political situation in Nagpur, where non-Brahmins had started a counter-agitation against the Brahmin sympathizers of the RSS. 'Almost daily anti-RSS processions and public meetings were held and slogans such as "hang Golwalkar" shouted in the streets,' recounted D. P. Mishra.

> Although these demonstrations were being organised in the name of the Congress, they had an overwhelming non-Brahman preponderance. Hindu Sabhaites and other supporters of the RSS got nervous in view of the incidents of the previous February. A number of them came in deputation to me with a request to stop the demonstrations. I had to tell them that while the government was determined to maintain law and order, it would be unfair to those who disagreed with the RSS not to allow them to express their views. Besides, I warned them, complete suppression of their sentiments might lead to sudden outbursts of violence.[15]

---

12. Ibid., pp. 96-97.

13. Delhi Police Records, File No. 405, p. 37, NMML, New Delhi.

14. Ibid., File No. 404, p. 8.

15. D. P. Mishra, *The Nehru Epoch: From Democracy to Monocracy*, Vikas Publishing House Pvt Ltd, New Delhi, 1978, p. 63.

When satyagraha was launched, Golwalkar seemed to assume that a significant section of Hindus, particularly refugees from Pakistan, would rise up in favour of the RSS. There was, however, no trace of any such support. Instead, he now confronted the scary prospect of being held responsible for triggering a repeat of violent attacks by non-Brahmins on RSS men and their Brahmin supporters. Even a hunger strike, in such a situation, would be fraught with grave dangers; it could simply turn out to be a suicide mission.

This would help explain his unconditional retreat on 19 January 1949 when Hindu Mahasabha leader G. V. Ketkar, acting as a third-party well-wisher, met him in Seoni jail and drew his attention to the worsening situation in Nagpur and some other areas.[16] And when Ketkar told him that this was his last visit and he would not come again if the meeting failed to produce any result, Golwalkar quickly took out his letter-writing pad and wrote: 'All my brother swayamsewaks, having been apprised by Shri G.V. Ketkar of the general situation in the country and the attitude of the Government regarding the present movement of the Rashtriya Swayam Sewak Sangh, of the wide sympathy and good will shown and expressed by a number of prominent third-party citizens, I deem that the time has come for discontinuing the present movement in order to promote a congenial atmosphere and also to bring about an atmosphere for the sympathetic efforts of these third party friends for solving the present dead-lock.'[17]

II

The failure of the satyagraha dampened the spirits of RSS men, but it lit up Congress leaders. It made it plain that Golwalkar no longer enjoyed any significant mass support, and his cadres were

16. Ibid., p. 64.

17. D. P. Mishra Papers, I & II Insts., Subject File No. 19 (Unbanning of the RSS), p. 111, NMML, New Delhi.

now more of a nuisance than a threat to the nation. With the RSS drifting into political irrelevancy, Nehru was taken over by more urgent issues: celebration of 26 January 1949 as Remembrance Day, for it was on this day in 1930 that India had taken the Independence Pledge for the first time; preparations for Gandhi's first death anniversary on 30 January; and finalization and adoption of the Constitution of India. There were also more particular factors. One was the presence of a large number of students in various jails—they had been the most enthusiastic participants in the RSS-led satyagraha, and they had to be sent back to their schools and colleges.

'You know my views regarding the R.S.S.,' Nehru said in his speech at Ramlila Maidan on 26 January 1949, a week after Golwalkar's withdrawal of satyagraha. 'There are many youngsters in the R.S.S., mere children, in fact. Now it is obvious that we cannot get annoyed with children. After all, they are our children, who have to shoulder the responsibilities of the nation. But when a childish attitude is brought to bear on important issues, the results are absolutely wrong. I am amazed to see the extent to which the R.S.S. is wrong in its basic policies. [...] Well, the matter has ended. I am not really bothered about the R.S.S., but I will repeat what I said earlier. I am constantly searching everywhere to see in which direction the new India that is shaping up will look and what it will do.'[18]

In line with prevailing sentiment, Patel held an inter-provincial conference on 29 January 1949. It was decided that all students should be released from prison 'with the exception of only those—understood to be very few in number—who were actively organising the Sangh activities'.[19] No mercy was shown

18. *Selected Works of Jawaharlal Nehru*, Second Series, Volume IX, Jawaharlal Nehru Memorial Fund, New Delhi, 1990, pp. 17-18.

19. Ministry of States, 'P' Branch, File No. 16(2)-P/49, 'Inter-Provincial Conference on R.S.S. held on Saturday, the 29th January 1949', p. 74, NAI, New Delhi.

to government servants who had taken part in the RSS activities because any 'consideration shown to them would destroy the whole fabric of administration'.[20] As for general people other than students and government servants, it was resolved that 'those who gave an undertaking of good behavior for the future should be released'.[21]

It was also decided in the conference that Golwalkar could be allowed—if he made a formal request or on the request of third parties—'to meet his colleagues so as to consider the new situation that has arisen'. Such a request could be accepted only if Golwalkar agreed formally to four conditions: that the RSS would frame and publish a written constitution, that it would abjure secrecy and all unconstitutional methods, that it would declare 'unquestioned allegiance' to the national flag and that it would accept 'the conception of a Secular Democratic State for India'.[22]

While circumstances generated by the failure of satyagraha were working in his favour, Patel himself seemed to be extremely worried, and he tried in every conceivable way to ensure that the conditions being laid down for starting a dialogue with the RSS addressed all the concerns of Nehru. He feared the spread of half truth that might cause misunderstanding among Congress leaders. It was, therefore, also decided in the conference that the decisions should be kept secret until Patel himself explained them in full detail in the Legislative Assembly.[23]

Nehru agreed with Patel's initiatives, but remained skeptical about the RSS. 'The Home Minister has discussed future policy in regard to the R.S.S. with Premiers,' he wrote to Chief Ministers on 3 February 1949.

---

20. Ibid.
21. Ibid.
22. Ibid., p. 75.
23. Ibid.

> Naturally we are anxious that our young men and students who have been misguided enough to participate in this movement [satyagraha] should not suffer. It is therefore desirable that these young men should be released. If they function wrongly again then action has to be taken. In regard to others, there should be no hurry in releasing them and the situation should be closely watched. A great deal is said about negotiations with the R.S.S. leaders. So far as we are concerned, there is not much room or anxiety for negotiation. It must be remembered that the R.S.S. is an organisation which has always said something and done something else. [...] For the present, therefore, it is best to watch events and developments and not in any way to encourage the R.S.S. leaders to imagine that we are anxious for some kind of a settlement with them.[24]

In writing this, Nehru certainly had not abandoned his quest for a secular, democratic nation. That remained one of the basic premises of all his policies right down to the last breath of his life. But it now assumed another character. From the sorrow and tragedy of the post-Partition communal riots and Gandhi's murder, some hope had started emerging. There was calm in India, attacks on Muslims had stopped and refugees had been housed. The nation appeared firmly moving on a secular, democratic path, and the communal forces were fast becoming the lunatic fringe of Indian politics. Furthermore, the inter-provincial conference had made it clear to the RSS that no talks could begin unless it formally accepted the conception of a secular, democratic state for India and abjured its secrecy and all its unconstitutional methods. Henceforth, national reconstruction and reconciliation became the central tenet of Nehru's domestic and foreign policies.

---

24. *Selected Works of Jawaharlal Nehru*, Second Series, Volume IX, Jawahrlal Nehru Memorial Fund, New Delhi, 1990, p. 303.

III

Inside Seoni jail, Golwalkar was in despair. The conditions laid down for revoking the ban on the RSS and releasing him from prison had put his whole vision of a Hindu Rashtra at stake. For, one of the conditions required him to formally announce his unequivocal acceptance of India as a secular, democratic nation. His aim, as spelt out in *We or Our Nationhood Defined*, was to replace a secular and nationalist Indian government with that which would accord the status of second-class citizenship to minorities. In a democratic set-up, this could not be accomplished by an organization that functioned—as these conditions expected—with total openness and transparency in its aims and practice. He wanted to take advantage of the new situation, and yet—as events would show later—he remained adamant to retain the essence of the old system.

At the time, however, public interest centred primarily on the attempt at democratic self-assertion. The conditions, whose value was ultimately to be measured by the national mood evolved in the aftermath of Mahatma Gandhi's assassination, were nothing less than an extremely generous offer of the government to the RSS. No support could have been achieved if Golwalkar opposed them too openly. He, therefore, appeared to bow to the government's conditions and enthusiastically welcomed the initiative of T. R. Venkatarama Sastri, an RSS sympathizer of Madras, and B. G. Khaparde, a former minister of the Central Provinces, to act as third-party negotiators in order to bring about a speedy settlement. As well-wishers and personal friends of Golwalkar, they had obtained Patel's nod to help frame a constitution for the RSS and persuade its chief to make adjustments according to the four conditions laid down by the inter-provincial conference.[25]

---

25. D. P. Mishra, *The Nehru Epoch: From Democracy to Monocracy*, Vikas Publishing House Pvt Ltd, New Delhi, 1978, p. 65.

On 13 February 1949, Sastri and Khaparde met with Golwalkar in jail and discussed the contours and basic principles of the proposed constitution. 'At the time of departure and termination of the interview,' said the jail report on the meeting, 'Golwalkar gave a blank cheque to his interviewers by saying that he would not let them down and would agree to any compromise that may be brought about by them with the Government.'[26] Sastri then put in long hours for weeks drafting a constitution in consultation with some senior leaders of the RSS and took it to Golwalkar for approval on 10 March 1949. After having gone through it, Golwalkar gave his approval in writing.[27]

However, the draft constitution and the accompanying letter that Golwalkar sent to Patel were ambiguous with regard to some of the critical conditions laid down by the inter-provincial conference, and this put off the government. 'You have stated in your letter that the RSS has in the past adhered to the principles laid down in the draft constitution,' Union Home Secretary H. V. R. Iengar wrote to Golwalkar on 3 May.

> One of these is that the Sangh adheres to 'peaceful and legitimate means' for the realisation of its ideals. Unfortunately the history of RSS activities in recent times shows that this profession has in practice been systematically violated by your followers. Incidents have occurred in all provinces and many states where the methods adopted by the Sangh were anything but peaceful and legitimate, and where the advancement of the interests of Hindu religion and culture took the form of violence against those who happened to profess some faith other than Hinduism. Government feel, therefore, that a positive and explicit declaration in the constitution for the abjuration of violence would be necessary.[28]

---

26. D. P. Mishra Papers, I&II Insts., Subject File No. 19 (Unbanning of the RSS), p. 24a, Manuscript Section, NMML, New Delhi.

27. Ibid., p. 2.

28. Ibid., pp. 53-55.

Iengar also demanded that the RSS constitution must specifically declare allegiance to the national flag and the Constitution of India, define the role of the sarsanghchalak and lay down the principle of election as the means to elect office-bearers. 'On the organizational side, the various committees of the RSS at all levels seem to contain a substantial element of persons who are virtually nominated from above,' Iengar wrote. 'This is a principle of organisation which is fraught with great danger and the Government of India consider that the democratic elective principle should be unequivocally recognized and acted upon. In particular, the functions of the Sar Sangh Chalak have not been defined with any degree of precision; in the interests of democratic working, these functions should be specifically listed, and all vestiges of a dictatorial character should be removed.'[29]

As a quick settlement with the government seemed elusive, Golwalkar flew into rage and shot off an angry letter to Patel on 17 May, calling for an 'impartial tribunal' to prove charges against the RSS.[30] Iengar responded by reminding Golwalkar that the government was the 'final judge' and that it chose not to prosecute the RSS, thinking that it would mend its ways. 'I am to repeat that the Government of India have ample evidence in their possession implicating both the RSS and its individual members in systematic acts of violence,' Iengar wrote on 24 May. 'They held their hand for a long time hoping that the organisation would mend its ways and they took action only when their patience was exhausted. [...] The Government of India had expected that you would appreciate the constructive approach which they made to the draft constitution of the RSS but find that you have either misunderstood that approach or are deliberately adhering to the

29. Ibid.

30. D. P. Mishra, *The Nehru Epoch: From Democracy to Monocracy*, Vikas Publishing House Pvt Ltd, New Delhi, 1978, p. 72.

objectionable features of your constitution in the hope that they will enable you to carry on the activities of the RSS on the same undesirable lines as in the past.'[31]

These tensions complicated Golwalkar's position. He tried to be careful in his next letter to Patel written on 1 June, but here, too, he did not offer any rethink on key matters. Instead, he sought to take a high moral ground. 'I am a plain man, brought up in an organisation wherein the sense of high and low does not predominate and wherein, therefore, there is no occasion to study and use "a style" of language suitable for addressing "rulers" and masters,' he wrote. 'Hence I could use only plain and straightforward expressions for expressing what I believe to be right and true. All the same I beg to be excused for having unwittingly offended the government by a direct expression of the truth.'[32]

There is no doubt about the basic facts. Patel's desire to revoke the ban on the RSS was intense, but he didn't want to do this without ensuring that all the concerns of Nehru were addressed. Golwalkar, too, was desperate to see the ban lifted, but he didn't want to put his whole political future at stake. For all of his seeming eagerness to comply with the demands of the government, he retained strong convictions about the old RSS culture and practice he had so meticulously shaped over the past decade.

Yet, his correspondence with the Home Ministry seemed to make him unsure of himself. On 29 May, days before he wrote his last letter to Patel, Golwalkar secretly tried to send a letter to his colleague Balasaheb Deoras, who was practically acting as the leader of the RSS, asking him to shore up support from outside the jail by organizing 'a strong, well-prepared and well-planned

31. D. P. Mishra Papers, I&II Insts., Subject File No. 19 (Unbanning of the RSS), p. 59, Manuscript Section, NMML, New Delhi.

32. D. P. Mishra, *The Nehru Epoch: From Democracy to Monocracy*, Vikas Publishing House Pvt Ltd, New Delhi, 1978, pp. 76-77.

movement' to build pressure on the government. But his letter, along with his entire correspondence with the government which he tried to smuggle out of jail, were intercepted by the authorities.[33] 'I immediately informed Patel of Golwalkar's unsuccessful attempt to send out instructions for re-starting the movement,' Mishra recounted.[34] Patel's response was quick: 'I think we have succeeded in catching Golwalkar on the wrong foot. [...] Now, in the light of Golwalkar's reply to me and with the evidence of these intercepts, we can easily turn the tables on Golwalkar.'[35] On the instructions of the Home Minister, Mishra shifted Golwalkar from Seoni to Betul jail on 7 June 1949. For a couple of days, no visitor could meet him. It was only on 19 June that Golwalkar's parents were allowed to see him in the new jail.[36]

These developments seemed to produce a sense of panic and led Golwalkar to start working again. He now turned to Pandit Mauli Chandra Sharma to ensure speedy settlement of the whole issue. Sharma was a former Congress leader who had shifted to the Hindutva camp and was a personal friend of Vasantrao Oak. Before long, Sharma visited Betul jail carrying a copy of the typed draft constitution that Mishra had prepared after incorporating all of Iengar's suggestions. Without raising any questions, Golwalkar took the document, copied it in his own handwriting, signed and handed it over to Sharma.[37]

The next day, Mishra flew down to Delhi to hand over the signed copy of the Sangh's draft constitution to Patel, who had already obtained Nehru's consent for revoking the ban and releasing the RSS men. Nehru's view was that 'the less we have

33. Ibid., p. 77.
34. Ibid., p. 80.
35. Ibid.
36. Ibid., pp. 80-81.
37. Ibid., pp. 82-83.

of these bans and detentions, the better' and that the government could 'always take action, when necessity arises'.[38] Patel acted with surprising speed once Mishra gave him the revised document signed by Golwalkar on 11 July 1949.[39] He read it carefully and compared it with Iengar's letters. 'I heaved a sigh of relief when he raised his head and expressed his complete satisfaction with what I had brought,' Mishra reminisced. 'He immediately rang up Nehru telling him that Golwalkar had accepted the conditions imposed by the Government and that he was ordering the release of RSS prisoners. Nehru approved [...].'[40]

By late 11 July 1949, the government communiqué revoking the ban on the RSS was ready.[41] In the morning of 12 July, the Home Ministry sent a telegram to provincial governments, informing them about the Centre's decision following Golwalkar's acceptance of all the conditions and asking them to release the RSS men.[42] The communiqué was officially issued in the evening.[43] Golwalkar was released from jail on 13 July.[44]

38. *Selected Works of Jawaharlal Nehru*, Second Series, Volume XII, Jawaharlal Nehru Memorial Fund, New Delhi, 1991, p. 453.

39. P. N. Chopra & Prabha Chopra (ed.), *Inside Story of Sardar Patel: The Diary of Maniben Patel (1936-50)*, Vision Books, New Delhi, 2001, p. 285.

40. D. P. Mishra, *The Nehru Epoch: From Democracy to Monocracy*, Vikas Publishing House Pvt Ltd, New Delhi, 1978, p. 83.

41. P. N. Chopra & Prabha Chopra (ed.), *Inside Story of Sardar Patel: The Diary of Maniben Patel (1936-50)*, Vision Books, New Delhi, 2001, p. 285.

42. JN (SG) Papers (Post-1947), File No. 26, Part I, p. 186, Telegram of July 12, 1949, Manuscript Section, NMML, New Delhi.

43. Ibid.

44. Ranga Hari, *The Incomparable Guru Golwalkar*, Prabhat Paperbacks, New Delhi, 2018, p. 170.

IV

It was a depressingly changed scene to which Golwalkar returned from jail. The idea of secular democracy had risen above the turmoil of the past and become the spirit of the age. The policy of reconciliation had begun to show results, refugees' lives had stabilized, and their hatred against Muslims had dissolved. The East Punjab High Court had upheld Godse's death sentence, awarded earlier by the trial court in Delhi. Princely states had given up their dreams of independent existence. The preparation of the draft constitution was in an advanced stage, and everyone seemed to be waiting for its adoption. Gradually, the government had acquired solidity and authority, and people could feel that the nation was on a reliable foundation. These changes were not so much a matter of specifics as the reflection of an improvement in the psychological climate in the country. Supporters of a Hindu Rashtra still moved around in society but they had been markedly thrown back. Although there was nothing dramatic in the turn of events, it did appear as if India, after years of social crisis and communal strife, was beginning to return to normalcy.

Viewed in political terms, Golwalkar's situation was hopeless. The domestic tranquility—the absence of which in the wake of Partition had let him emerge as the messiah of a Hindu Rashtra—now made him look like a failed and half-forgotten leader of a ragtag unit of volunteers who might be of little importance. The political climate that favoured pro-Hindu and anti-Muslim elements had changed. His organization had been wrecked, and most of the pracharaks, who had pledged celibacy and fanned out in different parts of the country as his emissaries, had returned to the routine of everyday life or had dispersed.

Golwalkar, however, was not discouraged by the situation. He appeared on the scene full of confidence but double faced. To his cadres, he postured as an unchanged man, as the longed-for rescuer of the idea of a Hindu Rashtra that had been sinking since the ban on the RSS, but in his public speeches, he avoided risks of embracing the idea openly. Instead, he now kept his views nuanced so as not to appear violating the conditions that had led to his release. Talking to media-persons at the RSS headquarters on 18 July, for example, he asserted that the authority of the government must be respected. 'It is our own Government,' he said, 'and therefore it has lifted the ban on the R.S.S. It is unlikely that the ban will be lifted in Pakistan.'[45] To provincial organizers and the regional chiefs of the RSS on 30 July, however, he categorically denied having given any undertaking or assurance to the government.[46]

Evidently, therefore, he seemed to believe that his political fate as well as the future of the RSS would be dependent upon how skillfully he played the two contradictory positions. But, of course, if he were to be effective, he needed a powerful ally. In the given situation, it was not difficult for him to figure out who that ally could be. Without the proactive role of Patel, the ban would not have been revoked and he would still be languishing in jail. Although Patel had been firm in forcing him to accept the conditions of the government, it did not affect the warmth of their relationship. On 18 July, Golwalkar wrote to Patel, expressing his gratitude to him and requesting a meeting. 'There are some feelings which cannot be expressed in writing,' he wrote. 'As it is, I am experiencing such a feeling [for you]. I cannot write even a fraction of it in the letter, and, therefore, it would only be appropriate for me to see you and express my feeling in person.'[47]

Patel's reply came within days. 'How much happiness I have

45. *The Times of India*, 19 July 1949.

46. *The Times of India*, 31 July 1949.

47. Sardar Patel Papers, 'Correspondence with Shri Golwalkar & R.S.S. Celebrities', File No. 8/38, p. 68 (original letter in Hindi), NAI, New Delhi.

felt after revoking the ban on the RSS can be explained only by those who were with me at that time,' read the letter dated 21 July. 'I am particularly delighted that in this way the god has given me yet another opportunity to work on my ideas regarding the future role of the Sangh which I had expressed in Jaipur and Lucknow over a year back.'[48] At Jaipur, on 17 December 1947, Patel had appreciated 'the enthusiasm' of the RSS men but asked them to divert it 'into constructive channels', and in Lucknow, on 6 January 1948, he had referred to them as 'patriots' who should be 'won over by Congressmen by love'.

Clearly, Patel had his own plans about the RSS. He still wanted RSS men to join the Congress. The entry of 3 August 1949 in the diary on Patel's daily activities by his daughter Maniben, for example, reads: 'Glad at release of Golwalkar—ready to welcome in Congress. Bapu's [father's] task to make their entry easy.'[49] His letter to Golwalkar also indicates that he was trying to use the latter's gratitude as a lever to extract from him a statement asking members of the RSS to enter the Congress. Moreover, Patel seemed convinced that as a 'well disciplined organisation' the RSS could be used strategically against communists. While explaining the unbanning of the Sangh, T. G. Sanjevi, the Intelligence Bureau director considered close to Patel, told a US diplomat that the government found it 'expedient to use the RSS as a buffer against communism'.[50]

Yet, Patel tried to manage his RSS plan as discreetly as possible so that it would not alarm Nehru, who, despite agreeing to revoke the ban on the RSS, still looked at it with utmost suspicion. 'As

48. Ibid., pp. 66-67 (original letter in Hindi).

49. P. N. Chopra & Prabha Chopra (ed.), *Inside Story of Sardar Patel: The Diary of Maniben Patel (1936-50)*, Vision Books, New Delhi, 2001, p. 298.

50. Records of the US State Department Relating to the Internal Affairs of India, 1945-1949, Image No. 160: India, Library of Congress, Washington DC.

you know, the ban on the RSS has been removed,' he wrote to chief ministers on 20 July 1949.

> This does not mean that we are convinced about the bona fides of the RSS movement, although they have promised to behave in future. All it means is that we feel that we must gradually relax the abnormal measures that we have taken in restricting the normal liberties of the individual and the group whatever that might be. We do not propose to relax in the slightest our vigilance and we shall take instant action whenever necessary. But such action loses its value when it becomes a normal action of the state. We have been criticised a great deal for our restriction of civil liberties. That criticism may be justified in vacuo, but it is to be considered in relation to the extraordinary circumstances which we have had to face during the past two years. We were compelled to take that action because the safety and security of the State and the great majority of our people were concerned.[51]

Nor did Nehru believe in Patel's idea that the RSS should be used as 'a buffer against communism'. When a reporter posed this question during a press conference on 5 August, Nehru said, 'So, so far as we are concerned, although all kinds of barriers and bans which existed generally have been removed, and in the case of the R.S.S. nearly all of them have been discharged from prison, we do not frankly trust the R.S.S. very much and we shall keep a very vigilant outlook in regard to it.'[52]

Aware of Nehru's views, Patel tried to act as the guarantor of Golwalkar's good conduct. He seemed to believe that with that guarantee, Nehru might reconsider his position on Golwalkar

51. JN (SG) Papers, Post-1947, File No. 26, Part II, p. 261, Manuscript Section, NMML, New Delhi.

52. *Selected Works of Jawaharlal Nehru*, Second Series, Volume XII, Jawaharlal Nehru Memorial Fund, New Delhi, 1991, p. 14.

and allow Patel to go ahead with his plans on the RSS. That's why Patel immediately updated Nehru the day he met Golwalkar at Birla House in Bombay on 16 August 1949. In a carefully-worded letter, he informed Nehru that he told Golwalkar about 'the pitfalls' which the RSS should avoid and asked him to eschew 'destructive methods' and 'adopt' a constructive role. 'I found him quite receptive and full of understanding,' he wrote. 'I have a feeling that he will not give us any trouble and will now adapt himself to the new requirements.'[53]

But Nehru remained unchanged. In fact, he flew into a rage when, merely a few days later, he got to know that R. K. Patil, a protégée of Patel and the commissioner of food production, had decided to seek help from RSS volunteers in the newly launched grow-more-food campaign. 'I am told that you are meeting Shri Golwalkar, the leader of the R.S.S. and that it has been announced that you have invited the R.S.S. to cooperate in the food campaign and give volunteers for it,' he wrote to Patil on 22 August. 'We want everybody's cooperation in this business. But we have to be careful how to associate ourselves with the R.S.S. Any close association in this matter may be exploited for a wrong purpose and party politics may come into play.'[54]

Yet, Nehru seemed to be under pressure as conservatives in the Congress shared Patel's affection for the RSS. Perhaps it was this pressure that led Nehru to meet Golwalkar on 30 August.[55] This was their second meeting and the first since the assassination of Mahatma Gandhi. To Nehru, it must have been a very awkward occasion. For, the meeting lasted just 15 minutes and 'no subject was discussed in

53. JN (SG) Papers, Post-1947, File No. 27, Part II, p. 356, Manuscript Section, NMML, New Delhi.

54. JN (SG) Papers, Post-1947, File No. 28, p. 35, Manuscript Section, NMML, New Delhi

55. *The Times of India*, 31 August 1949.

detail', although Golwalkar told the news agency, P.T.I., that 'he would be meeting the Prime Minister sometimes afterward'.[56] RSS sources claim there were a few more meetings in later days, but there is no conclusive evidence that they ever met again.

Patel, however, was adamant. His desires that had long lain just below the surface pulled into the open on 10 October 1949 when, taking advantage of Nehru's absence abroad, he got the Congress Working Committee to pass a resolution authorizing the entry of RSS men into the party.[57] On his return from the US, Nehru moved quickly, launched a campaign against 'the communalism of the RSS', and, to the humiliation of Patel, forced the Congress to rescind the resolution.[58] Although Patel had established considerable grip over the party organization, Gandhians were firmly against his initiative, and it was amongst them that Nehru found his most enthusiastic support. Their resentment towards Patel's initiative was bitter. It became implacable when K. G. Mashruwala, the most prominent follower of Mahatma Gandhi at the time, revealed on 2 December 1949 that 'a few volunteers of R.S.S. from Wardha and surrounding parts' observed on 27 November the 'terahvin'—last rites of Hindus performed on the thirteenth day after the death—for Godse and Apte, who had been hanged on 15 November 1949.[59]

Golwalkar was in a bind. The tumult caused by Gandhi's assassination had subsided, but the shadow of the assassin had lengthened and hung over the RSS, to which Godse belonged. This

---

56. Ibid.

57. Christophe Jaffrelot, *The Hindu Nationalist Movement and Indian Politics 1925 to the 1990s: Strategies of Identity-Building, Implantation and Mobilisation*, Hurst & Company, London, 1996, p. 90.

58. Ibid.

59. Sardar Patel Papers, 'Correspondence with Shri Golwalkar & R.S.S. Celebrities', File No. 8/38, p. 29, 'KG Mashruwala to V. Shankar, Private Secretary, Deputy Prime Minister', NAI, New Delhi.

fundamental change in climate made Golwalkar deeply unsettled about his future course. Nehru's firm stance worried him, but his faith in Patel restrained him. He could see fissures between the top two Congress leaders, but his new circumstances, clouded by the stigma of Gandhi's assassination, made it impossible for him to exploit them to his advantage.

Jana Sangh

Of all the myths that would swirl around the RSS, none was greater than the fable that Nathuram Godse had left the Sangh long before he killed Mahatma Gandhi. The foundation for this myth was laid down in an article published by a reputed English journal, the *Economic Weekly*, on 4 February 1950, two and a half months after the execution of Godse and Apte and just when Golwalkar and his cadres were desperately looking for a way to remove the stigma of the assassination. In a manner that scarcely aroused any suspicion, the article, titled 'The R.S.S.', sought to sanitize the Sangh's past by pushing a notion aimed at separating the RSS from Gandhi's assassin. The notion was based on one of the claims Godse had made in the court that he had broken with the RSS and joined the Hindu Mahasabha several years before he pulled the trigger. Godse's claims had been fundamentally directed at absolving all his co-accused and the organizations he had been associated with and establishing that he alone had been responsible for the murder. The court had found no merit in them.[1]

Yet, the article, in keeping with the claims made by Godse, tried to build a line of argument that would serve the RSS to

1. See for detail Dhirendra K. Jha, *Gandhi's Assassin: The Making of Nathuram Godse and His Idea of India*, Vintage, Penguin India, New Delhi, 2021.

cover its past tracks. Without referring to Gandhi's assassin, it took his claims further and sought to establish that the RSS and the Hindu Mahasabha existed in total separation since the late 1930s—meaning thereby that Godse couldn't have remained a member of the RSS after he joined the Mahasabha. In fact, the article, authored by D. V. Kelkar, declared that not only did the RSS and Hindu Mahasabha exist separately, but even that there was discord between the two after Savarkar became the president of the Mahasabha in December 1937.

At the time of publication, the article was perceived as an extremely straightforward account, as a mere description of interactions between the supreme leaders of the two Hindutva organizations, Hedgewar of the RSS and Savarkar of the Mahasabha. 'The cleavage between the two became clearer as years went by,' it claimed, 'until Veer Savarkar, in a speech at Panwel, openly attacked R.S.S. neutrality in respect of Hindu Mahasabha work and said: "The epitaph for the R.S.S. volunteer will be that he was born, he joined the R.S.S. and he died without accomplishing anything."'[2]

This quote of Savarkar soon became the most commonly cited evidence for the purported severing of ties between the two Hindutva outfits—a severance so imperative as to make Godse's claim of exiting the RSS upon joining the Hindu Mahasabha look natural. Strangely, however, Kelkar's failure to cite any evidence in support of his claims in the article seemed to pique no one's attention. The question of provenance in this case was all the more important because the author confessed in the same article that he had been a close associate of Hedgewar's[3]—a fact that leaves enough room for suspicion that Kelkar, out of sympathy for the RSS, might deliberately have twisted historical facts to help the Sangh exonerate itself from the charges of Gandhi's murder.

2. D. V. Kelkar, 'The R.S.S.', *Economic Weekly*, 4 February 1950, p. 133.

3. Ibid., p. 132.

Golwalkar's followers—and, later, some of his adversaries and objective researchers—parroted this distorted presentation of history, including the Savarkar quote. The myth persisted, even though the available archival records show that such a split never happened, that the RSS and the Hindu Mahasabha always had close connections, and sometimes even overlapping membership, and that Godse killed Gandhi as a member of the RSS.[4]

A fake narrative of such a large proportion could not have been possible without encouragement or even direct support from the RSS, and it fitted with the organization's penchant for making myths to hide the sordid events of its past. That Kelkar's claim was a lie and that the RSS distanced itself from the Mahasabha only after it was unbanned were noted by J. A. Curran, Jr., the American researcher who is credited with the first serious attempt to study the RSS. Curran must have been aware of the sensitivity of the issue as he did his field research in India during 1949-50—in the immediate aftermath of the removal of the ban on the RSS—and even referred to Kelkar's article in the *Economic Weekly*. 'Since the lifting of the ban,' he noted, 'Golwalkar has discouraged the practice, which had been common prior to 1947 and today still exists to a limited degree, of Sangh members holding office or even membership in the Mahasabha.'[5] These observations are significant because Curran had been given full access in the RSS, right from Golwalkar down to ordinary swayamsevaks.[6]

Kelkar's article, therefore, laid the foundation for one of the most comprehensive efforts at myth-making in the history of modern India. But it did not stop at that. Besides trying to clean

4. See for detail Dhirendra K. Jha, *Gandhi's Assassin: The Making of Nathuram Godse and His Idea of India*, Vintage, Penguin India, New Delhi, 2021.

5. J. A. Curran, Jr., *Militant Hinduism in Indian Politics: A Study of the R.S.S.*, Institute of Pacific Relations, New York, 1951, p. 64.

6. Ibid., p. 3.

up issues related to Gandhi's assassination, it also romanticized every aspect of the RSS, its leadership and its cadres. 'It would be unjust for the present writer not to be cognizant of the determined spirit not only of its founder and the present Sar Sangh Chalak, but also of the R.S.S. rank and file,' Kelkar wrote. 'It is not an exaggeration to state that the thousands and lakhs who are pledged to the Sangh have sacrificed their career, wealth and earthly pleasures for a cause.'[7]

II

Once Golwalkar had given up his dream of becoming an apostle of the Hindu Rashtra, he came to regard himself as someone whose spiritual leadership the nation awaited. He postured as if the principal objective of his life was to achieve spiritual greatness rather than grabbing power and holding it in perpetuity. With mythological ancient rishis in mind, he tried to model himself as a saint—an image that has stuck in the minds of his followers. At the time, Golwalkar was in his mid-40s and had spent barely nine out of his 33 years as the sarsanghchalak.

His decision was perhaps not surprising, and it was telling, as ever, that he could not deal calmly when the new era confronted him squarely with new constraints. In a traditional Hindu society, it would go a long way in the makeover of his image left shattered in the wake of the assassination of Gandhi who had been an object of popular adulation. Besides glorification of his personality, the new image, it must have occurred to him, would help at concealment of his past activities and aspirations.

After he came out of jail, there appeared a series of biographies on him by his followers, seemingly written under his own supervision, all trying to cover his past tracks and stylize his persona

7. D. V. Kelkar, 'The R.S.S.', *Economic Weekly*, 4 February 1950, p. 138.

as a sage, sometimes comparing him even with Mahatma Gandhi and a Christian saint. The first two biographies were written by his closest aides within a year or so of his release—Shri Gangadhar Indurkar's *Guruji: Rashtriya Swayamsevak Sangh ke Sarsanghachalak Shri Madhav Sadashiv Golwalkar Ji Ka Jeevan Charitra,* published in 1949, and Jagat S. Bright's *Guruji Golwalkar & R.S.S.,* which appeared in 1950. Both these accounts made careful attempts to obscure the trail of Golwalkar's past life and glorify his personality as a saintly character. They did not mention a word about *We or Our Nationhood Defined* or his views on minorities and the Hindu Rashtra. Nor did they say anything about his activities during most of the 1940s in Delhi, Punjab, the United Provinces, the Central Provinces, Bombay Presidency and a whole lot of princely states, including Alwar and Bharatpur.

Instead of basing their arguments on facts, these biographers preferred to write allegorically, as if dealing not with a human being but with an object of worship. 'With his long flowing hair Guruji is a remarkable sage of ancient times,' wrote Bright. 'His slight build and saintly eyes remind us of Mahatma Gandhi who charmed the masses not long ago. His eyes are piercing but nevertheless possess an irresistible charm and milk of human kindness. His frank laugh indicates the purity of his soul. His gait is quick and surprisingly striding like Saint Thomas popularly known as the "Saint in a Hurry". Golwalkar is a saint in a hurry too. He has to do a lot to carry out his programme successfully.'[8] At another place in the book, the author talked of a 'halo or divinity' which was so 'discernible around his personality'.[9]

Indurkar, who wrote in Hindi, also employed a similarly unrestrained, poetic language to glorify Golwalkar's life. These

8. Jagat S. Bright, *Guruji Golwalkar & R.S.S.*, New India Publishing Co., Delhi, 1950, p. 26.

9. Ibid., p. 27.

initial biographies helped to crystallize the themes that would later shape Golwalkar's legend—a born genius who brought blessings for his family, a sage who gave up his spiritual quests for the sake of uniting Hindus, a fighter who would not waver despite all odds. In fact, Golwalkar saw the production of about half a dozen biographies, all seemingly written under his guiding will, during his lifetime after his release from the jail. Part of these efforts could be explained by Golwalkar's own preference to cover his past tracks, but they also appeared to be driven by his desire of being seen as a saint.

The account of Hemendra Nath Pandit, a pracharak based in Kolkata, reveals some of the hidden aspects of Golwalkar's attempts to be seen as a saint and the myth-making by his followers. 'At a Press conference in Delhi he once said that he took only a fourth part of the quantity of food normally consumed by an average adult,' Pandit reminisced. 'His admirers would tell you that he takes only one meal a day. It has been my experience, however, to see him sit by the side of some of us on at least two occasions at Nagpur and take two full meals at 12 noon and 9 P.M. besides tea and tiffin at the usual hours.'[10]

Pandit, who attended the Akhil Bharatiya Pratinidhi Sabha (the All India Delegates' Conference) of the RSS in 1950, also talked of the efforts 'to make the young swayamsevaks believe that Golwalkar is the incarnation of Lord Krishna himself'. In his memoir, which he wrote after leaving the RSS in the late 1950s, he narrated a story of a pracharak telling swayamsevaks in West Bengal that 'Madhava of Mahabharat' had incarnated in the form of Golwalkar 'to lead Hindus to victory'.[11] Madhav, the first name of Golwalkar, is also one of the many names of Lord Krishna.

10. Hemendra Nath Pandit, *The End of A Dream: An Inside View of the R.S.S. Today*, Rabindra Nath Hore, Calcutta, 1950, p. 12.

11. Ibid., pp. 16-17.

Pandit also mentioned how Mahatma Gandhi's favourite devotional song, 'Ram Dhun', which sought to promote Hindu-Muslim unity by identifying 'Ishwar' of Hindus with 'Allah' of Muslims, was distorted to create a godly image of Golwalkar and Hedgewar. 'Mahatma Gandhi's favourite "Ram Dhun" has undergone a change in the RSS,' he wrote. 'The line *Ishwara Allah tere nam* is considered objectionable and the Sangh therefore has its own reading as *Keshava Madhava tere nam*.'[12] Keshav, another name of Lord Krishna, was also the first name of Hedgewar.

Golwalkar's efforts to be seen as a man of strong spiritual tendencies accounted for the curiously histrionic character of his existence. This evidently led him to carry himself in such a manner as to suit the image he thought of himself. In his pre-sainthood phase, by Pandit's account, Golwalkar was very 'fond of being photographed' and extremely desirous of his photographs being circulated widely.[13] But now, as he endeavoured to hide behind an overtly exaggerated spiritual image, he jealously took care to appear being averse to publicity. For instance, on 8 April 1956 in Delhi, Golwalkar 'threatened to leave a public meeting held to felicitate him on his 51st birthday, at the Ramlila grounds, if press photographers insisted on taking his picture'.[14]

III

Still, the prosaic truth about his personal position in the RSS mattered greatly. Pandit noted this hidden desire of Golwalkar in August 1949 during a meeting of RSS representatives from different provinces called in Nagpur to 'consider and pass' the new draft constitution. Pandit was a participant. 'One article provided that

12. Ibid., p. 17.

13. Ibid., p. 13.

14. *The Times of India*, 9 April 1956.

the Sarkaryavah (General Secretary) was to nominate the Kendriya Karyakari Mandal or the Central Executive,' he recounted.

> After it was passed someone remarked: 'The status of the Sarkaryavah now becomes similar to that of the President of the Congress.'
>
> 'So I am now completely out of the whole thing,' said Shri Golwalkar jocularly. Immediately one pracharak came out fawningly: 'You will be in the position of Mahatma Gandhi.'
>
> Golwalkar was mighty pleased; but feeling that he might not be able to conceal his joy, he laughed aloud but did not add even one word by way of comment.[15]

Similarly, he kept his old institutional façade—and the sense of authority he derived from it—intact. When senior RSS leaders met in Nagpur in January 1950 to consider whether the RSS should launch a separate political party or support an existing one, it was Golwalkar who had the last word. In his short opening speech, he explained 'to the members the delicacy of the subject' and asked them not to take a decision that would hamper 'the progress of the R.S.S. Sangh'.[16] Accordingly, the RSS leaders refrained from taking any decision on the issue.[17]

Partly, the reason for this was his cautious approach in the immediate aftermath of the removal of the ban on the RSS. But the principal reason was his secret hope for a split in the Congress. He seemed to believe that sooner or later the rift in the Congress would lead Patel to replace Nehru as the prime minister, thus offering a massive opportunity to the RSS to strike off fetters and regain its old shape. Intelligence officials recorded that in a meeting

---

15. Hemendra Nath Pandit, *The End of A Dream: An Inside View of the R.S.S. Today*, Rabindra Nath Hore, Calcutta, 1950, p. 14.

16. Delhi Police Records, File No. 557, p. 26, Manuscript Section, NMML, New Delhi.

17. Ibid., p. 27.

with 'his lieutenants from Delhi, East Punjab and Rajasthan States' in the last week of August 1949 at Delhi, Golwalkar said that a 'rift between the Right and Left wings of the Congress was bound to widen and the RSS should try to re-organise their forces during this transitory period'.[18]

That explains why he maintained a silence for the whole of 1950 on the issue of launching a political outfit and did not let the RSS leaders take any position on it. Nor did he respond to overtures by Dr. Syama Prasad Mookerjee, who had left the Hindu Mahasabha in December 1948 and who, after resigning from the Nehru cabinet in April 1950, was trying hard to reach out to him with his proposal to jointly float a new party. In the beginning of August 1950, for example, Mauli Chandra Sharma, after a long discussion with Mookerjee, wrote to Bhaiyaji Dani, suggesting a secret meeting of Golwalkar with the former Hindu Mahasabha leader in Delhi. But Golwalkar hid behind his public posturing. 'The response from Bhaiyaji Dani on August the 8th was not encouraging,' noted an intelligence report. 'Stressing that the R.S.S.S. abhorred underhand dealings and made no difference between profession and practice, Bhaiyyaji Dani pointed out that the social work in which the Sangh was engaged made it obligatory for the organisation to keep itself aloof from politics. He added however that Golwalkar may meet Dr. Mukherji in due course, as he had regard for the latter as a learned and dutiful man, but in the meeting it would not be possible for Golwalkar to discuss politics.'[19]

By the end of 1950, however, the circumstances changed. Patel, instead of meeting Golwalkar's expectations of carrying out a coup

18. Delhi Police Records, File No. 76, p. 4, Manuscript Section, NMML, New Delhi.

19. JN (SG) Papers, Post-1947, File No. 53, Part I, p. 42, Manuscript Section, NMML, New Delhi.

in the Nehru cabinet, died on 15 December 1950. Golwalkar was in Nagpur that day. On learning that Ravi Shankar Shukla, the chief minister of the province, would be flying to Bombay to attend Patel's funeral, Golwalkar requested him for a seat in the plane. Shukla agreed, and Golwalkar managed to reach Bombay to pay his personal homage to the departed leader.[20]

Shortly thereafter, 'sometime in the winter of 1950-51', noted K. R. Malkani, the editor of *Organiser*, 'Shri Madhav Rao, RSS leader, asked Dr. Bhai Mahavir [Punjab-based RSS leader], Balraj Madhok and myself to sit together and produce some working paper for a new political party'.[21] Accordingly, the three RSS leaders met and discussed the whole issue, and Malkani prepared a note. 'We met again, discussed this note,' Malkani recalled. 'Now Balraj was also asked to prepare a note, which he did.'[22] The two notes, which were sent to Golwalkar, marked the beginning of what appeared to be a long and cautious negotiation with Mookerjee, resulting in the formation of the Bharatiya Jana Sangh.

While Golwalkar held forth loquaciously about a section of the RSS desiring to take part in politics, he never spoke about his own hidden political ambition, just as he never spoke in public about his secret desire to politically exploit the rift between Patel and Nehru. Did he consider the possibility of a crackdown from Nehru? In the situation after the death of Patel, it would be far more exceptional if he did not. Golwalkar appeared extremely guarded about his public reaction on the Sangh's political aspirations. While addressing the concluding session of the Akhil Bharatiya Pratinidhi Sabha of the RSS in March 1951, for example, he said that 'the RSSS as a

20. D. P. Mishra, *The Nehru Epoch: From Democracy to Monocracy*, Vikas Publishing House Pvt Ltd, New Delhi, 1978, 194.

21. K. R. Malkani Papers, 'The first preparatory note before founding of Bharatiya Jan Sangh', p. 1, Manuscript Section, NMML, New Delhi.

22. Ibid.

body has no opinion over the election tangles' and that it was 'not possible for the RSSS to issue any direction in this connection'.[23] Such public observations often led intelligence officers to believe that the RSS was divided over the question of taking part in the election. 'A section led by B.K. Oak and other R.S.S. stalwarts like Dharam Vir and Madho Rao Mulley are in favour of R.S.S.'s participation in the elections,' said a report, 'while the other group led by the R.S.S. chief, M.S. Golwalkar, are opposed to it.'[24]

Mookerjee, who had been intently preparing for the upcoming general elections, having initiated the process of formally launching a new party with the help of the RSS, did sometimes consider the possibility that a hidden plot might lie behind these confusing messages from Golwalkar. During a meeting with a senior Hindu Mahasabha leader, Mahant Digvijay Nath, in the last week of March 1951, Mookerjee conveyed his fear that he anticipated a struggle for leadership with Golwalkar. 'He further expressed that he was stuck between the devil and the deep sea and did not know what to do,' said an intelligence report. 'In fact, Dr. S.P. Mookerjee expressed repentance on his having organised a new party. Mahant Digvijay Nath told the Doctor that he must now stick to his guns and any going back would make the confusion worst confounded.'[25]

Mookerjee was, however, relieved of his stress in April, when, following lengthy negotiations, a conference was held in Calcutta to inaugurate the Bharatiya Jana Sangh in Bengal and he was declared its president.[26] During the next couple of months, the

23. Delhi Police Records, File No. 552, p. 103, Manuscript Section, NMML, New Delhi.

24. Ibid., p. 95.

25. Ibid., p. 105.

26. Myron Weiner, *Party Politics in India: The Development of a Multi-Party System*, Princeton University Press, Princeton, 1957, pp. 190-191.

formation of party units in different provinces was in full swing. Not much time was left for the general elections, which were to start in December 1951 and extend through early 1952. Finally, on 21 October, the Bharatiya Jana Sangh was officially established on the national level at a convention in New Delhi, with Mookerjee as its all-India president.[27]

In the past, the RSS never controlled the Hindu Mahasabha, even though many of its swayamsevaks were its members and the two organizations were often seen working together. In the case of the Jana Sangh, although Mookerjee was the face and the leader, RSS men occupied key positions in party units at provincial and district levels. And yet, in the absence of any legal and constitutional arrangement between the RSS and the Jana Sangh, the leaders of both the organizations could deny that they were one.[28]

IV

In the election, the Jana Sangh fared miserably. It won only three seats in the Lok Sabha—two from Bengal, including that of Mookerjee, and one from Rajasthan. The Election Commission had set a level of 3 per cent of the total vote in the Lok Sabha election as the minimum to be polled by a party to qualify it as a national party. With 3.06 per cent of the total vote, the Jana Sangh managed to achieve this status by a narrow margin. The party was thus allowed to have its election symbol—*deepak* (lamp)—reserved for the exclusive use of its candidates everywhere in the country.[29]

---

27. Abhishek Choudhary, *Vajpayee: The Ascent of the Hindu Right 1924-1977*, Picador India, New Delhi, 2023, p. 90.

28. Myron Weiner, *Party Politics in India: The Development of a Multi-Party System*, Princeton University Press, Princeton, 1957, p. 194.

29. Craig Baxter, *TheJana Sangh: A Biography of an Indian Political Party*, Oxford University Press, Delhi, 1971, p. 93.

In provincial legislatures, the party won a total of thirty-three seats. In several provinces, it could not even open its account. The debacle was particularly shocking in East Punjab, where, due to a strong RSS base, the party had expected to achieve major successes and fielded ten candidates for the Lok Sabha and sixty-six for the provincial legislature but could not win a single seat.[30]

Electoral rout was followed by bitter clashes when its leaders of non-RSS background discovered that the Sangh was quietly scheming to control the party from the outside. In a meeting of thirty top party leaders held at the Jana Sangh office in Delhi on 18 May 1952, Mauli Chandra Sharma, who was one of the two general secretaries, 'disclosed with heavy heart that RSS on the strength of which they had counted much had not only deceived them but that the RSS people were acting as fifth columnists in the party'.[31] He claimed that the RSS workers were using the party as 'a stage for vilification of the govt. but they do not owe allegiance to the Jan Sangh and always give priority to their RSS work. He suggested that the Jan Sangh should have no connection with RSS organisation.'[32]

Sharma's vitriolic attack on the RSS forced Mookerjee to intervene. He said that 'the Jan Sangh had no connection with the RSS organisation but that individual RSS workers were members of the Jan Sangh and in case any of such worker who is found doing any mischief should be kicked out of the party'.[33] Clearly, Mookerjee was aware of his party's real source of strength. It was only natural for him to dismiss Sharma's allegation with a resigned shrug, instead of seizing the chance for a strong effort to save the

30. Ibid., p. 98.

31. Delhi Police Record, File No. 142, V Inst, p. 95, Manuscript Section, NMML, New Delhi.

32. Ibid., pp. 95-96.

33. Ibid., p. 96.

independence of the Jana Sangh. That in itself was indicative of his growing dependence on the RSS.

When the Jana Sangh delegates assembled for the party's first annual session at Kanpur in December 1952, Mookerjee was retained as the president and Mauli Chandra Sharma as one of the two general secretaries. The post of the other general secretary, however, went to Deen Dayal Upadhyaya, a pracharak from UP and a close confidant of Golwalkar.[34] It was also decided in the session that the Jana Sangh would join the agitation already started by the Praja Parishad—a party that had been formed by Balraj Madhok and other RSS men in Jammu and Kashmir—for the total integration of the Muslim-majority state into India.[35] As part of this agitation, Mookerjee entered Kashmir on 11 May 1953. He was promptly arrested and detained. On 23 June, while in detention, he died of heart attack, although many in the Jana Sangh and the RSS interpreted it as a murder.[36]

Because of the leadership vacuum caused by Mookerjee's sudden death, the RSS succeeded in making greater inroads in the party. In August, Mauli Chandra Sharma was made the interim president, but Deen Dayal Upadhyaya was given sole executive authority over the party's organizational structure.[37] The RSS men in the Jana Sangh, however, looked at Sharma's appointment as a temporary arrangement while the party searched for another all-India leader like Mookerjee. After Sharma had assumed office on a temporary basis, Balraj Madhok wrote in the *Organiser* that the successor of Mookerjee 'must be a living link between *dharma* as

34. Walter K. Andersen and Shridhar D. Damle, *The Brotherhood in Saffron: The Rashtriya Swayamsevak Sangh and Hindu Revivalism*, Westveiw Press, Boulder and London, 1987, p. 159.

35. Ibid.

36. Ibid., p. 160.

37. Ibid., pp. 160-161.

represented by the R.S.S. and *artha* and *kama* as represented by the Jana Sangh'.[38]

This was the first public acknowledgement of the Sangh's aspirations to run the new party and an indication that the RSS cadres were no longer ready for any compromise. During the Jana Sangh's annual session in January 1954, as no suitable national leader could be found, Sharma was confirmed as the new president of the party. Upadhyaya, with his firm control on the levers of power in the Jana Sangh, continued as the general secretary. After the session, the *Organiser* wrote: 'The man who stood head and shoulders above all others, and who in a way dominated the whole session was the lean, thin, unassuming Din Dayal Upadhyay, the young General Secretary of the young Organisation.' It also expressed hope that Sharma 'will succeed in securing the willing cooperation of the Swayam Sevak Sangh workers who form the core of the Jan Sangh'.[39]

But Sharma could not win the confidence of the RSS cadres. With Upadhyaya acting as their ring-leader, the RSS men in the Jana Sangh started a full-scale assault. By the account of R. H. Tupkary, who started attending the shakha just before the assassination of Mahatma Gandhi as a young swayamsevak in Nagpur and quickly became close to the RSS brass, the turn of events in the Jana Sangh became possible because of 'Golwalkar's consent'.[40] For some time Sharma fought to protect the rights of the party president.[41] Eventually, he lost all vestiges of control and

38. *Organiser*, 15 August 1953.

39. *Organiser*, 8 February 1954.

40. R. H. Tupkary, *RSS Revalued: Insider's Critical Assessment*, Notion Press, Chennai, 2018, p. 262.

41. Walter K. Andersen and Shridhar D. Damle, *The Brotherhood in Saffron: The Rashtriya Swayamsevak Sangh and Hindu Revivalism*, Westveiw Press, Boulder and London, 1987, p. 161.

launched into a tantrum. On 3 November 1954, disclosing that the Jana Sangh was 'dominated by the R.S.S.', he resigned from both the presidentship and the membership of the party. 'While wholeheartedly subscribing to the objects for which the Jana Sangh was founded, for which I shall continue to work in whatever field I can, it is not possible for me to continue my association with it so long as its present set-up lasts,' he declared.[42]

Upadhyaya did not immediately become president upon Sharma's resignation. The crown fell on Prem Nath Dogra, the former leader of the Praja Parishad, but the command of the party was practically entrusted to Upadhyaya, who rendered it subordinate to—and eventually all but subsumed by—the RSS.

V

During 1954, as he was busy in conquering the Jana Sangh, Golwalkar faced a massive personal shock. His father, who was about seventy, died on 20 July 1954. This was the first major tragedy the family had suffered since the death of his elder brother, Amrit, in 1918. Golwalkar was in Bhopal, the capital of Madhya Pradesh, when he learnt that his father had passed away. He immediately rushed back but could reach Nagpur only on 22 July. He, therefore, could not take part in the funeral rites of his father.[43]

Soon after, he endured a second shock—one of his lieutenants in Nagpur, Madhukar Dattatreya Deoras or Balasaheb, walked out of the RSS. Along with his younger brother, Murlidhar Dattatreya Deoras or Bhaurao, Balasaheb had been among the first to become a pracharak. While Bhaurao worked as the in-charge of the United

---

42. *The Times of India*, 4 November 1954.

43. Ranga Hari, *The Incomparable Guru Golwalkar*, Prabhat Paperbacks, New Delhi, 2018, pp. 208-209.

Provinces, Balasaheb Deoras operated from the RSS headquarters. He was arrested along with Golwalkar on 2 February 1948.[44] Like other RSS leaders, he was also released six months later. Between November 1948 and July 1949, while Golwalkar was in jail for a second time, Deoras managed all the affairs of the RSS and acted practically as the organization's main leader. When the talks with the government seemed to go nowhere and Golwalkar felt jittery, he tried to send a secret letter to Deoras for shoring up support from outside by re-launching the swayamsevaks' satyagraha.[45]

All the while Deoras acted as a loyal lieutenant of Golwalkar and a committed leader of the RSS. During the ban period, he never cared about money while helping pracharaks returning from different parts of the country.[46] It was largely in recognition of his role during the ban that, when in March 1950 the RSS formed its central executive as per its new constitution, Deoras was made the treasurer of the organization.[47] At the time of the first general elections, he, like most office-bearers of the RSS, indulged in a considerable amount of wishful thinking and imagined the Jana Sangh candidates doing much better than a more objective appraisal would have allowed. In his enthusiasm, he spent liberally for the election purposes of some of the candidates in the Vidarbha area of the Central Provinces. When he ran out of money, he borrowed from private lenders.[48]

Deoras seemed to understand that he was doing all that for

---

44. *The Times of India*, 3 February 1948.

45. D. P. Mishra, *The Nehru Epoch: From Democracy to Monocracy*, Vikas Publishing House Pvt Ltd, New Delhi, 1978, p. 77.

46. Sanjeev Kelkar, *Lost Years of the RSS*, Sage Publications India Pvt Ltd, New Delhi, 2011, p. 102.

47. Delhi Police Record, File No. 556, p. 1, Manuscript Section, NMML, New Delhi.

48. R. H. Tupkary, *RSS Revalued: Insider's Critical Assessment*, Notion Press, Chennai, 2018, p. 266.

the benefit of the RSS. But Golwalkar had many more pressing priorities, particularly during the desperate early years after the ban was revoked on the RSS. After the elections, when Golwalkar made it clear to him that the RSS as an organization would have nothing to do with the debts he had incurred, he became apoplectic, and they wrangled over finances.[49] By Tupkary's account, Deoras also felt frustrated because Golwalkar did not let him join the Jana Sangh and forced him to work for the RSS in Nagpur.[50] The rift widened so much during the post-election years that Deoras and Golwalkar were not even on 'talking terms' and required 'some intermediary to talk to each other in the form of exchange of written notes on a notebook'.[51]

Soon it became untenable. Deoras had emerged as the figure many within the RSS wished to invest with power, while Golwalkar was an object of adulation for swayamsevaks. They were two very different types, with distinct ideas and aspirations. As working together became impossible, Deoras, along with his younger brother Bhaurao, quit the RSS late in 1954.

49. Ibid.

50. Ibid., p. 267.

51. Ibid., p. 266.

The Fantasy of a Hindu Rashtra

With all his fancies of establishing the Hindu Rashtra turning to dust, Golwalkar seemed inhibited and inflicted by a sense of awkwardness. The first general election had established Nehru's sway over the country, and secularism had emerged as the norm of the Indian political system. In some respects, Golwalkar was unprepared for the leadership role in the new political and social environment. As the RSS chief, he had learned to work hard and to concentrate on results, but he lacked a natural touch for operating in the richly diverse cultural context that the secular, democratic system continually presented him. That he felt awkward was not due solely to the stigma of leading an organization of Hindu supremacists. Rather, his idea of a Hindu Rashtra suffered from a vague feeling that it represented part of the wrong turn the nation might have taken had leaders like Gandhi and Nehru not come in the way.

All the available sources show that Golwalkar, at this stage, displayed a singular indecisiveness, a fear of fixing on any one course. He was certainly eager to chart out a mass action programme for the RSS, but he exhibited no desire to take any risks. Thus, in the campaign for banning cow slaughter, which the RSS launched in late 1952, it is not hard to detect the escape motivation of Golwalkar. The same is true for much of his public behaviour during Nehru's lifetime.

The issue of cow protection had always been close to the RSS, but this was the first time it decided to build a campaign around it. The RSS observed 26 October 1952 as 'Anti-Cow Slaughter Day' and its swayamsevaks brought out processions in several parts of Delhi 'with banners, slogans and bedecked cows, arousing popular sentiments in favour of cow protection'.[1] These processions culminated in a public meeting that was presided over by RSS sarkaryavah Bhaiyaji Dani and attended by leaders of the Jana Sangh, the Hindu Mahasabha and 'other Hindu organisations'. It was the first mass movement against the government's policies since the ban on the RSS had been revoked, and yet Dani, reflecting Golwalkar's fears, declared that the campaign was 'not against the Government' and that it was 'the spontaneous expression of the sentiment of the crores of Indians'.[2] Interestingly, the public meeting where Dani made this claim was attended not even by lakhs but by just about 5,000 people.[3]

As expected, the results of this first expression of anti-cow slaughter sentiment were meagre. But the silence had been broken. Golwalkar's success was due in considerable part to his being the first to take up the issue. These initial moves resulted in a similar preoccupation overtaking other Hindutva organizations and gradually led Golwalkar into the wings of the political centre stage. Soon he became part of a joint effort to start a wider movement against cow slaughter. On 6 December 1952, Jana Sangh president Mookerjee inaugurated the 'Cow Protection Exhibition' at Ramlila Grounds in Delhi. The next day, a public meeting was organized

---

1. Delhi Police Records, File No. 553, p. 95, Manuscript Section, NMML, New Delhi.

2. Ibid.

3. Ibid.

at the venue. It was attended by about 20,000 people, mostly RSS men from Delhi as well as the neighbouring districts of Rohtak, Hansi, Sonipat, Karnal, Kurukshetra, Ghaziabad, Meerut, Saharanpur, Patiala and Gurgaon. As if emboldened by the mobilization and bursting through the political barriers of many years, Golwalkar's accusations against Nehru came tumbling out as he addressed the public meeting. An intelligence report on his speech said, 'Shri M.S. Golwalkar repudiated the Prime Minister's statement that the campaign was a "political stunt". He added that about two crores of signatures on the Memorandum for ending cow slaughter showed how the masses felt on the issue and presented a challenge which the Government could not ignore.'[4]

As everything with him turned to excess—his fears, his self-confidence, or even his rapture at seeing a good turnover in the rally—the number of signatories that he mentioned in his speech was an exaggeration of an unimaginable kind. To be sure, two crores of signatories in 1952 would have meant almost 6 per cent of the country's total population of 36 crore as per the census of 1951. In reality, the cow protection activists had collected barely 4,72,687 signatures in Delhi and its neighbourhood, the sole focal point of the campaign. That Golwalkar lied deliberately is borne out by the fact that he had already been informed about the actual figure during the RSS central executive's three-day meeting held in Delhi between 6 and 8 December.[5]

The RSS central executive meeting also revealed another bitter truth about Golwalkar—despite the political passion he showed at the rally, he still looked for ways to escape alternatives he felt to be threatening. Whereas other Hindutva organizations, particularly the Ram Rajya Parishad, favoured launching of a nationwide satyagraha on the issue, the RSS meeting, which was presided over

4. Ibid., p. 152.

5. Ibid., p. 162.

by Golwalkar, resolved to stay away from any confrontation with the government. 'It was, therefore, decided,' an intelligence report on the meeting said, 'to appoint a Sub-Committee to press upon various State Assemblies to enact legislation through non-official Bills.'[6]

By and large, therefore, his cadres never displayed mass anger on the street, and the anti-cow slaughter movement never assumed any serious proportion while Nehru was alive. Their activities consisted almost entirely of token protests and small meetings. Intelligence records of 1953 and 1954 talk primarily of incidents of small groups of five or six protesters getting intercepted outside the residence of Nehru as they carried milk and butter and shouted slogans like *'Gau hatya band ho'* [Cow slaughter should stop] and 'Panditji, *dudh khao, makhan khao'* [Panditji, drink milk, eat butter].[7]

Among the Hindutva groups, however, Golwalkar's restraint often created frustration and even led some of them to chart their own separate ways. In June 1954, for example, Swami Karpatri, president of the Ram Rajya Parishad, issued a statement threatening to detach his party from the anti-cow slaughter movement of 'the RSS and the Jana Sangh' and vowing 'to launch his "satyagraha" campaign separately'.[8] Golwalkar responded to Karpatri's threat in his own peculiar manner. On 8 August 1954, he called an 'all party meet' in Delhi with the stated objective to bring together 'all the Hindu organizations interested in the protection of cow'.[9] This time, even the Hindu Mahasabha joined the Ram Rajya Parishad in boycotting Golwalkar's call.[10]

---

6. Ibid.

7. Ibid., File No. 148, V Inst, pp. 1a, 2, 9, 10, 19.

8. Ibid., File No. 127, p. 3.

9. Ibid., p. 13a.

10. Ibid., p. 16.

With such turbulence becoming commonplace, and Golwalkar still not ready to embrace the same degree of risk as he had done before the assassination of Mahatma Gandhi, the cow protection movement could achieve nothing.

II

The downward spiral of the Sangh's appeal that began with the assassination of Mahatma Gandhi was yet to reverse. The Nehru cult glistened like a film of oil on the vast sea of masses in which the possibility of spreading a vision as different as that of the RSS was limited in scope. As options for the RSS continued to remain narrow, Golwalkar picked up the routines of organizational multiplication.

He may have had this objective in mind when he inaugurated the first Saraswati Shishu Mandir—an RSS school aimed at imparting education in line with Hindutva ideology—in 1952 at Gorakhpur in UP.[11] Set up at the behest of Golwalkar's close aide Nanaji Deshmukh, this school marked the beginning of the establishment of a series of Saraswati Shishu Mandir schools in different parts of the country.[12] The same year, the RSS also started the Vanavasi Kalyan Ashram—Tribal Development Centre—at Jashpur in the tribal-dominated district of Bastar in the Central Provinces.[13] It soon became the model for setting up similar Ashrams in several other tribal areas with a clear objective to involve the tribal people in the Sangh's pan-Hindu agenda through a series of social works and promotional activities. Years later, the RSS formed centralized agencies for their coordination—Vidya

11. *Organiser*, 12 November 1978.

12. Walter K. Andersen & Shridhar D. Damle, *The RSS: A View to the Inside*, Penguin Viking, Gurgaon, 2018, p. 33.

13. Ibid., p. 35.

Bharati for Saraswati Shishu Mandir schools and Akhil Bharatiya Vanvasi Kalyan Ashram for the tribal centres.

More organized efforts were visible in the setting up of a trade union centre—initially as a wing of the Jana Sangh—by Golwalkar's associate and a pracharak, Dattopant Bapurao Thengadi. A resolution to this effect was passed by the Jana Sangh at its all-India session at Jodhpur in January 1955, and the Bharatiya Mazdoor Sangh (BMS) was formed the following July.[14] The founding conference declared it to be the labour front of the Jana Sangh. Subsequently, however, the BMS avoided any reference to the Jana Sangh and gave credit exclusively to the RSS for its formation.[15]

The BMS adopted the saffron flag and rejected foreign symbols and signs associated with international working-class movements. It asked its activists to study and depend on ancient Indian writings instead of literature on foreign labour movements. It rejected both Marxism and capitalism, calling 'the maximum production' as 'the national duty of labour' and 'equitable distribution of the fruits of labour' as 'the legitimate rights of workers'.[16]

Another organization that was added to the Sangh Parivar, or the family of the RSS, around this time was Bhonsala Military School, which had been set up in 1937 at Nasik by Hindu Mahasabha leader Moonje. The takeover of the school was done through a quiet operation by Babasaheb Ghatate, a close associate of Golwalkar. The school had a rumbustious history in which Hindu communal politics had drawn heavily from fascist pedagogical practices Moonje had encountered during his visit to Rome in 1931. In his diary, Moonje describes his meeting with

14. Kiran Saxena, 'The Hindu Trade Union Movement in India: The Bharatiya Mazdoor Sangh', *Asian Survey*, July 1993, Vol. 33, No. 7, p. 687.

15. Ibid.

16. Ibid., p. 689.

Mussolini and visit to the Military College, the Central Military School of Physical Education, the Fascist Academy of Physical Education and Balilla and Avanguardisti organizations in Italy. On his return, he began to contact all those who could support his idea of starting a military school for Hindus. In 1934, he established the Central Hindu Military Education Society (CHMES) on the lines of the Italian regime's Central Military School for Physical Education. It was under the aegis of the CHMES that Bhonsala Military School was eventually set up in 1937. Moonje's decision to name the school after the royal family of Nagpur emanated from his old loyalty to the Bhonsalas.

According to Ghatate, who was a member of the CHMES right from the beginning, Moonje worked hard and within a short span of time collected 'lakhs of rupees' from Hindu princes and businessmen for the school. 'But more important was the sympathetic attitude of the Commanders-in-Chief and Viceroys of India which he had won by dint of his honest and sincere contacts and his dynamic personality,' he added.[17] In reality, however, the school promised these benefactors what they secretly desired. To the British, Moonje assured it would provide loyal soldiers who would be dedicated to the Raj alone, and to Hindu princes and businessmen he made no secret of the fact that the school would herald militarization of Hindus.

The school ran smoothly for almost a decade and, with Moonje in the picture, there was no interruption in the flow of students and funds. The scenario changed after the assassination of Mahatma Gandhi. Moonje could hardly do anything now to insulate his school from the popular revulsion that the assassination touched off against the Hindu Mahasabha and the RSS. Moonje died on

17. M. N. Ghatate, 'Dr. BS Moonje–Tour of European Countries', in N. G. Dixit (ed.), *Dharmaveer Dr. BS Moonje Commemoration Voume*, Birth Centenary Celebration (1872-1972), Centenary Celebration Committee, Nagpur, 1972, p. 69.

4 March 1948, five weeks after the murder of Gandhi. 'After the death of Dr. Moonje in 1948, the school gradually started declining,' Ghatate reminisced. 'The money stopped flowing in and so the students as there was no person in the school's society [CHMES] who would put in efforts like those of the parent of the institute.'[18]

Though Ghatate was part of the society, the RSS in general had nothing to do with it or the school that it ran. For some time after Moonje's death, there was complete confusion, with no one to look after the school. By the early 1950s, Bhonsala Military School had gone in deep financial crisis, though it still remained a potent institute from the point of view of Hindutva ideology. According to Ghatate, the strength of the students came down to 50 by 1953 and the media started writing that the school would be closed down for want of funds and enrolment. 'I stepped in at this stage,' he wrote.

> I requested the managing body to give me two years' time for my trial before the school was finally closed and assets were handed over to the government. The management agreed to this. I moved all around, especially in Bihar, Uttar Pradesh, Hyderabad and other places and admitted boys from there. Gradually the number on roll increased to 150 by 1955. Maintenance grant was sanctioned by the Education Department and the sapling so fondly planted by Dr. Moonje gathered strength by this manuring and has developed into what it is today.[19]

With Ghatate acting as Nagpur's point man in the revival exercise of Bhonsala Military School, its management was silently taken over by men belonging to the RSS. 'The shift took place during the period between 1953 and 1956,' recounted Major (Retd.) Prabhakar Balwant Kulkarni, who witnessed the quiet takeover

18. Ibid.

19. Ibid.

and who remained attached to the school since 1956. 'The Central Hindu Military Education Society had life members who used to elect the governing body of Bhonsala Military School. Along with the revival of the school, the composition of Society's life members also started changing. New members who joined now were all RSS men.'[20]

In a way, the association of Kulkarni—who had been an active member of the RSS since the late 1930s—with the school seems to have been part of the larger takeover design of the RSS. 'One day in early 1956, Guruji and Babasaheb Ghatate called me for a meeting and asked me to join Bhonsala Military School. I agreed and joined the school as an instructor on 12 June 1956,' he said. 'From 12 June 1956 to 31 May 1988, I worked for the school. During this period I held several posts: instructor, supervisor, principal and commandant. For five years between 1998 and 2003, I worked as the secretary of the Central Hindu Military Education Society.'[21]

The acquisition of Bhonsala Military School, which was completed by the end of the 1950s, constituted an unlikely expansion of the RSS. Nehru's secular hegemony had bewildered Golwalkar and forced him to keep the RSS in leash. But it could not stop him from auguring a feat of self-invention so important to provide a hydra-like structure to his organization, the implication of which remained little understood at the time.

III

Golwalkar seemed to believe that his years of waiting had ended when China invaded India in 1962. The war across the high-

---

20. Major (Retd.) Prabhakar Balwant Kulkarni was interviewed on 21 November 2015 at Nasik, Maharashtra.

21. Ibid.

altitude terrain of the Himalayas began in the middle of October, and the better resourced Chinese forces quickly moved in a vast tract of mountainous land of India. Although China announced a ceasefire on 21 November and withdrew from most of the captured territory, it retained a part of the Aksai Chin region of Kashmir. The war stopped thereafter, but the Himalayan border region continued to remain tense. To Nehru, who had dreamt of a great Indo-Chinese alliance, this unexpected invasion shattered all his hopes.

Golwalkar, who had been pushed into the background, seemed to find in India's gloom an opportunity to make himself politically relevant. Displaying a nationalistic belligerence, he posed as someone Nehru could count on. He offered the Sangh's 'support to the Government in its efforts to drive out the aggressors'.[22] His strident propaganda was also pointedly aimed at Indian communists whom he called agents of Chinese communist regime. On 23 December, he addressed a rally in Delhi and accused India's communists of indulging in 'subversive activities in Assam and Bengal and telling the people that the Chinese were coming to India to liberate the oppressed millions'.[23] He also attacked communists for asking people to 'rally around Nehru' and declared that they were 'not friends of Nehru but only opportunists'.[24]

A month later, as the nation celebrated its Republic Day event on 26 January 1963 in the shadow of the Chinese invasion, the RSS tried to steal the show. What provided it an opportunity to do so was the government's decision to give up the usual pageantry and pomp of the Republic Day and convert that year's event into a citizens' march. This shift was, in fact, Nehru's idea, since the Ministry of Defence, the nodal ministry for the Republic Day

22. *The Times of India*, 21 December 1962.

23. *The Times of India*, 24 December 1962.

24. Ibid.

function, was contemplating dropping the event altogether that year in view of the constraints caused by the China war. On 10 December 1962, Nehru wrote a detailed note to Defence Minister Y. B. Chavan, in which he opposed the move to drop the Republic Day celebrations and proposed the idea of the citizens' march. 'I agree that the Republic Day ceremony should avoid all unnecessary expenditure,' Nehru wrote.

> Also that there should be no movement of troops from different parts of the country to Delhi, but I do not understand that why there should not be any parade. That parade will only consist of some troops in Delhi itself, and, chiefly, it should be a civil parade, which can be joined in by a large number of our people. The Home Guards, the NCC will of course be there, as well as any other volunteer units in Delhi. Students, both college and school, may join it as well as trade unions and the other numerous organizations in Delhi. All these persons need not be drilled. It does not matter if they are not in step and they need not be trained for it. They should march en masse. I am sure this will be good and will have a strong effect on those who join it and on those who see it.[25]

The following day, he pressed the idea in the meeting of the Congress Parliamentary Party (CPP). 'It was suggested that we should give up the parade, I did not like that idea but we are converting the parade into much less of a military function and much more of a civil function,' he said. 'So the present idea is that the Members of Parliament be asked also to participate in the parade in a block as Members of Parliament.'[26]

Since the Republic Day event was to be primarily a show of various sections of local people, the Mayor of Delhi, Nuruddin

25. *Selected Works of Jawaharlal Nehru*, Second Series, Volume Eighty, Jawaharlal Nehru Memorial Fund, New Delhi, 2019, p. 608.

26. Ibid., pp. 513-514.

Ahmed, was made responsible for the mobilization of civilians. Ahmed worked in a non-partisan manner and invited people of every section, every sociological and political colouration, and tried to develop its dynamism as a movement unifying the entire country. He personally contacted all the trade unions, colleges and schools and motivated ward representatives of Delhi to ensure a successful citizens' march.

At the time, the RSS was desperate to gain legitimacy. It still faced serious credibility crisis even though the ban that was imposed on it after the assassination of Mahatma Gandhi had long been lifted. Ahmed might not have seen any reason to discriminate against the Bharatiya Mazdoor Sangh, the central trade union organization affiliated to the RSS. He invited the BMS along with other central trade union organizations of the time—the Indian National Trade Union Congress, All India Trade Union Congress and the United Trade Union Congress—and requested them to send their respective contingents for the citizens' march. It would seem that Ahmed's invitation to the BMS was seen by the RSS as a window of opportunity. For, the RSS began hectic efforts to mobilize its members not just from Delhi but also from neighbouring districts of UP for the Republic Day event.[27]

'More than 100,000 people joined the citizens' march and raised slogans renewing their resolve to safeguard India's honour and integrity against Chinese treachery and aggression,' said a report published in the *Hindustan Times*. 'The Armed Forces parade was on a small scale this year, reminding the people that the bulk of the forces were at the front guarding against further Chinese encroachments. Even the citizens' march was shorn of pomp and pageantry because of the national emergency and the need for austerity and economy.'[28]

27. Ibid., p. 396.

28. *Hindustan Times*, 28 January 1963.

It was an extraordinary Republic Day event in which even Members of Parliament marched solemnly in unison past the saluting base. Nehru and his cabinet colleagues led the contingent of MPs. 'The front line of their column comprised Mr. Satya Narayan Sinha, Minister for Parliamentary Affairs, Mr. Y.B. Chavan, Minister for Defence, Mr. Hukam Singh, Speaker of the Lok Sabha, Mr. Nehru, Mr. Morarji Desai, Minister for Finance, and Mr. Jagjivan Ram, Minister for Transport and Communications,' said another newspaper report. 'Mr. Sinha and Mr. Jagjivan Ram at two extremities held the National Flag aloft. Mr. Nehru and others folded their hands in salutation as they walked past the President's dais.'[29]

The RSS managed to sneak in about two thousand of its swayamsevaks 'in their full organizational uniform', and they marched along with other citizens of Delhi.[30] The role they cast themselves in was that of nationalist citizens, forming part of the contingent of the Bharatiya Mazdoor Sangh. For, they didn't carry any banner or a placard or even a bhagwa flag of the RSS. Their contingent might just have got mixed up in the massive crowd of over one lakh people, and they might not have looked conspicuous because the administration had, in any case, invited the BMS. This might have been the reason why most of the newspapers, except *Hindustan*,[31] a Hindi daily, failed to take note of their presence, even though the RSS men joined the march in their full uniform. In order to meet the conditions laid down for citizens joining the march, these RSS men carried the national flag instead of their own bhagwa flag.[32] This was perhaps the first time when, stoked by its desperate need to seek legitimacy, the RSS was forced to show some respect to the national flag in public.

---

29. *The Times of India*, 27 January 1963.

30. *Organiser*, 4 February 1963.

31. *Hindustan*, 28 January 1963.

32. Ibid.

Many in the Congress were watching the participation of the RSS men with concern. Nor was Nehru blind to the mechanisms whereby it had sneaked into the citizens' march. 'Some Congressmen came to me a day before and said that RSS people are collecting men with uniforms from Ghaziabad and Meerut and other places, we do not have so many uniforms. I said, "Look, I cannot stop the RSS from coming in, it is wrong to prevent anything,"' Nehru told the CPP on 27 January. He added that no dress code had been prescribed to civilians for their participation in the citizens' march. 'Also I said no bands, private bands of parties. For the rest they can come in any dress or uniform or not, I cannot hold that.'[33]

Nehru mentioned in the CPP meeting that the rumour was that twenty-five thousand RSS men would come, but, despite the fanfare, only two thousand did. 'We cannot stop them,' he said. 'What can we do about that? The matter was in the hands of Government only till the people came. After that it was not directly in the Government's hands. It had been handed over to the Mayor who had made very good arrangements.'[34]

In later years, a rumour swirled out from this curious episode of contemporary history—that Nehru invited the RSS to take part in the Republic Day parade of 1963 and that the Sangh participated in it as a separate contingent. The author of this rumour has never been traced, but the organization that benefited from it is obvious.

IV

Golwalkar did not really understand that Nehru was a secular democrat and always conscious, even after a brutal setback from

---

33. *Selected Works of Jawaharlal Nehru*, Second Series, Volume Eighty, Jawaharlal Nehru Memorial Fund, New Delhi, 2019, p. 396.

34. Ibid., p. 397.

China, of being one. No matter what Golwalkar presumed, the heart and soul of Nehru still deemed to lie where it used to in the past. As events were shortly to show, there was no change in his attitude towards Golwalkar, the RSS and their vision of a Hindu Rashtra. A crucial characteristic of this attitude was firmness—something that he maintained even after suffering a debacle from what seemed to be a socialist country at the very end of his career. Thus, for example, he became furious when he learned that senior Congress leader and former Madhya Pradesh chief minister K. N. Katju had taken part in a programme of the RSS. In a strongly-worded letter to Katju on 21 February 1963, Nehru reacted sharply, saying 'you were not right in attending the camp of the RSS'.[35]

For three days beginning 24 February, Golwalkar vacationed in Kathmandu, the capital of Nepal, where he met King Mahendravir Vikramshah and Prime Minister Tulsi Giri. Upon his return on 27 February, he wrote a very endearing letter to Nehru, detailing his Nepal visit and seeking a meeting with him.[36] Nehru replied courteously on 1 March, thanking him for informing him about his talks with the King and the Prime Minister of Nepal, but saying nothing about Golwalkar's request for a meeting.[37]

Days later, the Nehru government quietly rejected the passport application of Golwalkar, who was now planning to visit Burma. When Jana Sangh leader Atal Bihari Vajpayee raised the issue in Parliament and sought an explanation from the government, Deputy Minister for External Affairs Dinesh Singh said on 18

35. *Selected Works of Jawaharlal Nehru*, Second Series, Volume 81, Jawaharlal Nehru Memorial Fund, New Delhi, 2019, p. 112.

36. Ranga Hari, *The Incomparable Guru Golwalkar*, Prabhat Paperbacks, New Delhi, 2018, pp. 254-255.

37. *Selected Works of Jawaharlal Nehru*, Second Series, Volume 81, Jawaharlal Nehru Memorial Fund, New Delhi, 2019, p. 692.

March: 'It will not be in the public interest to disclose the reasons.'[38] Vajpayee then took the matter to Nehru. He met the Prime Minister on 3 August 1963 and requested him to review the government's decision on Golwalkar's passport issue. But Nehru remained unchanged. After Vajpayee left, he wrote to Home Minister Lal Bahadur Shastri informing him about the meeting and telling him, 'I do not think it is necessary or desirable to open this issue now and to issue a passport to him [Golwalkar] to go abroad.'[39]

Similarly, when Nehru learned about the book *Why Hindu Rashtra*, which contained 'extracts from speeches of Golwalkar', his response was as firm as ever. On 9 May 1963, he wrote to Shastri: 'I hope you will have this book examined and if necessary take action against it.'[40] Shastri forwarded Nehru's letter to Law Minister A. K. Sen with his noting: 'The book has aroused a lot of comments and some of the references to non-Hindus are somewhat unfortunate. Such books also give a handle to the propaganda made against us abroad.'[41] The Law Ministry examined the book and suggested on 22 February 1964 that 'prudence lies in favour of ignoring the publication rather than giving further publicity to it by taking action against it, whether under the Indian Penal Code or under the Defence of India Rules'.[42] But Nehru did not deviate from the line and continued to push the matter. Hours before Nehru's death on 27 May 1964, Minister of State for Home J. L. Hathi informed CPI leader Hiren Mukherjee

38. Ibid., p. 323.

39. *Selected Works of Jawaharlal Nehru*, Second Series, Volume 83, Jawaharlal Nehru Memorial Fund, New Delhi, 2019, p. 1.

40. *Selected Works of Jawaharlal Nehru*, Second Series, Volume 82, Jawaharlal Nehru Memorial Fund, New Delhi, 2019, p. 1.

41. Ibid., p. 2.

42. Ibid., pp. 2-3.

during Question Hour in Parliament that the government was 'considering the question of banning some books by the RSS leader, Mr. Golwalkar'.[43]

For almost everyone who knew him, Nehru embodied the ideals of secularism and democracy, and these underpinned his capacity for leadership. During a conversation with young diplomats of the Ministry of External Affairs in December 1963, Nehru, on being asked what would happen 'if the Communists are elected to power', challenged their basic assumptions. 'Communists, communists, communists,' Nehru said. 'Why are all of you so obsessed with communists and communism: What is it that communists can do that we cannot do and have not done for the country: Why do you imagine the communists will ever be voted into power at the Centre!' Then, after a long pause, he added: '*The danger to India, mark you, is not communism. It is Hindu right wing communalism.*'[44]

V

At the end of the Nehru regime, of all the factors that made Golwalkar deeply unsettled, none seemed to generate more anxiety—or more panic—than his book, *We or Our Nationhood Defined.* More than two decades after its publication, the book still potentially threatened to turn his situation instable. Its reprinting had been stopped after the assassination of Gandhi, but, as J. A. Curran noted in 1951, despite the conciliatory tone in Golwalkar's speeches delivered after the removal of the ban on the RSS, the 'genuine ideology of the Sangh' had continued to be based on the book. '*We* can be described as the R.S.S. "Bible",' Curran

43. *The Times of India*, 28 May 1964.

44. Y. D. Gundevia, *Outside the Archives*, Sangam Books, Hyderabad, 1984, pp. 209-210. (Emphasis is by the author)

wrote. 'It is the basic primer in the indoctrination of the Sangh volunteers. Although this book was written twelve years ago, in a national context different from the contemporary one, the principles contained in it are still considered entirely applicable by the Sangh membership.'[45] On the basis of his field research and widespread interaction with the RSS leaders and cadres, he concluded that the 'philosophy' of Golwalkar's 1939 book 'forms the foundation for contemporary R.S.S. plans and activities'.[46]

Curran's conclusion was echoed again in 1956 when two biographies were published to mark the completion of Golwalkar's fiftieth birth anniversary. B. N. Bhargava, one of these biographers, called *We or Our Nationhood Defined* 'an unassailable exposition' of the doctrine of 'nationhood' and asserted: 'Subsequent developments have established beyond all doubt the truth of his [Golwalkar's] thesis.'[47] N. H. Palkar, the other biographer, claimed that what Golwalkar wrote in his book 'is the only proper way to look at the question of minorities' in India and that 'this alone can ensure stable and peaceful national life'.[48]

Thus, despite stopping its reprinting, the book continued to carry the core of the RSS ideology as it had been prior to the assassination of Mahatma Gandhi. The book, however, remained out of public discourse all these years until it was dragged up in 1962 by P. Kodanda Rao, a Bangalore-based social activist and rationalist who was highly regarded by the political and social leaders of the time.

---

45. J. A. Curran, Jr., *Militant Hinduism in Indian Politics: A Study fo the R.S.S.*, Institute of Pacific Relations, New York, 1951, p. 28.

46. Ibid., p. 33.

47. B. N. Bhargava, *Shri Guruji: The Man & His Mission*, Bharat Prakashan (Delhi) Ltd., New Delhi, 1956, pp. 13-14.

48. N. H. Palkar, *Shri Ma Sa Golwalkar*, published by N. H. Palkar, Mumbai, 1956, p. 63.

That year, on having discovered some of the contents of *We or Our Nationhood Defined*, Rao wrote to Golwalkar to ascertain whether he had modified his views on minorities since the publication of the book or he still held them. Rao waited for a while, but Golwalkar neither acknowledged the receipt of his letter nor replied to it.[49] Rao then wrote to Nehru and Shastri on 9 June 1962, acquainting them with the communal contents of the book.[50] He also started reflecting on the book's anti-minority contents in his write-ups for several English dailies and journals.

Up until then, Golwalkar maintained silence on the book, believing that it would remain forgotten. For a long while, the absence of the book from public debate conferred seemingly unestimable benefits on Golwalkar but was now, under the aegis of Kodanda Rao, threatening to bring those benefits to naught. Acutely conscious of the uncensored expression of his views in the book, he seemed to start looking for a way to escape the threat that it posed. The opportunity came in May 1963 during the week-long celebration of V. D. Savarkar's eightieth birth anniversary in Bombay. As part of the celebration, Golwalkar addressed a public meeting on 15 May, when he claimed that he was not the author of *We or Our Nationhood Defined* and that it was really an abridged translation of Babarao's Marathi book, *Rashtra Mimansa*. His claim was recorded by Savarkar's official biographer Dhananjay Keer: 'Golwalkar [...] said that the book *We* which was read by the RSS was the abridgement done by him [Golwalkar] of the work *Rashtra Mimansa* of Babarao Savarkar. [...] He said that it was most befitting on his part to acknowledge publicly the debt of gratitude.'[51]

49. P. Kodanda Rao Papers, Sub. File No. 37, p. 9., Manuscript Section, NMML, New Delhi.

50. Ibid., pp. 2-3.

51. Dhananjay Keer, *Veer Savarkar*, Popular Prakashan, Bombay, 1966, p. 527.

This claim was nothing but a lie. It also exemplified the paranoid attitude of Golwalkar who scrambled for an escape route when confronted with the danger of being called out. That is the only way to explain the fake narrative that he churned out on 15 May 1963. Golwalkar had definitely drawn inspiration from *Rashtra Mimansa* and used it as one of his main sources. He acknowledged Babarao's influence in his book's preface, which also mentioned that an English translation of *Rashtra Mimansa* would be out separately. 'In compiling this work, I have received help from numerous quarters, too many to mention,' Golwalkar wrote in the preface to *We or Our Nationhood Defined*. 'I thank them all heartily; but I cannot help separately naming one and expressing my gratefulness to him—Deshbhakta GD Savarkar. His work Rashtra Meemansa in Marathi has been one of my chief sources of inspiration and help. An English translation of this work is due to be shortly out and I take this opportunity of directing the reader to that book for a more exhaustive study of the subject.'[52]

Thus, while writing his book, Golwalkar had no confusion regarding its authorship. He used Babarao's Marathi book as a source and even endorsed it, but made it clear that *We or Our Nationhood Defined* was his own work, not an abriged translation. Even biographical accounts on Golwalkar and his own writings prior to May 1963 do not in any way support his claims. On the contrary, they make his turnaround look like an afterthought and a completely arbitrary and false hypothesis which even Golwalkar did not have in mind all these years after writing the book. In 1944, for example, the Hindi translation of *Rashtra Mimansa* was published, and Golwalkar wrote its introduction. Interestingly, nowhere in the introduction, which in a way was his own testimony, did he give even a faint suggestion of anything similar to what he claimed

52. M. S. Golwalkar, *We or Our Nationhood Defined*, Bharat Publications, Nagpur, 1939, p. 4.

later in 1963—that *Rashtra Mimansa* was the original book and his own its mere abridged translation.[53]

Nor are the critical formulations of Golwalkar's book—especially its prescription of Nazi treatment of Jews as a model to be applied to Indian Muslims—to be found anywhere in *Rashtra Mimansa*. There is not a word in Babarao's book about the Nazi regime, nor about its treatment of Jews.[54] It is unlikely that Babarao knew anything about the Nazi government when he wrote his book, which was published in 1934, only a year after Hitler came to power. In fact, the Nazi hostility towards Jews reached a critical point with the Kristallnacht pogroms in 1938—a year before Golwalkar's book was published—in which Jewish homes, synagogues, hospitals and schools were ransacked across Germany. Hundreds of Jews were killed, and thousands arrested and sent to concentration camps. These pogroms set the stage for the murder of an unfathomable number of Jewish people in the years to follow. Similarly, Hitler's aggressive steps towards rebuilding the German military and expanding the Third Reich across Europe—which included the aggression towards Austria and Czechoslovakia that Golwalkar refers to in his book—began in 1935, a year after *Rashtra Mimansa* was published.

Golwalkar did not repeat the lie in any of his subsequent speeches. Perhaps, in view of the many discrepancies which it carried, he did not want to over-emphasize the claim to avoid provoking independent evaluation of its validity. After his death in 1973, the Sangh's efforts to deny the influence of Nazism on its ideology forced its supporters into the strangest of postures, ranging from a complete silence on *We or Our Nationhood Defined*

53. G. D. Savarkar, *Rashtra Mimansa Wa Hindustan Ka Rashtra-Swaroop*, Shakti Prakashan, Jabalpur, 1944, pp. 3-33.

54. See for detail Durgatanay, *Rashtra Mimansawa Hindustanchen Rashtraswaroop*, Published by Vaidyaratna Vishnu Ganesh Kelkar, Nasik, 1934.

to loosely constructed arguments aimed at excluding Golwalkar from the possibility of ever writing the book.

The question of Golwalkar's authorship of this book was also complicated by some non-RSS writers in later years. In their writings, the complexity of his thinking as enshrined in *We or Our Nationhood Defined* is not always evident as they seem to accept the claim that Golwalkar was not its author—the claim from which the Sangh's argument of having no Nazi influence on its ideology was derived. For example, in his book *Makers of Modern India*, historian Ramachandra Guha, while deliberating on Golwalkar, says absolutely nothing about *We or Our Nationhood Defined.* It neither finds mention in Guha's description of Golwalkar's life-history nor in the excerpts curated from the RSS leader's work to portray his political and social views.[55] Political scientist Jyotirmaya Sharma, in his book *Terrifying Vision: M.S. Golwalkar, the RSS and India*, goes to the extent of declaring, without even examining the veracity of Golwalkar's claims, that he 'did not write *We or Our Nationhood Defined*' and that Babarao Savarkar 'originally wrote the book'.[56]

In some respects, such writings have helped the warped pro-RSS historians' attempts to take advantage of the distance in time to excuse Golwalkar and hide Nazi influence on the ideology of the Sangh.

---

55. Ramachandra Guha, *Makers of Modern India*, Viking, New Delhi, 2010, pp. 370-384.

56. Jyotirmaya Sharma, *Terrifying Vision: M.S. Golwalkar, the RSS and India*, Viking, New Delhi, 2007, p. xix.

'I Am Not in Politics'

For Golwalkar, there appeared to be no future, illusory or otherwise, under the overwhelming presence of Nehru, who commanded insurmountable legitimacy across communities, including Hindus. Nehru's death on 27 May 1964, therefore, ended his constant state of perturbation. Golwalkar, now some fifty-eight years old, suddenly saw a way out of a hopelessly blocked life. Finding that he still had prospects for a future, he set out to do what he was best at—establishing a mechanism to use religion for political mobilization of Hindus. On 29 August, merely three months after Nehru's death, Golwalkar held a meeting with a select group of religious leaders in Bombay and set up the Vishwa Hindu Parishad, or World Hindu Council.[1]

More than any single organization floated by the RSS so far, this one seemed to be the closest to Golwalkar as his vision—or, to be more accurate, the idea of a Hindu Rashtra—drew its vital sustenance from political use of religion. In keeping with this vision, the VHP sought to draw upon the dense network of sadhus, their maths and ashrams and associations formed by monastic orders for developing political Hinduism, that is, religious

1. Ranga Hari, *The Incomparable Guru Golwalkar*, Prabhat Paperbacks, New Delhi, 2018, p. 264.

mobilization of Hindus to capture political power in the country.

Structurally, the VHP was conceived as a two-tier body—while a group of RSS men acted as the core of the organization, a vast network of sadhus formulated a Hindu perspective on social as well as political issues. In the beginning, this network of sadhus was a loose structure, but later it was given a formal shape under the name of 'Margdarshak Mandal'. It was in accordance with this objective that Golwalkar appointed one of his close associates and a senior pracharak, S. S. Apte, as the first general secretary of the VHP and Swami Chinmayananda, an influential sadhu close to him, its first president.[2] The collaboration between Apte and Chinmayananda symbolized the association of RSS pracharaks and Hindu sadhus, an association that formed the cornerstone of the VHP.

Raising the Hinduism-in-danger bogey, Apte gave a clear hint of the political agenda of the VHP right after the Bombay meeting in 1964. 'The world has been divided into Christian, Islamic and Communist, and all these three consider the Hindu society as a very fine rich food on which to feast and fatten themselves,' he said. 'It is therefore necessary in this age of competition and conflict to think of, and organize, the Hindu world to save itself from the evil eyes of all the three.'[3]

Golwalkar's decision not to use the Jana Sangh to involve sadhus and monastic orders for consolidating Hindu masses but to launch a separate outfit that could claim to be operating outside the sphere of politics was a shrewd tactical move aimed at cleverly bypassing the constraints of the contemporary government's secularist approach. The VHP, as it turned out, gave the RSS an opportunity to identify itself with the Hindu monastic groups and enabled it to lobby for their views among a larger audience.

---

2. Ibid.
3. *Organiser*, Diwali Special, 1964, p. 15.

In course of time, this identification became critical in setting the ground for invoking Hinduism to polarize voters for the political benefits of the Sangh's electoral outfit.

Until the formation of the VHP, the Hindu Mahasabha and the Ram Rajya Parishad had been the leading political forums for politically-motivated sadhus. The Mahasabha, for instance, had enrolled in its ranks Mahant Digvijay Nath, the religious head of Gorakshapeeth temple of Gorakhpur in UP. The Ram Rajya Parishad was itself headed by a Hindu religious leader, Swami Karpatri. The Shankaracharya of Puri, Niranjandev Teerth, a prominent sadhu of the time, was another leader of this party. In its initial days, the VHP, like the Hindu Mahasabha and the Ram Rajya Parishad in earlier time, could attract only sadhus who were in search of a platform and greater legitimacy. But it persisted and, in course of time, started gaining roots among Hindu monastic orders and became an extremely powerful vehicle for the political use of sadhus.

II

In December 1964, the RSS published a slim 42-page book to provide 'glimpses of the Sangh's philosophy and programme, the progress it has made and the confidence it enjoys'.[4] Titled *Sangha Darshan*, the book turned out to be the Sangh's first systematic attempt to cover its tracks by creating a fake narrative about its history. It called Hedgewar the 'Doctor of the Nation'[5] and presented him as that compound of politician and theoretician that made someone the only possible saviour for a nation. The book gave all credit for the formation of the RSS to Hedgewar and

4. *Sangha Darshan*, Prakashan Vibhag, Rashtreeya Swayamsevak Sangh, Bangalore, 1964.

5. Ibid., p. 2.

talked nothing about the role played by Moonje, Babarao Savarkar and other Hindu Mahasabha leaders. It claimed that Hedgewar, after a long contemplation, concluded that 'rousing of national consciousness and building up of national solidarity' were the only guarantee for national survival and 'the only effective weapon for a nation in bondage to shake off its fetters'.[6]

Thus, the rationale of the RSS was explained by the idea of a special mission: the sense of taking part in national regeneration, of inculcating patriotism among youth, of being the agent of an ideal. 'There is therefore absolutely no place in the Sangh for negative feelings such as hatred against non-Hindus,' the book claimed. 'The Sangh seeks self-reformation to generate strength, believing that we are ourselves responsible for our downfall.'[7]

Sangha Darshan also asserted that the RSS had absolutely nothing to do with politics and that the inner values it preached included patriotism, devotion, character, amity and sacrifice. 'There is also no place for political rivalry or bitterness in the Sangh, because the Sangh has kept itself scrupulously aloof from the day-to-day political activities,' the book claimed. 'It does not believe that national oneness can be achieved through elections or political propaganda.'[8]

The book reinforced all the myths that later swirled around Golwalkar, from his being a child prodigy to a professor in the BHU to a Hindu saint comparable to Swami Vivekananda. 'The only surviving darling son of his parents, as a boy Sri Guruji showed signs of extraordinary talents,' it continued.

> Later, after doing his M.Sc., he was for some time professor in the Benaras Hindu University. He was respectfully called Guruji by his beloved students and the epithet stuck to him in later

6. Ibid., p. 9.
7. Ibid., p. 26.
8. Ibid.

> years. But his was not the spirit to be cribbed and cabined in the confines of service. He resigned and returned to Nagpur. He did his L.L.B., but never practiced law. He had by then come under the magnetic influence of Doctorji. That was like Narendra [original name of Swami Vivekananda] meeting Sri Ramakrishna. The result was equally epoch-making![9]

Of special significance was the book's portrayal of Golwalkar as someone who had reached the lofty heights of Indian culture and had all through thought long and hard so that he could offer not only an interpretation of the present but also an outline for the future. 'With his finger constantly on the nation's pulse, with his unceasing concern for the good of the country, Sri Guruji is eminently the leader qualified to guide the nation,' it said. 'Rising above the lures of position or power or personal glory his single-minded devotion is to the nation as a whole. His utterances therefore carry the ring of harsh truth. He is fearless in his espousal of the nation's cause and makes no concession to any individual or party.'[10]

The book doesn't mention the name of its author, but as it was published by the Karnataka unit of the RSS it is safe to assume that Golwalkar's close aide Yadavrao Joshi, a pracharak and chief of the Sangh's state unit, played a key role in the production of *Sangha Darshan*. The picture of the RSS that emerged from the book's narrative showed that Joshi and his friends succeeded in large part in weeding out the uncomfortable episodes of the Sangh's history and reclaiming a new identity for the RSS, its founder Hedgewar and Golwalkar. Equally evident was the anxiety lurking behind the front of the bold words of *Sangha Darshan* to make the narrative fully believable to others. Perhaps it was this anxiety that resulted in the book being so pretentious in its approach and ambiguous in its language.

---

9. Ibid., pp. 34-35.

10. Ibid., p. 35.

III

In May 1965, while attending an RSS camp in Nagpur, Golwalkar received the news of Bhaiyaji Dani's death.[11] Dani had gone to Indore for some RSS work and died of a heart attack. Golwalkar seemed to be closer to Dani than to any other colleague in the RSS. He had been responsible in many important respects for Golwalkar's rise in the RSS. It was Dani who had first brought Golwalkar, then a lab assistant in the Zoology department of the BHU, into contact with the RSS. He helped Golwalkar get the important assignment of translating Babarao Savarkar's *Rashtra Mimansa* into English, cemented his relationship with the elite Hindutva group of Nagpur, guarded his ascension to the top post of the RSS upon Hedgewar's death and served him loyally as the sarkaryavah, or general secretary, of the RSS for most of the years since the mid-1940s. With Dani's abrupt passing, Golwalkar lost a confidant who practically ran the RSS for him.

At the same time, Golwalkar was also losing some of his sense of direction. The cause that had fuelled him for almost a quarter of a century was ebbing. Lal Bahadur Shastri, the new prime minister, was not as stiff in dealing with the RSS as Nehru, but there had not been any significant change in the overall political climate. Golwalkar's aspirations still remained tempered, even a year after Nehru's death. The bad time, therefore, continued for Golwalkar. Dani's death seemed to make it worse.[12] He expressed the paralyzing sense of his grief to his friend Hanuman Prasad Poddar, the editor of the Hindu spiritual journal *Kalyan*. 'The death of Bhaiyaji Dani is a big setback for our organisation,' he wrote to Poddar on 5 June 1965. 'For me, with his death, it is

---

11. Ranga Hari, *The Incomparable Guru Golwalkar*, Prabhat Paperbacks, New Delhi, 2018, p. 270.

12. Ibid.

as if the ground has moved from under my feet.'[13]

In this season of intense crisis, one of the main tasks before Golwalkar was to select a new sarkaryavah in place of Dani. Golwalkar had long been focusing on ideological issues and constantly traveling, while the day-to-day running of the organization, the main responsibility of a sarkaryavah, had been left to Dani. Since 1962, Balasaheb Deoras, who had already returned to the RSS fold in 1960 after getting realigned with Golwalkar largely due to Dani's efforts, had been working as sah-sarkaryavah, or joint general secretary.[14] While assisting Dani in the micro-management of the RSS, Deoras quickly revived his connections with most prominent members of the organization. Although circumstances surrounding Deoras' elevation as sarkaryavah after Dani's death remain somewhat unclear, it seems likely that, in the absence of a more suitable person for the job, Golwalkar, already discomposed at the loss of his closest friend, didn't have much of a choice on the issue.

Dani's death coincided with a sudden deterioration in Golwalkar's health. According to Ranga Hari, 'Non-stop travels, four to five programmes each day, open and endless sessions of discussions and advancing age led to weakening of Guruji's health.'[15] It must have added to the void created by the absence of Dani's friendship. In the beginning of July 1965, Golwalkar, on the advice of his associates, agreed to go for a month-long recuperation at a naturopathy centre at Pattambi in Kerala.[16] It was at Pattambi that summer that he checked and cleared the manuscript of the compilation of his

13. *Shri Guruji Samagra,* Vol. 7, pp. 257-258, Suruchi Prakashan, New Delhi.

14. Sanjeev Kelkar, *Lost Years of the RSS,* Sage Publications India Pvt Ltd, New Delhi, 2011, p. 108.

15. Ranga Hari, *The Incomparable Guru Golwalkar*, Prabhat Paperbacks, New Delhi, 2018, p. 270.

16. Ibid.

select speeches and discussions, which had been made ready and brought to him by Yadavrao Joshi.[17] Later, in February 1966, the compilation was published under the title *Bunch of Thoughts.*

One might suspect that *Bunch of Thoughts* was Golwalkar's way of camouflaging some of the uncensored expressions of his views enumerated in *We or Our Nationhood Defined.* The new book took some of Golwalkar's beliefs as mentioned in *We or Our Nationhood Defined,* diluted what he considered internal enemies and went silent on Nazis and the use of their anti-Jew model to deal with minorities in India. It, however, still affirmed that Hindus alone were true lovers of the nation and that Muslims, Christians and Communists were internal threats. 'Have those who remained here changed at least after [the Partition of India]?' it asked. 'Has their old hostility and murderous mood, which resulted in widespread riots, looting, arson, raping and all sorts of orgies on the unprecedented scale in 1946-47, come to a halt at least now? It would be suicidal to delude ourselves into believing that they have turned patriots overnight after the creation of Pakistan. On the contrary the Muslim menace has increased a hundredfold by the creation of Pakistan which has become a springboard for all their future aggressive designs on our country.'[18]

In *Bunch of Thoughts,* Golwalkar also maintained ambiguity on his communal theory of history, including the thousand years of the Hindu nation's continuous struggle, as enumerated in *We or Our Nationhood Defined.* He, in fact, made it so vague in the new book that an ordinary reader could hardly make out that it had anything to do with what Golwalkar originally meant by it. Yet, *Bunch of Thoughts* retained the philosophy of *We or Our Nationhood Defined,* promising Hindus that, were they determined

17. Ibid., p. 271.

18. M. S. Golwalkar, *Bunch of Thoughts,* Vikrama Prakashan, Bangalore, 1966, pp. 167-168.

enough, they alone would have the exclusive right to lay down the terms of national identity.

At many places, Golwalkar cited unverifiable personal experiences as evidence to augment his arguments. Sample this: 'Once I asked a Christian missionary why they abused our sacred scriptures, gods and goddesses. He said frankly, "Our aim is to knock out the faith from the heart of the Hindu. When his faith is shattered, his nationalism is also destroyed. A void will be created in his mind. Then it becomes easy for us to fill that void with Christianity."'[19]

Along with all the jumbled thoughts, the book contains some deep insights, born directly of Golwalkar's profound irritationality with modern, progressive ideas. Women's liberation was, for example, anathema to him. He believed they were misled by modernity. Referring to a couplet that states 'a virtuous lady covers her body', he lamented: 'But "modern" women think that "modernism" lies in exposing their body more and more to the public gaze. What a fall!'[20]

At another place in the book, he gave an utterly bizarre argument, mocking Indians for imitating the West's use of the word 'mummy' for mother. 'Do we know what the word originally conveyed?' he asked. 'In Egypt, there are massive cemeteries entombing their old kings. They are called pyramids. The corpses placed inside are called "mummies"! And here we address our living, loving mothers as mummies!'[21] Golwalkar also chided 'educated mothers who have spare time and energy' for wasting it 'in gossip of fashionable clubs'.[22] Demands for equality seemed ludicrous to him: 'There is now a clamour for "equality

19. Ibid., p. 182.

20. Ibid., pp. 452-453.

21. Ibid., p. 453.

22. Ibid., p. 456.

for women" and their "emancipation from man's domination"! Reservation of seats in various positions of power is being claimed on the basis of their separate sex, thus adding one more "ism"—"sexism!"—to the array of casteism, communalism, linguism, etc.'[23]

The convoluted style of *Bunch of Thoughts* may make it hard to read, but it does convey a remarkably clear picture of its author, who in his constant fear of getting unmasked by *We or Our Nationhood Defined* actually ends up unmasking himself.

IV

Hardly had Golwalkar finished checking the manuscript of *Bunch of Thoughts* than an overwhelming moment took over him. In the afternoon of 5 September 1965, while he rested at Limaye's home in Sangli, a young swayamsevak came scampering with a message: someone from the Prime Minister's Office had called to inform that Lal Bahadur Shastri would want to speak with Golwalkar urgently.[24] The swayamsevak, Bapusaheb Pujari, was Sangli's only RSS member who had a telephone connection at his residence—the reason why the PMO called at his number.

Shortly thereafter, Golwalkar was at Pujari's residence speaking with Shastri on the phone. Pujari sat nearby jotting down the conversation.

'You know about the war with Pakistan,' Shastri, according to Pujari, told Golwalkar. 'I want support from you.'

'Thank you, Shastriji, but I am not a leader of any party. I am sarsanghchalak of the RSS and a renunciant. How can I be of any use to you?' Golwalkar asked.

23. Ibid., p. 156.

24. Bapusaheb Pujari was interviewed on 14 October 2019 at Sangli in Maharashtra.

'I have called leaders of all political parties tomorrow at 10 a.m. I invite you for the meeting,' Shastri said.

'But how can I reach Delhi tomorrow morning from such a long distance?'

'Please reach Bombay tonight. Seats will be reserved for you and your attendant in the first flight for Delhi tomorrow morning,' said Shastri.

By Pujari's account, the conversation took place around 4 p.m., and Golwalkar, excited by his conversation with the Prime Minister, cancelled all his appointments and started off for Bombay—380 km northwest of Sangli—around 7 p.m. in a car.

Although he reached Delhi in time, the meeting got delayed and took place on the night of 6 September 1965. 'Leaders of all political parties who conferred with the Prime Minister, Mr. Lal Bahadur Shastri, tonight for two hours gave their full support to the action taken by the Government to thwart Pakistani aggression,' reported the *Times of India*, adding that Golwalkar was among the opposition leaders who attended the meeting.[25] The war with Pakistan had begun in April 1965 following the neighbouring country's aggression on Jammu and Kashmir. By the beginning of September, India's victory seemed beyond question. The mood was, therefore, upbeat when Shastri met political leaders.

Golwalkar's behaviour during the following months suggests that he revelled in the attention he had begun once again to attract and tried hard to emerge from the anonymity that had so long concealed and depressed him. He took an optimistic and aggressive tone as he set out to strengthen the hands of the Shastri government in India's war against Pakistan. On 8 September, he issued a formal appeal to 'brother swayamsevaks', asking them to cooperate with the government in every possible way. 'Work like serving the injured and the sick, order and peace, citizens' security

25. *The Times of India*, 7 September 1965.

can be done on non-government basis,' his statement said. 'Special attention will have to be paid towards keeping the moral of people high, awakening high sense of national pride and resolve to fight on firmly till the final victory.'[26]

Two days later, on 10 September, he addressed a rally of swayamsevaks at Bombay and said that 'India should move forward and consolidate advantage' it had gained in the war 'because the world opinion would favour only the powerful and the strong' nations. 'Even a just cause like ours has not been accepted or understood by the world,' he said, according to a report published in the *Times of India*. 'They will realize the truth only if we are strong and powerful. [...] Pakistan had been committing mischief on India's borders for the last 18 years because she thought that India was not strong enough to stop this. Pakistan never realized that the patience of even a peaceful country like India could be exhausted.'[27]

Bodyguards, RSS volunteers and acolytes encased him as he moved around the states bordering Pakistan. On 19 September, his speech in the border state of Gujarat was broadcast by All India Radio from its Vadodara station. 'It is my request to all countrymen,' Golwalkar said, 'that we should wish for victory, pray for victory, work ceaselessly and make sacrifice of the highest order. You should exhibit courage and fortitude.'[28] He then went to Punjab, another border state, and spoke before the Army jawans at Ambala cantonment on 15 October.[29] A month later, on 12 November, he met Shastri again.[30]

---

26. Ranga Hari, *The Incomparable Guru Golwalkar*, Prabhat Paperbacks, New Delhi, 2018, p. 273.

27. *The Times of India*, 11 September 1965.

28. Ranga Hari, *The Incomparable Guru Golwalkar*, Prabhat Paperbacks, New Delhi, 2018, p. 274.

29. Ibid.

30. Ibid.

It would be incorrect, however, to infer from this that Shastri sought to appease Golwalkar. With all his humility and patience, Shastri worked in his own style—patiently and with broad consultation among all major interest groups. At a time of a national crisis, he wished to see Indians united as rapidly as possible. The Hindu right constituted a significant grouping, and Golwalkar as the head of the Sangh Parivar could be a useful resource.

Yet, the warm reception that Golwalkar received from Shastri, though scarcely of a political nature, seemed to mean quite a lot to him. Increasingly, he appeared bent upon making an impression on Shastri. Golwalkar wanted, of course, to make use of his proximity to Shastri for his own ends. But he probably also felt a genuine respect for a man who, despite being the Prime Minister, was ready to treat him as an equal and as a leader of national importance. Shastri's sudden death on 11 January 1966 must, therefore, have shocked Golwalkar in the same manner as the demise of Sardar Patel did fifteen years back.

V

By early 1966, with Indira Gandhi becoming the prime minister, the biggest change occurring in the Nehru family, and in the Congress party, was the rise of a second generation. As Nehru's daughter, Indira Gandhi had inherited a secular and progressive outlook and a distinctive awareness of her relationship to the past. As a politician, having been with her father during his most trying days after Partition, having travelled across many countries alongside him and having worked as the president of the Congress in 1959 and a minister under Shastri, she had learned the threat communal forces could pose to the secular and democratic structure of the country. These qualities served to endear her to an electorate which preferred to see Nehru in her, but they also made her insufferable for Hindu conservatives in her own party and Hindu communalists outside.

Before long they colluded and tried to present one of the earliest threats to her regime. In their campaign to outflank Indira Gandhi through appeals to Hindu religion, they found the emotive issue of cow slaughter a useful resource. The demand for a ban on cow slaughter had gone dormant after Nehru had rejected it firmly. But within months of Indira Gandhi assuming charge, the issue was revived—first innocuously by a small group of sadhus and then rather seriously when those operating from the background opted to come out in the open. Of this latter group, Golwalkar, to whom cow protection was among his favourite ideas, was the most significant figure. He still seemed to be guided by the bloated self-image acquired during the Shastri era. The rise of Hindu conservatives in the Congress might have further added to his confidence.

The agitation for cow protection had a muted revival. On 2 April 1966, when Indira Gandhi was barely two months in office, a small group of sadhus sat on dharna outside her residence demanding a ban on cow slaughter. Similar dharnas were also witnessed outside the residences of some of her cabinet colleagues and in front of Parliament and Secretariat. The protesting sadhus were promptly rounded up and sent to jail.[31] By the end of July, with the commencement of the Monsoon session, they launched a fresh dharna outside Parliament. This time, Sunder Singh Bhandari, an old RSS hand and Jana Sangh MP, garlanded the protesting sadhus and assured them of his party's full support to their demand. Congress MP Govind Das, who was also present on the occasion, declared that if the government did not concede the demand, many sadhus would start fasts unto death.[32]

During the next two weeks, it became clear that there was more to this agitation than what was apparent. On 10 August, the

31. *Organiser*, 31 July 1966.

32. Ibid.

news agency PTI reported that 'a committee consisting of several MPs' had been formed to secure the legal ban on cow slaughter. Another PTI report on 16 August claimed that Golwalkar and some prominent Hindu religious leaders 'have decided to go on a fast unto death if the Union Government does not legally ban cow slaughter throughout the country'.[33]

The report instantly brought Golwalkar in the centre of the emotive cow slaughter issue. It also revealed the Hindu Right's strategy ahead of the general elections due in early 1967. In the secular quarters, therefore, it evoked as much ridicule as bitterness. For a few days after the publication of the PTI report, Golwalkar seemed to remain unsure of himself; he neither supported nor contradicted it. Perhaps he expected that his supporters would come out and beg him to give up the idea of a fast unto death, as had happened when Mahatma Gandhi had announced his decision to go on an indefinite fast. But there was no trace of any such welling up of emotions. As he confronted the scary prospect of being left in the lurch and the serious possibility of actually sitting on an indefinite fast, Golwalkar appeared to be filled with anxiety.

On 20 August, therefore, he told a gathering of RSS men at Nagpur that the media report of him committing to undertake a fast was not correct. 'I have not said that, nor has any such proposal been made to me,' he said. 'But if any such proposal is put before me, the matter will have to be thought over. We do not quite believe in fasting. Recourse to that method is all right for the sadhus, but not others. In the political sphere particularly, I think that this remedy should be scrupulously eschewed. So far as I am concerned, I am not in politics, and so if I undertake a fast, it should be pardonable. But I have made no such announcement.'[34]

---

33. P. Kodanda Rao Papers, Sub. File No. 28, p. 2, Manuscript Section, NMML, New Delhi.

34. *Organiser*, 28 August 1966.

Yet, alongside his upwelling sense of self-preservation was his aching desire to be seen as someone never afraid of undertaking an indefinite fast. Proof of this is the tale he told to the RSS men in the same meeting. He claimed to have once done on his own a thirteen-day fast as an 'experiment'. Golwalkar said: 'I stopped eating, but continued my normal activity—my reading and writing, going to the *shakha*, cycling four-five miles a day etc. This routine continued for some thirteen days, and I didn't seem any the worse for that. A few friends came and reproached me: "What are you doing? Stop it." I acquiesced and sat down with them to have my meals—yes, meals, not orange juice!'[35] The 'orange juice' pun was aimed at ridiculing Mahatma Gandhi's way of breaking his fast.

The anecdote later became a staple item of the Golwalkar legend. Yet, what was significant in this tale was this: when the time for subjecting himself to an indefinite fast came he backed out, citing his lack of belief in fasting as the reason. It would seem that the public activity represented to him principally a means for unburdening himself through his rhetorical speeches, and he simply could not think of taking upon himself the actual rigour of pulling the movement by undertaking a fast. Nor did he want anyone to link his activity with the politics of the Hindu Right.

Golwalkar, therefore, felt irritated when Kodanda Rao issued a statement on 22 August, saying that a ban on cow slaughter was 'demanded only by Hindus' and that if 'the religious sentiments of Hindus are to prevail, we may as well declare India as a Hindu State and install the Hindu Matadhipathis and sadhus in the seats of political power and say good-bye to secularism'.[36] On 3 September, Golwalkar wrote an angry letter to Rao: 'I hope you appreciate that none of those persons, who have been reported

35. Ibid.

36. *Deccan Herald*, 23 August 1966.

to undertake "fast unto death" for securing legal ban on cow-slaughter, are in even a distant way interested in elections and politics of that sort. [...] About myself, you may go on attributing any motives to me and try to give me a bad name, to your heart's content and I will not say a word about it. I am used to such things.'[37]

VI

On 25 September, three weeks after Golwalkar wrote to Kodanda Rao, the RSS, VHP, Jana Sangh, Hindu Mahasabha, Ram Rajya Parishad, Arya Samaj and several sadhus and monastic associations, including the Bharat Sadhu Samaj, which had been founded by Congress leader and Home Minister Gulzarilal Nanda, announced the formation of the All Party Anti-Cow-Slaughter Campaign Committee—Sarvadaliya Goraksha Maha-abhiyan Samiti (SGMS).[38] The umbrella organization was headed by Prabhudatt Brahmachari, an Allahabad-based sadhu who had contested against Nehru as the joint candidate of all Hindutva parties and lost by a huge margin in the 1952 election. During the Sangh's low-pitch anti-cow slaughter movement of the 1950s, he had developed a close relationship with Golwalkar.

While Golwalkar was part of the supreme committee of the SGMS, many of his colleagues, including Hans Raj Gupta and V. P. Joshi, became members of its executive body.[39] Golwalkar's friend Hanuman Prasad Poddar was made treasurer. Rajendra Singh or Rajju Bhaiyya, the UP RSS leader who later became

37. P. Kodanda Rao Papers, Sub. File No. 28, p. 5, Manuscript Section, NMML, New Delhi.

38. Christophe Jaffrelot, *The Hindu Nationalist Movement and Indian Politics: 1925 to the 1990s*, Hurst & Company, London, 1993, p. 206.

39. Akshaya Mukul, *Gita Press and the Making of Hindu India*, HarperCollins Publishers India, New Delhi, 2015, p. 303.

the sarsanghchalak, assisted in managing the funds and reported directly to Poddar.[40] Soon, the SGMS gave a call for a rally in Delhi to be held on 7 November 1966. Golwalkar played a key role in the preparation for the rally—a fact that was recognized by Poddar in his letter to the RSS chief dated 20 October. 'RSS swayamsevaks are ideal, skilled, dutiful and true people. The training at Shri [Prabhudatt] Brahmachari's place [in Allahabad] was really useful. The entire credit goes to the swayamsevaks. They have been preparing for weeks,' said the letter, which also gave the RSS men credit for organzing public meetings at Deoria and some other places in UP in the run-up to the Delhi rally.[41]

After weeks of preparations, the SGMS managed to organize a massive rally of more than one lakh men, including a large number of sadhus, in front of Parliament on 7 November. Initially, the demonstration remained peaceful, but around 1.30 p.m., following a provocative speech by Jana Sangh MP Swami Rameshwaranand, the crowd went berserk.[42] Violence spread in the entire area as protestors attacked Parliament, All India Radio and neighbouring buildings. When the crowd surged, police resorted to firing after repeated teargas bursts and lathi-charges failed to stop the violent mobs from trying to get into 'Parliament House and All India Radio and attacking buildings along the way and setting fire to over 100 cars and a dozen buses'.[43] Seven persons were killed and about 140 injured in the police firing. A few kilometres away, the enraged protesters attacked the residence of Congress president K. Kamaraj. Although Kamaraj escaped safely, his residence was

---

40. Ibid.

41. Hanuman Prasad Poddar to M. S. Golwalkar, 20 October 1966, cited in Akshaya Mukul, *Gita Press and the Making of Hindu India*, HarperCollins Publishers India, New Delhi, 2015, p. 308.

42. Abhishek Choudhary, *Vajpayee: The Ascent of the Hindu Right, 1924-1977*, Picador India, New Delhi, 2023, p. 208.

43. *Patriot*, 8 November 1966.

ransacked and partly burnt and one of his staff members was seriously injured.[44] By the evening, the army was called in and curfew imposed.[45]

Indira Gandhi, with her resolute stance, struck back decisively. The violence and arson put those who had organized the rally and supported the prohibition of cow slaughter on the back foot. The three-hour mob rule—the first of its kind by sadhus in the national capital—was seen as a well-planned attempt to discredit parliamentary democracy. Guljarilal Nanda, the union Home Minister, tried to extricate himself from the mess by telling the Lok Sabha that 'it was the highly inflammatory speech of Swami Rameshwaranand that had converted the till then comparatively peaceful assembly of sadhus and people campaigning for a ban on cow slaughter into a violent and destructive mob in Parliament street.'[46] Two days later, Indira Gandhi sacked Nanda.[47]

Once again, the heat was on the RSS. 'We saw the R.S.S. hand in 1948 also when that dastardly act took place,' Congress MP I. K. Gujral said in the Rajya Sabha, referring to the assassination of Mahatma Gandhi. 'After that we were assured that it was a cultural organisation. It will only confine itself to culture and then the Jan Sangh was formed. [...] The R.S.S. has always been active. It has been organizing this trouble quite for some time there and we have been demanding from the Government again and again that the R.S.S. should either be declared political or it should be banned.'[48] Over the next few days, hundreds of members of the

44. *The Times of India*, 8 November 1966.

45. *Patriot*, 8 November 1966.

46. Ibid.

47. *Patriot*, 10 November 1966.

48. Rajya Sabha Debates, 7 November 1966, Column 1758; accessed on 10 August 2023: https://rsdebate.nic.in/bitstream/123456789/520136/1/PD_58_17111966_8_p1649_p1790_7.pdf

RSS and the Jana Sangh were arrested and put behind bars. On 9 November, Minister of State for Home J. L. Hathi, told the Lok Sabha that 'the main leaders and organizations of the anti-cow slaughter demonstration on Monday, which had resulted in violence and arson, were the Jana Sangh and the RSS'.[49]

Golwalkar's confidence acquired during the reign of Lal Bahadur Shastri was based on his conviction that as a cultural organization the RSS had broken free from the system of monitoring exercised by the Election Commission on political parties. He seemed to believe that because of its peculiar status, the RSS could do anything in the name of honouring Hindu culture and tradition and get away with it. But when the demand for declaring the RSS a political party arose, he got perturbed. For a while, he kept quiet, apparently hoping that the demand would die down on its own. The issue, however, gained huge momentum on 26 November, when, during a reception at Press Club of India in New Delhi, Indira Gandhi told media persons that her 'Government was considering whether to declare the Rashtriya Swayam Sewak Sangh a political party'.[50]

Golwalkar was in a renewed state of flux. In a secular, democratic set-up, he had always suffered from political awkwardness; with Indira Gandhi's remarks, he now entered a period of groping and searching. Yet he made one explicit, forthright declaration on 12 December: that the RSS was not 'a political body' and that it was 'an organisation to make young men of the country physically strong through ordinary exercises'.[51]

49. *Patriot*, 10 November 1966.

50. *The Hindu*, 27 November 1966.

51. *The Hindu*, 14 December 1966.

Pilgrim's Progress

After the abortive anti-cow slaughter rally of 1966, the RSS seemed to vanish from the political arena, but a few months later its outfit Jana Sangh was in full resurgence. In the general elections of February 1967, the Congress barely managed to get a majority in the Lok Sabha and was reduced to a minority in several states. The Jana Sangh benefitted greatly from the drop in Congress support as did socialists and other parties in the opposition. Although Indira Gandhi was again sworn in as the prime minister, the dissension within the ranks of the Congress made the situation extremely difficult for the party in most of the north Indian states.

In an astonishingly short time, the tentative, dispute-ridden, back-of-the-envelope relationship that had prevailed among the Jana Sangh, socialists and a section of the Congress came to an end. In its place rose a muddled, mutually resentful engagement that led to the emergence of coalition governments in several north Indian states, including Bihar, Uttar Pradesh, Punjab and Madhya Pradesh. The coalition, called the Samyukta Vidhayak Dal (SVD) or United Legislators Party, seemed fragile from the beginning as the top leaders representing mutually antagonistic ideologies rarely spoke, while mid-level and lower-level functionaries fumed at one another over perceived slights and failures to cooperate.

Yet, it provided an opportunity to many swayamsevaks to occupy ministerial berths as the Jana Sangh joined the governments almost everywhere. For the first time, the party got a chance to spread its tentacles inside the state apparatus. This tendency was most visible in Uttar Pradesh, where the Jana Sangh used its education portfolio to promote the RSS's Saraswati Shishu Mandir schools, while its cooperative portfolio was used to pack the committees and administrative posts with swayamsevaks.[1] Nevertheless, the SVD governments remained dangerously unstable, and within months it was apparent that the internecine feud among the constituents, especially between the Jana Sangh and the communists, would not let them survive for long.

Meanwhile, with remarkable political instinct, Indira Gandhi, having probably felt the sting of cow protectionists' condescension in the general elections, considered a new approach to deal with Golwalkar and the SGMS. On 29 June 1967, she formed a high-power committee to recommend 'appropriate practical steps' to direct the policy of the government for cow protection.[2] Headed by former Chief Justice of India A. K. Sarkar, the committee was asked to examine 'the question of cow protection in the light of all the proposals of the Sarvadaliya Goraksha Mahabhiyan Samiti and others on the subject, including the one for a total ban on the slaughter of cow and its progeny'.[3] The committee consisted of eleven members, the majority of them being chief ministers and ministers from states and experts, including National Dairy Development Board chairman Dr. V. Kurien. Golwalkar and Puri Shankaracharya Niranjandev Teerth, both prominent leaders of the

1. Christophe Jaffrelot, *The Hindu Nationalist Movement and Indian Politics: 1925 to the 1990s*, Hurst & Company, London, 1993, p. 225.

2. *The Times of India*, 30 June 1967.

3. Ibid.

SGMS, were also made part of the panel.[4]

Kurien presented perhaps the greatest obstacle to those advocating a legal ban on cow slaughter. He was particularly hostile towards the Shankaracharya of Puri, the most aggressive proponent of the ban in the committee. 'For some inexplicable reason, the Shankaracharya and I took a spontaneous and mutual dislike to one another,' recounted Kurien in his memoir.

> I still recall my first meeting with him. He strode into the room, bare-chested, carrying an ankush (trident) in one hand and a rolled up deerskin tucked under his other arm. He walked up to the chair next to me, spread out his deerskin on the seat and sat down. In those days I used to be a heavy smoker and I thought to myself that if he did not need permission to carry a deerskin, I did not need permission to smoke and I continued smoking. Unfortunately, each time I took a puff and exhaled the smoke, it would move in his direction. The Shankaracharya glared at me, made some angry noises, snatched up his ankush and deerskin and moved down a few chairs away from me. He continued to glower at me from his new position and I continued to smoke. Justice Sarkar, who was watching this little sideshow delightedly, leaned forward, tapped me on the shoulder and said, "Dr Kurien, may I have a cigarette too?"[5]

Kurien often 'locked horns and got into heated arguments' with the Shankaracharya during the meetings of the committee.[6] By contrast, Golwalkar, according to Kurien, was a reticent personality 'but when he got angry fire spewed out of his eyes'.[7] In the meetings, Golwalkar 'argued passionately for banning cow

4. Ibid.

5. Verghese Kurien (As told to Gouri Salvi), *I too Had a Dream*, Roli Books, New Delhi, 2005, p. 182.

6. Ibid., p. 183.

7. Ibid., pp. 183-184.

slaughter'.[8] By Kurien's account, the committee met regularly and interviewed scores of people from all fields to get opinions of all shades on cow slaughter.[9]

Within months it became clear that Indira Gandhi had played her card well. For, by the end of 1967, the participation of Golwalkar and the Shankaracharya in the meetings of the committee—largely because of their inability to put forth any logical argument in favour of banning cow slaughter—became infrequent. Perhaps, they wanted a quick decision by the committee, but were repeatedly mortified and outraged to find the direction the panel was taking. Months later, on 5 July 1968, while the process of collection of experts' opinions was still on, Golwalkar and the Shankaracharya, along with one more member of the panel, former Calcutta High Court judge Rama Prasad Mukerji, announced their decision to boycott meetings of the cow protection committee.[10] Explaining their decision, the Shankaracharya alleged the committee 'was not functioning properly and even went beyond its jurisdiction'.[11] They also threatened to revive the anti-cow slaughter agitation—a threat that could never be carried out during Golwalkar's lifetime. At that point, the issue of cow protection was a lost cause.

II

Golwalkar's problems as the supreme leader of the Sangh Parivar compounded in the last quarter of 1967 when John D. Smith, an American detective who had worked in India as a CIA agent, defected to Soviet Union and made it public through a press

8. Ibid., p. 184.

9. Ibid., p. 183.

10. *The Times of India*, 6 July 1968.

11. Ibid.

conference in October.[12] The damning revelations that he made about the CIA's activities in India during the 1950s and 1960s forced Hindu Right parties and organizations to reckon with global politics to a greater extent than ever before. His revelations came mainly in the form of a series of articles published by the Russian weekly *Literaturnaya Gazeta* in November and reproduced in India in the form of a booklet by the Communist Party of India in December.

Among his varied revelations, Smith spoke of the RSS's 'close ties with the CIA'.[13] He also hinted that the CIA had provided 'large sums of money' for organizing the anti-cow slaughter rally in Delhi in November 1966 and that the attempt to assassinate Congress president Kamaraj on that afternoon had been the work of the RSS. 'The assassination attempt had been organised by the RSS,' he claimed.[14]

Jana Sangh members protested, but Golwalkar remained silent. Like most other RSS leaders, he seemed to be severely shaken by revelations in Russia. An assault by the government or a political party would have been tolerable, but this was more than any conventional attack, since it threatened to kill whatever image the RSS had been left with after the assassination of Mahatma Gandhi. Despite all the odds that the RSS had faced, many still believed Golwalkar and his cadres to be nationalists. The revelations had called this belief into question. They made it appear as if the RSS was no more than an organization of anti-national opportunists who could easily be suborned by any international agency and made to act as pawns in the hands of forces inimical to the country.

12. *The Times of India*, 25 October 1967.

13. John D. Smith, *I was a CIA Agent in India*, Communist Party Publication, New Delhi, 1967, p. 34.

14. Ibid., pp. 34-35.

At least on one occasion, Golwalkar had himself given access to J. A. Curran, who figured in Smith's revelations as one of the most important CIA agents in India. In fact, Curran was the first 'outsider', or non-RSS member, who was given full access by Golwalkar at the time the ban was revoked and the RSS seemed struggling for an image makeover. Curran himself acknowledged this in the book he wrote on the RSS. 'The gratitude the author owes to R.S.S. members for their assistance in his research cannot be exaggerated,' read his book's preface. 'In every echelon of this organization, from Mr. Golwalkar, its leader, down to the newest recruits, the story was generally the same. Opportunities were constantly provided to ask numerous questions about plans and activities, as well as to observe the Sangh's operation. The bulk of this study is based on a year and a half of frequent association with the R.S.S.'[15]

Smith's wife, Mary L. Smith, herself a CIA agent in India, worked directly under Curran.[16] 'He [Curran] was considered one of the most experienced intelligence agents of the CIA in India,' Smith wrote.

> He had been here over seven years and knew the country very well. Curran was born in China, grew up in Burma and was educated in the States. He had been approached by the CIA when he was still a student, and they gave him a special grant. The CIA sent him to India to 'study sociology'. After graduating Jack [Curran] was sent to Delhi with the Diplomatic Service. He was with the Embassy's political group for six years but did not hold any important post. However, he was highly regarded by high ranking members of the diplomatic staff. It was said that

15. J. A. Curran, JR., *Militant Hinduism in Indian Politics: A Study of the R.S.S.*, Institute of Pacific Relations, New York, 1951, p. 3.

16. John D. Smith, *I was a CIA Agent in India*, Communist Party Publication, New Delhi, 1967, p. 26.

> Curran was personally acquainted with Allen Dulles [Deputy Director of CIA]. The latter considered him the most valuable man that the US intelligence ever had in India.[17]

Smith's revelations gave rise to a number of questions. Did Golwalkar know that Curran was a CIA operative? Did they remain in touch even after the completion of Curran's research? How close were they at the time of the anti-cow slaughter rally? Golwalkar might not have had anything to do with the CIA and his cooperation with Curran might just have been limited to the latter's book, but the revelation stimulated the Opposition as it came only months after a *New York Times* report had stirred India's political climate by claiming that the Indian government had been investigating secret American funding to the Jana Sangh and other right-wing parties.

The *New York Times* report, which was published on 13 June 1967, claimed that the Central Bureau of Investigation (CBI) probed the CIA's activities during the elections held in February 1967 and discovered that the US had contributed large sums of money primarily to the right-wing parties, including the Jana Sangh, and their candidates.[18] The report caused an upheaval in Parliament. The Jana Sangh and other parties named in the report denied allegations and sought an enquiry into the entire issue by an independent tribunal.[19] Home Minister Y. B. Chavan admitted that an enquiry had indeed been conducted into the activities of the foreign agencies in India during the elections. 'The methods by which foreign money is coming into this country to influence political parties should be studied and measures taken to end such inflow,' Chavan said, but refused to divulge the findings, saying

17. Ibid., p. 14.

18. *The New York Times*, 13 June 1967.

19. *The Times of India*, 15 June 1967.

the enquiries were yet to be completed.[20]

The issue gradually petered out, but with John Smith's revelations it got revived. On 5 December, CPI MP S. A. Dange tabled a motion in the Lok Sabha to discuss 'CIA activities in India, as revealed by the ex-CIA personnel, John Smith'.[21] Responding to the motion, Chavan, while calling Smith's account as part of an international propaganda, told Parliament that 'a further enquiry might be ordered into the alleged use of foreign funds in the general election after the Government had arrived at some tentative conclusions on the report recently submitted by the Intelligence Bureau'.[22]

Chavan, therefore, seemed to suggest that there might be some degree of truth in the CIA's involvement with right-wing organizations. Nonetheless, for reasons that are not altogether clear, the government never came out with any report. Smith's allegations, too, passed quickly as occasional moments of distress for the RSS, Jana Sangh and other Hindu Right parties.

III

Golwalkar was at the RSS camp in Allahabad on the morning of 11 February 1968 when he received news of Deen Dayal Upadhyaya's murder. Upadhyaya's abandoned body had been found on railway tracks near the Mughalsarai station in eastern UP.[23] Golwalkar fell into a long silence; Upadhyaya was 'dearer than life to him'.[24] Only five weeks back, he had had a long conversation with

20. *The Times of India*, 20 June 1967.

21. *The Times of India*, 6 December 1967.

22. *The Times of India*, 13 December 1967.

23. *The Times of India*, 12 February 1968.

24. Ranga Hari, *The Incomparable Guru Golwalkar*, Prabhat Paperbacks, New Delhi, 2018, p. 287.

Upadhyaya, who, days after becoming the president of the Jana Sangh, had come to meet and pay his obeisance to him.[25] The shock that followed the news of Upadhyaya's murder seemed more depressing to Golwalkar than all the emotions of the past few months. Upadhyaya had always made his loyalty to Golwalkar his watchword and prided himself on being a pracharak of the RSS. For Golwalkar it was the gravest imaginable blow.

He came out of the RSS camp and proceeded for a last glimpse of Upadhyaya to Varanasi where the body had been kept. Ranga Hari, Golwalkar's biographer and a pracharak since 1951, observed the signs of him cracking. 'On seeing that lifeless body,' Ranga Hari noted, 'the only words that came out of his lips were, "Oh! What has happened…" Caressing that still, lifeless face with his right hand, he looked at his face once again, the last time in life, turned back and went away.'[26] Later in the day, the body was flown to Delhi, where the cremation was held on 12 February.[27] When *Organiser* editor K. R. Malkani asked Golwalkar for a condolence message, he replied: 'The wound is deep. Very deep. I do not know when it will heal or if ever it will heal. Words fail me. The pain is benumbing. I simply can't write though I would very much like to.'[28]

As the months passed, Golwalkar started blending his RSS activities with his pilgrimages and meeting with Hindu religious leaders. The management of the organization fell increasingly on Deoras, who was re-elected unanimously as sarkaryavah for another term on 25 March 1968.[29] Golwalkar's association with

---

25. Ibid.

26. Ibid.

27. *The Times of India*, 13 February 1968.

28. K. R. Malkani Papers, Correspondences with M. S. Golwalkar, p. 26, Manuscript Section, NMML, New Delhi.

29. *The Times of India*, 26 March 1968.

religious leaders like Tukdoji Maharaj, Prabhudatt Brahmachari, Niranjandev Teerth and Swami Amurtananda—the last being the head of the Ramakrishna Math at Nagpur—increased. So did his travels to Hindu religious places, the highest point of his pilgrimage being his visit to Badrinath in the Himalayas in September 1968.

His lifestyle, marked by his constant association with religious heads and priestly people, became more and more driven by orthodox Hindu rituals and values. These were the themes that formed part of the repertory of his earlier years, when he openly defended the varnashrama system, the four-fold division of the Hindu caste system, calling it the 'best order for achieving human happiness' and 'a supreme and scientific social order based on the division of labour.'[30] Back then these themes went unnoticed, but their repetition in early 1969, when Golwalkar said that 'the caste system had been created by God and everyone should do his duty according to his caste', caused massive protest.[31] The opposition became so widespread that on 15 February 1969, the Bombay unit of the RSS had to cancel Golwalkar's visit 'due to the present atmosphere in the city'.[32]

The issue came up again two months later when Parliament unanimously denounced the Shankaracharya of Puri for justifying untouchability at a convention on 29 March 1969. Just when all members of the Lok Sabha joined the Home Minister in criticizing the Shankaracharya, a Congress MP, supported by communist and socialist members, claimed that Golwalkar had also expressed similar views.[33] In Pune, as per a *Times of India* report, effigies of

30. B. N. Bhargava, *Guruji: The Man and His Mission*, Bharat Prakashan, Delhi, 1956, pp. 50, 63.

31. *The Times of India*, 7 February 1969.

32. *The Times of India*, 16 February 1969.

33. *The Times of India*, 3 April 1969.

the Shankaracharya and Golwalkar were taken out in a rally 'in protest against their views on untouchability and "chaturvarya"'.[34] The next day in Parliament, the Jana Sangh and Congress MPs clashed over Golwalkar's views 'on the soundness of the caste system'. The provocation this time came from Congress MP Amrit Nahata who equated Golwalkar with the Shankaracharya of Puri and 'used a derisive epithet to describe both'.[35]

More disturbing than the endless criticism of his views on the caste system, at least from the point of view of Golwalkar, was Indira Gandhi's frontal attack on his vision of a Hindu Rashtra. A report in the *Times of India* said that in the meeting of the standing committee of the National Integration Council on 16 October 1969 'the Prime Minister read a recent statement by Mr. Golwalkar that a strong India could be built only on the basis of Hindu Rashtra and asked what was the comment of the Jana Sangh spokesman'. The Jana Sangh MP and former RSS leader, Prof. Mahavir, stunned by the attack, fell back on the usual play of words and claimed that by 'the term Hindu Rashtra' Golwalkar 'meant only the Bharatiya-Rashtra'.[36]

In open debates, there seemed to be no aspect of Golwalkar's vision that did not create trouble for the RSS or its outfits. Everywhere outside the Sangh circles, he was accused of leading the forces bent upon causing communal and caste division in the country. There was also a pervasive confusion about what direction the government would take to curb the activities of the RSS. Golwalkar's new tormentor, Indira Gandhi, appeared firm, and that was unnerving.

34. *The Times of India*, 14 April 1969.

35. *The Times of India*, 15 April 1969.

36. *The Times of India*, 17 October 1969.

IV

In August 1969, while on a tour to Sirsi in Karnataka, he noticed a lump on the left side of his chest.[37] At first he did not make much of it and continued with his frequent tours. The lump kept swelling, causing him pain. One day in April 1970, while attending a meeting of the RSS, he could not speak, nor could he stand properly. Doctors examined him but did not find anything unusual.[38] A month later, another doctor at Poona examined the lump and told Golwalkar that it could be malignant. A biopsy showed that he was suffering from cancer. He was operated on 1 July at Tata Cancer Hospital in Bombay.[39]

A few weeks later, Golwalkar resumed his tours. In spite of the visible changes in his look, his weakening body and his rapidly graying hair and beard, he seemed to retain an unusual desire for travel. The abuse of his physical potential and consumption of his energy reserves might have exacerbated his rapid aging, showing up in the sudden graying and his shattered appearance—every year he seemed to age not a year but several years. The consistency with which he took up and carried out his travels during this period revealed that however shadowy he looked outwardly, he was still the man he had been before cancer struck him.

What is so staggering about him in those last years was not so much the consistency in pursuing his travelling obsession as his retention of the fears that had driven him during the years after the unbanning of the RSS. His anxieties about a crackdown by the government appear to have been justified. Certainly, there was a rumour that the government was contemplating introducing

37. Prof. Dharmavir, *Guru Golwalkar*, Hind Pocket Books Pvt Ltd, 1974, p. 132.

38. Ranga Hari, *The Incomparable Guru Golwalkar*, Prabhat Paperbacks, New Delhi, 2018, p. 309.

39. Ibid., p. 312.

a bill in Parliament seeking to ban the Sangh.[40] Also, the state offices of the RSS began receiving notices from the income-tax department seeking tax on their fund collections.[41] On what seems to have been Golwalkar's instructions, Jana Sangh leader Vajpayee met Indira Gandhi twice to request her rescind the income-tax notices.[42] Golwalkar also occasionally tried to get in touch with the prime minister, but like her father, she was unresponsive to him.[43]

As might be expected in this situation, he wrote a long, endearing letter to Indira Gandhi, giving her 'complete credit' for India's victory in the war with Pakistan and the liberation of Bangladesh in December 1971. 'From the beginning you tried to mediate and showed your commitment to peace,' he wrote to her on 22 December.

> But when war became unavoidable for the security of India, you inspired the defence forces to face it bravely and successfully called upon people to perform their moral duty to achieve this national honour. Despite the opposition from so-called friendly countries, their attempts to build pressure on us by threatening to stop their assistance, their efforts to intensify the crisis by supplying weapons to Pakistan, your decision to take independent position and deal with the threat with utmost patience and firmness was commendable. This has increased India's self-esteem and respect, and the entire nation feels excited to greet you.[44]

The following year in August, while the Jana Sangh was demanding a uniform civil code, Golwalkar embarked on a different argument,

40. Ibid., p. 313.

41. Ibid.

42. Abhishek Choudhary, *Vajpayee: The Ascent of the Hindu Right, 1924-1977*, Picador India, New Delhi 2023, p. 271.

43. Ibid.

44. *Shri Guruji Samagra*, Volume 7, Suruchi Prakashan, New Delhi, p. 149.

one that contradicted the Sangh Parivar's stand: he argued that a uniform civil code for citizens of all religions was 'not necessary' in itself. 'The important thing is to infuse a spirit of intense patriotism and brotherhood among all citizens, Hindus and non-Hindus, and make them love this motherland according to their own religion,' he said.[45] It is questionable whether Golwalkar had a genuine change of heart on the question of minorities, especially Muslims, or he took the changed position cunningly in order to ingratiate himself with Indira Gandhi in his desperate attempt to stop her from banning the RSS or forcing it to pay its income tax dues.

This was Golwalkar in the final phase of his life: a man who lived continuously under the fear of a crackdown, and who worried, considering the short time he might have left, about how such a government action could be forestalled. At least in part, he seemed to succeed in his efforts. Indira Gandhi might not have been impressed by his efforts to endear himself to her. But there is no evidence that she made any serious attempt to push her anti-RSS plans for the time Golwalkar was alive.

V

All the while, Golwalkar's medical condition was worsening. Chronic over-exertion was exacting its toll. In September 1972, another boil was detected on the left side of his chest. There was also disorientation in his speech while addressing an RSS camp in Jaipur, and it took him three hours to become normal.[46] When he was brought to Bombay's Tata Cancer Hospital for examination, doctors suggested radiation therapy, saying the new boil was a sign of the spread of cancer. The radiation therapy began in the last week of October and continued for over a fortnight. He returned to

45. *The Motherland*, 21 August 1972.

46. Ranga Hari, *The Incomparable Guru Golwalkar*, Prabhat Paperbacks, New Delhi, 2018, pp. 335-336.

Nagpur on 12 November. In a month, his courage and confidence returned, and he resumed his tour on 29 December.[47] For two and a half months, he kept travelling, returning to Nagpur intermittently.

It is true that in the preceding years, contempt for his western-educated adversaries had been Golwalkar's strength. How else could he have risen out of nowhere and won so much support of orthodox Hindus that his vision of a Hindu Rashtra posed a real threat to India at one point? His successes among rulers of the Hindu princely states may also have been partly based on that. But now that the ground reality had changed and as he tried desperately at the fag-end of his life to present himself as the vanguard of Hinduism, he often mocked western-educated people for cutting themselves from Hindu culture and tradition. Sometimes, he even told fictitious tales to bolster his arguments, and when listeners took this as a joke, he insisted that he meant what he said. Shyam Shridhar Pandharipande, son of Anna Pandharipande, Golwalkar's old friend and a colleague in the organization, recalled that the RSS chief, while addressing a meeting of swayamsevaks at Nagpur 'sometime in late 1972', told a story that only 'thoughtless morons' could have believed.[48]

It was a meeting of local swayamsevaks. Shyam, who had completed his third-year training in the RSS and was twenty at the time, also attended it. 'Guruji was speaking with contempt about English-educated people, saying how they were unaware of our glorious past and our magnificent Hindu culture,' he recounted, adding that Golwalkar, in order to support his argument, narrated a story about an Indian Foreign Service officer with Chaturvedi as his surname—Chaturvedi means one who has the knowledge of four Vedas. 'Once this Chaturvedi was transferred as India's ambassador to Germany, the country which has high regard for

47. Ibid., p. 349.

48. Based on an interview with Shyam Shridhar Pandharipande at Nagpur on 15 September 2020.

ancient Hindu texts, including Vedas,' Golwalkar, according to Shyam, said.

> So when the German government came to know that one Mr. Chaturvedi would be coming to take charge as India's ambassador, it arranged a very great welcome ceremony for him. It got a large tent erected which had four entrances, representing four Vedas—Rig Veda, Sama Veda, Yajur Veda and Atharva Veda. These entrances were decorated with colourful flowers in ancient Indian style. When Mr. Chaturvedi reached the venue, he was ushered in and taken to the dais. Ministers and senior officials were also present there. The person who conducted the programme praised him in his welcome address and, while inviting him to deliver his speech, said that since he was Chaturvedi the people present in the function would like him to enlighten them on four Vedas in a nutshell. Chaturvedi, who was suited-booted and had put up a tie, fumbled. He didn't know anything about Vedas and couldn't tell anything about them. He sweated and cut a sorry figure. See, this is the state of our educated people. This shows that they have complete lack of understanding of our ancient culture and values, our ancient texts and epics.[49]

All clapped and laughed, but Shyam was shocked. He knew that no government in any country would organize a public ceremony to welcome a new ambassador. 'On my way back from the meeting, I kept thinking about the story Guruji had told,' he recalled later. 'I won't say Guruji lied, but the story had given rise to several questions. Did Guruji intentionally narrate a fake story or did he do so because of his ideological confusion? How many of those in the audience who clapped and laughed in scorn and ridicule knew of Vedas? Could most of the swayamsevaks present in the meeting even tell the names of four Vedas in proper order?'

49. Ibid.

According to Shyam, these questions kept haunting him for several days, and finally he decided to quit the RSS.[50]

By this time, Golwalkar's physical decline was unmistakable. Things were getting bad. He looked frail and shattered. He was still hailed, of course, whenever he addressed the RSS men, still spoken of with reverence, and treated with that devotion which he had by now accepted as his right; but the question of who would succeed him was also whispered about. When a journalist, during one of his short visits to Nagpur in February 1973, asked him about his successor, Golwalkar replied: 'Why not you?'[51] This was surely a sign of his growing irritation. His subordinates, of course, knew the answer to the journalist's question—Balasaheb Deoras, the sarkaryavah, was already calling the shots.

Golwalkar still went on a few more organized tours. But after 14 March 1973, the illness incapacitated him.[52] His weight decreased sharply and he became very weak. Two days later, doctors proclaimed that the cancer had reached his lungs.[53] His decision to stop making public speeches came after a painful experience on 25 March, when he addressed the Akhil Bharatiya Pratinidhi Sabha—All India Delegates' Conference—sitting in a chair. He suffered breathlessness after every one or two sentences and his speech was interrupted by frequent bouts of cough.[54]

It demonstrated how spent he was. He had no reserves left. His energy level became very low, and even the ingestion of food and liquid became painful. From this point on, an irrevocable end stared straight in his face. The direction of events finally slipped from Golwalkar's hands.

---

50. Ibid.

51. Ranga Hari, *The Incomparable Guru Golwalkar*, Prabhat Paperbacks, New Delhi, 2018, p. 350.

52. Ibid., p. 349.

53. Ibid., p. 352.

54. Ibid.

Project and Projection

On 2 April 1973, over two months before his death, Golwalkar wrote and signed his last will and testament—a set of three letters addressed to swayamsevaks. At Nagpur, by this time, his hope of physical recovery had slipped away, and now he prepared to die. His tremendous consciousness of the mission that had accompanied him for three and a half decades, and had only been obscured but never given up, was now bowing to the inevitable. The mythological conception he seemed to have had of himself could not be reconciled with the stark reality of human life made unbearable by the agony of cancer. As the letters show, he was now worried, considering the short time he was left with, about his own posthumous reputation.

Golwalkar opened his first letter with the religious invocation, *Om*, a sacred syllable considered the most important of all Hindu mantras. He then proceeded to name Deoras as his successor: 'I have discussed the matter with members of Akhil Bharatiya Karyakari Mandal, all of whom are workers with long-standing experience and as sanghchalaks have been organizing work in various states. As the present sarsanghchalak, it is my responsibility to set forth the decision arrived at after the due discussion with them all. In the fulfillment of that responsibility, I hereby declare that after my body turns cold, the office of sarsanghchalak shall be filled by Madhukar Dattatreya—alias Balasaheb—Deoras, who is well known to all.'[1] He also directed the RSS men to obediently follow Deoras for future guidance: 'I have full confidence that all swayamsevaks, young and old, will strive their utmost, in word, thought and deed, under the guidance of the new sarsanghchalak to complete the Sangh's mission.'[2]

In the second letter, he explicitly advised not to construct any memorial for him or to perform his last rites: 'The physicians seem to feel that my body may not survive for long. [...] After life has fled, decorating the corpse etc. would appear funny and meaningless. Likewise, it is unnecessary to idolize or raise memorials to anyone except the founder who was the embodiment of the mission of the Sangh.'[3]

The third letter was meant specifically for swayamsevaks: 'In my long tenure, it is not unlikely that I have caused mental agony to many workers, due to my idiosyncrasies or shortcomings and defects. With folded hands I seek forgiveness of one and all.'[4]

Never before had a speech or a write-up attributed to him conveyed such despair and exhaustion. Because of the excruciating pain caused by cancer, he had apparently assumed—as the very first letter suggests—that he would not survive 'more than a few days'.[5] But as weeks passed, and still he remained alive, Golwalkar looked around to dispose of the stuff that he owned.

On 19 April, he got an advocate to prepare a private will, by which he donated his parental house at Ramtek to a newly-started

1. Prof. Dharmavir, *Guru Golwalkar*, Hind Pocket Books Pvt Ltd, 1974, pp. 140-141.

2. Ibid., p. 141.

3. Ibid., p. 142.

4. Ibid., pp. 141-142.

5. Ibid., p. 140.

outfit of the RSS, the Bharatiya Utkarsh Mandal.[6] To his cousin, Vasudev Ramchandra Golwalkar, he sent his personal items of worship, including utensils, a woolen sheet, socks and a silk dhoti worn at the time of worship. He also wrote to him, suggesting the way the worship would be done: 'Please offer one set of *bilwa* leaves [*aegle marmelos* species] and light an incense stick every morning, and in the evening, just light the incense stick. That is enough, nothing more needs to be done.'[7]

In the last week of May, Golwalkar's condition began to deteriorate rapidly, and within days he was on his deathbed. He died around 9 p.m. on 5 June 1973.

II

His legacy, however, was to endure. He had extended the RSS across the entire country, and its network of allied organizations—the Sangh Parivar—had penetrated almost every aspect of Indian society. In the years following his death, Golwalkar assumed the position of the demi-god of Hindutva politics. His ascetic self-imagining did not only survive, but developed deep roots and gave him a mythical posthumous life during what remained of the twentieth century and during the first quarter of twenty-first century.

Many of his acolytes and followers went on to become ministers and chief ministers in several states, and two of them—Atal Bihari Vajpayee and Narendra Modi—acquired even more power and became the prime ministers of the country. When Vajpayee, the first RSS man to become prime minister, described his earliest

---

6. 'Vaseeyatnama', cited in Ranga Hari, *The Incomparable Guru Golwalkar*, Prabhat Paperbacks, New Delhi, 2018, p. 354.

7. Ranga Hari, *The Incomparable Guru Golwalkar*, Prabhat Paperbacks, New Delhi, 2018, pp. 354-355.

meeting with Golwalkar, in 1940, there was a strong spiritual overtone to it. 'Shri Guruji had come to Gwalior station,' Vajpayee recalled later. 'I was also among those who reached there to welcome him. When I met him he looked at me as if he recognized me. In fact, there was no reason of recognizing, as it was our first meeting. But that meeting left a lasting influence on me. It was at that time that I decided to work for the nation.'[8]

Modi, the second RSS man to head the central government, described Golwalkar in a mystical, pantheistic and supra-nationalistic context. In his book *Jyotipunj*, which has biographical accounts of sixteen people who most influenced him, the largest chapter is on Golwalkar. He put Golwalkar at an unattainable height of spiritual being: 'The fragrance of unbroken, continuous, attentive meditation of an ascetic can be felt even today. Attaining or even knowing the life of Guruji is beyond our capacity.'[9]

Golwalkar's ideological effects went very deep in the rank and file of the RSS, and possibly this was his most enduring legacy. His book, *We or Our Nationhood Defined*, had totally transformed the entire relationship of the RSS cadres to politics. To an unimaginable extent, it had alienated the followers of the RSS from mainstream democratic politics and oriented them toward a political programme based on the anti-Semitic model for dealing with India's minorities, especially Muslims, and achieving the ideal of a Hindu Rashtra. Later, prompted by the fear of the Nehru government, Golwalkar publicly lied in order to give the impression that the views expressed in *We or Our Nationhood Defined* were not really a reflection of his thought. Even RSS leaders, on several occasions after Golwalkar's death, sought to distance him from his book.

---

8. *Organiser*, 12 March 2006.

9. Narendra Modi, *Jyotipunj*, Prabhat Prakashan, New Delhi, 2015, p. 75. (First published in Gujarati in 2007)

Yet, the separation has always been artificial. The RSS could never really give up Golwalkar's vision, nor could it ever try to alter the transformation his book had brought about in the nature and orientation of its cadres. This must be said even though the RSS and its sympathizers have repeatedly tried to excuse Golwalkar and deny the Nazi influence, engendered by his book, on its ideology. The strength of his legacy to exercise his spell even after his death is displayed in the dilemma that successive RSS leaderships have faced: if they advertise the abandonment of Golwalkar's ideological project, there would be a questioning of their own legitimate claim to be in the leadership of the RSS; and if they speak or write openly in its defence, they would have to incur massive public criticism.

It is not accidental that since 2014, when the Bharatiya Janata Party, the RSS's electoral wing that succeeded the Jana Sangh, won absolute majority in the Lok Sabha and Modi became the prime minister, India has been confronting a political project that seeks to promote Hindu authoritarianism along the lines laid down by *We or Our Nationhood Defined*. The project is premised on the same old idea of Golwalkar that India must be a Hindu Rashtra and minorities must subscribe to Hindu primacy—a position that threatens the very foundation of Indian democracy in which all citizens of every faith have equal standing.

The period has witnessed massive efforts to steer the national discourse to treat Muslims as the 'other'. Hate speeches, overt Islamophobia, lynchings and violent attacks on Muslims in the name of cow protection and 'love jihad'—described by Hindu supremacists as a ploy contrived by Muslim men to lure young Hindu women into marriage and conversion into Islam—have become frequent. These as well as the BJP government's efforts to push forward its Hindu majoritarian agenda, including a citizenship law seen to directly discriminate against Muslims, have started eroding and subjugating the secular, democratic vision that Golwalkar could not defeat in his lifetime.

For the first time since Independence, Golwalkar's promise of denying Muslims citizens' rights is being lived out, from the legislature to the rhythms of their daily lives. Of 240 legislators of the BJP in the 543-member Lok Sabha, not one is a Muslim. In the previous Lok Sabha, the BJP had over three hundred legislators but none was a Muslim. Politically, the Muslims have been virtually invisibilised during the last one decade. Efforts of the Sangh Parivar to direct hate towards the minority community as a means of consolidating political power have further marginalized and ghettoized Muslims on the ground. Even renting or buying properties in Hindu-majority areas is increasingly becoming difficult for Muslims. This has usually been achieved by legislative means, through the enactment of new laws or the reinterpretation of existing ones, but it is also the result of a social consensus by the Hindu supporters of the RSS and the BJP. Its effects are vast; the terror it spreads enormous. All this enjoys such widespread approval in the Sangh Parivar because it corresponds to Golwalkar's ideas and the historical destiny he set out for the RSS—to convert India into a Hindu Rashtra.

Acknowledgements

My sincerest appreciation goes to Anil Rajimwale and Krishna Jha, whose exceptional translation from Marathi and Bengali documents was essential for the creation of the book. Much that is most interesting within it is, in large part, a direct result of their translations, which they did with perceptivity and accuracy.

I have worked intermittently on this book for more than six years. On many occasions, while researching and writing, I faced daunting challenges that I could not have overcome without considerable help from numerous individuals, some of them outstanding. I cannot acknowledge them all here, but I must thank certain persons whose contributions to my work were very specific: Ramesh Shiledar, Shyam Pandharipande, Partha Chatterjee, Samik Bandyopadhyay, Arun Shourie, Sudheendra Kulkarni, Lata Bhise, Asmita Hulyalkar, Shruti Ganapatye, Kalrav Joshi, Narendra K. Bar, Hartosh Singh Bal, Sushant Singh, Basharat Peer, Shahid Tantray, Anant Purushottam Padhye, Chandrashekhar Deshpande, Rahul Bhatia, Mukund Madhav Jha, Abhishek Choudhary, Akshaya Mukul, Vaibhav Vats, Samar Khadas, Ashok Parashar, Rajeshwar Thakare, Ratinath Mishra, Yugal Rayalu, Dilip Deodhar, Milind Pakhale, Anant Bagaitkar, Dhruv Kumar, Sharad Khare, Vinayak Kanitkar, Pradeep Rawat, Bal Mane, Satish Kamat, Sunil Chowke,

Uma Nabar, Narendra Wable, Anil Gupta, Janardan Limaye and Ravindra Biwalkar.

I am indebted to the staff of National Archives of India (New Delhi), Nehru Memorial Museum and Library (New Delhi), Maharashtra State Archives (Mumbai), West Bengal State Archives (Kolkata), UP State Archives (Lucknow), National Gandhi Museum (New Delhi), Mumbai Marathi Grantha Sangrahalaya (Mumbai), Gokhale Institute of Politics and Economics (Pune), Maharashtra Sahitya Parishad Library (Pune), Rajaram Sitaram Dixit Library (Nagpur) and Banaras Hindu University Library (Varanasi).

My agent, Shruti Debi, made the book immeasurably better than it would have been without her suggestions. And Elizabeth Kuruvilla was meticulous and unsparing in her editing. I owe them both, as always, a very great deal.

There are many senior members of the RSS who helped me with valuable insights and information, though only on the condition that they would neither be quoted nor acknowledged. I hope to soon be able to publicly thank them in print, without fear that such recognition might bring them harm. They know who they are, and I am grateful to them.

Bibliography

ARCHIVAL MATERIALS, PRIVATE PAPERS AND REPORTS

AICC Papers, Manuscript Section, NMML, New Delhi.

B. S. Moonje Papers, Manuscript Section, NMML, New Delhi.

D. P. Mishra Papers, Manuscript Section, NMML, New Delhi.

Gandhi Murder Trial Papers, NAI, New Delhi.

G. D. Khosla Papers, Manuscript Section, NMML, New Delhi.

Golwalkar Papers, Microfilm Section, NMML, New Delhi.

Hindu Mahasabha Papers, Manuscript Section, NMML, New Delhi.

Jawaharlal Nehru (SG) papers, Manuscript Section, NMML, New Delhi.

K. R. Malkani Papers, Manuscript Section, NMML, New Delhi.

Mountbatten Papers, Microfilm Section, NMML, New Delhi.

N. B. Khare Papers, NAI, New Delhi.

P. Kodanda Rao Papers, Manuscript Section, NMML, New Delhi.

Sardar Patel Papers, NAI, New Delhi.

Savarkar Papers, Microfilm Section, NMML, New Delhi.

Shri Jugal Kishore Khanna, Oral History Transcripts, Manuscript Section, NMML, New Delhi.

University Calendar for 1930-31, Banaras Hindu University, Varanasi.

Government of India, Home Department (Political), File No. 88/33, 1933, NAI, New Delhi.

Government of India, Home Department (Political), File No. 220-P/42 (Sec), 1942, NAI, New Delhi.

Government of India, Home Department (Political), File No. 190-P (S), 1943, p. 26, NAI, New Delhi.

Government of India, Political Department ('P' Branch), File No. 190-P (S), 1943-44, NAI, New Delhi.

Government of India, Home Political (I), File No. NA-F-5-12, 1946, NIA, New Delhi.

Government of India, Home Department, File No. 28/5/46–Pol (I), NAI, New Delhi.

Government of India, Home Department (Political), File No. 22/3/1947-Poll. (I), NAI, New Delhi.

Government of India, Home Department (Political), File No. 18/6/46, NAI, New Delhi.

Government of India, Ministry of States, File No. 74-p/48, Vol I (Secret), 1948, NAI, New Delhi.

Government of India, Ministry of States–Political Branch, File No. 74(1)–P/48, NAI, New Delhi.

Government of India, Ministry of States, 'P' Branch, File No. 16(2)-P/49, NAI, New Delhi.

The Defence of India Act, 1939 and The Rules Made Thereunder, Manager of Publications, Government of India Press, 1943.

Reference: PF710182, National Archives, London, UK.

Reference: DO 133/60, Foreign Office Files for India, Pakistan and Afghanistan, 1947-1964, The National Archives, London, UK.

Reference: FO 371/69729, Foreign Office Files for India, Pakistan and Afghanistan, 1947-1964, The National Archives, London, UK.

Records of the US State Department Relating to the Internal Affairs of India, 1945-1949, Image No. 160: India, Library of Congress, Washington DC.

File: 60 D(g), Part III, 1938, Home Special Department, Maharashtra State Archives, Mumbai.

File No. W-602/40, Home (Poll) Department, West Bengal State Archives, Kolkata.

File No. 21/40, Home (Poll) Department, Confidential, West Bengal State Archives, Kolkata.

Government of United Provinces, Extracts from Weekly Report No. 27, 5 July 1946, CID Records, UP State Acrhives, Lucknow.

Delhi Police Records, VIII Inst., File No. 417, Manuscript Section, NMML, New Delhi.

Delhi Police Record, File No. 405, Manuscript Section, NMML, New Delhi.

Delhi Police Records, V Inst., File No. 137, Manuscript Section, NMML, New Delhi.

Delhi Police Record, File No. 413, Manuscript Section, NMML, New Delhi.

Delhi Police Record, File No. 409, Manuscript Section, NMML, New Delhi.

Delhi Police Records, File No. 416, Manuscript Section, NMML, New Delhi.

Delhi Police Records, File No. 414, Manuscript Section, NMML, New Delhi.

Delhi Police Records, IX Inst., File No. 528, Manuscript Section, NMML, New Delhi.

Delhi Police Records, V Inst., File No. 138, Manuscript Section, NMML, New Delhi.

Delhi Police Records, File No. 519, Manuscript Section, NMML, New Delhi.

Delhi Police Records, File No. 407, Manuscript Section, NMML, New Delhi.

Delhi Police Records, IX Inst., File No. 527, Manuscript Section, NMML, New Delhi.

Delhi Police Records, File No. 404, Manuscript Section, NMML, New Delhi.

Delhi Police Records, IX Inst., File No. 518, NMML, New Delhi.

Delhi Police Records, File No. 405, NMML, New Delhi.

Delhi Police Records, File No. 557, Manuscript Section, NMML, New Delhi.

Delhi Police Records, File No. 76, Manuscript Section, NMML, New Delhi.

Delhi Police Records, File No. 552, Manuscript Section, NMML, New Delhi.

Delhi Police Record, File No. 142, V Inst, Manuscript Section, NMML, New Delhi.

Delhi Police Record, File No. 556, Manuscript Section, NMML, New Delhi.

Delhi Police Records, File No. 553, Manuscript Section, NMML, New Delhi.

Delhi Police Records, File No. 148, V Inst, Manuscript Section, NMML, New Delhi.

Delhi Police Records, File No. 127, Manuscript Section, NMML, New Delhi.

Justice J. L. Kapur, Report of Commission of Inquiry into Conspiracy to Murder Mahatma Gandhi, Part I & II, New Delhi, Government of India, 1969.

Sardar Patel's Correspondence, 1945-50, Volume IV, Navajivan Publishing House, Ahmedabad, 1972.

Shri Guruji Samagra, Vol. 5, Suruchi Prakashan, Delhi.

Shri Guruji Samagra, Vol. 6, Suruchi Prakashan, New Delhi, 2014.

Shri Guruji Samagra, Vol. 7, Suruchi Prakashan, New Delhi.

Shri Guruji Samagra, Volume 10, Suruchi Prakashan, New Delhi.

SWJN, Second Series, Volume Four, Jawaharlal Nehru Memorial Fund, New Delhi, 1986.

SWJN, Second Series, Volume VIII, Jawahrlal Nehru Memorial Fund, New Delhi, 1989.

SWJN, Second Series, Volume IX, Jawahrlal Nehru Memorial Fund, New Delhi, 1990.

SWJN, Second Series, Volume XII, Jawahrlal Nehru Memorial Fund, New Delhi, 1991.

SWJN, Second Series, Volume Eighty, Jawaharlal Nehru Memorial Fund, New Delhi, 2019.

SWJN, Second Series, Volume 81, Jawaharlal Nehru Memorial Fund, New Delhi, 2019.

SWJN, Second Series, Volume 83, Jawaharlal Nehru Memorial Fund, New Delhi, 2019.

SWJN, Second Series, Volume 82, Jawaharlal Nehru Memorial Fund, New Delhi, 2019.

CWMG, Volume. LXXXIX, The Publications Division, Government of India, 1983.

CWMG, Vol. XC, The Publications Division, Government of India, New Delhi, 1984.

NEWSPAPERS AND JOURNALS

Bombay Chronicle
Daily Mirror
Deccan Herald
Frontline
Hindustan
Hindustan Times
Illustrated Weekly of India
Kesari
News Chronicle
Organiser
Panchjanya
Patriot
People's Age
Sakal
The Caravan
The Hindu
The Hitavada
The Leader
The Motherland
The New York Times
The Times of India

BOOKS AND PRERIODICALS

Abhishek Choudhary, *Vajpayee: The Ascent of the Hindu Right 1924-1977*, Picador India, New Delhi, 2023.

Acharya Balarao Savarkar, *Swatantryaveer Savarkar: Hindu Mahasabha Parva*, Vol. II, Swatantryaveer Savarkar Rashtriya Smarak, Mumbai, 2020.

Akbar S. Ahmed, *Jinnah, Pakistan and Islamic Identity: The Search for Saladin*, Routledge, London & New York, 1997.

Akshaya Mukul, *Gita Press and the Making of Hindu India*, HarperCollins Publishers India, New Delhi, 2015.

Alex von Tunzelmann, *Indian Summer: The Secret History of the end of an Empire*, Simon & Schuster UK Ltd, London, 2007.

Alan Campbell-Johnson, *Mission with Mountbatten*, Robert Hale Limited, London, 1951.

Anis Kidwai, *In Freedom's Shade*, Penguin Books, New Delhi, 2011.

Antony Copley, *Religion in Conflict: Ideology, Cultural Contact and Conversion in Late Colonial India*, Oxford University Press, Delhi, 1997.

A. S. Bhide (ed.), *Whirlwind Propaganda: Extracts from President's Diary of His Propagandist Tours, Interviews from December 1937 to October 1941*, All India Hindu Mahasabha, Bombay, 1941.

Ashis Nandy, *At the Edge of Psychology: Essays in Politics and Culture*, Oxford University Press, Delhi, 1980.

Balraj Madhok, *R.S.S. and Politics*, Hindu World Publications, Delhi 1980.

Bhaiya Ghatate, *Shri Babasaheb Ghatate Yanche Atmakathan*, Shri Babasaheb Apte Smarak Samiti, Nagpur, 1997.

Bipan Chandra, *Communalism in Modern India*, Vikas Publishing House, Delhi, 1987.

B. N. Bhargava, *Shri Guruji: The Man & His Mission*, Bharat Prakashan (Delhi) Ltd., New Delhi, 1956.

B. V. Deshpande and S. R. Ramaswamy, *Dr Hedgewar: The Epoch-maker*, Sahitya Sindhu, Bangalore, 1981.

C. H. Philips and Mary Doreen Wainwright (ed.), *The Partition of India: Policies and Perspectives 1935-1947*, George Allen and Unwin Ltd, London, 1970.

Chetan Bhatt, *Hindu Nationalism: Origins, Ideologies and Modern Myths*, Oxford, New York, 2001.

Clemens Six, *Secularism, Decolonisation, and the Cold War in South and Southeast Asia*, Routledge, London and New York, 2018.

Christophe Jaffrelot, *The Hindu Nationalist Movement and Indian Politics, 1925 to 1990s*, Hurst & Company, London, 1996.

Craig Baxter, *The Jana Sangh: A Biography of an Indian Political Party*, University of Pennsylvania Press, Philadelphia, 1969.

C. V. Mathew, *The Saffron Mission: A Historical Analysis of Modern Hindu Missionary Ideologies and Practices*, Indian Society for Promoting Christian Knowledge, Delhi, 1999.

Damodar Trayambak Sabnis, *Swargiya Ke. Ba. Hedgewar: Ojharte Darshan*, Arvind Prakashan, Nagpur, 1940.

David Ludden (ed.), *Making India Hindu: Religion, Community and the Politics of Democracy in India*, Oxford University Press, Delhi, 1996.

Dhirendra K. Jha, *Gandhi's Assassin: The Making of Nathuram Godse and His Idea of India*, Penguin India, New Delhi, 2021.

D. G. Tendulkar, *Mahatma: Life of Mohandas Karamchand Gandhi*, Volume Eight, The Publications Division, New Delhi, 1963.

Dhananjay Keer, *Veer Savarkar*, Popular Prakashan, Bombay, 1966.

D. N. Gokhale, *Krantiveer Babarao Savarkar*, Mangal Sahitya Prakashan, Pune, 1947.

D. P. Mishra, *The Nehru Epoch: From Democracy to Monocracy*, Vikas Publishing House Pvt Ltd, New Delhi, 1978.

D. R. Goyal, *Rashtriya Swayamsevak Sangh*, Radhakrishna Prakashan, Delhi, 1979.

Dr. Shrirang Arvind Godbole (ed.), *Yugpravartak Dr. Hedgewar*, Sanskritik Jagaran Mandal, Pune, 2014.

D. S. Harshe, *Adarsh Hindu Sanghatak: Ka. Bha. Limaye*, published by Sudha Dattatreya Harshe, Satara, 1981.

'Durgatanaya' [Pseudonym of Ganesh Damodar Savarkar], *Rashtra Mimansa Wa Hindusthanchen Rashtraswaroop*, published by Vaidyaratna Vishnu Ganesh Kelkar, Nasik, 1934.

D. V. Kelkar, 'The R.S.S.', *Economic Weekly*, 4 February 1950.

G. Parthasarathi (ed.), *Jawaharlal Nehru: Letters to Chief Ministers, 1947-1964*, Volume I, Jawaharlal Nehru Memorial Fund, New Delhi, 1985.

George E. Jones, *Tumult in India*, Dodd, Mead & Company, New York, 1948.

G. D. Savarkar, *Rashtra Mimansa Wa Hindustan Ka Rashtra-Swaroop*, Shakti Prakashan, Jabalpur, 1944.

Gyanendra Pandey, *Remembering Partition: Violence, Nationalism and History in India*, Cambridge University Press, 2001.

Hemendra Nath Pandit, *The End of A Dream: An Inside View of the R.S.S. Today*, Rabindra Nath Hore, Calcutta, 1950.

H. M. Patel, *Rites of Passage: A Civil Servant Remembers*, Rupa & Co., New Delhi, 2005.

Ian Copland, *State, Community and Neighbourhood in Princely North India, c. 1900—1950*, Palgrave Macmillan, New York, 2005.

Indra Prakash, *A Review of the History and Work of the Hindu Mahasabha and the Hindu Sanghatan Movement*, Dharmarajya Press, Delhi, 1952.

J. A. Curran, Jr., *Militant Hinduism in Indian Politics: A Study of the R.S.S.*, Institute of Pacific Relations, New York, 1951.

Jagat S. Bright, *Guruji Golwalkar & R.S.S.*, New India Publishing Co., Delhi, 1950.

J. N. Sahni, *Fifty Years of Indian Politics: 1921-1971*, Allied Publishers, New Delhi, 1971.

John Wilson, *Indian Caste*, Vol. II, Times of India Office, Bombay, 1877.

Jawaharlal Nehru, *The Discovery of India*, Penguin India, New Delhi, 2008.

Jawaharlal Nehru, *An Autobiography*, Oxford University Press, New Delhi, 1982.

Jawaharlal Nehru, *Letters to Chief Ministers*, Volume 1, Jawaharlal Nehru Memorial Fund, New Delhi, 1985.

John D. Smith, *I was a CIA Agent in India*, Communist Party Publication, New Delhi, 1967.

Jyotirmaya Sharma, *Terrifying Vision: M.S. Golwalkar, the RSS and India*, Viking, New Delhi, 2007.

Kiran Saxena, 'The Hindu Trade Union Movement in India: The Bharatiya Mazdoor Sangh', *Asian Survey*, July 1993, Vol. 33, No. 7.

K. N. Panikkar, *Communalism in India: History, Politics and Culture*, Manohar, Delhi, 1991.

Larry Collins and Dominique Lapierre, *Freedom at Midnight*, Vikas Publishing House Pvt Ltd, Delhi, 1975.

Leah Renold, *A Hindu Education: Early Years of the Banaras Hindu University*, Oxford University Press India, Delhi, 2006.

Louis Fischer, *The Life of Mahatma Gandhi*, HarperCollins Publishers, London, 2019.

Manik Chandra Vajpayee & Shridhar Paradkar, *Partition-Days: The Fiery Saga of RSS*, Suruchi Prakashan, Delhi, 2002.

Manuben Gandhi, *Last Glimpses of Bapu*, Shiva Lal Agarwala & Co. (P) Ltd., Agra, 1962.

Marzia Casolari, 'Hindutva's Foreign Tie-up in the 1930s: Archival Evidence', *Economic and Political Weekly*, 22 January 2000.

Maulana Abul Kalam Azad, *Indian Wins Freedom: An Autobiographical Narrative*, Orient Longman, Bombay, 1964.

Michael Edwards, *The Last Years of British India*, World Publishing Company, New York, 1965.

M. J. Akbar, *India: The Siege Within*, Penguin Books, 1985.

M. N. Ghatate, 'Dr. BS Moonje—Tour of European Countries', in N. G. Dixit (ed.), *Dharmaveer Dr. BS Moonje Commemoration Voume*, Birth Centenary Celebration (1872-1972), Centenary Celebration Committee, Nagpur, 1972.

Morarji Desai, *The Story of My Life*, Vol. One, Macmillan India, Delhi, 1974.

M. S. Golwalkar, *We or Our Nationhood Defined*, Bharat Publications, Nagpur, 1939.

M. S. Golwalkar, *Bunch of Thoughts*, Vikrama Prakashan, Bangalore, 1966.

M. S. Dixit, *Mi Ma Shri*, Utkarsh Prakashan, Pune, 2004.

Mushirul Hasan, 'Adjustment and Accommodation: Indian Muslims after Partition', in K. N. Panikkar (ed.), *Communalism in India: History, Politics and Culture*, Manohar Publications, New Delhi, 1991.

Myron Weiner, *Party Politics in India: The Development of a Multi-Party System*, Princeton University Press, Princeton, 1957.

Nandini Gondhalekar and Sanjoy Bhattacharya, 'The All India Hindu Mahasabha and the End of British Rule in India, 1937-1947', *Social Scientist*, July-August, 1999, Vol. 27, No. 7/8.

Narendra Modi, *Jyotipunj*, Prabhat Prakashan, New Delhi, 2015.

Narhari N. Kirkire, *Sangliche Diwas (1937-1945)*, N. N. Kirkire (publisher), Satara, 2008.

Neela Vasant Upadhye (ed.), *DV Gokhale: Vyaktitva va Krititva*, Navachaitanya Prakashan, Mumbai, 2013.

N. H. Palkar, *Shri Ma Sa Golwalkar*, published by N. H. Palkar, Mumbai, 1956.

N. H. Palkar, *Dr. Hedgewar: Patraroop-Vyaktidarshan*, Archana Prakashan, Indore, 1989.

Nicholas Goodrick-Clarke, *Hitler's Priestess*, New York University Press, New York and London, 1998.

Philip Ziegler, *Mountbatten: The Official Biography*, Collins, London, 1985.

P. N. Chopra & Prabha Chopra (ed.), *Inside Story of Sardar Patel: The Diary of Maniben Patel (1936-50)*, Vision Books, New Delhi, 2001.

Pralay Kanungo, *RSS's Tryst with Politcs: From Hedgewar to Sudarshan*, Manohar, New Delhi, 2002.

Prof. Dharmavir, *Guru Golwalkar*, Hind Pocket Books Pvt Ltd, 1974.

Pyarelal, *Mahatma Gandhi: The Last Phase*, Volume X, Navajivan Publishing House, Ahmedabad, 1958.

I. H. Qureshi, 'A Case Study of the Social Relations between the Muslims and the Hindus, 1935-47', in C. H. Philips and Mary Doreen Wainwright (ed.), *The Partition of India: Policies and Perspectives*, George Allen and Unwin Ltd, London, 1970.

Raj Kumar, *Annie Besant's Rise to Power in Indian Politics 1914-1917*, Concept Publishing House, Delhi, 1981.

Rajeshwar Dayal, *A Life of Our Times*, Orient Longman, Hyderabad, 1998.

Ramachandra Guha, *Gandhi: The Years that Changed the World, 1914-1948*, Penguin Random House India, Gurgaon, 2018.

Ramachandra Guha, *Makers of Modern India*, Viking, New Delhi, 2010.

Ram Lall Dhooria, *I Was A Swayamsewak*, Sampradayikta Virodhi Committee, New Delhi, 1976.

Ranga Hari, *The Incomparable Guru Golwalkar*, Prabhat Paperbacks, 2018.

R. H. Tupkary, *RSS Revalued: Insider's Critical Assessment*, Notion Press, Chennai, 2018.

Richard Symonds, *In the Margins of Independence: A Relief Worker in*

India and Pakistan (1942-1949), Oxford University Press, London, 2001.

Robert Payne, *The Life and Death of Mahatma Gandhi*, Rupa & Co., Calcutta, 1997.

Sangha Darshan, Prakashan Vibhag, Rashtreeya Swayamsevak Sangh, Bangalore, 1964.

Sanjeev Kelkar, *Lost Years of the RSS*, Sage Publications India Pvt Ltd, New Delhi, 2011.

Savitri Devi, *A Warning to the Hindus*, Hindu Mission, Calcutta, 1939.

S. H. Deshpande, 'My Days in the RSS', *Quest*, July-August 1975.

Shail Mayaram, *Resisting Regimes: Myth, Memory and the Shaping of a Muslim Identity*, Oxford University Press, Delhi, 1997.

Shri Gangadhar Indurkar, *Guruji: Rashtriya Swayamsevak Sangh ke Sarsanghchalak Shri Madhav Sadashiv Golwalkar ka Jeevan Charitra*, Sangh Vastu Bhandar, Delhi, 1949.

Sir Francis Tuker, *While Memory Serves*, Cassell and Company Ltd, London, 1950.

Sucheta Mahajan, *Independence and Partition: The Erosion of Colonial Power in India*, Sage Publications Pvt. Ltd., New Delhi, 2000.

Sumit Sarkar, *Modern India: 1885-1947*, Macmillan Publishers India Ltd, Delhi, 2013.

Swami Akhandanand Smorone, Ramakrishna Mission Ashram, Sargachhi, Murshidabad, 2020.

Swami Niramayanand, *Swami Akhandanand Ke Sannidhya Mein*, Ramakrishna Math, Nagpur, 2015.

Tapan Ghosh, *The Gandhi Murder Trial*, Asia Publishing House, Bombay, 1974.

Thomas Blom Hansen, *The Saffron Wave: Democracy and Hindu Nationalism in Modern India*, Oxford University Press, New Delhi, 1999.

Vasudev Balwant Gogate, *Hotson-Gogate: Atmavritta*, published by Anil Vasudev Gogate, Pune, 2006.

V. D. Savarkar, *Hindutva: Who is a Hindu?*, Hindi Sahitya Sadan, New Delhi, 2005.

Verghese Kurien, *I too Had a Dream*, Roli Books, New Delhi, 2005.

Walter K. Andersen and Shridhar D. Damle, *The Brotherhood in Saffron: The Rashtriya Swayamsevak Sangh and Hindu Revivalism*, Westview Press, Boulder and London, 1987.

William Gould, *Religion and Conflict in Modern South Asia*, Cambridge University Press, New York, 2012.

William Gould, *Hindu Nationalism and the Language of Politics in Late Colonial India*, Cambridge University Press, New York, 2004.

Yasmin Khan, *The Great Partition: The Making of India and Pakistan*, Penguin Books India, New Delhi, 2007.

Y. D. Gundevia, *Outside the Archives*, Sangam Books, Hyderabad, 1984.

Index

N

P

Q

R